D0065224

Taking SIDES

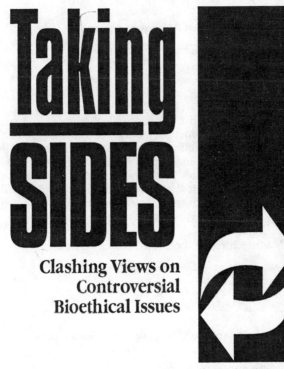

Clashing Views on Controversial Bioethical Issues

Sixth Edition

Edited, Selected, and with Introductions by

Carol Levine

The Dushkin Publishing Group, Inc.

For Hannah and Amy

Photo Acknowledgments

Part 1   Win McNamee/Sipa Press
Part 2   Digital Stock
Part 3   Middlesex Memorial Hospital
Part 4   World Health Organization photo by J. Mohr
Part 5   Middlesex Memorial Hospital

Cover Art Acknowledgment

Charles Vitelli

Library of Congress Cataloging-in-Publication Data

Main entry under title:
    Taking sides: clashing views on controversial bioethical issues/edited, selected, and with introductions by Carol Levine.—6th ed.
    Includes bibliographical references and index.
    1. Medical ethics. 2. Bioethics. I. Levine, Carol, *comp.*
    R724.T35
    1-56134-328-5

174'.2—dc20
94-47618

174.2
T

c1, 6ᵗʰ ed.

The Dushkin Publishing Group, Inc.

PREFACE

This is a book about choices—hard and tragic choices. The choices are hard not only because they often involve life and death but also because there are convincing arguments on both sides of the issues. An ethical dilemma, by definition, is one that poses a conflict not between good and evil but between one good principle and another that is equally good. The choices are hard because the decisions that are made—by individuals, groups, and public policymakers—will influence the kind of society we have today and the one we will have in the future.

Although the views expressed in the selections in this volume are strong—even passionate—ones, they are also subtle ones, concerned with the nuances of the particular debate. *How* one argues matters in bioethics; you will see and have to weigh the significance of varying rhetorical styles and appeals throughout this volume.

Although there are no easy answers to any of the issues in the book, the questions will be answered in some fashion—partly by individual choices and partly by decisions that are made by professionals and government. We must make them the best answers possible, and that can only be done by informed and thoughtful consideration. This book, then, can serve as a beginning for what ideally will become an ongoing process of examination and reflection.

Changes to this edition   Although I have retained the basic structure of the fifth edition, I have made some significant internal changes. There are six entirely new issues: *Is It Ethical to Clone Human Embryos?* (Issue 3); *Is It Ethical to Treat Short Children With Human Growth Hormone?* (Issue 9); *Is There a Gender Bias in Medicine and Research?* (Issue 14); *Should Newborns Be Screened for HIV Infection?* (Issue 15); *Is It Unfair to Tie Health Insurance to Employment?* (Issue 19); and *Should Health Insurance Companies Have Access to Information from Genetic Testing?* (Issue 20). In addition, both the question and the selections have been changed in Issue 6 (*Should Physicians Be Allowed to Assist in Patient Suicide?*), Issue 10 (*Should HIV-Infected Surgeons Be Allowed to Operate?*), and Issue 13 (*Will Fetal Tissue Research Encourage Abortions?*), although the general topics appeared in the previous edition. Also, one of the selections for Issue 2 (*Is There a Moral Right to Abortion?*) has been changed to bring a fresh perspective to the debate.

In all, 19 new readings are included in this edition. Part introductions, issue introductions, and postscripts have been revised as necessary.

A word to the instructor   An *Instructor's Manual With Test Questions* (multiple-choice and essay) is available through the publisher, and a general guidebook,

Using Taking Sides in the Classroom, which discusses methods and techniques for using the pro/con approach in any classroom setting, is also available.

Acknowledgments   I received helpful comments and suggestions from the many users of *Taking Sides* across the United States and Canada. Their suggestions have enhanced the quality of this edition of the book and are reflected in the new selections and issues.

Special thanks go to those who responded with specific suggestions for the sixth edition:

James G. Anderson
Purdue University

Hessel Bouma III
Calvin College

Thomas A. Easton
Thomas College

Robert E. Farmer
Barry University

Mark Gedney
Framingham State College

Alan Gross
University of Minnesota

Allen Haney
Rice University

Morris J. Holtzcaw
Eckerd College

Peter J. Kajenski
Community College of
  Vermont

Lawrence R. Krupka
Michigan State University

James C. Marker
University of Wisconsin

Donald Marquis
University of Kansas

Donald W. Munro
Houghton College

Malcolm S. Munson
Greenville Technical College

Betty J. Odello
Los Angeles Pierce College

Robert F. Rizzo
Canisius College

Robin Alice Roth
University of Scranton

Mark Sheldon
Indiana University

Maryella Sirmon
University of South Alabama

Louis Suarez
Lorain County Community
  College

Lee Usnick
University of Oklahoma

Robert Wilson
San Jose State University

For this edition, Ben Munisteri was an invaluable researcher, commentator, critic, and one-person support system. He also prepared the *Instructor's Manual*. Both of us have benefited immeasurably from Lauri Posner's careful work on previous editions. Marna Howarth, Julie Rothstein, and Sarah Gill of the Hastings Center staff responded to inquiries efficiently, promptly, and with great good humor. For their assistance in previous editions, which gave me a solid base from which to proceed, I want to thank Paul Homer, Eric Feldman, and Arthur Caplan. I would particularly like to thank Daniel Callahan, director of the Hastings Center, and Willard Gaylin, now retired, for their early encouragement in this project.

Carol Levine

CONTENTS IN BRIEF

CONTENTS

Law student Jim Persels believes that the use of long-acting contraceptive
technologies as requirements for probation for women convicted of child
abuse or drug use serves to protect the unborn. The American Medical Association's board of trustees argues that such demands threaten a person's
fundamental right to refuse medical treatment, to procreate, and to be protected from cruel and unusual punishment.

Philosopher Bonnie Steinbock argues for a pro-choice position based on the
moral status of the fetus and the pregnant woman's moral right to bodily self-
determination. Psychologist Sidney Callahan asserts that pregnant women
have a moral obligation to carry their fetuses to term.

Law professor John A. Robertson contends that cloning human embryos raises no novel ethical problems. Theologian Richard A. McCormick argues that human embryo cloning calls into question basic premises about the sanctity of life and the uniqueness of individuals.

Professor of religious studies Thomas A. Shannon maintains that surrogacy encourages the treatment of women and children as commodities rather than as persons worthy of respect. Attorney Carmel Shalev argues that women as autonomous and responsible individuals ought to be free to enter legally binding surrogate contracts.

Physician Bernard C. Meyer argues that physicians who adhere to a rigid formula of truth telling fail to appreciate the differences in patients' readiness to hear and understand the information. Philosopher Sissela Bok argues that the harm resulting from disclosure is less than physicians may think and is outweighed by the benefits.

Bioethicist Franklin G. Miller and his colleagues believe that physician-assisted suicide relieves patients of suffering and allows them to be self-determining. Physician and lawyer David Orentlicher argues that physician-assisted dying violates the principle of the inalienable right to life, which at the very least means that a person should not have his life taken by another.

Physician Joanne Lynn and professor of religious studies James F. Childress claim that nutrition and hydration are not morally different from other life-sustaining medical treatments that may be withheld or withdrawn. Professor of religion Gilbert Meilaender asserts that removing the ordinary human care of feeding aims to kill and is morally wrong.

Physician Mark Siegler argues that confidentiality must often be compromised to ensure complete and proper medical treatment. Physician Michael H. Kottow argues that any kind of breach of patient confidentiality causes serious harms.

Pediatrician David B. Allen argues that it is ethical to use growth hormone to bring short children into the normal range for height. Pediatrician John D. Lantos asserts that widespread use of growth hormone will provide unfair advantages to some children at the expense of other, untreated children.

Nursing professor Inge B. Corless asserts that restricting the practice of HIV-infected health care workers rather than implementing universal protections to prevent infection actually puts patients at greater risk of infection. Philosopher Carson Strong believes that physicians infected with HIV should be restricted from certain procedures, particularly those involving an open wound.

Physician Steven H. Miles believes that physicians' duty to follow patients' wishes ends when the requests are inconsistent with what medical care can reasonably be expected to achieve. Philosopher Felicia Ackerman contends that decisions involving personal values, such as those regarding quality of life, should be made by the patient or family, not by the physician.

Jerod M. Loeb and his colleagues, representing the American Medical Society's Group on Science and Technology, assert that concern for animals cannot impede the development of methods to improve the welfare of humans. Philosopher Tom Regan argues that those who support animal research fail to show proper respect for animals' inherent value.

Bioethicist Douglas K. Martin argues that the option to donate fetal tissue for therapeutic use may well influence some women to choose abortion. Bioethicists Dorothy E. Vawter and Karen G. Gervais contend that knowledge of the option to donate tissue is not an incentive for a woman to abort a fetus she would otherwise carry to term.

Philosopher and medical ethicist Ruth Macklin argues that the traditional focus on men—in both medicine and research—violates the principle of distributive justice. Physician Andrew G. Kadar argues that women actually receive more medical care and benefit more from medical research than men do.

Pediatrician and county health commissioner Mark S. Rapoport believes that the knowledge that a baby may be HIV-infected benefits the baby's health.

Pediatrician Alan R. Fleischman argues that mandatory testing is detrimental to the development of the trusting relationship that is essential for providing services to both mother and child.

Pediatric surgeon Michael R. Harrison asserts that anencephalic newborns should be treated as brain-dead rather than as brain-absent so that their organs can be transplanted. Philosopher John D. Arras and pediatric neurologist Shlomo Shinnar argue that the current definition of brain death reflects sound public policy and good ethics.

Attorney Lori B. Andrews believes that donors, recipients, and society will benefit from a market in body parts so long as owners retain control over their bodies. Ethicist Thomas H. Murray argues that the gift relationship should govern the transfer of body parts.

Philosopher Daniel Callahan believes that people who have lived a full natural life span should be offered care that relieves suffering but not expensive life-prolonging technologies. Sociologist Amitai Etzioni argues that rationing health care for the elderly would invite restrictions on health care for other groups.

Philosopher Nancy S. Jecker asserts that injustice in the distribution of jobs linked to health insurance have compromised justice in health care. Political scientist David A. Rochefort believes that employment-based health insurance offers policymakers a ready-made structure for achieving their objectives of universality and cost constraint.

The American Council of Life Insurance and the Health Insurance Association of America assert that denying insurers access to genetic test results could lead to higher premiums for most policyholders. Thomas H. Murray, a professor of biomedical ethics, warns that genetic tests will likely be used by insurance companies to increase the price of or even deny people access to health insurance.

Professor of history and philosophy of science Evelyn Fox Keller warns that the Human Genome Project's beneficent focus on "disease-causing genes" may lead to the abuse of inherently ambiguous standards of normality. Professor of humanities Daniel J. Kevles and professor of biology Leroy Hood maintain that a resurgence of negative eugenics as a result of this project is highly unlikely.

INTRODUCTION

Medicine and Moral Arguments

Carol Levine

In the fall of 1975, a 21-year-old woman lay in a New Jersey hospital—as she had for months—in a coma, the victim of a toxic combination of barbiturates and alcohol. Doctors agreed that her brain was irreversibly damaged and that she would never recover. Her parents, after anguished consultation with their priest, asked the doctors and hospital to disconnect the respirator that was artificially maintaining their daughter's life. When the doctors and hospital refused, the parents petitioned the court to be made her legal guardian so that they could authorize the withdrawal of treatment. After hearing all the arguments, the court sided with the parents, and the respirator was removed. Contrary to everyone's expectations, however, the young woman did not die but began to breathe on her own (perhaps because, in anticipation of the court order, the nursing staff had gradually weaned her from total dependence on the respirator). She lived for 10 years until her death in June 1985—comatose, lying in a fetal position, and fed with tubes—in a New Jersey nursing home.

The young woman's name was Karen Ann Quinlan, and her case brought national attention to the thorny ethical questions raised by modern medical technology: When, if ever, should life-sustaining technology be withdrawn? Is the sanctity of life an absolute value? What kinds of treatment are really beneficial to a patient in a "chronic vegetative state" like Karen's? And, perhaps the most troubling question, who shall decide? These and similar questions are at the heart of the growing field of biomedical ethics or (as it is usually called) *bioethics*.

Ethical dilemmas in medicine are, of course, nothing new. They have been recognized and discussed in Western medicine since a small group of physicians—led by Hippocrates—on the Isle of Cos in Greece, around the fourth century B.C., subscribed to a code of practice that newly graduated physicians still swear to uphold today. But unlike earlier times, when physicians and scientists had only limited abilities to change the course of disease, today they can intervene in profound ways in the most fundamental processes of life and death. Moreover, ethical dilemmas in medicine are no longer considered the sole province of professionals. Professional codes of ethics, to be sure, offer some guidance, but they are usually unclear and ambiguous about what to do in specific situations. More important, these codes assume that whatever decision is to be made is up to the professional, not the patient. Today, to an ever-greater degree, laypeople—patients, families, lawyers, clergy, and others—want to and have become involved in ethical decision making not only in individual cases, such as the Quinlan case, but also in large societal decisions, such as how to allocate scarce medical resources, including high-technology machinery, newborn intensive care units, and the expertise of physicians. While questions about the physician-patient relationship and individual cases are still prominent in bioethics (see, for example, the issues on truth telling and assisting dying patients in suicide), today the field covers a broad range of other decisions as well, such as the harvesting and transplantation of organs, equity in access to health care, and the future of animal experimentation.

This involvement is part of broader social trends: a general disenchantment with the authority of all professionals and, hence, a greater readiness to challenge the traditional belief that "doctor knows best"; the growth of various civil rights movements among women, the aged, and minorities—of which the patients' rights movement is a spin-off; the enormous size and complexity of the health care delivery system, in which patients and families often feel alienated from the professional; the increasing cost of medical care, much of it at public expense; and the growth of the "medical model," in which conditions that used to be considered outside the scope of physicians' control, such as alcoholism and behavioral problems, have come to be considered diseases.

Bioethics began in the 1950s as an intellectual movement among a small group of physicians and theologians who started to examine the questions raised by the new medical technologies that were starting to emerge as the result of the heavy expenditure of public funds in medical research after World War II. They were soon joined by a number of philosophers who had become disillusioned with what they saw as the arid abstractions of much analytic philosophy at the time and by lawyers who sought to find principles in the law that would guide ethical decision making or, if such principles were not there, to develop them by case law and legislation or regulation. Although these four disciplines—medicine, theology, philosophy, and law —still dominate the field, today bioethics is an interdisciplinary effort, with political scientists, economists, sociologists, anthropologists, nurses, allied health professionals, policymakers, psychologists, and others contributing their special perspectives to the ongoing debates.

The issues discussed in this volume attest to the wide range of bioethical dilemmas, their complexity, and the passion they arouse. But if bioethics today is at the frontiers of scientific knowledge, it is also a field with ancient roots. It goes back to the most basic questions of human life: What is right? What is wrong? How should people act toward others? And why?

While the *bio* part of *bioethics* gives the field its urgency and immediacy, we should not forget that the root word is *ethics*.

APPLYING ETHICS TO MEDICAL DILEMMAS

To see where bioethics fits into the larger framework of academic inquiry, some definitions are in order. First, *morality* is the general term for an individual's or a society's standards of conduct, both actual and ideal, and of the character traits that determine whether people are considered "good" or "bad." The scientific study of morality is called *descriptive ethics*; a scientist —generally an anthropologist, sociologist, or historian—can describe in empirical terms what the moral beliefs, judgments, or actions of individuals or societies are and what reasons are given for the way they act or what they believe. The philosophical study of morality, on the other hand, approaches the subject of morality in one of two different ways: either as an analysis of the concepts, terms, and methods of reasoning (*metaethics*) or as an analysis of what those standards or moral judgments ought to be (*normative ethics*). Metaethics deals with meanings of moral terms and logic; normative ethics, with which the issues in this volume are concerned, reflects on the kinds of actions and principles that will promote moral behavior.

Because normative ethics accepts the idea that some acts and character traits are more moral than others (and that some are immoral), it rejects the rather popular idea that ethics is relative. Because different societies have different moral codes and values, ethical relativists have argued that there can be no universal moral judgments: What is right or wrong depends on who does it and where, and whether or not society approves. Although it is certainly true that moral values are embedded in a social, cultural, and political context, it is also true that certain moral judgments are universal. We think it is wrong, for example, to sell people into slavery—whether or not a certain society approved or even whether or not a person wanted to be a slave. People may not agree about what these universal moral values are or ought to be, but it is hard to deny that some such values exist.

The other relativistic view rejected by normative ethics is the notion that whatever feels good *is* good. In this view, ethics is a matter of personal preference, weightier than one's choice of which automobile to buy, but not much different in kind. Different people, having different feelings, can arrive at equally valid moral judgments, according to the relativistic view. Just as we should not disregard cultural factors, we should not overlook the role of emotion and personal experience in arriving at moral judgments. But to give emotion ultimate authority would be to consign reason and rationality —the bases of moral argument—to the ethical trash heap. At the very least, it would be impossible to develop a just policy concerning the care of vulnerable persons, like the mentally retarded or newborns, who depend solely on the vagaries of individual caretakers.

Thus, if normative ethics is one branch of philosophy, bioethics is one branch of normative ethics; it is normative ethics applied to the practice of medicine and science. There are other branches—business ethics, legal ethics, journalism ethics, and military ethics, for example. One common term for the entire grouping is *applied and professional ethics*, because these ethics deal with the ethical standards of the members of a particular profession and how they are applied in the professionals' dealings with each other and the rest of society. Bioethics is based on the belief that some solutions to the dilemmas that arise in medicine and science are more moral than others and that these solutions can be determined by moral reasoning and reflection.

ETHICAL THEORIES

If the practitioners of bioethics do not rely solely on cultural norms and emotions, what are their sources of determining what is right or wrong? The most comprehensive source is a theory of ethics—a broad set of moral principles (or perhaps just one overriding principle) that is used in measuring human conduct. Divine law is one such source, of course, but even in the Western religious traditions of bioethics (both the Jewish and Catholic religions have rich and comprehensive commentaries on ethical issues, and the Protestant religion has a less cohesive but still important tradition) the law of God is interpreted in terms of human moral principles. A theory of ethics must be acceptable to many groups, not just the followers of one religious tradition. Most writers outside the religious traditions (and some within them) have looked to one of three major traditions in ethics: teleological theories, deontological theories, and natural law theories.

Teleological Theories

Teleological theories are based on the idea that the end or purpose (from the Greek *telos*, or end) of the action determines its rightness or wrongness. The most prominent teleological theory is *utilitarianism*. In its simplest formulation, an act is moral if it brings more good consequences than bad ones. Utilitarian theories are derived from the works of two English philosophers: Jeremy Bentham (1748–1832) and John Stuart Mill (1806–1873). Rejecting the absolutist religious morality of his time, Bentham proposed that "utility"—the greatest good for the greatest number—should guide the actions of human beings. Invoking the hedonistic philosophy of Epicurean Greeks, Bentham said that pleasure (*hedon* in Greek) is good and pain is bad. Therefore, actions are right if they promote more pleasure than pain and wrong if they promote more pain than pleasure. Mill found the highest utility in "happiness," rather than pleasure. (Mill's philosophy is echoed, you will recall, in the Declaration of Independence's espousal of "life, liberty, and the pursuit of happiness.") Other utilitarians have looked to a range of utilities, or goods (including friendship, love, devotion, and the like) that they believe ought to be weighed in the balance—the utilitarian calculus.

Utilitarianism has a pragmatic appeal. It is flexible, and it seems impartial. However, its critics point out that utilitarianism can be used to justify suppression of individual rights for the good of society ("the ends justify the means") and that it is difficult to quantify and compare "utilities," however they are defined.

Utilitarianism, in its many forms, has had a powerful influence on bioethical discussion, partly because it is the closest to the case-by-case risk/benefit ratio that physicians use in clinical decision-making. Joseph Fletcher, a Protestant theologian who was one of the pioneers in bioethics in the 1950s, developed utilitarian theories that he called *situation ethics*. He argued that a true Christian morality does not blindly follow moral rules but acts from love and sensitivity to the particular situation and the needs of those involved. He has enthusiastically supported most modern technologies on the grounds that they lead to good ends.

Other writers in this volume who use utilitarian theories to arrive at their moral judgments are John A. Robertson, who supports cloning to help infertile couples; Bernard C. Meyer, who defends withholding the truth from dying patients on the grounds that it leads to better consequences than truth telling; and Jerod M. Loeb and his colleagues, who defend animal research.

Deontological Theories

The second major type of ethical theory is *deontological* (from the Greek *deon*, or duty). The rightness or wrongness of an act, these theories hold, should be judged on whether or not it conforms to a moral principle or rule, not on whether it leads to good or bad consequences. The primary exponent of a deontological theory was Immanuel Kant (1724–1804), a German philosopher. Kant declared that there is an ultimate norm, or supreme duty, which he called the "Moral Law." He held that an act is moral only if it springs from a "good will," the only thing that is good without qualification.

We must do good things, said Kant, because we have a duty to do them, not because they result in good consequences or because they give us pleasure (although that can happen as well). Kant constructed a formal "Categorical Imperative," the ultimate test of morality: "I ought never to act except in such a way that I can also will that my maxim should become universal law." Recognizing that this formulation was far from clear, Kant said the same thing in three other ways. He explained that a moral rule must be one that can serve as a guide for everyone's conduct; it must be one that permits people to treat each other as ends in themselves, not solely as means to another's ends; and it must be one that each person can impose on himself by his own will, not one that is solely imposed by the state, one's parents, or God. Kant's Categorical Imperative, in the simplest terms, says that all persons have equal moral worth and that no rule can be moral unless all people can apply it autonomously to all other human beings. Although on its own Kant's Categorical Imperative is merely a formal statement with no moral content at all, he gave some examples of what he meant: "Do not commit suicide," and "Help others in distress."

Kantian ethics is criticized by many who note that Kant gives little guidance on what to do when ethical principles conflict, as they often do. Moreover, they say, his emphasis on autonomous decision making and individual will neglects the social and communal context in which people live and make decisions. It leads to isolation and unreality. These criticisms notwithstanding, Kantian ethics has stimulated much current thinking in bioethics. In this volume, the idea that certain actions are in and of themselves right or wrong underlies, for example, Sissela Bok's appeal to truth telling; Michael H. Kottow's defense of medical confidentiality as an absolute obligation; and

John D. Lantos's rejection of growth hormone to treat short children without a hormone deficiency.

Two modern deontological theorists are philosophers John Rawls and Robert M. Veatch. In *A Theory of Justice* (1971), Rawls places the highest value on equitable distribution of society's resources. He believes that society has a fundamental obligation to correct the inequalities of historical circumstance and natural endowment of its least well off members. According to this theory, some action is good only if it benefits the least well off. (It can also benefit others, but that is secondary.) His social justice theory has influenced bioethical writings concerning the allocation of scarce resources.

Veatch has applied Rawlsian principles to medical ethics. In his book *A Theory of Medical Ethics* (1981), he offers a model of social contract among professionals, patients, and society that emphasizes mutual respect and responsibilities. This contract model will, he hopes, avoid the narrowness of professional codes of ethics and the generalities and ambiguities of more broadly based ethical theories.

Natural Law Theory

The third strain of ethical theory that is prominent in bioethics is *natural law theory*, first developed by St. Thomas Aquinas (1223–1274). According to this theory, actions are morally right if they accord with our nature as human beings. The attribute that is distinctively human is the ability to reason and to exercise intelligence. Thus, argues this theory, we can know the good, which is objective and can be learned through reason. References to natural law theory are prominent in the works of Catholic theologians and writers; they see natural law as ultimately derived from God, but knowable through the efforts of human beings. The influence of natural law theory can be seen in this volume in Sidney Callahan's pro-life feminist opposition to abortion and in Gilbert Meilaender's arguments against removing food and water from dying patients.

Theory of Virtue

The *theory of virtue*, another ethical theory with deep roots in the Aristotelian tradition, has recently been revived in bioethics. This theory stresses not the morality of any particular actions or rules but the disposition of individuals to act morally, to be virtuous. In its modern version, its primary exponent is Alasdair MacIntyre, whose book *After Virtue* (1980) urges a return to the Aristotelian model. Gregory Pence has applied the theory of virtue directly to medicine in *Ethical Options in Medicine* (1980); he lists temperance in personal life, compassion for the suffering patient, professional competence, justice, honesty, courage, and practical judgment as the virtues most desirable in physicians. Although this theory has not yet been as fully developed in bioethics as the utilitarian or deontological theories, it is likely to have particular appeal for physicians—many of which have resisted formal ethics education on the grounds that moral character is the critical factor and that one can best learn to be a moral physician by emulating one's mentors.

Although various authors, in this volume and elsewhere, appeal in rather direct ways to either utilitarian or deontological theories, often the various types are combined. One may argue both that a particular action is immoral in and of itself and that it will have bad consequences (some commentators say even Kant used this argument). In fact, probably no single ethical theory is adequate to deal with all the ramifications of the issues. In that case we can turn to a middle level of ethical discussion. Between the abstractions of ethical theories (Kant's Categorical Imperative) and the specifics of moral judgments (always obtain informed consent from a patient) is a range of concepts—ethical principles—that can be applied to particular cases.

ETHICAL PRINCIPLES

In its four years of deliberation, the National Commission for the Protection of Human Subjects of Biomedical and Behavioral Research grappled with some of the most difficult issues facing researchers and society: When, if ever, is it ethical to do research on fetuses, on children, or on people in mental institutions? This commission—which was composed of people from various religious backgrounds, professions, and social strata—was finally able to agree on specific recommendations on these questions, but only after they had finished their work did the commissioners try to determine what ethical principles they had used in reaching a consensus. In their Belmont Report (1978), named after the conference center where they met to discuss this question, the commissioners outlined what they considered to be the three most important ethical principles (respect for persons, beneficence, and justice) that should govern the conduct of research with human beings. These three principles, they believed, are generally accepted in our cultural tradition and can serve as basic justifications for the many particular ethical prescriptions and evaluations of human action. Because of the principles' general acceptance and widespread applicability, they are at the basis of most bioethical discussion. Although philosophers argue about whether other principles— preventing harm to others or loyalty, for example—ought to be accorded equal weight with these three or should be included under another umbrella, they agree that these principles are fundamental.

Respect for Persons
Respect for persons incorporates at least two basic ethical convictions, according to the Belmont Report. Individuals should be treated as autonomous agents, and persons with diminished autonomy are entitled to protection. The derivation from Kant is clear. Because human beings have the capacity for rational action and moral choice, they have a value independent of anything that they can do or provide to others. Therefore, they should be treated in a way that respects their independent choices and judgments. Respecting

autonomy means giving weight to autonomous persons' considered opinions and choices, and refraining from interfering with their choices unless those choices are clearly detrimental to others. However, since the capacity for autonomy varies with age, mental disability, or other circumstances, those people whose autonomy is diminished must be protected—but only in ways that serve their interests and do not interfere with the level of autonomy that they do possess.

Two important moral rules are derived from the ethical principle of respect for persons: informed consent and truth telling. Persons can exercise autonomy only when they have been fully informed about the range of options open to them, and the process of informed consent is generally considered to include the elements of information, comprehension, and voluntariness. Thus, a person can give informed consent to some medical procedure only if he or she has full information about the risks and benefits, understands them, and agrees voluntarily—that is, without being coerced or pressured into agreement. Although the principle of informed consent has become an accepted moral rule (and a legal one as well), it is difficult—some say impossible—to achieve in a real-world setting. It can easily be turned into a legalistic parody or avoided altogether. But as a moral ideal it serves to balance the unequal power of the physician and patient.

Another important moral ideal derived from the principle of respect for persons is truth telling. It held a high place in Kant's theory. In his essay "The Supposed Right to Tell Lies from Benevolent Motives," he wrote: "If, then, we define a lie merely as an intentionally false declaration towards another man, we need not add that it must injure another...; for it always injures another; if not another individual, yet mankind generally.... To be truthful in all declarations is therefore a sacred and conditional command of reasons, and not to be limited by any other expediency."

Other important moral rules that are derived from the principle of respect for persons are confidentiality and privacy.

Beneficence

Most physicians would probably consider beneficence (from the Latin *bene*, or good) the most basic ethical principle. In the Hippocratic Oath it is used this way: "I will apply dietetic measures for the benefit of the sick according to my ability and judgment; I will keep them from harm and injustice." And further on, "Whatever houses I may visit, I will comfort and benefit the sick, remaining free of all intentional injustice." The phrase *Primum non nocere* (First, do no harm) is another well-known version of this idea, but it appears to be a much later, Latinized version—not from the Hippocratic period.

Philosopher William Frankena has outlined four elements included in the principle of beneficence: (1) One ought not to inflict evil or harm; (2) one ought to prevent evil or harm; (3) one ought to remove evil or harm; and (4) one ought to do or promote good. Frankena arranged these elements in hierarchical order, so that the first takes precedence over the second, and so on. In this scheme, it is more important to avoid doing evil or harm than to do good. But in the Belmont Report, beneficence is understood as an obligation—first, to do no harm, and second, to maximize possible benefits and minimize possible harms.

The principle of beneficence is at the basis of Franklin G. Miller and his colleagues' support of allowing physicians to assist some patients in suicide, of Joanne Lynn and James F. Childress's defense of withholding fluids and nutrition from some dying patients, and of David Orentlicher's opposition to physician-assisted suicide.

Justice

The third ethical principle that is generally accepted is justice, which means "what is fair" or "what is deserved." An injustice occurs when some benefit to which a person is entitled is denied without good reason or when some burden is imposed unduly, according to the Belmont Report. Another way of interpreting the principle is to say that equals should be treated equally. However, some distinctions—such as age, experience, competence, physical condition, and the like—can justify unequal treatment. Those who appeal to the principle of justice are most concerned about which distinctions can be made legitimately and which ones cannot (see the issue on gender bias in medicine and research).

One important derivative of the principle of justice is the recent emphasis on "rights" in bioethics. Given the successes in the 1960s and 1970s of civil rights movements in the courts and political arena, it is easy to understand the appeal of "rights talk." An emphasis on individual rights is part of the American tradition, in a way that emphasis on the "common good" is not. The language of rights has been prominent in the abortion debate, for instance, where the "right to life" has been pitted against the "right to privacy" or the "right to control one's body." The "right to health care" is a potent rallying cry, though it is one that is difficult to enforce legally. Although claims to rights may be effective in marshaling political support and in emphasizing moral ideals, those rights may not be the most effective way to solve ethical dilemmas. Our society, as philosopher Ruth Macklin has pointed out, has not yet agreed on a theory of justice in health care that will determine who has what kinds of rights and—the other side of the coin—who has the obligation to fulfill them.

WHEN PRINCIPLES CONFLICT

These three fundamental ethical principles—respect for persons, beneficence, and justice—all carry weight in ethical decision making. But what happens when they conflict? That is what this book is all about.

On each side of the issues included in this volume are writers who appeal, explicitly or implicitly, to one or more of these principles. For example, in Issue 1, Jim Persels sees beneficence as paramount and would approve under some circumstances involuntary implantation of long-acting contraceptives as a way to prevent child abuse. The American Medical Association sees such a policy as an intrusion into the protected doctor-patient relationship and the autonomy of the individual.

Some of the issues are concerned with how to interpret a particular principle: Whether, for example, it is more or less beneficent to allow a physician to assist in suicide, or whether patients can best be protected from HIV transmission in a health care setting by putting restrictions on HIV-infected practitioners or by using a voluntary system of education on infection control.

Will it ever be possible to resolve such fundamental divisions—those that are not merely matters of procedure or interpretation but of fundamental differences in principle? Lest the situation seem hopeless, consider that some consensus does seem to have been reached on questions that seemed equally tangled a few decades ago. The idea that government should play a role in regulating human subjects research was hotly debated, but it is now generally accepted (at least if the research is medical, not social or behavioral in nature, and is federally funded). And the appropriateness of using the criteria of brain death for determining the death of a person (and the possibility of subsequent removal of their organs for transplantation) has largely been accepted and written into state laws. The idea that a hopelessly ill patient has the legal and moral right to refuse treatment that will only postpone dying is also well established (though it is often hard to exercise because hospitals and physicians continue to resist it). Finally, nearly everyone now agrees that health care is distributed unjustly in this country—a radical idea only a few years ago. There is, of course, sharp disagreement about whose responsibility it is to rectify the situation—the government's or the private sector's.

In the decade since the first edition of this book was published, the dominance of principles as the foundation of bioethics has been challenged. Several philosophers have pointed out, as already noted, that the "mid-level" principles are not grounded in a unified moral theory. Other writers have described the philosophical mode of argument as too arid and abstract, and they have called for the inclusion of other forms of discourse, such as public policy, emotion-based reasoning, and narrative or "storytelling."

Besides the virtue theory, already described, two other candidates have their defenders. The ethics of caring has been presented as an alternative to traditional bioethics reasoning. Women, it is claimed, embody an ethic of caring, which is itself a prime aim of healing relationships. An ethic of caring would focus on relationships rather than autonomy, on reconciliation rather than winning an argument, and on nurturing rather than imposing dominance. While the absence of caring relationships is clearly a problem in modern health care, this view has been severely criticized by many, including women, as failing to provide a sufficient basis for replacing ethical principles.

Another mode of analysis that is being revived is casuistry. Although associated with the Middle Ages and religious thinking, casuistry is simply a way of reaching consensus on principles by focusing on concrete cases—the clearest ones first, and then the harder ones. The casuist reaches principles from the bottom up, rather than deciding cases from the top (principles first) down.

A final form of analysis is clinical ethics. Its practitioners focus on the clinical realities of moral choices as they emerge in ordinary health care. It is not antithetical to principles but brings abstractions back to reality by measuring proposed solutions against the real world in which doctors and patients live and work.

Edmund Pellegrino, a distinguished physician and ethicist, has seen many changes in the 50 years he has been involved in medicine. Looking toward the future, he does not see the death of principles, but he does foresee some changes. "Physicians and other health workers must become familiar with shifts in contemporary moral philosophy," he says, "if they are to maintain a hand in restructuring the ethics of their profession." But clinicians, too, must change, to "provide a reality check on the nihilism and skepticism of contemporary philosophy. Medical ethics is too ancient and too essential . . . to be left entirely to the fortuitous currents of philosophical fashion or the unsupported assertion of clinicians."

Although there is consensus in some areas, in others there is only controversy. This book will introduce you to some of the ongoing debates. Whether or not we will be able to move beyond opposing views to a realm of moral consensus will depend on society's willingness to struggle with these issues and to make the hard choices that are required.

PART 1

Choices in Reproduction

Few bioethical issues could be of greater significance than questions concerning reproduction. Advances in medical technology, such as in vitro fertilization and cloning human embryos, and changes in social mores that have made surrogate mothering more acceptable have opened new possibilities to infertile couples. Nevertheless, these practices challenge established family patterns. Our enhanced understanding of fetal development creates new pressures to control the mother's behavior. New long-acting forms of contraception seem tailor-made for situations in which courts or legislatures wish to limit a person's reproduction. The centuries-old debate about abortion takes on new significance in the modern era, when abortion is safe and legal but still highly controversial. The issues in this section come to grips with some of the most perplexing and fundamental questions that confront medical practitioners and society.

■ Should Courts Be Permitted to Order
   Women to Use Long-Acting Contraceptives?

■ Is There a Moral Right to Abortion?

■ Is It Ethical to Clone Human Embryos?

■ Should Commercial Surrogate Motherhood
   Be Banned?

ISSUE 1

Should Courts Be Permitted to Order Women to Use Long-Acting Contraceptives?

YES: Jim Persels, from "The Norplant Condition: Protecting the Unborn or Violating Fundamental Rights?" *The Journal of Legal Medicine* (vol. 13, 1992)

NO: American Medical Association, from "Board of Trustees Report: Requirements or Incentives by Government for the Use of Long-Acting Contraceptives," *Journal of the American Medical Association* (April 1, 1992)

ISSUE SUMMARY

YES: Law student Jim Persels believes that the use of long-acting but reversible contraceptive technologies as requirements for probation for women convicted of child abuse or drug use serves to guard the unborn while simultaneously limiting the intrusion on the individual's privacy rights and the state's burden of supervision.

NO: The American Medical Association's board of trustees opposes the use of long-acting contraceptives either as a condition of probation or as an incentive to women to get off welfare because such demands threaten a person's fundamental right to refuse medical treatment, to procreate, and to be protected from cruel and unusual punishment.

In December 1990 the Food and Drug Administration approved the use of Norplant as a contraceptive for American women. Although Norplant is the first long-acting contraceptive to be marketed and the first new birth control method developed in 25 years, in the future other products will undoubtedly be approved, some of them for men.

Norplant works in this way: Six small silicone tubes, each about the size of a matchstick, are inserted under the skin of a woman's upper arm with a local anesthetic. The procedure takes about 10 to 15 minutes. The tubes release a synthetic version of the hormone progestin, which suppresses ovulation. Because she does not produce ova (eggs), the woman is infertile. The hormones also act in other ways to inhibit fertilization. The hormones are released at a steady pace over five years. When the tubes are removed, also a relatively simple procedure, the woman again becomes fertile.

Norplant has been widely used around the world. It is extremely effective, with a failure rate of only 0.3 percent to 0.6 percent in one year and 1.5

percent over five years. It has several advantages over other contraceptive options, the primary one being the guaranteed compliance of the user while the tubes are in place. In addition, there are relatively few side effects, although headaches, acne, and irregular menstrual bleeding do occur among some women. Women with a history of diabetes, hypertension, cardiovascular disease, and some other diseases should not use Norplant because the additional hormones present some risks. Except for its high cost ($350 for the device, plus $150 to $650 for the insertion, counseling, and checkups), Norplant seems to be almost entirely a good-news story, and nearly 1 million American women have chosen this method of birth control over others that require either partner participation (condom), daily usage (oral contraceptives), or insertion before intercourse (diaphragm).

There is, however, a controversial aspect to this contraceptive. Because it does not require constant monitoring and is nearly foolproof, Norplant is an appealing candidate for use as a method of controlling the reproduction of women whom courts or others deem unfit to be mothers, either because they have been convicted of child abuse or because they are drug users. The use of Norplant could be required as a condition of probation. In addition, Norplant may be used as an incentive to women on welfare or as a condition of receiving further benefits to induce them to have fewer children and thus to lower welfare costs.

Mandatory sterilization of convicted criminals or other socially "undesirable" people has a long history in the United States. The case of *Buck v. Bell*, in which the Supreme Court upheld the sterilization of a young woman, assumed to be retarded but later proved not to be, is a legal benchmark in this area. Decided in 1927, it has never been overturned. Other courts have upheld a fundamental right to procreate.

The question of whether or not Norplant can be used in the modern context arose in 1991 when Judge Howard Broadman suggested in his California court that Darlene Johnson, a woman convicted of abusing two of her children, might reduce her prison sentence if she agreed to accept Norplant. In Kansas that same year a legislator proposed a variation on this idea: Drug-abusing fertile women could be placed on probation only if they accepted Norplant. The ethical question raised by these proposals is whether or not the interests of the state in reducing child abuse or welfare costs justifies the imposition of a temporary form of contraception.

Jim Persels believes that the Johnson case and the Kansas legislation are harbingers of more defensible uses of the imposition of Norplant and that under some conditions the state is justified in imposing this technology. The board of trustees of the American Medical Association, on the other hand, claim that the state's interests in protecting children can be best served by less intrusive means and that government benefits should not be made contingent on the acceptance of a health risk.

YES

THE NORPLANT CONDITION: PROTECTING THE UNBORN OR VIOLATING FUNDAMENTAL RIGHTS?

INTRODUCTION

The children are at risk. Approximately 1,727,000 cases of child abuse are reported annually. Studies show that more than 25 of each 1,000 children in the United States suffer some form of abuse or neglect. In addition, there has been a dramatic increase in the number of babies born to drug-abusing mothers. Some experts now estimate that as many as 375,000 infants affected by maternal drug use are born each year. The prevalence of crack cocaine has ignited this explosion. Crack cocaine is the drug of choice for many women of childbearing age because it is relatively inexpensive and can be smoked rather than injected. Infants born to mothers that are addicted to cocaine are subject to premature birth, low birth weight, and withdrawal symptoms. Furthermore, these infants demonstrate neurobehavioral problems, congenital disorders and deformities, and have a tenfold greater risk of dying of sudden infant death syndrome than babies not so affected.

This wholesale maiming of our children has recently motivated a judge in California and a legislator in Kansas in their attempts to use a newly approved medical technology to deal with the problem. That new technology is Norplant, a highly effective contraceptive implant that renders a woman infertile for up to five years or until the device is removed. A California appellate court is currently considering the case of *People v. Johnson*, in which a superior court judge ordered that Norplant be implanted in a convicted child abuser as a condition of probation. Similarly, during the 1990 session of the Kansas legislature, a legislator introduced a bill [House Bill 2255] that would mandate the implantation of Norplant as a condition of probation for drug-abusing fertile women.

The defense in the *Johnson* case and the opponents of the Kansas Norplant bill claim that court-ordered contraception violates the individual's right of privacy. Specifically, they argue that the Norplant condition is an unconstitutional intrusion on the fundamental right of procreation. In contrast, the states argue that the condition is valid for two reasons. First, the implantation of Norplant in child-abusing and drug-using women facilitates achievement of the state's probationary goal of rehabilitation by greatly reducing the risk of an untimely childbirth. This factor has been identified as one of the key risk factors for child abuse and neglect. Second, Norplant furthers the states' compelling interest in protecting the welfare of their children.

The purpose of this commentary is to discuss whether the state has the power to use this new contraceptive technology to defeat an individual probationer's fundamental right of procreation....

THE FUNDAMENTAL RIGHT OF PROCREATION

The seminal case that articulated a fundamental right of procreation was *Skinner v. Oklahoma.* Jack Skinner was a chicken thief and an armed robber. His crimes landed him in the Oklahoma penal system. His record of three felony convictions brought him under the heavy hand of the Oklahoma Habitual Criminal Sterilization Act.

This law defined an "habitual criminal" as one who was convicted three or more times for crimes "amounting to felonies involving moral turpitude." The law further provided that the Oklahoma attorney general could initiate proceedings against the habitual criminal for a judgment that such person be rendered

sexually sterile. The issues in a proceeding under this act were narrow and well-defined. The trier of fact had to decide whether the defendant was an "habitual criminal" and, if so, whether he "may be rendered sexually sterile without detriment to his or her general health." If the answer to both inquiries were affirmative, the court could then "render judgment to the effect that said defendant be rendered sexually sterile" by vasectomy [a surgical procedure that prevents sperm from being ejaculated] for males or salpingectomy [surgical removal of the fallopian tubes] for females. Jack Skinner qualified under both criteria and was sentenced to be sterilized. The Oklahoma Supreme Court affirmed by a five to four decision, and the United States Supreme Court granted the petition for certiorari.

The Court found that Oklahoma's law was fatally flawed because it ran afoul of the Equal Protection Clause of the fourteenth amendment. Justice Douglas noted many inconsistencies in the act. For instance, under the law, a man that broke into a chicken coop and stole chickens was a felon. Therefore, he could be sterilized after his third conviction. Ironically, however, an embezzler that feloniously appropriated significant sums of money from a bailor could not be sterilized under the law regardless of the number of times he was convicted for that crime. The Court reasoned that because the two crimes were intrinsically the same, the availability of this most serious sanction for one crime and not the other was inequitable under the fourteenth amendment. Justice Douglas characterized the nature of the violated right by stating, "[w]e are dealing here with legislation which involves one of the basic civil rights of man. Marriage and procreation are fundamental to the very existence and survival of the race."

Later decisions of the Supreme Court expanded and shaped the fundamental right of procreation that was initially expounded in *Skinner.* ...

The Court has demonstrated its willingness to permit states to interfere with the fundamental right of procreation only when two criteria have been met. First, the state must be able to show a compelling interest. Second, the state must demonstrate that there are no more effective or less intrusive means than that chosen to protect the interest. ...

Against the backdrop of these precedents and the great national debate over abortion, the fundamental right of procreation has been steadily eroded during the past 10 to 15 years by the decisions of an increasingly conservative Supreme Court. It is in light of this hostile environment that the use of contraception as a condition of probation must be considered.

CONTRACEPTION AS A CONDITION OF PROBATION

Probationary conditions include a variety of restrictions on the liberty of convicted persons. In general, the restrictions are, or should be, tailored to relate to the crime for which the person was convicted. This section defines probation and its legitimate uses in the criminal justice system. Further, this section focuses on one probationary condition that has been considered in a few state courts, that of remaining childless or having no additional children during the probationary period. This discussion leads to consideration of the Norplant condition.

A. Nature and Goals of Probation
Probation is the suspension of a convicted defendant's sentence before its execution. In *Griffin v. Wisconsin,* the Court likened probation to imprisonment, stating it is "a form of criminal sanction imposed by a court upon an offender after verdict, finding, or plea of guilty." ...

B. State Decisions Mandating Contraception as a Condition of Probation
People v. Johnson is the first case involving a probationary restriction on conception that mandated a specific contraceptive modality. Several other state cases, however, have ruled on probationary conditions that have generally required probationers to remain childless or have no additional children during the probationary period. In each of these cases, the courts have ruled that probationary conditions mandating that a probationer remain childless were void.

In *People v. Dominguez,* the trial court placed a woman who was convicted of second-degree robbery on probation. The woman was unmarried, had two illegitimate children, and was pregnant with a third. One probationary restriction was that she remain childless until she was married. Accordingly, when she later became pregnant again without being married, the trial court revoked her probation. On appeal, however, a California appellate court overturned the probationary condition, concluding that it was unreasonable. The court articulated a test that voided a condition of probation if it "(1) has no relationship to the crime of which the offender was convicted, (2) relates to conduct that is not in itself criminal, and (3) requires or forbids conduct that is not reasonably related to future criminality." Applying the test in this case, the court found no relation between the woman's future pregnancy and her crime. In addition, the court noted that there was no demonstrable evidence that unmarried, pregnant women were predisposed to commit crimes. Nor was there any rational basis for believing that poor, unmarried women tend to commit crimes upon becoming pregnant.

In sum, when the underlying crime is not child abuse, courts have generally struck down the probationary condition that the defendant remain childless, reasoning that the nexus between the crime and the condition is too tenuous. The nexus is more substantial, however, where the offense is related to abuse of a child.

In *State v. Livingston,* a woman allowed her seven-month-old child to be seriously burned when she placed him on a space heater. She was convicted of child abuse and placed on probation. As a condition of her probation, the trial court required that the defendant remain childless for five years. On appeal, however, an Ohio appellate court voided this condition of probation. The court said that a test of reasonableness should be applied in determining the validity of conditions of probation. While conceding that trial courts have considerable discretion in imposing probationary conditions, the court said that the condition failed here because it imposed arbitrary conditions that severely constrained the defendant's exercise of liberty. It also noted that the condition was unreasonable because it was only remotely related to the crime for which she was convicted and the rehabilitative goals of probation.

Similarly, in *Howland v. State,* a Florida appellate court held that a condition of probation that prohibited a man who was convicted of child abuse from fathering a child was void. The court admitted that the condition of probation could reasonably relate to future criminality in the form of further child abuse if the defendant were allowed to have custody of or to have contact with the child. In this case, however, those possibilities were foreclosed by other valid conditions of probation.

These concerns also arise in cases of child endangerment. In *State v. Mosburg,* a mother who abandoned her two-hour-old baby was convicted of endangering her child. As a condition of her probation, the trial court prohibited Ms. Mosburg from becoming pregnant during her probationary period. The appellate court found that the condition was an undue intrusion on her right to privacy, however, and remanded the case to the court below for deletion of the probationary condition.

In its analysis, the *Mosburg* court discussed some of the preceding cases but relied most significantly on the California case of *People v. Pointer. Pointer* helps focus the reasoning in this line of cases. In *Pointer,* Ruby Pointer was the mother of two young children. A strict adherent to a macrobiotic diet consisting only of grains, legumes, and vegetables, she imposed this dietary regime on her children. Despite repeated warnings by her physician and intervention by Children's Protective Services, Ms. Pointer continued to restrict the children's diet. As a result, the state removed the children to a foster home. Ms. Pointer later abducted the children and took them to Puerto Rico. Nearly a year later, the Federal Bureau of Investigation discovered Ms. Pointer and her children and subsequently returned them to California. Because of the macrobiotic diet, one of the children was seriously underdeveloped, and the other had suffered severe growth retardation and permanent neurological damage.

On these facts, Ms. Pointer was convicted of the felony of child endangerment and sentenced to five years probation. The conditions of probation included one year in county jail, participation in a counseling program, a ban on contact with her children or custody of any children without court approval, and a prohibition against conception during the probationary period. Ms. Pointer appealed the decision, claiming that the latter condition was an unconstitutional invasion of her fundamental right of procreation.

In applying the three-part *Dominguez* test, the *Pointer* court determined that the condition was reasonable because there was a direct nexus between the condition and the crime and possible future criminality. In arriving at that conclusion, the court distinguished *Pointer* from cases in other jurisdictions where courts had held that the challenged condition lacked the requisite relation to child abuse or to future criminality. The court noted that "those cases relied heavily upon the fact that the abuse could be entirely avoided by removal of any children from the custody of the defendant. This case is distinguishable, however, because of evidence that the harm sought to be prevented by the trial court may occur before birth." After concluding that the crime-condition nexus and the condition-future criminality nexus satisfied the *Dominguez* test, the court had to decide whether the condition was "impermissibly broad."

The court found that the condition clearly infringed on the fundamental right of procreation because it inhibited Ms. Pointer's power to choose to conceive and give birth to additional children.

The court further noted that it was equally clear that "the condition must be subjected so special scrutiny to determine whether the restriction is entirely necessary to serve the dual purposes of rehabilitation and public safety." It relied on *Parrish v. Civil Service Commission* to conclude that "[i]f available alternative means exist which are less violative of a constitutional right and are narrowly drawn so as to correlate more closely with the purpose contemplated, those alternatives should be used."

Applying the *Parrish* test, the court found that the condition was not designed to afford any rehabilitative purpose. Instead, it was designed to protect the public by preventing injury to an unborn child. According to the court, this purpose could be served by less intrusive means. It suggested that those means might include periodic pregnancy testing and, should Ms. Pointer become pregnant, close supervision by both her physician and her probation officer. In addition, if a child was born during her probation, the child could be removed to a foster home if necessary.

The appellate court further noted that the trial judge made it clear that he would uphold every condition of the probation and, if any was violated, Ms. Pointer would be sent to prison. It concluded that this threat posed a danger that Ms. Pointer might seek a clandestine abortion should she become pregnant during her probationary period. The potential for this result and the availability of less intrusive means of achieving the goals of probation led the court to reverse and remand the case for resentencing that would exclude the condition that prohibited conception.

Dominguez, Pointer, and their progeny provide the framework of precedent for the current initiatives....

FACTORING THE NORPLANT TECHNOLOGY INTO THE STATE INTEREST VERSUS INDIVIDUAL RIGHTS EQUATION

The underlying question in this privacy analysis is whether Norplant technology tips the scale in favor of state interests when balanced against the individual's fundamental right of procreation. In resolving this issue, *People v. Johnson* and H.R. 2255 must be considered separately because they address different behaviors. In the case of a drug-abusing pregnant woman, the fetus may be harmed in utero by the drugs that the woman ingests. Thus, there is a clear nexus between the crime of drug abuse and the welfare of any infant that may be born to the woman who ingests drugs during her pregnancy. In the case of a child-abuser, however, the nexus may not be so clear.

People v. Johnson
Darlene Johnson beat her children with a belt and electrical extension cord. She was subsequently convicted of child abuse. In applying the *Dominguez* test to these facts, the inclusion of Norplant as a probationary condition would seem to have little or no influence on the decision whether the prohibition on conception is unconstitutionally intrusive. The test makes a condition of probation invalid if it (1) has no relationship to the crime of which the offender was convicted, (2) relates to conduct that is not in itself criminal, and (3) requires or forbids conduct that is not reasonably related to future criminality and does not serve the statutory ends of probation.

Ms. Johnson sets forth four arguments to show that the condition fails the *Dominguez* test because it is neither directly related to child abuse nor to the prospect that she would engage in similar unlawful conduct in the future. First, she points out that there was no evidence that she inflicted similar treatment on her youngest child; nor was there any evidence that she mistreated any of them as infants. Second, she argues that the Norplant condition is unreasonable because it is unrelated to the rehabilitative goals of probation.... Third, she stresses that she is already required to undergo counseling and education that are specifically designed to help her cope with the stress of parenting and to teach her acceptable means of disciplining her children. Finally, she reasons that, should she become pregnant, the nine month gestation period would allow her time to complete her rehabilitation before another child is born. Thus, there would be no risk of an infant being born before she was fully rehabilitated....

Ms. Johnson also invokes her fundamental right of procreation as protected by the California and United States Constitutions. The trial court recognized the fundamental right but reasoned that it could be limited in certain circumstances. The court concluded that the defendant's constitutional rights should be balanced against the state's interests in protecting her unconceived children and ensuring that Ms. Johnson's rehabilitation was effective. In this case, the trial court held that the state's interests were more compelling than those of the individual. It is in the application of this balancing test that the unique characteristics of Norplant may have an impact in the outcome of the analysis.

1. Probationer's Reduced Expectation of Privacy

Before considering the impact of Norplant, the effect of probationary status in relation to fundamental rights should be examined. Ms. Johnson argues that "[a] probationer has the right to enjoy a significant degree of privacy, or liberty, under the Fourth, Fifth and Fourteenth Amendments to the federal Constitution." Ms. Johnson recognizes that a prisoner must forego some of her privacy rights because of the necessity for orderly administration of the prison system. She distinguishes probationers, however, on the basis that there is "[n]o parallel justification [that] supports depriving a defendant under the supervision of the probation system of fundamental human rights."

In contrast, the state argues that a probationer has an expectation of privacy that is less than that of an ordinary law abiding citizen. The Supreme Court has explicitly recognized a reduced expectation of privacy in probationers. "To a greater or lesser degree, it is always true of probationers ... that they do not enjoy 'the absolute liberty to which every citizen is entitled, but only ... conditional liberty properly dependent on observance of special [probation] restrictions.' " "Supervision, then, is a 'special need' of the State permitting a degree of impingement upon privacy that would not be constitutional if applied to the public at large." This reduced expectation of privacy must be considered in balancing state interests against individual rights.

2. The Balancing Test

Factoring in this reduced expectation of privacy, the scale tips slightly toward the state. The use of Norplant to enforce the probationary condition arguably could tip the scale further to the state's side. The probationer has been convicted of a crime. She could often be incarcerated for that crime. If incarcerated, the prisoner loses a wide array of rights, including not only the right of procreation but also the right of sexual expression. A probationer who has been ordered to practice contraception is in a significantly better position than the prisoner. Though she has temporarily given up the right of procreation, she has retained the right to associate with persons other than fellow criminals, to move freely in society, and to sexual expression.

Using standard contraceptive methods, this invasion of privacy could still be substantial. Periodic pregnancy checks or supervision of appropriate contraceptive use could seriously broaden the restraints on the probationer's liberty. In addition, the probationer must always be concerned that if her attempts at contraception fail, the court may revoke her probation and send her to prison. This is where the new technology may play a role. Once the Norplant was in place, the requirement for supervision would be obviated, and the probationer would not have to worry about being held in violation of probation. Courts would have to accept an inadvertent pregnancy as a failure of the technology for which the probationer is not responsible. Therefore, there would be no willful violation of the probation. In all likelihood, however, given the effectiveness of Norplant, this would happen only rarely. In addition, while the implantation does involve an invasion of bodily integrity, it is relatively minor because the procedure is required only once every five years. Further, it avoids the intrusiveness related to court monitoring that is required when other forms of contraception are used.

The intrusion would be great, however, on those women that could not medically tolerate the drug. This factor would make it imperative that any woman on whose behalf the Norplant condition is ordered receive a complete medical exam before implantation and ongoing medical care during her probation. No woman for whom Norplant was contraindicated or who had a major risk factor should be a candidate for a probationary condition mandating the implantation of Norplant.

The final factor that may make Norplant attractive as a condition of probation is its reversibility. When the probation ends and the Norplant capsules are removed, there is very little, if any, lingering restraint on the woman's ability to conceive if she so desires.

To win its argument for imposition of the Norplant condition, the state must first establish a reasonable nexus between the condition, child abuse, and the potential for future similar crimes. Once the state has demonstrated this nexus in a given case, the technological advantages of Norplant may become a factor in the analysis. Arguably, Norplant reduces the extent of the intrusion on the individual's fundamental rights because of its effectiveness, safety, ease of compliance, and reversibility. These unique characteristics tip the scale toward the state when this balancing test is applied in select cases.

3. Limiting the Probation Condition
The courts should be very selective in their application of the condition because it is an intrusion on the probationer's right of procreation. Norplant becomes the least invasive alternative only if the probationer is one who has been convicted of multiple offenses or particu-

larly egregious crimes that could result in her imprisonment. The woman who has failed at one or more previous courses of counseling, education, or other less intrusive measures may also fall into this category. The first time offender who may be rehabilitated by other means should not be a candidate for the Norplant condition. In addition to this limitation, all women should be medically evaluated before the condition is imposed. The condition should be ruled out for any woman for whom the drug is contraindicated. Additionally, any woman who receives the implant should receive medical supervision throughout the probationary period. Within the framework of these constraints, the Norplant condition may be an effective state tool in the battle against the problem of child abuse.

The Future for the Use of the Norplant Condition Against Child Abuse
The future of the Norplant condition in combating child abuse must be considered in light of three different factors. First, child abuse is gaining national attention as a major problem in society. Some legislators and judges have been proposing extremely serious sanctions for this crime. Similarly, courts have found that sterilization as an aspect of a plea bargain in child abuse cases is constitutional. Second, the Supreme Court has become increasingly active in restricting freedom of procreative choice. Third, the composition of the United States Supreme Court, with the retirement of Justices Brennan and Marshall and their replacement by the current administration's appointees, will be decidedly conservative for many years to come. Under these circumstances, it is not unreasonable to predict that the Norplant condition will become a viable weapon in the

justice system's battle against child abuse at some point in the future....

Kansas House Bill 2255

The purported intent of this bill is analogous to *People v. Pointer* in that both relate to situations where the newborn may be injured if the mother were to conceive. House Bill 2255 focuses on babies of mothers that use illegal drugs. The nexuses between the condition and the crime and the condition and future criminality in these cases are easy to identify. In *Pointer*, the nexus was that the mother persistently adhered to a macrobiotic diet, thereby putting any child that she may conceive at risk of in utero injury. For drug-abusing mothers, the nexus lies in the fact that the newborn is infused with the drugs that the mother uses during the pregnancy. Balancing the state interest against individual rights, it seems clear that the compelling state interest in protecting the newborn from maternal drug abuse outweighs the probationer's reduced expectation of privacy as it relates to the right of procreation.

House Bill 2255 is fatally flawed, however, because it is broadly drafted to include a wide range of drug-related crimes. A more narrowly drafted bill may well survive legislative scrutiny. Such a bill would limit imposition of the condition to drug-abusing fertile women and exclude nonusers such as possessors and traffickers. Again, considering the changing orientation of the Supreme Court and the high visibility of the "war on drugs," it is very possible that legislation of this type will become law in the future.

CONCLUSION

Child abuse and the terrible consequences of maternal drug abuse are at epidemic proportions in this country. In attempts to deal with this problem, a judge in California and a legislator in Kansas have proposed using a new contraceptive technology, Norplant. The use of this new drug delivery system to prevent probationers from conceiving during the probationary period runs headlong into the constitutionally protected fundamental right of procreation. The right is not absolute, however, and it has suffered significant erosion during the past decade. The increasingly conservative face of the United States Supreme Court means that this weakening of the fundamental right of procreation will likely continue.

Although these crimes against children have very high visibility with the public, it is improbable that either of the pioneering initiatives discussed above will succeed in gaining acceptance for the Norplant condition. The judge in California picked the wrong defendant on whom to impose the condition. Her conviction for child abuse was her first for that crime, and less intrusive alternative methods of rehabilitation had not been tried in her case. In addition, insufficient attention was given to a medical determination of whether she was an appropriate candidate for the implant. Similarly, the bill in the Kansas legislature is too broad to gain acceptance. It opens an expansive spectrum of drug-related crimes to the Norplant condition. A bill drafted to impose the condition only on drug users would have a much better chance of passage.

The issue, however, is not likely to die with these fledgling initiatives. Norplant and other contraceptive technologies on the research horizon are becoming increasingly appealing to lawmakers as tools to ensure compliance with conditions of probation that mandate contraception. They serve to safeguard the unborn while simultaneously limiting both the intrusion on an individual's privacy rights and the state's burden of probationary supervision. Accordingly, Norplant and the contraceptive technologies that will follow are likely to find their place as judicially imposed shields to help protect the children.

American Medical Association

BOARD OF TRUSTEES REPORT: REQUIREMENTS OR INCENTIVES BY GOVERNMENT FOR THE USE OF LONG-ACTING CONTRACEPTIVES

In December 1990, the Food and Drug Administration approved Norplant Contraceptive System (levonorgestrel) for long-term contraceptive use by women....

In the future, other long-acting contraceptives may be approved for use in the United States, and some of them may be for use by men....

Court-ordered use of Norplant or other long-acting contraceptives raises serious constitutional and policy concerns. Financial incentives offered by the government are troublesome as well on both constitutional and policy grounds.

COURT-ORDERED USE OF LONG-ACTING CONTRACEPTIVES

Court-ordered insertion of Norplant or other long-acting contraceptives probably violates multiple constitutional provisions. Each of these provisions is considered in turn.

Right to Refuse Medical Treatment

For more than two centuries, the common law has considered any medical treatment performed without the patient's consent to constitute a battery, excusable only in emergency circumstances. In the last 30 years, the common law has developed the doctrine of informed consent to medical treatment and its corollary right to refuse treatment....

A constitutional right to refuse treatment also has been recognized by the Supreme Court in criminal contexts. In *Winston v Lee*, the Court held that a state could not compel a criminal defendant to undergo surgery for the removal of a bullet lodged 2.5 cm deep in his chest. In addition to the health risks posed by the surgery, the Court found that the surgery would constitute a "severe" intrusion into the defendant's interests in "personal privacy and bodily integrity." The Supreme Court has found that compelled blood tests or stomach pumping, and even physically noninvasive medical procedures like the breath-testing devices for intoxication (eg, Breathalyzer test) and urinalysis, implicate constitutional concerns about an individual's personal privacy and bodily integrity.

The right to refuse medical treatment reflects in part the fact that treatments pose both benefits and risks to the patient. Because individuals have varying views about the different benefits and risks, each person is entitled to choose which benefits and risks to accept and which to forgo. A person ordered to use a long-acting contraceptive may wish to continue having children and therefore see no health benefit in the contraceptive. With any long-acting contraceptive, some health risks exist, and there may be increased risks of serious illnesses such as myocardial infarction, stroke, and cancer. In the case of Norplant, users appear to be very safe in terms of immediate health risks. However, data are lacking on the long-term risks of Norplant use. Given the possible role of hormone-based contraceptives in the development of breast cancer, it may be particularly important to preserve the freedom to refuse long-acting contraceptives.

Cruel and Unusual Punishment

In several cases, courts have considered whether forced medical treatment violates the Eighth Amendment's prohibition against cruel and unusual punishment. Courts have upheld the imposition of medical treatment when the treatment can be justified as being in the patient's health interest or when the treatment would protect the health or safety of others. Thus, for example, a prison may re-

quire vaccinations for incoming inmates or psychotropic medications for prisoners who are suffering from a mental disorder and are either gravely disabled or a threat to themselves or others. On the other hand, courts have tended to disapprove forced medical treatment when the treatment is aimed solely at behavioral control or punishment.

Long-acting contraceptives cannot be justified as therapeutic for persons who have committed child abuse. These medications do nothing to treat the abuser's abusive tendencies. Similarly, they are hard to justify as a means of protecting others. Preventing child abusers from having more children may avoid the stress that can come from having a large family, but the concern can also be met by providing better support services, including day-care programs and parenting skills training. Long-acting contraceptives would prevent the abuse of any future children, but it would do so by precluding the man or woman from having the children. Such an approach may constitute a more severe response to the problem of child abuse than is constitutionally appropriate. Many of those who would be forced to use a long-acting contraceptive would not have had any additional children even if permitted to procreate. Of those men and women who would have additional children, many may not abuse the children. In short, for every person who would be prevented by contraception from abusing another child, there might well be several people denied the right to procreate who never would have abused another child.

Alternative approaches to the problem of child abuse are less intrusive than forced contraception. While no child should face a risk of abuse by his or her parents, the needs of children may be better met by enacting safeguards to protect the child, not preventing the child from being born. The child's needs may be served by providing close supervision of the parents, appropriate treatment and social services, and foster placement care when necessary.

Right to Procreate

The right to procreate has been recognized for nearly 50 years by the US Supreme Court as one of society's "basic civil rights." In a 1942 decision, the Court rejected an Oklahoma law that provided for sterilization of those who were convicted of multiple felonies involving "moral turpitude." During the past few decades, the Court has reasserted the right to procreate in its decisions about the right to privacy. According to the Court, individuals must have "independence in making certain kinds of important decisions." At the core of the privacy right have been matters concerning marriage and procreation. Government interference with such inherently private and personal matters has been viewed as antithetical to basic concepts of individual liberty in a free society. When a foreign government prohibits couples from having more than one or two children, citizens of this country react with outrage. Under US Supreme Court rulings, as well as decisions of state supreme courts, individuals have the right to control contraception and, to a large extent, pregnancy.

Recent Supreme Court decisions have suggested that the Court may allow states to impose greater limits on the right of women to terminate pregnancy. In *Webster v Reproductive Health Services* and *Rust v Sullivan*, the Court suggested that the states may increasingly be permitted to regulate abortions. Nevertheless, these rulings do not necessarily affect the right to become pregnant. Indeed, the principles underlying *Webster* and *Rust* would argue against state-mandated contraception. In each case, the decision reflected a desire to give the states greater authority to advance their interest in preserving potential life. Such an interest would not be served by preventing certain women or men from having children.

The State's Interests

The state may infringe on a fundamental constitutional right only if it does so to further a compelling state interest and the state's action is narrowly tailored to further its compelling interest....

Important policy reasons counsel caution when considering state-mandated contraception. If parents convicted of child abuse could be forced to use long-acting contraceptives, it is likely that cultural and other prejudices would influence whether a particular person was ordered to have a long-acting contraceptive imposed. Historically, members of minority groups and the lower socioeconomic classes have been disproportionately subject to reporting and prosecution of child abuse. Similarly, women who use illicit drugs during pregnancy are more likely to be reported for their drug use if they are poor or black.

An analogy can be drawn between long-acting contraceptives for child abusers and involuntary sterilization of the mentally handicapped. Similarly, an analogy can be drawn with mandatory use of antiandrogens (eg, medroxyprogesterone acetate) [substances that decrease levels of male hormone] for male sex offenders. However, neither of these two practices provides adequate support for court-ordered use of long-acting contraceptives. Involuntary sterilization of the mentally handicapped has been characterized by serious abuses and injustices in the past. Many of the mentally handicapped have been deprived unfairly of their reproductive capacity. It is not clear that involuntary sterilization has any role in the care of the mentally handicapped, unless the sterilization serves a therapeutic purpose. For example, a mentally handicapped woman may have severe heart disease for which pregnancy would pose a high risk of cardiac compromise. When there are circumstances in which involuntary sterilization may be justified, it must be justified in terms of protecting the health or other interests of the sterilized person. As discussed above, the involuntary use of a long-acting contraceptive cannot be supported on the grounds that it serves the interests of the person who receives it.

Use of antiandrogens for male sex offenders is also controversial. Proponents of antiandrogen use base their advocacy on the therapeutic role of antiandrogens in controlling inappropriate sexual desires and therefore preventing recidivism of male sex offenders. While there is some evidence that antiandrogens may have a role in the treatment of male sex offenders, other studies have failed to demonstrate a therapeutic benefit from the drugs. In addition, involuntary use of antiandrogens raises many of the same legal concerns as does use of a long-acting contraceptive. In the one reported case involving court-ordered antiandrogens for criminal sexual conduct, a Michigan appeals court rejected their use. If there is a role for antiandrogens for male sex offenders, it is on therapeutic grounds. Since long-acting contraceptives do not have a therapeutic role, their mandatory use cannot be justified by analogy to antiandrogens.

Consent to Court-Ordered Contraception

When a person is convicted of child abuse and a long-acting contraceptive is imposed as a condition of probation, the defendant technically consents to the contraceptive when the terms of probation are accepted. In general, defendants may reject probation in favor of a prison sentence, although some courts have held that defendants have no right to refuse probation.

However, as courts have recognized, a defendant's "consent" to the conditions of probation is more illusory than real. The alternative of incarceration prevents the acceptance of probationary terms from being willing or voluntary. Even if consent were truly voluntary, courts are limited by constitutional and statutory considerations in the kinds of probationary terms that can be imposed. The defendant's acceptance of a probationary condition does not prevent the defendant from appealing the condition as unconstitutional or otherwise invalid legally. Indeed, since the time that procreative rights were recognized by the US Supreme Court, appellate courts have consistently refused to permit forced contraception or sterilization as a condition of probation.

Similar concerns apply to long-acting contraception as part of plea bargaining. In addition, plea bargaining takes place in an inherently coercive environment that lacks the procedural safeguards of trial proceedings. There is too great a risk that contraception would be offered in a plea bargain for inappropriate reasons. Prosecutors enjoy broad discretion regarding who is charged with child abuse and what kind of penalty is pursued. Cultural and other prejudices could too easily influence the decision to threaten a person with a jail sentence in order to secure the person's agreement to accept contraception. In some cases in which incarceration ordinarily would not even be a possibility, the prosecutor could threaten incarceration to ensure that contraception was accepted.

Contraception should also not be part of negotiations with child welfare authorities. Child welfare authorities can use the threat of criminal prosecution to coerce the individual's acceptance of contraception; the discretion of child welfare authorities to refer cases for criminal prosecution can be affected by their social and cultural biases.

FINANCIAL INCENTIVES TO USE LONG-ACTING CONTRACEPTIVES

There can be an appropriate role for financial subsidies for women (and someday for men) who use long-acting contraceptives. The poor may have to forgo the option of a long-acting contraceptive for lack of medical insurance or personal funds to pay the cost of the contraceptive. Consequently, government subsidies for the costs of inserting long-acting contraceptives like Norplant and for follow-up visits to the physician are desirable. Use of Norplant is covered by Medicaid in at least 43 states; its use and that of other long-acting contraceptives should be covered by Medicaid in all states (*New York Times*, March 20, 1991:A28). Similarly, the use of long-acting contraceptives should be covered by private medical insurance.

However, it would not be appropriate to tie the amount of a person's welfare payment or other government benefits to his or her decision to use a long-acting contraceptive. Individuals should not be required to assume a potentially serious health risk as a condition of receiving government benefits, particularly when those benefits may be needed for basic human needs like housing, clothing, and food.

Tying the amount of a person's welfare benefits to his or her decision to use a contraceptive may well be unconstitutional. While the government is not obligated to provide welfare, it may not condition the receipt of welfare benefits on the waiver of important fundamental rights. For example, welfare recipients cannot be forced to give up their benefits if they exercise their right to vote. Similarly, while the government may subsidize the costs of contraception, courts might not permit the government to increase welfare benefits for those who use contraception since the practical effect would be to reduce a person's welfare benefits if he or she declined contraception. Tying benefits to contraceptive use would result in penalties for people who refused contraception as an exercise of their right to refuse medical treatment or their right to procreate. The government should not be able to withhold public benefits in order to penalize people who exercise their constitutional rights in a way that is distasteful to government officials.

RECOMMENDATIONS

The Board of Trustees recommends the following:

1. Involuntary use of long-acting contraceptives because of child abuse raises serious questions about a person's fundamental rights to refuse medical treatment, to be free of cruel and unusual punishment, and to procreate. The state's compelling interest in protecting children from abuse may be served by less intrusive means

than imposing contraception on parents who have committed child abuse. The needs of children may be better met by providing close supervision of the parents, appropriate treatment and social services, and foster placement care when necessary. There is not sufficient evidence to demonstrate that long-acting contraceptives are an effective social response to the problem of child abuse. Before long-acting contraceptives are considered as a response to individual cases of child abuse, the issue needs to be addressed by society broadly. Society must be careful about taking shortcuts to save resources when constitutional rights are involved.

2. Serious questions are raised by plea bargains or negotiations with child welfare authorities that result in the use of long-acting contraceptives. Such agreements are made in inherently coercive environments that lack procedural safeguards. In addition, cultural and other biases may influence decisions made by the state to seek the use of a long-acting contraceptive.

3. If welfare or other government benefits were based on the use of long-acting contraceptive agents, individuals would be required to assume a potentially serious health risk before receiving their benefits. Government benefits should not be made contingent on the acceptance of a health risk.

4. Individuals should not be denied access to effective contraception because of their indigence. Use of long-acting contraceptives should be covered by Medicaid and other health insurance programs, both public and private.

5. Long-acting contraceptives may be medically contraindicated. Assessing the health risks of long-acting contraceptives is substantially outside the purview of courts and legislatures.

POSTSCRIPT

Should Courts Be Permitted to Order Women to Use Long-Acting Contraceptives?

At the time of her sentencing, Darlene Johnson agreed to the Norplant implantation but later changed her mind. In addition to the implantation, her sentence included one year in jail and three years probation. Two months after the decision, Judge Broadman was shot at in his courtroom by a man who claimed to be angry about the Johnson decision. As a result of this incident and the publicity surrounding his decision, Judge Broadman removed himself from the case. The district attorney's office then asked for an appeal on the grounds that Johnson did not voluntarily agree to the implantation. The appeal was dismissed in April 1992 at the request of her lawyers because she had violated the terms of her probation by testing positive for drug use and was sentenced to five years in prison. The Norplant order never became effective and was never adjudicated. The Kansas legislation was defeated, as were similar proposals introduced in other states.

In 1991 a Texas judge ordered the implantation of Norplant as part of a plea bargain agreement. A woman who pleaded guilty to injuring her hospitalized 10-month-old daughter was ordered to serve 10 years probation, including 5 years of using Norplant and participation in parenting classes. In addition, she was denied unsupervised visits with her other children for 10 years. In Baltimore a 1993 plan to offer Norplant in high school clinics has failed to attract many young women. Health officials believe that misinformation about side effects and accusations by some black leaders that the program is genocidal and would lead to promiscuity have contributed to its failure.

In 1994 a class action suite was filed by 400 women who had used Norplant and who claimed that removing the contraceptive when they wanted to become pregnant was painful and difficult. Some of the women said that they required surgery and that they have been left with extensive scars as a result.

Another long-acting contraceptive, Depo-Provera, was approved by the Food and Drug Administration in 1992. Depo-Provera is an injectable drug that prevents pregnancy for three months. Like Norplant, it has side effects for some women; but it does not require implantation or removal.

In "Norplant: The New Scarlet Letter?" *Journal of Contemporary Health Law and Policy* (vol. 8, 1992), Michael T. Flannery presents legal arguments for and against the use of Norplant and concludes, "Implantation of Norplant will remain a sentencing option available to the courts." Also see Anita Hardon,

"Norplant: Conflicting Views on Its Safety and Acceptability," in *Issues in Reproductive Technology (I): An Anthology* edited by Helen B. Holmes (Garland Publishing, 1992). See also Madeline Henley, "The Creation and Perpetuation of the Mother/Body Myth: Judicial and Legislative Enlistment of Norplant," *Buffalo Law Review* (vol. 41, no. 2, 1993). Finally, *Norplant and Poor Women* edited by Sarah E. Samuels and Mark D. Smith (Henry J. Kaiser Family Foundation, 1992) contains essays on the potential for coercion and other issues relating to poor, minority women.

ISSUE 2

Is There a Moral Right to Abortion?

YES: Bonnie Steinbock, from *Life Before Birth: The Moral and Legal Status of Embryos and Fetuses* (Oxford University Press, 1992)

NO: Sidney Callahan, from "Abortion and the Sexual Agenda: A Case for Prolife Feminism," *Commonweal* (April 25, 1986)

ISSUE SUMMARY

YES: Philosopher Bonnie Steinbock argues for a pro-choice position based on two independent considerations: the moral status of the fetus, which she claims begins when the fetus has a capacity for conscious experience; and the pregnant woman's moral right to bodily self-determination.

NO: Psychologist Sidney Callahan asserts that a woman's moral obligation to continue a pregnancy arises from both her status as a member of the human community and her unique life-giving female reproductive power.

Abortion is the most divisive bioethical issue of our time. The issue has been a persistent one in history, but in the past 20 years or so the debate has polarized. One view—known as "pro-life"—sees abortion as the wanton slaughter of innocent life. The other view—"pro-choice"—considers abortion as an option that must be available to women if they are to control their own reproductive lives. In the pro-life view, women who have access to "abortion on demand" put their own selfish whims ahead of an unborn child's right to life. In the pro-choice view, women have the right to choose to have an abortion—especially if there is some overriding reason, such as preventing the birth of a child with a severe genetic defect or one conceived as a result of rape or incest.

Behind these strongly held convictions, as political scientist Mary Segers has pointed out, are widely differing views of what determines value (that is, whether value is inherent in a thing or ascribed to it by human beings), the relation between law and morality, and the use of limits of political solutions to social problems, as well as the value of scientific progress. Those who condemn abortion as immoral generally follow a classical tradition in which abortion is a public matter because it involves our conception of how we ought to live together in an ideal society. Those who accept the idea of abortion, on the other hand, generally share the liberal, individualistic ethos of contemporary society. To them, abortion is a private choice, and public policy ought to reflect how citizens actually behave, not some unattainable ideal.

This is what we know about abortion practices in America today: It has been legal since the 1973 Supreme Court decision of *Roe v. Wade* declared that a woman has a constitutional right to privacy, which includes an abortion. It is seven times safer than childbirth, although there are some unknown risks—primarily the effect of repeated abortions on subsequent pregnancies. Abortion is common: Each year about 1.5 million abortions are performed. That is, one out of four pregnancies (and half of all unintended pregnancies) end in abortion. About 90 percent of all abortions are performed within the first 12 weeks of pregnancy by a method called suction aspiration. Eighty percent of the women who have abortions are unmarried, and nearly 63 percent are between the ages of 15 and 24. (In comparison, however, in 1965 there were between 200 thousand and 1.2 million illegal abortions, and 20 percent of all deaths from childbirth or pregnancy were caused by botched abortions.) Although the number of abortions performed in 1990 was about 10 percent higher than in 1980, the number of live births increased by 16 percent. In 1990 the national fertility rate (the number of live births per 1,000 women of reproductive age) was the highest since 1972. American women are having more babies and about the same number of abortions.

If abortion today is legal, safe, and common, it undeniably involves the killing of fetal life, and so the question remains: Is it ethical? At the heart of the issue are two complex questions. Does the fetus have a moral status that entitles it to life, liberty, and the pursuit of happiness as guaranteed by the Constitution? And even if it does, does a woman's rights to the same freedoms outweigh those of the fetus?

The selections that follow are written from two different feminist perspectives. Bonnie Steinbock believes that consideration of both the moral status of the fetus and a pregnant woman's right to bodily self-determination is necessary to establish the moral status of abortion. She places the beginning of a fetus's status as a potential human at the point when the capacity for conscious experience develops, sometime toward the end of the second trimester. Her criteria support a liberal stance on abortion. Sidney Callahan seeks to broaden what she sees as feminists' excessively narrow focus on "rights." She argues that women, as members of the human community with unique life-giving powers, have a moral obligation not to terminate a pregnancy and that society should provide the support that women need to enhance their lives.

YES

Bonnie Steinbock

ABORTION

Nearly two decades after the Supreme Court ruled in *Roe* v. *Wade*[1] that a woman has a constitutional right to terminate her pregnancy, abortion remains one of the most divisive and emotionally charged issues in America. Pro-lifers march with posters of macerated fetuses; pro-choicers use a bloody coat hanger as their symbol of the days of illegal abortions. But behind the drama and the emotion are claims that can be subjected to philosophical scrutiny. Is the unborn a human being, with a right to life like any other human being, as pro-lifers maintain? If it is, then very few abortions, if any, could be justified. For we do not generally think that it is morally permissible to kill children because they are unwanted or illegitimate or severely handicapped. On the other hand, if the fetus[2] is not a child, but only part of the pregnant woman's body, then restrictive abortion laws would be as difficult to justify in a pluralistic society as laws against contraception. For restrictive abortion laws impose enormous physical, emotional, and financial burdens on women. Even legal moralists, who hold that society has the right to enforce its moral beliefs through law, could not justify the imposition of such heavy burdens. Only the assumption that the unborn is a human being like any other, entitled to the law's protection, could justify the prohibition of abortion. Thus, the moral status of the unborn is central to the abortion debate....

Few writers on abortion come to the topic with a fully open mind, and I am no exception. I believe that the decision to have an abortion is one that belongs to the pregnant woman—not the state, not her doctor, not her husband. My pro-choice position is based on two independent considerations: the moral status of the fetus and the pregnant woman's moral right to bodily self-determination. I believe that both are necessary to an adequate treatment of abortion, yet many writers on abortion focus on only one aspect, while ignoring or downplaying the other. Thus, some opponents of abortion talk about the fetal right to live, or the wrongness of depriving a potential human being of its future life, without even mentioning the fact that a particular woman must carry and bear the fetus for it to have a future life.[3] On the other side, some feminists regard the inquiry into the status of the fetus as irrelevant to the problem of abortion.[4] The central questions, from a feminist perspective, are not about the abstract individual rights of fetuses but how to create the social conditions that make possible the fulfillment of reproductive responsibilities....

But these questions, important as they are, do not go "beneath the surface of the abortion dispute." *They change the subject.* The issue is whether abortion is a morally permissible choice. This question would remain, even if poverty, racism, or sexism were eliminated. In such a world, there would presumably still be contraceptive failures and unwanted pregnancies. It goes without saying that women ought to be recognized as fully autonomous choosers; the question is whether abortion is a choice that autonomous choosers are morally permitted to make. It is hard to see how one can answer this question without responding to the claim that abortion is the killing of a human being, with a right to life.

The interest view responds to this claim by arguing that embryos and early fetuses lack moral status. We are not morally required to consider their interests because, prior to becoming conscious and sentient, fetuses do not *have* interests. The defense of this claim requires some factual investigation as to when sentience occurs. More important, I will need to explain why sentience is essential to moral status. After all, if allowed to grow and develop, the nonconscious, nonsentient fetus will become conscious and sentient. It has been argued that its potential to acquire these characteristics gives the fetus a present interest in continued existence, and makes abortion seriously wrong....

CRITERIA FOR MORAL STATUS

The Conservative Position

...[T]here are two parts to the extreme conservative position. First, it attaches moral significance to the genetic humanity of the fetus; second, it argues that this humanity is present from conception onward. Either part can be challenged independently. For example, Baruch Brody takes what might be called a modified conservative position. Like Noonan, Brody bases the moral status of the unborn on its being human. However, he does not agree that humanity begins at conception. Brody argues that a functioning brain is essential for being human. When the brain stops functioning, the person dies and goes out of existence. On the same reasoning, the fetus "comes into humanity" when its brain begins to function.[5] In other words, the beginning of brain function marks a radical discontinuity in the life of the unborn. The human being who begins when brain function starts is not identical with the embryo whose brain has not yet begun to function.

Even if one accepts the thesis of radical discontinuity (a thesis that most conservatives would reject as inconsistent with the reality of continuous physical development), it is not clear why this should be marked by the emergence of brain waves. The beginning of brain function, taken as a physiological occurrence, is not different from any other change in the fetus. The significance of brain function lies rather in its connection with mental states such as conscious awareness. Brody suggests this when he says, "One of the characteristics essential to a human being is the capacity for conscious experience, at least at a primitive level. Before the sixth week, as far as we know, the fetus does not have this capacity. Thereafter, as the electroencephalographic evidence indicates, it does. Consequently, that is the time at which the fetus becomes a human being."[6]

The phrase "capacity for conscious experience" is ambiguous. It might refer to the physiological ability of a being to have conscious experiences *at some point* in its development. The fetus at six weeks after conception (eight weeks g.a. [gestation age]) certainly has the capacity for conscious experience in this sense, but so does the single-celled zygote. Obviously, this is not what Brody intends. In another sense of "capacity," a being has the capacity for an experience *x* if *x* occurs, given the appropriate stimulus. A frog has the capacity to feel pain if, on being subjected to certain kinds of stimuli, the frog feels pain. However, in this sense of "capacity," neither a zygote nor a 6-week-old fetus has the capacity for conscious experience. The emergence of brain waves is only a necessary, not a sufficient, condition of conscious experience.

What further development is necessary for the fetus to feel pain, arguably the most primitive form of conscious experience? ... Admittedly, the evaluation of pain in the fetus is difficult, both because pain is a subjective phenomenon and because we do not have access to the fetus *in utero* to perform behavioral tests. Nevertheless, from what we do know about the physiology of pain perception, it seems reasonable to conclude that the fetus during the first trimester, and probably well into the second trimester, is not sentient. The neural pathways are not sufficiently developed to transmit pain messages to the fetal cortex until 22 to 24 weeks of gestation. If the early fetus is not sentient, it

is unlikely to have conscious awareness of any kind. Certainly the ability to feel pain would precede more highly developed cognitive states, such as thoughts, emotions, and moods.

To summarize, brain function has no significance if taken as a purely physiological development in the fetus. Brain function is significant only because it is a necessary condition for mental states, such as sentience, conscious awareness, beliefs, and memories. However, brain function is not a sufficient condition for even the most rudimentary mental states. Thus, Brody's claim that the emergence of brain waves marks the beginning of human life is not tenable. If the capacity for conscious experience is a necessary condition of humanity, the fetus does not become human until sometime toward the end of the second trimester. This criterion for moral status supports a liberal, rather than a conservative, stance on abortion. ...

A conscious, sentient newborn ordinarily has a life worth living, a life he enjoys, a life that is a good to him. Continuing to live is certainly *in* the baby's interest, because of the value to him of his life *right now.* A right to life protects his interest in his life. I conclude that there is no conceptual bar to ascribing to newborns a right to life.[7] Nor is there any conceptual bar to ascribing a right to life to the nearly born fetus. A late-gestation fetus is conscious and sentient. It is possible that it has pleasurable experiences. If so, it has an interest in continuing to live, an interest that can be protected by a right to life. By contrast, embryos and preconscious fetuses do not have lives that they value, lives that are a good to them. Life is no more a good to an embryo than it is to a plant or a sperm. Thus, the importance of sentience is not primarily that abortion causes pain to the sentient fetus. That problem might be taken care of with an anesthetic. The relevance of sentience is that a sentient being can have a life it values, and that we can protect for its own sake.

Some antiabortionists consider it callous and unfeeling to deny moral status to the preconscious fetus. But the charge of callousness makes sense only if we persist in thinking of embryos and fetuses as being just like babies, only smaller. In fact, I think that this is how many opponents of abortion do regard the fetus. For example, the film *The Silent Scream* purported to show a 12-week fetus struggling to get away from the abortionist's scalpel, and opening its mouth in "a silent scream." Critics of the film charged that normal fetal movements were speeded up to make it look as if the fetus were recoiling in pain. But even if the film was not doctored, such movements are not by themselves evidence of pain. A mimosa plant shrinks from touch, but no one claims that the mimosa feels pain. The reason is that a plant lacks the nervous system necessary for the experience of pain. Similarly, the fetal nervous system at 12 weeks is not sufficiently developed to carry and transmit pain messages. Insofar as opposition to abortion is based on factual error, or worse, deliberate misrepresentation of the facts, it must be rejected out of hand.

A more sophisticated conservative position acknowledges that zygotes, embryos, and early fetuses do not suffer from being aborted, nor does death deprive them of happy lives. Nevertheless, it maintains that even a zygote has an interest in not being killed. This interest in continued existence does not derive from the kind of life it has *now,* but rather on the kind of life it *will* have, if it is allowed to develop and grow. Such arguments are known as arguments from potential. If successful, they can support the conservative proposal that genetic humans ought to be treated as normative persons.

THE ARGUMENT FROM POTENTIAL

There are different versions of the argument from potential, but the basic idea is that it is wrong to kill, or otherwise prevent the development of, a human fertilized egg because it possesses the potential to be a descriptive person. As Stephen Buckle expresses it, "It is, potentially, just like us, so we cannot deny it any rights or other forms of protection that we accord ourselves."[8] A fertilized egg does not now have any of the properties of a person. It isn't even sentient. But this does not matter because, left alone and allowed to develop, the zygote will become a person. Buckle says, "The fertilized egg is not 'just like us' only in the sense that it is not *yet* just like us. Therefore, the argument concludes, we should not interfere with its natural development towards being a rational, self-conscious being. On its strongest interpretation, the argument is thought to establish that we should treat a potential human subject as if it were already an actual human subject."[9]

The Logical Problem

A standard objection to the argument from potential is that it involves a logical mistake. The mistake consists in thinking of a "potential person" as a kind of person, and, on this basis, ascribing to "potential persons" the rights of other persons. But potential persons are not persons; they do not now have the characteristics of persons....

It is a logical error to think that potential personhood implies possession of the rights of actual persons. However, the argument from potential need not be based on this logical mistake. Like the defender of the genetic humanity criterion, the defender of the argument from potential can be understood as making a normative proposal: that potential persons *ought* to have the same rights as actual persons. Understood this way, the argument is not based on a logical confusion, but is rather in need of defense. Why should beings who are potentially "just like us" be entitled to the same protection as we are?

A Future Like Ours

Don Marquis argues that abortion is seriously immoral, for the same reason that killing an innocent adult human being is immoral.[10] What makes killing wrong is not primarily the effects on other people, or the threat to the fabric of society. What makes killing wrong is the effect on the victim. The loss of one's life is one of the greatest losses one can suffer. The loss of one's life deprives one of all the experiences, activities, projects, and enjoyments that would otherwise have constituted one's future. When I am killed, I am deprived of all of the value of my future. Abortion deprives the fetus of its future, a future just like ours. Hence, abortion is prima facie seriously morally wrong.

Marquis maintains that this is not an argument based on the wrongness of killing potential persons, since the central category is not *personhood* at all, but the category of having a valuable future like ours. However, if we ask what it is that makes "a future like ours" valuable, the answer is likely to be in terms of our capacity to enjoy our lives and derive meaning from them, to envisage a future and to make plans about it, to have relationships with others. In other words, the very capacities that make us people are what enable us to have a valuable future. So the notion of personhood, and the special wrongness of killing persons, is implicit in Marquis's account.

On the interest view, only beings that have already begun to experience their lives have an interest in the continuation of their lives. Only sentient beings can be harmed or wronged by being killed. Marquis calls this the *discontinuation account*. He concedes that it is intelligible, but holds that it is inferior to his "future-like-ours" account of the wrongness of killing. The value of one's present life is irrelevant, Marquis argues. What matters is the future of which one is deprived by death. Whether one has immediate past experiences or not does not work in the explanation of what makes killing wrong....

Contraception and the Moral Status of Gametes

The strongest objection to the argument from potential is that it seems to make contraception, and even abstinence, prima facie morally wrong. If the objection to abortion is that it deprives the zygote of "a future like ours," why, it may be asked, cannot the same complaint be made of contraceptive techniques that kill sperm, or prevent fertilization? Why don't gametes have "a future like ours"? Why aren't unfertilized eggs and sperm also potential people? John Harris makes the point this way:

> To say that a fertilized egg is potentially a human being is just to say that if certain things happen to it (like implantation), and certain other things do not (like spontaneous abortion), it will eventually become a human being. But the same is

also true of the unfertilized egg and the sperm. If certain things happen to the egg (like meeting a sperm) and certain things happen to the sperm (like meeting an egg) and thereafter certain other things do not (like meeting a contraceptive), then they will eventually become a new human being.[11]

So, if abortion is seriously wrong because it kills a potential person, then the use of a contraceptive is equally seriously wrong. In using a spermicide, one commits mass murder! Indeed, even abstinence is wrong, insofar as it prevents the development of a new human being. Very few defenders of the potentiality principle are willing to accept this conclusion.[12] They must then give reasons why a zygote, but not a sperm or ovum, is a potential person.

Defenders of the potentiality criterion sometimes appeal to an enormous difference in probabilities. John Noonan points out that the chances of any particular sperm becoming a person are remarkably low. There are about two hundred million spermatozoa in a normal ejaculate, of which only one has a chance of developing into a zygote. By contrast, he estimates the chances of a zygote developing into a person to be about 80 percent. The difference is still impressive, even if we adjust Noonan's estimate to reflect more recent information on the miscarriage rate. A 1988 study found that 31 percent of all conceptions end in miscarriage, usually in the early months of pregnancy and often before women even know they are pregnant. Even this study probably underestimated the miscarriage rate by an unknown amount, since some fertilized eggs are so defective that they never make chorionic gonadotropin, the hormone that pregnancy tests measure, and are miscarried within days of fertilization.[13] This suggests that a given zygote's chance of becoming a person is about 50 percent, rather than the 80 percent chance Noonan gives it. Still, the zygote's one-in-two chance is a lot better than a sperm's one-in-two-hundred-million chance. The odds of an ovum's developing into a person are better than those of a sperm, but still much worse than those of a fertilized egg. If we think of potential in terms of statistical likelihood, a zygote has greater potential than a gamete. But it is not clear that the odds matter. Although the chances of any particular sperm becoming a person are infinitesimal, why should that prevent its being a potential person? Is not every entrant in a lottery a potential winner, even if the odds of winning are extremely low? Every gamete, it may be said, has the potential to develop into a person, even though very few do....

At this point, the debate seems to be at a standstill. Antiabortionists are convinced that there is an enormous moral difference between the product of conception and the ingredients of conception. Their opponents are convinced that the difference is one of degree, and lacking in moral importance. Neither side is obviously right or wrong. Yet the success of the argument from potential hinges on differentiating the zygote from its component gametes....

There is no question that abortion is for most women psychologically and emotionally different from contraception. Few women experience abortion as just another way to avoid motherhood. Abortion is the end of a specific pregnancy, and this termination can be psychologically distressing, even when it is felt to be necessary. Pregnancy affects a woman's body in concrete, noticeable ways, preparing her to carry and bear a child. The child she would have, if she did not abort, is thus likely to have for her a reality that no merely possible person can have. Some women are pleased at finding that they *can* bear a child, even if they realize that having a child at this point in their lives is unwise. In ending the pregnancy, they are likely to have mixed feelings. In addition, pregnancy is imbued with certain cultural meanings. It is ordinarily a joyous experience, and one that is associated with congratulations, gift-giving, and special treatment. As one woman expresses it, "Sadness at not being able to celebrate pregnancy, to enjoy the sense of specialness it brings, is an understandable response."[14] Once we understand this, we can see why so many women (and men) do not have the same attitude toward abortion as they do toward contraception. Unless one's religion forbids it, contraception is likely to be regarded as morally neutral, a sensible preventive health habit, like flossing your teeth. It has none of the sadness or sense of loss that often accompanies abortions. A view that equates abortion and contraception is remote from the experiences of most people.

Does this matter? Some philosophers deny that it does. They argue that people's intuitions or felt convictions have no moral significance. They remind us that some people "experience" blacks and women to be inferior to whites and men. They maintain that we should not try to account for such feelings in our moral theories. The appropriate response to feelings that do not accord with moral theory is, "So what?"

I do not agree with this total rejection of moral feelings. It *may* be that a feeling is mere prejudice, incapable of being supported by good reasons. I think that this can fairly easily be shown of racist

and sexist views. But from the fact that some strong convictions are indefensible, it does not follow that all are. A morality that is radically divorced from our deepest feelings, and disconnected from our experiences and emotions, cannot be practical or action-guiding. For all the reasons I have given above, I think we are justified in regarding abortion as morally more serious than contraception, and for thinking that abortion is a moral issue in a way that contraception is not. Still, I would not go so far as Rosalind Hursthouse, who argues that abortion is a choice that a completely wise and virtuous person would rarely make, because it usually displays a callous and light-minded attitude toward life.[15] This is unfair. A great many abortions occur because of contraceptive failure. A woman who is responsibly using a reliable contraceptive, and nevertheless gets pregnant, should not be labeled callous or light-minded. At the same time, this characterization might fit a woman who does not use contraceptives, repeatedly becomes pregnant, and has several abortions. I knew a sixteen-year-old girl who was about to have her third abortion. I asked her what seemed to be the problem. "Oh," she responded, "I can never remember to put in a diaphragm, and the pill makes me fat." We can acknowledge that her attitude toward sexuality, pregnancy, and potential human life is immature and superficial, without implying that the unborn has moral status. Abortion may be morally undesirable, in a way that contraception is not, without its being a *wrong to* the unborn....

Sentient Fetuses

What is the moral status of sentient fetuses? They have begun to have experiences, and so it is at least possible that they enjoy their lives. Obviously, the range and nature of their enjoyment is not very great, but perhaps late fetuses, like babies, are capable of sensuous pleasure, from sucking their thumbs, from the warmth of the womb, from the sound of their mothers' heartbeats, from motion as the mother moves around. Certainly in newborn nurseries the temperature is kept quite high, on the ground that this is what the baby was used to before birth. The ability to calm infants by motion is often attributed to this being a replication of the uterine environment. Studies have been done correlating fetal activity with extrauterine sound, leading researchers to claim that fetuses can not only hear inside the womb, but that they enjoy some kinds of sounds more than others. If all of this is right, then it seems plausible to say that late fetuses have, or have begun to have, lives in the biographical sense. Death deprives them of their lives, and so is a harm to them. Thus, it seems that life is *in* the interest of the conscious fetus, and it, like a newborn, can have a right to life.

On the other hand, fetuses, unlike born babies, dwell inside pregnant women. This has been dismissed by conservatives as "mere geography," but the geography is not insignificant. Any attempt to protect the life of a fetus may conflict with, or even endanger, the interests of the pregnant woman, including her life or health. There is a possibility of conflict that simply does not exist in the case of the newborn. For this reason, we cannot simply extend the right to life possessed by all human newborns to sentient fetuses.

To summarize, sentience is sufficient for minimal moral status. The interests of all sentient beings—persons, animals,

conscious fetuses, and babies—must be considered. However, some sentient beings may have lives that are more valuable than others. They occupy a higher place on the moral-status scale. For example, we have good reasons for extending normative personhood, and a right to life, to human infants, stemming both from their relation to other human persons and from their potential personhood. We do not have these reasons to extend normative personhood to nonhuman animals. Conscious fetuses, though substantially similar to newborns, and thus entitled to some legal protection, are located inside the pregnant woman's body. This makes it impossible to give them full protection without violating her right to privacy or bodily self-determination.

Embryos and preconscious fetuses are admittedly potential persons, but they do not have interests. Therefore, their interests cannot be considered in making the decision to abort. A pregnant woman who wishes to be responsible and conscientious in making a decision about abortion is not required to consider the child who might have been born. In order to justify having an abortion, she does not have to claim that her child would be miserable. She can acknowledge that, if she does not abort, the resulting child might well have a very happy life. Pro-lifers are quite right to cast scorn on the notion that all unplanned pregnancies result in unwanted children, or that all unwanted children necessarily have unhappy lives.[16] Instead, pro-choicers should respond that the happiness of the potential child is not determinative—indeed, not even relevant to the decision to abort. There is no obligation to bring happy people into the world, only an obligation to try to give the children one decides to bring into the world a decent chance at happiness. . . .

THE ARGUMENT FROM BODILY SELF-DETERMINATION

Thomson's Defense of Abortion

In 1971, Judith Jarvis Thomson published a genuinely novel defense of abortion.[17] She noted that most debates about abortion center on the moral status of the fetus: whether it is a person with a right to life. This is because people have generally thought that if we accept the premise that the fetus is a person, it follows that abortion is always wrong. The argument goes like this: All persons have a right to life. The fetus is a person, and so it has a right to life. The mother has the right to decide what happens in and to her body, but the right to life is stronger and more stringent than the mother's right to decide, and so outweighs it. So the fetus may not be killed; an abortion may not be performed.

It is this argument that Thomson wants to challenge. She argues that even if we grant the personhood of the fetus, abortion is not necessarily wrong. For it is possible that in at least some cases abortion does not violate the fetus-person's right to life. This is initially puzzling. If the fetus has a right to life, and abortion kills it, then how can abortion fail to violate its right to life? Thomson suggests that our perplexity stems from a failure to understand the nature of rights in general and the right to life in particular. In a nutshell, her argument is that having a right to life does not entitle a person to whatever he or she needs to stay alive, and in particular does not entitle him to the use of another person's body.

To illustrate this point, Thomson creates the following example:

> You wake up in the morning and find yourself back to back in bed with an unconscious violinist. He has been found to have a fatal kidney ailment, and the Society of Music Lovers has canvassed all the available medical records and found that you alone have the right blood type to help. They have therefore kidnapped you, and last night the violinist's circulatory system was plugged into yours, so that your kidneys can be used to extract poisons from his blood as well as your own.[18]

The director of the hospital, while acknowledging that it was very wrong of the Society to kidnap you, nevertheless refuses to unplug you, since to unplug you would be to kill him. Anyway, it's only for nine months. After that, the violinist will have recovered and can be safely unplugged. Thomson questions whether it is morally incumbent on you to accede to this situation. It would be very nice of you, of course, but do you *have* to stay plugged in to the violinist? What if it were not nine months, but nine years? Or longer still? What if the director were to maintain that you must stay plugged in forever, on the ground that the violinist is a person, and all persons have a right to life? Thomson suggests that you would regard this argument as "outrageous," and says that this suggests that something really is wrong with the plausible-sounding right-to-life argument presented above.

The violinist example, fantastic though it is, preserves some of the features of the pregnancy situation without making at all doubtful the personhood of the "victim." Given that the violinist is a person, with a right to life, do you murder him, do you violate his right to life, if you unplug yourself? If not, then we have, it seems, a case of terminating the life of an innocent person that is not a case of violating his right to life.

The violinist example is intended to demonstrate Thomson's central theme, that the right to life does not necessarily include getting whatever you need to live. To take a less fanciful example, I may need your bone marrow in order to live, but that does not give me a right to it. Even if you *ought* to be willing to donate, even if your refusal is selfish and mean, it does not follow that I have a right to your bone marrow, or that you may legitimately be compelled to donate.[19] The right to life does not imply a right to use another person's body.

However, it may be objected that the fetus *does* have a right to use the pregnant woman's body because she is (partly) responsible for its existence. By engaging in intercourse, knowing that this may result in the creation of a person inside her body, she implicitly gives the resulting person a right to remain. This argument would not apply in the situation most closely aligned with the violinist example—pregnancy due to rape. A woman who is pregnant due to rape does not voluntarily engage in sexual intercourse, and so cannot be said to have implicitly given the fetus permission to use her body.

On this analysis, even if abortion is ordinarily a grave wrong, it is permissible in the case of rape. Many antiabortionists wish to make such an exception, but they have been hard-pressed, on their own argument, to account for it. For antiabortionists maintain that the fetus is an innocent person. How can it be right to kill the fetus because its father is a rapist? The Thomson argument gives an answer: the fetus whose existence is caused by rape has no right to use the pregnant woman's body. Killing it does not violate its right to life.

But what about most pregnancies, which do not result from rape but from voluntary intercourse? Given that the presence of the fetus is due in part to the woman's own voluntary action, can she now eject it at the cost of its life? Thomson responds by saying that even where the woman voluntarily engages in sex, she may not be responsible for the presence of the fetus. She argues that responsibility for an outcome depends on what one has done to prevent it. She suggests that if a person has taken all reasonable precautions to prevent something from happening, then she has not been negligent, and should not be held responsible for its having occurred. So whether the woman can be said to have given the fetus a right to use her body would depend on such variables as whether she was using a reliable contraceptive that happened to fail.

Some critics of Thomson have taken her to task for concentrating exclusively on rights. The real question, they say, is not what constitutes giving the unborn person a right to use one's body, but rather the conditions that make aborting the fetus morally permissible. Thomson responds by saying that since her intention was to examine the right-to-life argument, she can hardly be faulted for concentrating on rights. However, she acknowledges that we can have moral obligations to help people, even when they do not have rights against us. Suppose that the violinist needed your kidneys only for an hour, and that this would not affect your health at all. Even though you were kidnapped, even though you never gave anyone permission to plug him into you, still you ought to let him stay: "it would be indecent to refuse."[20] Similarly, if pregnancy lasted only an hour, and posed no threat to life or health, the pregnant woman ought to allow the fetus-person to remain for that hour. She ought to do this even if the pregnancy was due to rape, and the fetus has no right to use her body. This conclusion is based on the principle (which Thomson calls "minimally decent Samaritanism") that if you can save a person's life without much trouble or risk to yourself, you ought to do it. In the real world, however, pregnancies do not last for only an hour, and they do involve considerable sacrifices.[21] Thomson concludes, "Except in such cases as the unborn person has a right to demand it—and we were leaving open the possibility that there may be such cases—nobody is morally *required* to make large sacrifices, of health, of all other interests and concerns, of all other duties and commitments, for nine years, or even for nine months, in order to keep another person alive."[22]

Thomson's analysis apparently justifies abortion only in a relatively narrow range of cases. Many unwanted pregnancies occur because contraception was not used at all, or only occasionally. In such cases, the woman *is* (partly) to blame, and so the resulting fetus may be said to have been given the right to use her body. If so, then abortion violates its right to life, and is impermissible. Mary Anne Warren writes, "This is an extremely unsatisfactory outcome, from the viewpoint of the opponents of restrictive abortion laws, most of whom are convinced that a woman has a right to obtain an abortion regardless of how and why she got pregnant."[23]

It seems to me that Warren is right. A successful defense of abortion cannot be based solely on the woman's moral right to decide what happens in and to her body. This yields a defense of abortion in a relatively narrow range of cases—namely, those in which the woman is absolved of responsibility for the presence of the unborn. By the same token, a defense of abortion based solely on the claim that presentient fetuses lack moral status is vulnerable to potentiality arguments. The strongest argument in favor of a liberal abortion policy combines both these approaches. This was the approach taken by the United States Supreme Court in *Roe* v. *Wade*.

NOTES

1. *Roe* v. *Wade*, 410 U.S. 113 (1973).
2. Technically, the term "fetus" refers to the unborn after eight weeks of gestation. Many writers on abortion use the term "fetus" to refer generally to the unborn throughout pregnancy. I will follow this convention except where necessary to distinguish the different phases of gestation.
3. A good example is Don Marquis, "Why Abortion is Immoral," *The Journal of Philosophy* 76:4 (April 1989), pp. 183–202.
4. See, for example, Sandra Harding, "Beneath the Surface of the Abortion Dispute," in Sidney Callahan and Daniel Callahan, eds., *Abortion: Understanding Differences* (New York and London: Plenum Press, 1984).
5. Baruch Brody, *Abortion and the Sanctity of Life* (Cambridge, Mass.: The MIT Press, 1975), p. 111.
6. Ibid., p. 83.
7. A similar argument is made by Carson Strong, "Delivering Hydrocephalic Fetuses," *Bioethics* 5:1 (January 1991), pp. 7–11.
8. Stephen Buckle, "Arguing from Potential," *Bioethics* 2:3 (July 1988), p. 227.
9. Ibid.
10. Don Marquis, "Why Abortion is Immoral," pp. 183–202.
11. John Harris, *The Value of Life: An Introduction to Medical Ethics* (London: Routledge & Kegan Paul, 1985), pp. 11–12.
12. R. M. Hare may be the only potentiality theorist who does not hinge his argument on a morally significant difference between embryos and gametes. On Hare's version of the argument from potential, abortion is *prima facie* morally wrong,

but so are contraception and abstention from procreation. See "Abortion and the Golden Rule," *Philosophy & Public Affairs* 4:3 (Spring 1975).

13. "Study Finds 31% Rate of Miscarriage," *The New York Times*, Wednesday, July 27, 1988, p. A14.

14. Angela Neustatter, with Gina Newson, *Mixed Feelings: the Experience of Abortion* (London: Pluto Press, 1986), p. 10.

15. I borrow this term from Rosalind Hurst-house, *Beginning Lives* (Oxford: Basil Blackwell in association with the Open University), 1987.

16. However, a recent study showed that more than a third of women denied abortions confessed to strongly negative feelings toward their children, and that children born to women whose requests for abortion were refused are much likelier to be troubled and depressed, to drop out of school, to commit crimes, to suffer from serious illnesses, and to express dissatisfaction with life than are the offspring of willing parents. See Natalie Angier, "Study Says Anger Troubles Women Denied Abortions," *The New York Times*, May 29, 1991, p. C10.

17. Judith Jarvis Thomson, "A Defense of Abortion," *Philosophy & Public Affairs* 1:1 (1971). Reprinted in Joel Feinberg, ed., *The Problem of Abortion*, 2nd edition (Belmont, Calif.: Wadsworth Publishing Company, 1984), pp. 173–187.

18. Ibid., p. 174.

19. The claim that individuals do not have a legal obligation to donate body parts to others, even when they are needed for life itself, has been upheld in several cases. The first recorded case, to my knowledge, is *Shimp* v. *McFall*, 10 Pa. D. & D.3d 90 (1978).

20. Thomson, "A Defense of Abortion," p. 182.

21. The burdens of even normal pregnancies are well detailed by Donald Regan, "Rewriting *Roe* vs. *Wade*," *Michigan Law Review* 77 (1979).

22. Thomson, "A Defense of Abortion," p. 184.

23. Mary Anne Warren, "On the Moral and Legal Status of Abortion," *The Monist* 57 (1973). Reprinted by Joel Feinberg, ed., *The Problem of Abortion*, p. 108.

NO   Sidney Callahan

ABORTION AND THE SEXUAL AGENDA: A CASE FOR PROLIFE FEMINISM

The abortion debate continues. In the latest and perhaps most crucial development, prolife feminists are contesting prochoice feminist claims that abortion
rights are prerequisites for women's full development and social equality.
The outcome of this debate may be decisive for the culture as a whole. Prolife feminists, like myself, argue on good feminist principles that women can
never achieve the fulfillment of feminist goals in a society permissive toward
abortion.

These new arguments over abortion take place within liberal political circles. This round of intense intra-feminist conflict has spiraled beyond earlier
right-versus-left abortion debates, which focused on "tragic choices," medical judgments, and legal compromises. Feminist theorists of the prochoice
position now put forth the demand for unrestricted abortion rights as a *moral
imperative* and insist upon women's right to complete reproductive freedom.
They morally justify the present situation and current abortion practices.
Thus it is all the more important that prolife feminists articulate their different feminist perspective.

These opposing arguments can best be seen when presented in turn. Perhaps the most highly developed feminist arguments for the morality and
legality of abortion can be found in Beverly Wildung Harrison's *Our Right
to Choose* (Beacon Press, 1983) and Rosalind Pollack Petchesky's *Abortion and
Woman's Choice* (Longman, 1984). Obviously it is difficult to do justice to
these complex arguments, which draw on diverse strands of philosophy and
social theory and are often interwoven in prochoice feminists' own version
of a "seamless garment." Yet the fundamental feminist case for the morality
of abortion, encompassing the views of Harrison and Petchesky, can be analyzed in terms of four central moral claims: (1) the moral right to control
one's own body; (2) the moral necessity of autonomy and choice in personal
responsibility; (3) the moral claim for the contingent value of fetal life; (4) the
moral right of women to true social equality.

1. The Moral Right to Control One's Own Body

Prochoice feminism argues that a woman choosing an abortion is exercising a basic right of bodily integrity granted in our common law tradition. If she does not choose to be physically involved in the demands of a pregnancy and birth, she should not be compelled to be so against her will. Just because it is *her* body which is involved, a woman should have the right to terminate any pregnancy, which at this point in medical history is tantamount to terminating fetal life. No one can be forced to donate an organ or submit to other invasive physical procedures for however good a cause. Thus no woman should be subjected to "compulsory pregnancy." And it should be noted that in pregnancy much more than a passive biological process is at stake.

From one perspective, the fetus is, as Petchesky says, a "biological parasite" taking resources from the woman's body. During pregnancy, a woman's whole life and energies will be actively involved in the nine-month process. Gestation and childbirth involve physical and psychological risks. After childbirth a woman will either be a mother who must undertake a twenty-year responsibility for child rearing, or face giving up her child for adoption or institutionalization. Since hers is the body, hers the risk, hers the burden, it is only just that she alone should be free to decide on pregnancy or abortion.

The moral claim to abortion, according to the prochoice feminists, is especially valid in an individualistic society in which women cannot count on medical care or social support in pregnancy, childbirth, or child rearing. A moral abortion decision is never made in a social vacuum, but in the real life society which exists here and now.

2. The Moral Necessity of Autonomy and Choice in Personal Responsibility

Beyond the claim for individual *bodily* integrity, the prochoice feminists claim that to be a full adult *morally*, a woman must be able to make responsible life commitments. To plan, choose, and exercise personal responsibility, one must have control of reproduction. A woman must be able to make yes-or-no decisions about a specific pregnancy, according to her present situation, resources, prior commitments, and life plan. Only with such reproductive freedom can a woman have the moral autonomy necessary to make mature commitments, in the area of family, work, or education.

Contraception provides a measure of personal control, but contraceptive failure or other chance events can too easily result in involuntary pregnancy. Only free access to abortion can provide the necessary guarantee. The chance biological process of an involuntary pregnancy should not be allowed to override all the other personal commitments and responsibilities a woman has: to others, to family, to work, to education, to her future development, health, or well-being. Without reproductive freedom, women's personal moral agency and human consciousness are subjected to biology and chance.

3. The Moral Claim for the Contingent Value of Fetal Life

Prochoice feminist exponents like Harrison and Petchesky claim that the value of fetal life is contingent upon the woman's free consent and subjective acceptance. The fetus must be invested with maternal valuing in order to become human. This process of "humanization" through personal consciousness and "sociality" can only be bestowed by the woman in whose body and psychosocial system a new life must mature. The meaning and value of fetal life are constructed by the woman; without this personal conferral there only exists a biological, physiological process. Thus fetal interests or fetal rights can never outweigh the woman's prior interest and rights. If a woman does not consent to invest her pregnancy with meaning or value, then the merely biological process can be freely terminated. Prior to her own free choice and conscious investment, a woman cannot be described as a "mother" nor can a "child" be said to exist.

Moreover, in cases of voluntary pregnancy, a woman can withdraw consent if fetal genetic defects or some other problem emerges at any time before birth. Late abortion should thus be granted without legal restrictions. Even the minimal qualifications and limitations on women embedded in *Roe v. Wade* are unacceptable —repressive remnants of patriarchal unwillingness to give power to women.

4. The Moral Right of Women to Full Social Equality

Women have a moral right to full social equality. They should not be restricted or subordinated because of their sex. But this morally required equality cannot be realized without abortion's certain control of reproduction. Female social equality depends upon being able to compete and participate as freely as males can in the structures of educational and economic life. If a woman cannot control when and how she will be pregnant or rear children, she is at a distinct disadvantage, especially in our male-dominated world.

Psychological equality and well-being is also at stake. Women must enjoy the basic right of a person to the free exercise of heterosexual intercourse and full sexual expression, separated from procreation. No less than males, women should be able to be sexually active without the constantly inhibiting fear of pregnancy. Abortion is necessary for women's sexual fulfillment and the growth of uninhibited feminine self-confidence and ownership of their sexual powers.

But true sexual and reproductive freedom means freedom to procreate as well as to inhibit fertility. Prochoice feminists are also worried that women's freedom to reproduce will be curtailed through the abuse of sterilization and needless hysterectomies. Besides the punitive tendencies of a male-dominated health-care system, especially in response to repeated abortions or welfare pregnancies, there are other economic and social pressures inhibiting reproduction. Genuine reproductive freedom implies that day care, medical care, and financial support would be provided mothers, while fathers would take their full share in the burdens and delights of raising children.

Many prochoice feminists identify feminist ideals with communitarian, ecologically sensitive approaches to reshaping society. Following theorists like Sara Ruddick and Carol Gilligan, they link abortion rights with the growth of "maternal thinking" in our heretofore patriarchal society. Maternal thinking is loosely defined as a responsible commitment to the loving nature of specific human beings as they actually exist in socially embedded interpersonal contexts. It is a moral perspective very different from the abstract, competitive, isolated, and principled rigidity so characteristic of patriarchy.

* * *

How does a prolife feminist respond to these arguments? Prolife feminists grant the good intentions of their prochoice counterparts but protest that the prochoice position is flawed, morally inadequate, and inconsistent with feminism's basic demands for justice. Prolife feminists champion a more encompassing moral ideal. They recognize the claims of fetal life and offer a different perspective on what is good for women. The feminist vision is expanded and refocused.

1. From the Moral Right to Control One's Own Body to a More Inclusive Ideal of Justice

The moral right to control one's own body does apply to cases of organ transplants, mastectomies, contraception, and sterilization; but it is not a conceptualization adequate for abortion. The abortion dilemma is caused by the fact that 266 days following a conception in one body, another body will emerge. One's own body no longer exists as a single unit but is engendering another organism's life. This dynamic passage from conception to birth is genetically ordered and universally found in the human species. Pregnancy is not like the growth of cancer or infestation by a biological parasite; it is the way every human being enters the world. Strained philosophical analogies fail to apply: having a baby is not like rescuing a drowning person, being hooked up to a famous violinist's artificial life-support system, donating organs for transplant—or anything else.

As embryology and fetology advance, it becomes clear that human development is a continuum. Just as astronomers are studying the first three minutes in the genesis of the universe, so the first moments, days, and weeks at the beginning of human life are the subject of increasing scientific attention. While neonatology pushes the definition of viability ever earlier, ultrasound and fetology expand the concept of the patient *in utero*. Within such a continuous growth process, it is hard to defend logically any demarcation point after conception as the point at which an immature form of human life is so different from the day before or the day after, that it can be morally or legally discounted as a nonperson. Even the moment of birth can hardly differentiate a nine-month fetus from a newborn. It is not surprising that those who countenance late abortions are logically led to endorse selective infanticide.

The same legal tradition which in our society guarantees the right to control one's own body firmly recognizes the wrongfulness of harming other bodies, however immature, dependent, different looking, or powerless. The handicapped, the retarded, and newborns are legally protected from deliberate harm. Prolife feminists reject the suppositions that would except the unborn from this protection.

After all, debates similar to those about the fetus were once conducted about feminine personhood. Just as women, or blacks, were considered too different, too underdeveloped, too "biological," to have souls or to possess legal rights, so the fetus is now seen as "merely" biological life, subsidiary to a person. A woman was once viewed as incorporated into the "one flesh" of her husband's person; she too was a form of bodily property. In all patriarchal unjust systems, lesser orders of human life are granted rights only when wanted, chosen, or invested with value by the powerful.

Fortunately, in the course of civilization there has been a gradual realization that justice demands the powerless and dependent be protected against the uses of power wielded unilaterally. No human can be treated as a means to an end without consent. The fetus is an immature, dependent form of human life which only needs time and protection to develop. Surely, immaturity and dependence are not crimes.

In an effort to think about the essential requirements of a just society, philosophers like John Rawls recommend imagining yourself in an "original position," in which your position in the society to be created is hidden by a "veil of ignorance." You will have to weigh the possibility that any inequalities inherent in that society's practices may rebound upon you in the worst, as well as in the best, conceivable way. This thought experiment helps ensure justice for all.

Beverly Harrison argues that in such an envisioning of society everyone would institute abortion rights in order to guarantee that if one turned out to be a woman one would have reproductive freedom. But surely in the original position and behind the "veil of ignorance," you would have to contemplate the possibility of being the particular fetus to be aborted. Since everyone has passed through the fetal stage of development, it is false to refuse to imagine oneself in this state when thinking about a potential world in which justice would govern. Would it be just that an embryonic life—in half the cases, of course, a female life—be sacrificed to the right of a woman's control over her own body? A woman may be pregnant without consent and experience a great many penalties, but a fetus

killed without consent pays the ultimate penalty.

It does not matter... whether the fetus being killed is fully conscious or feels pain. We do not sanction killing the innocent if it can be done painlessly or without the victim's awareness. Consciousness becomes important to the abortion debate because it is used as a criterion for the "personhood" so often seen as the prerequisite for legal protection. Yet certain philosophers set the standard of personhood so high that half the human race could not meet the criteria during most of their waking hours (let alone their sleeping ones). Sentience, self-consciousness, rational decision-making, social participation? Surely no infant, or child under two, could qualify. Either our idea of person must be expanded or another criterion, such as human life itself, be employed to protect the weak in a just society. Prolife feminists who defend the fetus emphatically identify with an immature state of growth passed through by themselves, their children, and everyone now alive.

* * *

It also seems a travesty of just procedures that a pregnant woman now, in effect, acts as sole judge of her own case, under the most stressful conditions. Yes, one can acknowledge that the pregnant woman will be subject to the potential burdens arising from a pregnancy, but it has never been thought right to have an interested party, especially the more powerful party, decide his or her own case when there may be a conflict of interest. If one considers the matter as a case of a powerful versus a powerless, silenced claimant, the prochoice feminist argument can rightly be inverted: since hers is the body, hers the risk, and hers the greater burden, then how in fairness can a woman be the sole judge of the fetal right to life?

Human ambivalence, a bias toward self-interest, and emotional stress have always been recognized as endangering judgment. Freud declared that love and hate are so entwined that if instant thoughts could kill, we would all be dead in the bosom of our families. In the case of a woman's involuntary pregnancy, a complex, long-term solution requiring effort and energy has to compete with the immediate solution offered by a morning's visit to an abortion clinic. On the simple, perceptual plane, with imagination and thinking curtailed, the speed, ease, and privacy of abortion, combined with the small size of the embryo, tend to make early abortions seem less morally serious—even though speed, size, technical ease, and the private nature of an act have no moral standing.

As the most recent immigrants from nonpersonhood, feminists have traditionally fought for justice for themselves and the world. Women rally to feminism as a new and better way to live. Rejecting male aggression and destruction, feminists seek alternative, peaceful, ecologically sensitive means to resolve conflicts while respecting human potentiality. It is a chilling inconsistency to see prochoice feminists demanding continued access to assembly-line, technological methods of fetal killing—the vacuum aspirator, prostaglandins, and dilation and evacuation. It is a betrayal of feminism, which has built the struggle for justice on the bedrock of women's empathy. After all, "maternal thinking" receives its name from a mother's unconditional acceptance and nurture of dependent, immature life. It is difficult to develop concern for women, children, the poor and the dispossessed—and to care about peace—and at the same time ignore fetal life.

2. From the Necessity of Autonomy and Choice in Personal Responsibility to an Expanded Sense of Responsibility

A distorted idea of morality overemphasizes individual autonomy and active choice. Morality has often been viewed too exclusively as a matter of human agency and decisive action. In moral behavior persons must explicitly choose and aggressively exert their wills to intervene in the natural and social environments. The human will dominates the body, overcomes the given, breaks out of the material limits of nature. Thus if one does not choose to be pregnant or cannot rear a child, who must be given up for adoption, then better to abort the pregnancy. Willing, planning, choosing one's moral commitments through the contracting of one's individual resources becomes the premier model of moral responsibility.

But morality also consists of the good and worthy acceptance of the unexpected events that life presents. Responsiveness and response-ability to things unchosen are also instances of the highest human moral capacity. Morality is not confined to contracted agreements of isolated individuals. Yes, one is obligated by explicit contracts freely initiated, but human beings are also obligated by implicit compacts and involuntary relationships in which persons simply find themselves. To be embedded in a family, a neighborhood, a social system, brings moral obligations which were never entered into with informed consent.

Parent-child relationships are one instance of implicit moral obligations arising by virtue of our being part of the interdependent human community. A woman, involuntarily pregnant, has a moral obligation to the now-existing dependent fetus whether she explicitly consented to its existence or not. No prolife feminist would dispute the forceful observations of prochoice feminists about the extreme difficulties that bearing an unwanted child in our society can entail. But the stronger force of the fetal claim presses a woman to accept these burdens; the fetus possesses rights arising from its extreme need and the interdependency and unity of humankind. The woman's moral obligation arises both from her status as a human being embedded in the interdependent human community and her unique lifegiving female reproductive power. To follow the prochoice feminist ideology of insistent individualistic autonomy and control is to betray a fundamental basis of the moral life.

3. From the Moral Claim of the Contingent Value of Fetal Life to the Moral Claim for the Intrinsic Value of Human Life

The feminist prochoice position which claims that the value of the fetus is contingent upon the pregnant woman's bestowal—or willed, conscious "construction"—of humanhood is seriously flawed. The inadequacies of this position flow from the erroneous premises (1) that human value and rights can be granted by individual will; (2) that the individual woman's consciousness can exist and operate in an *a priori* isolated fashion; and (3) that "mere" biological, genetic human life has little meaning. Prolife feminism takes a very different stance toward life and nature.

Human life from the beginning to the end of development *has* intrinsic value, which does not depend on meeting the selective criteria or tests set up by powerful others. A fundamental humanist assumption is at stake here. Either we are going to value embodied human life and humanity as a good thing, or take some variant of the nihilist position that assumes human life is just one more random occurrence in the universe such that each instance of human life must explicitly be justified to prove itself worthy to continue. When faced with a new life, or an involuntary pregnancy, there is a world of difference in whether one first asks, "Why continue?" or "Why not?" Where is the burden of proof going to rest? The concept of "compulsory pregnancy" is as distorted as labeling life "compulsory aging."

In a sound moral tradition, human rights arise from human needs, and it is the very nature of a right, or valid claim upon another, that it cannot be denied, conditionally delayed, or rescinded by more powerful others at their behest. It seems fallacious to hold that in the case of the fetus it is the pregnant woman alone who gives or removes its right to life and human status solely through her subjective conscious investment or "humanization." Surely no pregnant woman (or any other individual member of the species) has created her own human nature by an individually willed act of consciousness, nor for that matter been able to guarantee her own human rights. An individual woman and the unique individual embryonic life within her can only exist because of their participation in the genetic inheritance of the human species as a whole. Biological life should never be discounted. Membership in the species, or collective human family, is the basis for human solidarity, equality, and natural human rights.

4. The Moral Right of Women to Full Social Equality from a Prolife Feminist Perspective

Prolife feminists and prochoice feminists are totally agreed on the moral right of women to the full social equality so far denied them. The disagreement between them concerns the definition of the desired goal and the best means to get there. Permissive abortion laws do not bring women reproductive freedom, social equality, sexual fulfillment, or full personal development.

Pragmatic failures of a prochoice feminist position combined with a lack of moral vision are, in fact, causing disaffection among young women. Middle-aged prochoice feminists blamed the "big chill" on the general conservative backlash. But they should look rather to their own elitist acceptance of male models of sex and to the sad picture they present of women's lives. Pitting women against their own offspring is not only morally offensive, it is psychologically and politically destructive. Women will never climb to equality and social empowerment over mounds of dead fetuses, numbering now in the millions. As long as most women choose to bear children, they stand to gain from the same constellation of attitudes and institutions that will also protect the fetus in the woman's womb—and they stand to lose from the cultural assumptions that support permissive abortion. Despite temporary conflicts of interest, feminine and fetal liberation are ultimately one and the same cause.

Women's rights and liberation are pragmatically linked to fetal rights because to obtain true equality, women need (1) more social support and changes in the structure of society, and (2) increased self-confidence, self-expectations, and self-esteem. Society in general, and men in particular, have to provide women more support in rearing the next generation, or our devastating feminization of poverty will continue. But if a woman claims the right to decide by herself whether the fetus becomes a child or not, what does this do to paternal and communal responsibility? Why should men share responsibility for child support or child rearing if they cannot share in what is asserted to be the woman's sole decision? Furthermore, if explicit intentions and consciously accepted contracts are necessary for moral obligations, why should men be held responsible for what *they* do not voluntarily choose to happen? By prochoice reasoning, a man who does not want to have a child, or whose contraceptive fails, can be exempted from the responsibilities of fatherhood and child support. Traditionally, many men have been laggards in assuming parental responsibility and support for their children; ironically, ready abortion, often advocated as a response to male dereliction, legitimizes male irresponsibility and paves the way for even more male detachment and lack of commitment.

For that matter, why should the state provide a system of day care or child support, or require workplaces to accommodate women's maternity and the needs of child rearing? Permissive abortion, granted in the name of women's privacy and reproductive freedom, ratifies the view that pregnancies and children are a woman's private individual responsibility. More and more frequently, we hear some version of this old rationalization: if she refuses to get rid of it, it's her problem. A child becomes a product of the individual woman's freely chosen investment, a form of private property resulting from her own cost-benefit calculation. The larger community is relieved of moral responsibility.

With legal abortion freely available, a clear cultural message is given: conception and pregnancy are no longer serious moral matters. With abortion as an acceptable alternative, contraception is not as responsibly used; women take risks, often at the urging of male sexual partners. Repeat abortions increase, with all their psychological and medical repercussions. With more abortion there is more abortion. Behavior shapes thought as well as the other way round. One tends to justify morally what one has done; what becomes commonplace and institutionalized seems harmless. Habituation is a powerful psychological force. Psychologically it is also true that whatever is avoided becomes more threatening; in phobias it is the retreat from anxiety-producing events which reinforces future avoidance. Women begin to see themselves as too weak to cope with involuntary pregnancies. Finally, through the potency of social pressure and the force of inertia, it becomes more and more difficult, in fact almost unthinkable, *not* to use abortion to solve problem pregnancies. Abortion becomes no longer a choice but a "necessity." ...

New feminist efforts to rethink the meaning of sexuality, femininity, and reproduction are all the more vital as new techniques for artificial reproduction, surrogate motherhood, and the like present a whole new set of dilemmas. In the long run, the very long run, the abortion debate may be merely the opening round in a series of far-reaching struggles over the role of human sexuality and the ethics of reproduction. Significant changes in the culture, both positive and negative in outcome, may begin as local storms of controversy. We may be at one of those vaguely realized thresholds when we had best come to full attention. What kind of people are we going to be? Prolife feminists pursue a vision for their sisters, daughters, and granddaughters. Will their great-granddaughters be grateful?

POSTSCRIPT

Is There a Moral Right to Abortion?

Although the Supreme Court consistently upheld the legality of abortion in a series of cases in the early and mid-1980s, that trend was reversed in the last several years. The 1989 decision in *Webster v. Reproductive Health Services* upheld the constitutionality of Missouri's restrictive abortion statutes, thus giving more power to state legislatures and courts in regulating abortion. In 1991, in *Rust v. Sullivan*, the Court affirmed a Department of Health and Human Services regulation prohibiting federally funded family planning clinics from counseling or referring women for abortions. In March 1992, the Bush administration changed the regulation to allow physicians, but not nurses or counselors, to discuss abortion under some circumstances. And three days after he became president in 1992, Bill Clinton reversed restrictive federal policies on abortion—the ban on abortion counseling at federally financed clinics was lifted, as was a prohibition on aid to international family planning programs that are involved in abortion-related activities.

Planned Parenthood of Southeastern Pennsylvania v. Casey, the most significant of the more recent Supreme Court cases on abortion, was decided in June 1992. The ruling reaffirmed the constitutionality of *Roe v. Wade*, but it also declared that a woman's legal right to an abortion was not unduly restricted by the provisions of Pennsylvania's law. The law requires physicians to provide information about the nature, risks, and alternatives to abortion, as well as the gestational age of the fetus. It also imposes a 24-hour waiting period after the information is given before the abortion is performed. Finally, it requires the consent of a parent or a court in the case of young women under age 18 seeking abortion. For two articles critical of the *Casey* decision, see R. Alta Charo, "Life after *Casey*: The View from Rehnquist's Potemkin Village," *The Journal of Law, Medicine & Ethics* (Spring 1993), and Janet Benshoof, "Planned Parenthood v. Casey: The Impact of the New Undue Burden Standard on Reproductive Health Care," *Journal of the American Medical Association* (May 5, 1993).

For a history of the political and ethical issues surrounding abortion in the United States, see Eva R. Rubin's *The Abortion Controversy: A Documentary History* (Greenwood, 1994). In *Our Right to Choose* (Beacon Press, 1983), Beverley Wildung Harrison argues that women ought to decide whether or not to bear children on the basis of their own moral preparedness to become responsible mothers. For more recent arguments, see Cynthia R. Daniels, *At Women's Expense: State Power and the Politics of Fetal Rights* (Harvard University Press, 1993) and Ronald Dworkin, *Life's Dominion: An Argument About Abortion, Euthanasia, and Individual Freedom* (Alfred A. Knopf, 1993).

ISSUE 3

Is It Ethical to Clone Human Embryos?

YES: John A. Robertson, from "The Question of Human Cloning," *Hastings Center Report* (March/April 1994)

NO: Richard A. McCormick, from "Blastomere Separation: Some Concerns," *Hastings Center Report* (March/April 1994)

ISSUE SUMMARY

YES: Law professor John A. Robertson contends that it is reasonable to add human embryo cloning to the repertoire of infertility treatments and that cloning raises no novel ethical problems.

NO: Theologian Richard A. McCormick argues that human embryo cloning is not just another infertility technique for it calls into question basic premises about sanctity of life, wholeness, and the uniqueness of individuals.

When modern bioethics began in the 1950s, the notions of test-tube babies, frozen embryos, and women past menopause giving birth seemed to be science-fiction scenarios. Now that all these procedures are common, if not considered ethically acceptable, the frontier of reproductive technology has moved onward. Human cloning—also among the early reproductive hypotheticals—is still far off in the technological future. But recent experiments have brought it one step closer, amid much controversy.

The word *clone* comes from the Greek and simply means a twig. Plant a twig and you will get a tree that looks like the one from which the twig was cut. In the modern meaning, a clone is an identical copy. Techniques that split embryos are commonly used in the cattle industry to produce more identical animals, which lowers the cost of meat and dairy products.

But human cloning is different. Or is it? The experiment that set off the current controversy involved a technique known as *blastomere separation*, one of several possible cloning techniques. Once a fertilzed egg has divided into two separate cells, the protective coating around it is removed with an enzyme. The two cells are then separated and each is surrounded by an artificial protective coating. The cells continue to divide, and the result is two separate, identical embryos.

Researchers from George Washington University in Washington, D.C., reported at the October 1993 joint meetings of the American Fertility Society and the Canadian Fertility and Andrology Society that they had successfully multiplied 17 blastomeres into 48 clones. The embryos selected had been designated for destruction because they were abnormal, having come from eggs that had been fertilized by more than one sperm. None of the clones grew for more than six days. The researchers, Drs. Jerry Hall and Robert Stillman, saw their work as a modest step in infertility research, as one possible way to increase the likelihood of a successful pregnancy through in vitro fertilization (the process through which an egg is artificially fertilized outside of the woman's body and later implanted inside the woman), since the odds increase with the number of implanted embryos. The research has been approved by an institutional review board.

However limited the actual science or the researchers' intent, once the story hit the media, the reaction among the public and professionals was loud and strong. A *Time*/CNN poll found that 75 percent of survey respondents said no to the question, "Do you think human cloning is a good thing?" Nevertheless, when asked whether or not they approved of cloning to provide infertile couples using test-tube fertilization with more embryos to increase their chances of conceiving, 45 percent said yes.

The following selections illustrate two ways of looking at the issue. John A. Robertson places cloning among the spectrum of techniques already in use or contemplated to assist infertile couples, and he sees nothing extraordinary about it. Richard A. McCormick finds the idea of human cloning unsettling and threatening to basic values of human individuality and wholeness.

YES

John A. Robertson

THE QUESTION OF HUMAN CLONING

Some persons would argue that the idea of creating exact replicas of other human beings is so novel that there should be a moratorium on further research and development until a national consultative body evaluates the ethical acceptability of the procedure and develops guidelines for research and use of the technique. At the very least, to prevent abuses there should be strict rules about the circumstances in which cloning by embryo splitting occurs, and about the uses made of cloned embryos.

A closer look at the issues, however, suggests that the most likely uses of cloning are neither so harmful nor so novel that all research and development should now stop until the ethics of the practice are fully aired, or that governmental restrictions on cloning research or applications are needed. Indeed, there may be no particular need for guidelines beyond the full and accurate disclosure of risks and success rates that should always occur in assisted reproduction.

To assess the ethics of embryo splitting and the need for regulation, we must first ask who would use this technique if it were available and why, and then analyze the ethical issues that the likely demand for cloning would generate. We can then address the need for regulation of the embryo research that is essential if cloning by blastomere separation is to occur, and of the uses to which cloning techniques will be put....

THE DEMAND FOR CLONING

... The immediate impetus to develop cloning—and its most likely future use—is to enable infertile couples going through IVF [in vitro fertilization] to have a child.

To Increase the Number of Embryos Transferred. Initially the main demand for embryo splitting would come from couples undergoing IVF who cannot produce enough viable embryos to initiate pregnancy. In basic IVF practice, the highest rates of pregnancy occur with transfer of three to four embryos. Often more than that number of eggs has to be fertilized to produce enough viable embryos for transfer, with the excess frozen for use during a later cycle. Couples who produce only one or two embryos may thus have undergone an expensive and, for the woman, onerous procedure that has little chance of success.

Cloning by blastomere separation appears to be a reasonable step for such couples, if genetic heterogeneity of transferred embryos turns out not to be a key determinant of pregnancy success rates. Their goal is the birth of at least one child. If the prospective parents produce only two embryos, they would face the difficult choice of transferring those two in the hopes that a single pregnancy would result, or increasing their chances of having one child by splitting the blastomeres of one or both embryos.

If they produce only one embryo and embryo splitting has been shown to be safe and effective, they may opt to divide that embryo. Depending on the embryonic stage at which splitting is most successful, this could produce two embryos (if split at the two-cell stage), four (if split at the four-cell stage), or even eight (if two embryos are both split at the four-cell stage)....

Embryo Splitting to Avoid Subsequent Egg Retrieval. Other scenarios involving embryo splitting as a treatment for infertility can also be envisaged. Perhaps the next most likely scenario if cloning by blastomere separation is in fact effective would arise with a couple undergoing IVF who produce a sufficient complement of viable embryos to initiate a pregnancy—three or four—but who wish to avoid the expense and burdens of subsequent egg retrieval cycles. Not many IVF candidates are likely to find themselves in this position, since ovarian stimulation often produces ten or more eggs. Because the couple would need to split only one or two of the three or four viable embryos that they have produced, it is conceivable that many couples who produce only four embryos would opt for this procedure. Indeed, the demand for embryo splitting from this group might arise even if it turned out that successful implantation requires genetic heterogeneity of embryos and the procedure thus was not sought by the group that produces very few eggs....

Embryo Splitting as a Form of Life or Health Insurance. An often cited though highly unlikely demand for embryo cloning could arise from couples seeking insurance against disaster for any children that they have. That is, a couple might request that one or more blastomeres be split from embryos that will be transferred, so that the resulting clone can be frozen for later use in case the child born from the source embryo later dies or needs an organ or tissue transplant. In that case, embryos that are genetically identical to the child already born can be thawed and implanted in the mother (or a surrogate) to produce a genetically identical child to replace the dead child, or to serve as an organ or tissue donor for an existing child.

This scenario could occur, but it is unlikely for several reasons. First, few couples not otherwise undergoing IVF would choose to do so just to gain the hypothetical protection that identical backup embryos might provide. Second, couples that experience the death of a child may not, because of the sadness that it will engender, want to replace that child with a genetic twin, much less plan even before the first child is born to create a replica for that purpose. Third, couples undergoing IVF who produce enough embryos for transfer may not want to risk their viability by separating blastomeres for hypothetical insurance purposes. Fourth, a genetic replica of an existing child might not be necessary to provide needed organs or tissue, or there may not be sufficient time once organ failure in a child occurs to thaw, implant, and bring to term the cloned embryo to serve as an organ or tissue donor. Fifth, there may be medical reasons why a genetic twin will not be suitable as a donor, though in some cases, such as bone marrow or kidney transplantation, genetic homogeneity could provide an advantage.

Because so few couples—even those otherwise going through IVF—will request embryo splitting for this purpose, the use of cloned embryos as backup protection for existing children is likely to arise only with embryos that were created to enhance the efficiency of IVF. In situations of this kind, where the embryonic clones were *not* produced with the specific intention of insuring against disaster, parents might occasionally be glad of the opportunity to avail themselves of the stored cloned embryos to obtain tissue for transplant for an existing child, or to replace a child who has already died. Such scenarios are not impossible, but for the reasons stated above, they are not likely to be frequent.

Embryo Splitting to Obtain a Desirable Genome.   Ethicists have speculated that cloning by embryo splitting might occur to facilitate, or might result in, the selection of stored embryos deemed to be particularly desirable. They envisage scenarios whereby parents will try to sell clones of desirable children to other couples, or where an attractive or successful couple will clone many embryos for later sale or dissemination.

These speculations are highly fanciful. Most couples are not in the market for other peoples' genetic offspring, but prefer to have their own. If so, they can exercise some control over the genetic characteristics of offspring by mate or gamete selection, or by preimplantation or prenatal genetic analysis. Few couples who can have their own children would be so obsessed with having a perfect child that they would eschew their own reproduction in order to obtain a cloned embryo that appears to have a desirable genome.

Of course, if cloning by embryo splitting is perfected, one could routinely excise and store a cell from every embryo that is produced and transferred to the uterus (assuming that this will not impair the embryo's development). The children born of the source embryo could then be followed, and the excised cells of those that turn out to have good genomes or healthy lives might then be sought by persons in quest of donor embryos. The mere description of the procedure shows how complicated and unwieldy it would be as a means to produce particularly desirable embryos.

However, couples who cannot produce genetic offspring might wish to have some say in the characteristics of embryos donated to them. In addition to choice of hair and eye color, and assurances that there are no genetic defects, they might want to see what the embryo they choose would look like as a child or youth, if such information were available. But there is no particular reason why it would be available, or why it would necessarily have to be provided.

In any event, providing information about cloned embryos to prospective recipients would not itself lead to embryo splitting specifically for purposes of genetic selection. The couple undergoing IVF might clone to enhance IVF efficiency, but there would be no particular point in cloning embryos just to enable genetic selection of donor embryos to occur at some later time. If the sale of embryos is also prohibited, the financial incentives necessary to induce embryo splitting for later sale would not exist.

ETHICAL ISSUES: DESTRUCTION OF EMBRYOS

Cloning by blastomere separation raises a number of ethical issues. Some ethical concerns derive from the stark interference with natural reproduction, or the manipulation and destruction of embryos that cloning necessarily entails. However, those concerns are not unique to cloning, and have been voiced about embryo research, freezing, and discard, and about IVF generally. Since they are not deemed sufficient to justify banning or restricting those accepted forms of assisted reproduction, they should not be sufficient to ban cloning either....

There may be no way to answer the objections of persons who think that embryos are themselves persons and must be protected at all costs. The fact that embryo cloning might yield additional human lives will not assuage their concerns, for one is ordinarily not justified in killing one person in order to save several.[1] One can only point to the prevailing moral and legal consensus that views early embryos as too rudimentary in neurological development to have interests or rights.[2] On this view, splitting embryos can no more harm them than freezing or discarding them can. Nor is splitting embryos to enable one or more of them to implant and come to term inherently degrading or disrespectful of human life. Cloning embryos thus poses no greater harm to embryos than other IVF practices and should be permitted to the same extent that they are.

ETHICAL ISSUES: DELIBERATE TWINNING

Ethical objections that are unique to cloning arise from a concern that the intentional creation of genetic replicas of an existing person denies the uniqueness of resulting offspring. This could occur from causing more than one child with the same genome to be born simultaneously. It could also occur from causing more than one child with the same genome to be born at different points in time.

Is the intentional creation of twins who are born simultaneously morally objectionable? Identical twinning occurs naturally and is not generally thought to be harmful or disadvantageous to twins. If anything, being a twin appears to create close emotional bonds that confer special advantages. If this is true, then having twins as a result of embryo splitting should be no more harmful to offspring than having twins naturally.

Suppose, however, that having twins does sometimes pose rearing problems or even psychological conflicts for children. For example, some families may have trouble rearing two infants simultaneously. Or asymmetrical relations with parents or intense rivalry between twins may occur, resulting in psychological harm to one or both of the pair. Still, the fact that undesirable outcomes might occur for some twins is no basis for concluding that all embryo splitting is unethical and should be discouraged....

ETHICAL ISSUES:
LATER BORN TWINS

The second ethical issue unique to cloning by embryo splitting is the possibility of genetically identical siblings being born years apart in the same or different families. Are later born children harmed because a twin or triplet already exists? The claim rests on the notion that the later born child lacks the uniqueness or individuality that we deem essential to human worth and dignity, and that human individuality is largely determined by nature or genome rather than by nurture and environmental factors. Because phenotype and genotype do diverge, and because the environment in which the child will be raised will be different from that of his older twin, the child will still have a unique individuality. Physical characteristics alone do not define individuals, and there is no reason to think that personal identity will be wholly controlled by having an older twin.

Still, there could be special problems faced by such a child. Its path through life might be difficult if the later born child is seen merely as a replica of the first and is expected to develop and show the skills and traits of the first. This might be a special danger if the later born child is used as a replacement for an earlier born child who has died. However, it will be some years before the later born child is even aware of his genetic identity relative to an older sibling and the special expectations his parents might have.

But it is also as likely that the later born child will be loved and wanted for his own sake. His status as a later born twin (or triplet) could be seen as a special status, indeed, a unique or novel status that confers attention and love. It could also lead to close ties with the older twin, if the special bond that twins feel is genetically based. However, it could also lead to unique forms of sibling rivalry. Will the older twin feel that he is deficient because his parents wanted a newer version of him, or will he feel special and proud that his parents wanted another child like him? In any event, it is difficult to conclude that later or earlier born twins or triplets are likely to have such serious psychological problems that they should never be born at all. Even if one did so conclude, this would counsel against implanting cloned embryos only when a twin already exists, not against implanting two cloned embryos simultaneously or splitting embryos at all.

ETHICAL ISSUES: CLONING AS
LIFE OR HEALTH INSURANCE

Although cloning for the explicit purpose of providing parents with a replica for a lost child or as a source of organs or tissue for transplant for an earlier born child will not frequently occur, couples who have split embryos to treat infertility might occasionally be faced with thawing a cloned embryo for those purposes. Consider, for example, parents who request cloning to protect against the loss or death of a child, or who wish to thaw a cloned embryo to replace a dead child. Wanting a child to replace one who has died is not itself unethical. Nor does it become so merely because the new child will be a twin of the first. Although the parents may hope that the new child will develop and show the same traits as her deceased twin, they should very rapidly learn that the second child is different in some respects and similar in others, and would ordinarily come to treat and accept her as the individual that she is.

The use of cloned embryos as insurance against organ and tissue failure in an existing child presents a different set of issues. Here the concern is that the cloned embryo will be treated as an instrument or means to serve the needs of an older twin and will not be loved or respected for his own sake. As the Ayala case in California showed, however, a family can be motivated to have another child to provide an existing child with bone marrow and still treat the subsequent child with the love and respect that children deserve.

If this is so, thawing cloned embryos to provide tissue or organs for an existing child should also be ethically acceptable. The key is whether the child will be loved and accepted by the family that brings her into the world, not how or why she was conceived, nor even whether she was cloned for that purpose. As long as the child's interests are protected after birth occurs, it is hard to see how being cloned or thawed to provide organs for a twin is any worse than being conceived for that purpose. Even if it were, the risk that some cloned embryos might be used to provide tissue to existing children would not justify a ban on embryo splitting to treat infertility.

ETHICAL ISSUES: EMBRYO SPLITTING FOR GENETIC SELECTION

Scenarios involving embryo splitting for genetic selection are, as discussed above, extremely unlikely as long as overall demand for embryo donation is low and the buying and selling of embryos is not permitted. Since it is highly unlikely that a market in embryos will develop, there

will be little incentive for couples going through IVF to clone embryos in order to sell them in the future. This is true even if recipients of donated embryos are permitted to pay some of the costs of embryo production.

It is true that the small subset of infertile couples who are candidates for embryo donation might wish to know the actual characteristics of existing twins or triplets of the embryos they seek to "adopt." However, neither having nor satisfying this wish is itself immoral. Indeed, the right of adoptive parents to receive as full information as possible about the children whom they seek to adopt is increasingly recognized. There is no reason why the same principle should not apply to embryo "adoptions." Even though the couple seeking the embryos will be choosing them on the basis of expected characteristics, such a choice is neither invalid nor immoral. As long as the parents are realistic about what the information signifies, do not have unrealistic expectations about the child's perfection, and love the child for itself, seeking and providing such information prior to embryo donation should be ethically acceptable. If it were not, providing such information could be banned without requiring that embryo splitting to treat infertility also be banned.

REGULATORY ISSUES

This account of cloning by embryo splitting and the ethical issues it poses suggests that, contrary to initial impressions, there is no major ethical barrier to proceeding with further research in embryo splitting as a treatment or adjunct to IVF. Given the great utility that embryo splitting could have for infertile couples, a moratorium on embryo splitting research is both unnecessary and unjustified. . . .

As long as the research is for a valid scientific purpose, embryos that would otherwise be discarded can, with the informed consent of the couple whose gametes produced the embryos, ethically be used in research. Indeed, it should also be ethically acceptable to create embryos solely for research purposes when needed, even if there is no intent to place them in the uterus. Thus neither the lack of guidelines, the moral objections of some to any embryo research, or fears about where cloning research might lead justify forbidding researchers to take this next step. Researchers may not have the right to receive governmental or private funds for cloning, but if they are otherwise funded, their research should not be stopped because of objections to the use of embryos or to cloning itself.

ACKNOWLEDGMENTS

The author gratefully acknowledges the comments of Howard Jones, Joe Massey, and George Annas on an earlier draft.

NOTES

1. Judith Thomson, "The Trolley Problem," *Yale Law Journal* 94 (1985): 1395–1415.

2. American Fertility Society, "Ethical Considerations of the New Reproductive Technologies," special supplement, *Fertility and Sterility* 46 (1986); John A. Robertson, "In the Beginning: The Legal Status of the Early Embryo," *Virginia Law Review* 76 (1990): 437–517, at 440–50.

NO

Richard A. McCormick

BLASTOMERE SEPARATION: SOME CONCERNS

If one has no ethical misgivings about cloning by blastomere separation, then John A. Robertson's essay should be a corrective. It is breathtaking in the speed with which it subordinates every consideration to its usefulness in overcoming infertility. His thesis can be summarized as follows: if it aids otherwise infertile couples to have children, it is ethically acceptable.

In his words: "There is no major ethical barrier to researchers proceeding with further research in embryo splitting as a treatment or adjunct to IVF [in vitro fertilization]. Given the great utility that embryo splitting could have for infertile couples, a moratorium on embryo splitting research is both unnecessary and unjustified." These two sentences are different. The first is an ethical conclusion. The second leans much more toward policy. Robertson is concerned with both, as his title indicates. However, the second sentence (as well as his entire paper) reveals the shape of his moral reasoning: *anything* that is useful for overcoming infertility is ethically acceptable. Robertson might disown that conclusion but I find nothing in his paper to support such a disclaimer. Needless to say, I think a great deal more needs to be said. I shall gather this "more" under three titles: life, wholeness, individuality.

LIFE

What we may do to preembryos (embryos whose cells have not yet differentiated into placenta and fetus) depends on what we think of them. Robertson is unhesitating here. He cites "the prevailing moral and legal consensus that views early embryos as too rudimentary in neurological development to have interests or rights." Therefore, we do not harm preembryos by splitting, freezing, and discarding them. Indeed, there should be no ethical objection to creating preembryos solely for research purposes. Robertson's conclusion: "Thus neither the lack of guidelines, the moral objections of some to any embryo research, or fears about where cloning research might lead justify denying researchers the ability to take this next step [creating embryos for research]." In brief, *nothing* may be allowed to get in the way of preembryo research and destruction.

That is a bit fast for me, and I suspect may be for many others. When dealing with the preembryo in 1979 the Ethics Advisory Board said it was "entitled to profound respect." The Warnock Committee accorded it "special status." Neither of these groups regarded the preembryo as a person. Reviewing these and similar statements, the American Fertility Society's Ethics Committee states: "Therefore, we find a widespread consensus that the preembryo is not a person but is to be treated with special respect."[1] It based this "special respect" on the fact that the preembryo is a living, genetically unique human entity that "might become a person." Or again, it referred to the "high moral value attributed to each human preembryo."

Granted, terms like "special status," "profound respect," and "high moral value" are tantalizingly vague and unspecified in terms of practical implications. But they totally dissolve and disappear under Robertson's protocols.

I have discussed this matter with Robertson before and have little reason to believe that he found me persuasive. I argued that the potential of the preembryo for personhood makes powerful prima facie demands on us not to interfere with that potential. Under favorable circumstances the preembryo will move through developmental individuality, and then through functional, behavioral, psychic, and social individuality. In viewing the first stage one cannot afford to blot out subsequent stages. That is what it means to ascribe significance to potential. Robertson denied this in the past, as he does here. "If preembryos are not persons," he wrote, "then how we treat them is a matter of policy, not moral obligation."[2] Such a statement looks very much like a knockout blow to dogs, cats, and the rest of nature.

I must leave it to others to judge whether potential for personhood retains any bite at all in Robertson's perspectives. I think not. In this sense he is not following a consensus but trying to create one. In my judgment, potential should have bite. That is why I attached a qualifying footnote to the American Fertility Society's statement on preembryo research. It reads: "The matter is of such grave public importance that approval of preembryo research should depend on conformity with guidelines established at the national level."[3] As I write, a committee established by the National Institutes of Health is attempting to draw up such guidelines.

The matter is of "grave public importance" because it engages our basic attitude toward human life. What will be the effect of preembryo manipulation on personal and societal attitudes toward human life in general? Will there be further erosion of our respect? I say "further" because of the widespread practice of abortion. If preembryos may be manipulated, would we gradually extend this to embryos and fetuses? Robertson is far from reassuring here. For instance, he views pregnancy reduction in multifetal pregnancies with the casual detachment of a croupier.

WHOLENESS

It is shortsighted, I believe, to view a technology in isolation from its social context and impacts. One of the easiest ways to do this is to see the technology in terms of individual rights, desires, and choices. It was in this spirit that Susan

Jacoby regretted "the pervasive sense of entitlement that forms a crucial, largely unexamined backdrop to the debate over the ethics of cloning human embryos."[4]

Here Robertson is instructive. He states that couples who are candidates for embryo donation might wish to know the characteristics of the existing twins or triplets of the embryos they seek to adopt. His response: "However, neither having nor satisfying this wish is itself immoral.... Even though the couple seeking the embryos will be choosing them on the basis of expected characteristics, such a choice is neither invalid nor immoral."

I call this privatizing what is also and especially a social issue. How is cloning a social issue? It issues from and reinforces societal attitudes, which in turn generate societal policies and practices.

Our society has taken long strides down the road of positive eugenics, the preferential breeding of superior genotypes. The contemporary symbol of this is Robert Graham's Repository for Germinal Choice in Escondido, California, featured on the *MacNeil/Lehrer Newshour* on 30 December 1993. The sperm of Nobel laureates, among others, is gathered so that brighter people will be conceived. After all, brighter people are better people. Perhaps the most depressing aspect of this is that many see nothing wrong with it.

What is wrong with it? It harbors many problems. For example, what qualities are desirable, what defects intolerable? Who decides? But the most glaring defect in preferential breeding is the perversion of our own attitudes: we begin to value the person in terms of the trait that he or she was programmed to have. We reduce the whole to a part. Societies that do that will likely be strongly tempted to do a lot of very unacceptable things, especially to the debilitated, retarded, elderly, and marginalized. I believe it is naive to think that we can program for certain characteristics and continue for long to "love the child for itself" when it does not have them. Is it really surprising that it was retarded persons who were the unsuspecting recipients of radioactive food at the Fernald State School in Waltham, Massachusetts? Can we unblushingly argue that this was an example of loving them for their own sake?

We can easily discern the long eugenic strides our society has already taken. Barbara Katz Rothman has noted the erosion of the unconditional acceptance of the child implicit in "quality" thinking. "What," she asks, "does it do to motherhood, to women, and to men as fathers too, when we make parental acceptance conditional, pending further testing? We ask the mother and her family to say in essence, 'These are my standards. If you meet these standards of acceptability, then you are mine and I will love and accept you totally. After you pass this test.' "[5] China is embarking on a similar eugenic policy with its draft law to "avoid new births of inferior quality."

We have recently seen several cases of "wrongful life" where the child herself is the plaintiff.[6] Recent neonatal intensive care cases have revealed an alarming attitude on the part of some people, including physicians: a healthy child or a dead child. We have preimplantation diagnosis for some genetic defects.

All of this takes on added importance in light of the Human Genome Project. Let the Dor Yeshorim project be an example here.[7] Dor Yeshorim is the program of blood testing given to Orthodox Jews in New York (and Israel) to determine if they carry genes for three diseases: Tay-Sachs, cystic fibrosis, and Gaucher's disease. Those tested are given six-digit identification numbers. When a boy and girl want to date they can call the Central Office of Dor Yeshorim to see whether as a couple they are at risk of passing along these diseases to their children. If they are they will probably cease dating.

As the Human Genome Project progresses and more genes are added to the list, some people may become genetic wallflowers, in Gina Kolata's phrase, rejected by all prospective suitors because of their recessive genes. Rejection is the flip side of any preferential breeding. To forget this is to forget one of the most critical ethical dimensions of cloning by blastomere separation. It is to abstract the discussion from its profoundly eugenic social context. That is why I find Robertson's statement—"neither having nor satisfying this wish is itself immoral"—an impoverished account of the issues involved. Ethics is concerned not only with individual choices and acts. It is also and perhaps above all concerned with the cultural shifts and trends of which acts are but the symptoms. In this sense the desire to know—and reject—the characteristics of the preembryos they propose to adopt must be viewed as an early step toward designer children.

INDIVIDUALITY

Cloning by blastomere splitting creates the possibility of genetically identical siblings, even siblings born years apart and in the same or different families. Robertson asks, "Are later born children harmed because a twin or triplet already exists? The claim," he continues, "rests on the notion that the later born child lacks the uniqueness or individuality that we deem essential to human worth and dignity." Thus for Robertson the issue of individuality revolves around the feelings and self-awareness of the cloned person, whether the person will somehow be harmed by genetic identity with others.

That is a legitimate question, but I believe that there is another aspect of this issue that is missed if we emphasize only harm to the cloned person. It is harm to ourselves. It is increasingly easy to shatter our wonder at human diversity and individuality, especially perhaps in the era of the Human Genome Project, when we are tempted to collapse the human person into genetic data. It would be ironical were this to happen in an era that prides itself on treasuring uniqueness and diversity of all kinds (sexual, racial, ethnic, cultural).

In conclusion, it is important to note that once our culture views human persons as isolated and autonomous agents—as it does—then nearly anything becomes thinkable. We begin to consider certain desires or felt needs as rights and judge restrictions on them to be intrusive violations of rights. This can happen with reproductive technologies.

My implicit plea in the foregoing reflections is that we take our social insertion seriously. When we do we may see that cloning by blastomere separation is not just another technological tool to be judged in terms of its efficacy in facilitating fertility and its effects on those clones. We may be led to wonder, in Meg Greenfield's words, "what the moral blind spots of our own age are."[8] Perhaps we will begin to ponder what human cloning would be capable of doing to us, to our cherished sense of the sanctity, wholeness, and individuality of human life. This might do no more than give us pause. But it just may be a pause that refreshes.

NOTES

1. This statement and that of the Warnock Committee can be found in American Fertility Society, Ethics Committee, "Ethical Considerations of the New Reproductive Technologies," Supplement 2, *Fertility and Sterility* 53, no. 6 (1990): 35S.

2. See John A. Robertson, "What We May Do with Preembryos," *Kennedy Institute of Ethics Journal* 1, no. 4 (1991): 193–302; and my "The Preembryo as Potential: A Reply to John A. Robertson," pp. 303–5. Robertson's statement is found on p. 295.

3. See American Fertility Society, "Ethical Considerations," p. 63S.

4. Susan Jacoby, "Do We Have Fertility Rights?" *Minneapolis Star Tribune*, 28 November 1993.

5. Barbara Katz Rothman, "The Products of Conception: The Social Context for Reproductive Choices," *Journal of Medical Ethics* 11, no. 4 (1985): 188–92, at 190.

6. *Turpin* v. *Sortini* 119 Cal. App. 3d 690; Harbeson v. Parke Davis 746 Fed. 2d 517; 656 P 2d 483; 98 Wash. 2d 460.

7. See Gina Kolata, "Nightmare or the Dream of a New Era in Genetics?" *New York Times*, 7 December 1993.

8. Meg Greenfield, "The Radiation Experiments," *Newsweek*, 17 January 1994, p. 60.

POSTSCRIPT

Is It Ethical to Clone Human Embryos?

In September 1994 a National Institutes of Health (NIH) panel recommended that some kinds of research with human embryos can be conducted ethically and are worth federal support. Many other countries—including the United Kingdom, Canada, Spain, and Sweden—liberally permit such research, and Canada actively encourages it. Other countries—such as Australia, France, and Germany—have stringent requirements, but they do permit the research. Norway, on the other hand, bans it altogether.

The panel set certain limits for federally funded embryo research, including special scrutiny for research in which eggs are fertilized solely for research purposes. Furthermore, research would be limited to embryos 14 days from the first cell division. Before the NIH panel report can be implemented, it must be accepted by the NIH director, Dr. Harold Varmus. His advisory committee is expected to rule early in 1995. If it accepts the report, the NIH will then issue guidelines for federally funded research. (Researchers Drs. Jerry Hall and Robert Stillman, responding to the reaction to their work on cloning, have said that they will not proceed with this line of research until there are formal guidelines.)

For a view supporting research into human embryo cloning, see "On Attempts at Cloning in the Human," by Howard W. Jones, Jr., Robert G. Edwards, and George E. Seidel, Jr., *Fertility and Sterility* (March 1994). Existing voluntary guidelines can be found in the American Fertility Society's "Ethical Considerations of the New Reproductive Technologies," a special supplement of *Fertility and Sterility* (1986), and in supplement 2 of the same journal (1990).

ISSUE 4

Should Commercial Surrogate Motherhood Be Banned?

YES: Thomas A. Shannon, from *Surrogate Motherhood: The Ethics of Using Human Beings* (Crossroad Publishing, 1988)

NO: Carmel Shalev, from *Birth Power* (Yale University Press, 1989)

ISSUE SUMMARY

YES: Professor of religious studies Thomas A. Shannon maintains that surrogacy continues social devaluing of women and encourages women and children to be treated as commodities rather than as persons worthy of respect.

NO: Attorney Carmel Shalev argues that women as autonomous and responsible individuals ought to be free to enter legally binding contracts and that the real issue is not commercialism but power to control reproduction.

The desire to bear a child is a deep and natural one, and for the 2.4 million infertile married American couples, their inability to reproduce is often a source of sorrow and pain. But adoption is not an easy alternative today. Because of the availability of legal abortion and because an increasing number of unwed teenage mothers are choosing to keep their babies, there are fewer babies available through adoption agencies—particularly the nondisabled, white newborns that are in greatest demand. The new reproductive technologies of external fertilization and embryo transfer are available only to a few women who meet rigid medical criteria.

Under these circumstances, it is not surprising that, when the wife is infertile, some couples are turning to surrogate mothers—women who will bear the husband's baby for a fee and then give it up for legal adoption. This is the way it works: A broker (usually a lawyer) puts an infertile couple in contact with potential surrogates who have been recruited (usually through newspaper advertisements) and screened for medical and psychological characteristics. If the couple and the surrogate agree, they sign a contract specifying in detail the fee (usually $10,000), the surrogate's responsibilities to care for her health during pregnancy, the conditions under which she would have an abortion, the transfer of legal custody, and the like. The price tag is high. In addition to the surrogate's fee, the couple will have to pay the broker ($5,000 to $10,000), the doctor who performs the insemination, the doctor who delivers the baby, and other medical costs. The total costs can run to $30,000 or more.

In the past such arrangements were almost certainly carried out in secret, and probably without any money changing hands, between friends and relatives. But in 1980 Elizabeth Kane (a pseudonym), a married woman with three children, announced publicly that she had borne a baby for a fee. "It's the father's child," she is reported to have said. "I'm only growing it for him." Since then there have been an estimated 500 to 700 babies born by contract, and several firms are now engaged in matching would-be adoptive parents and willing surrogates.

Are these contracts legal? Most states have laws prohibiting baby selling: the offering, giving, or receiving anything of value for placing a child for adoption. But whether surrogate mother contracts are baby selling or just another form of private adoption has yet to be settled in the courts. Even if the contracts are proven to be legal, serious questions remain about whether they are enforceable—whether, for instance, a mother who decides to keep the baby when it is born can be forced to give it up. The 1987–88 Baby M case in New Jersey, which was played out in the glare of publicity, illustrated how divisive such court battles can be. In the end, the court declared the contract illegal but awarded custody of Baby M to her father and adoptive mother, William and Elizabeth Stern. Her biological mother, Mary Beth Whitehead, has visitation rights.

When any unusual social arrangement is introduced, people tend to see it either as a continuation of already existing patterns or as something completely novel, and therefore suspect. Those who support the idea of surrogate mothers see it as similar to other practices in which a child is reared by someone other than its genetic parents. They believe that, as long as the child is wanted and cared for, the practice is acceptable—even desirable.

Those who oppose the practice point not only to the legal uncertainties but also to the psychological and family stresses that will face the children, the surrogate, and the adoptive family.

In the following selections, Thomas A. Shannon argues that surrogacy reinforces the still prevalent cultural view that values women primarily for their reproductive function. Moreover, the right to reproduce does not include the right to obtain a child by whatever means one chooses. From a feminist perspective, Carmel Shalev claims that attempts to ban surrogacy are paternalistic. In her view, women should be free to make reproductive contracts and be expected to fulfill them.

YES

Thomas A. Shannon

SURROGATE MOTHERHOOD: THE ETHICS OF USING HUMAN BEINGS

HUMAN BODY USE

If anything is clear about surrogacy, it is that the practice involves the use of human bodies. Surrogacy can be located within the tradition of the use of bodies such as wet nursing, organ transplantation, blood donation, and participation in research. The practice also is located at the intersection of public and private behavior. These issues provide one level for the analysis of surrogacy.

First, using the distinction between private and public behavior to blunt a critique of surrogacy does not work. By its nature surrogacy touches on issues that are critical for the individual *and* society and its well-being. How individuals obtain blood or organs is not simply a question of individuals satisfying private needs. It is also a question of how and on what basis individuals are cared for and how society allocates resources. While there are no policies mandating that specific individuals participate in research, progress in medicine requires the participation of human subjects and social well-being is dependent on such participation.

Yet if structures that encourage such participation are coercive or manipulative, subjects will be harmed and may not continue to participate in research. Individuals may not give the gift of their organs if policies and practices allow other people to profit financially from their gift. . . .

Additionally, these historical analogies suggest that once one commercializes the human body, its parts or its use, problems enter in. First, one begins a process of reducing the body to an object. While it is certainly true that the body is objective and is correctly perceived as an object in some circumstances —a medical examination or operation—to experience it primarily as an object is to diminish its significance and, ultimately, the status of the person who is present to the world through the body. Even when dead, or present as an organ to be transplanted, the body is not simply an object, but, because of its transcendent relation to the person, is a sign of the person's presence in the world.[1] The human body and its separate parts maintain their own dignity, even when separate from the person.

Second, when, as Marx Wartofsky says, one begins "doing it for the money,"[2] a new relation is set up with the person and his or her body: alienation. Karl Marx and Wartofsky both see prostitution as the prototype of alienation. In this act one takes what is most intimate to one's self and then objectifies, prices, and sells it. This objectifies one's body and distances one's self from it, thereby destroying the psychosomatic unity. Ultimately this destroys one's self.

Third, the objectifying and pricing of the body leads to a loss of its dignity. In a fulfillment of the Cartesian vision, the body becomes an extended object, a machine whose parts are interchangeable with any other parts. The body is simply another object in the world alongside other objects; when one part wears out, we simply buy another. Clearly, we know from experience, as Thomas Murray noted, that body parts have a price.[3] Blood and sperm can legally be sold. Other parts are in fact bought and sold on a somewhat open market. To be sure, this is illegal at present, but it is done. But our society has drawn the line by being unwilling to establish a policy of selling bodies and their parts.

Should society allow the body to become commodified and seek its market value, the body would become an object and have a price rather than a dignity. This would substantively contribute to the loss of human dignity. Such a policy would enhance the already common experience of alienation by stating in a policy what many already believe to be true: that their personal worth is only equal to their market value. This experience and policies that reinforce it will only be destructive of human dignity and human solidarity in both the short and long run. Permitting surrogates to be paid contributes to the tendency to price the body and to alienate women from themselves and their bodies.

Additionally, given already prevalent social values, women are frequently seen as objects. Witness their reduction to their physical attributes, their complexion, their hair color, and their alleged ability to enhance the desirability of a product. The practice of surrogacy reinforces this objectification of the woman.

First, the physical appearance of the surrogate is important. Surrogates are selected from a photo album or from a personal interview. How she presents herself is critical. Second, a demonstrated capacity successfully to reproduce is required. Her value comes from a biological capacity. Third, in renting or selling her uterus, the woman is reducing herself to the status of an incubator. Obviously pregnancy is an objective biological process. But it is not only that, for an organic relation develops between fetus and woman that cannot be discounted or ignored. The fetus is not in the woman's body as are her kidneys or lungs or any other organ of her own body. Thus to make of herself only an incubator is to discount the biological processes that are occurring and their impact on her, even after the pregnancy is ended. Fourth, in so renting her uterus the surrogate is assuming the role of a reproductive prostitute.[4] The social and biological analogies between prostitution and surrogacy, even though somewhat harsh, are too obvious to ignore. The surrogate is valued for a biological service she can perform; she is not desired for her person; she is to exit when the job is done; and she is paid. Thus, like the prostitute, the surrogate takes a capacity intimate to herself, objectifies it, prices it, and puts it on the market. This alienates her from herself, makes her a commodity among other commodities, and destroys her dignity.

The practice of surrogacy will destroy women by making objects of them, giving them a price but not a dignity, reinforcing the already present valuing of women primarily for their physical characteristics, and defining their value primarily as an exchange value.

THE COERCION OF THE NURTURING PARENTS AND THE SURROGATE

Coercion is a difficult concept and one not uniformly applicable to each situation. This is especially true when considering cash or other economic incentives to engage in various activities, for money has a diminishing marginal utility. Some individuals who are extremely wealthy can never have enough and some extremely poor people are content with very little. In thinking about coercion and surrogacy, one has to examine thematic issues as well as the individual situation.

First, to what extent is childbearing itself coercive? Judith Blake's argument that our society has a pronatalist bias needs to be seriously considered.[5] For if it is the case that our status as adults and mature membership in human society depend on having a child, our society may indeed have a pronatalist bias. This bias will exert subtle and unsubtle pressures on women, particularly since they are socially marginalized to begin with. For a woman, then, childbearing can provide a double function. First, it gives her social value because she has fulfilled her function and, second, it confers upon her adult status. The more that these motiva-

tions—even though unconscious—drive a woman, the less free and more coerced her choice with respect to childbearing becomes regardless of whether she is a surrogate or not.

Second, acts become coercive when they contain the threat of harm. There are two sets of harms associated with childbearing, somewhat at odds with each other in the surrogacy context. Childbearing contains some risk of harms that may argue against bearing a child. A certain degree of morbidity is typically, though not always, associated with pregnancy and delivery. There is also a small, but real, risk of mortality. Even if one argues that there is a large dose of cultural conditioning in a woman's choice to have a child, that does not mitigate the harms that are part of that process. The other harm—social as opposed to physical—is the harm of childlessness. In addition to diminished social status, the woman may experience severe strains because of perceptions of a lack of self-worth, of personal failure, and the perception of rejection associated with childlessness. Thus the nurturing mother may be driven to a surrogate by a need to avoid the physical harms of the pregnancy for whatever reasons or to avoid the social harm of childlessness. Also the surrogate may be driven by the desire to have children so she can feel fulfilled and socially useful. Both may be coerced into acts and relations that otherwise they may not have chosen.

Third, the research of Philip Parker, M.D., shows that the primary motivation for surrogates is economic compensation.[6] While the lump-sum payment seems large—ten thousand dollars is the usually quoted fee—it averages out to about $1.50 an hour. We are not talking about an eight-hour shift, five days a week; one is pregnant twenty-four hours a day for about nine months. The fee is well below minimum wage and assumedly such a small amount could not be coercive.

Or could it? First, the worth of the money is determined by one's situation. For some, this may be their way out of a desperate situation, but for others it may simply be extra cash to augment an already comfortable situation. Second, the money is typically provided in one or two payments. A payment of five or ten thousand dollars may be more than an individual has ever received or seen at one time. Third, I suspect few people actually calculate the payment on a per-hour-of-pregnancy basis. Thus ten thousand dollars is perceived much differently than $1.50 an hour.

Finally, the purpose of the prohibition of pre- or immediately postbirth contracts for adoption is precisely designed to avoid any appearance of coercion at a time when the individual is vulnerable emotionally or physically. The prohibitions exist to give some psychological and moral space around the decision of whether or not to give a child up for adoption. Such contracts serve to diminish any coercive elements in this decision. One can argue that since the surrogate contract is made before pregnancy, it is at a sufficient distance from relinquishment of the child so that coercion is not a factor. However, the circumstances of the woman's life—economic, need for social affirmation, or fear of childlessness, for example—may be such that the offer is one she can refuse only with the greatest difficulty because her situation may have coercive elements in it. Additionally, the experience of pregnancy and birth may change the perspective of the woman completely and she may want to keep the child.

While the intent should always be to keep a contract, the situation of surrogacy may qualify such an intent. Many adoption agreements, for example, allow for a change of mind within a certain period of time. Such provisions, while surely difficult on the adopting couple, recognize the difficulty and complexity of the situation and attempt to make provision for it. Even though the surrogate, for example, typically agrees not to bond with the child, such a promise may be impossible to keep even biologically. The surrogate may find herself in a situation in which, if she keeps the contract, she may cause herself significant emotional damage but, if she does not, she will cause serious emotional damage to the genetic father and nurturing mother. Such a conflict may be so disruptive as to make the surrogate unable to make any choices or act in what others might consider a responsible fashion. Either choice produces harm and neither resolves the harms. Whatever choice is made by the woman or is made for her by the court might, in fact, be a coerced decision: a decision in which there are no alternatives, in which harm comes from the choice, and in which control for the choice is out of the surrogate's hands.

The coercive nature of childbearing is uncertain. Part of the uncertainty comes from not knowing the degree to which the culture overrides the choices of individuals and/or blunts their freedom. Also money has a diminishing marginal utility. As well, there is simply a paucity of data to help resolve the issue. Finally, the surrogate may find herself in a situation in which she had no choices whatsoever and all decision-making power is taken from her.

The coupling of an apparently large fee for being a surrogate with the identified primary economic motivation of surrogates creates a situation that is potentially coercive. The loss of such a fee by not being a surrogate may be experienced as an actual harm and thus be coercive. Otherwise the fee may serve as either an inducement or a bribe, neither of which are, of course, associated with high moral standards. Thus at best the fee responds to an articulated motivation of potential surrogates. As such it creates a context in which the potential surrogate may act against her own best interests and in fact may be coerced or unfairly induced. By being paid, the surrogate enters into a compromised context and becomes vulnerable if she is not aware of her own interests, needs, and motivations. Not paying a fee would eliminate many but not all of the moral concerns. Additionally, the harms that may come to the surrogate from either fulfilling the contract or from not fulfilling it may in fact so diminish her decision-making capacities that her choices are simply not free choices. The whole surrogacy process occurs within a context that has coercive elements attached to it. One must examine each case separately to accurately ascertain whether there are coercive elements in it and to what extent they are operative.

BABY SELLING

In the practice of surrogacy, a couple contracts for a woman to become pregnant and then relinquish the baby to them post-birth when the terms of the contract have been fulfilled, that is, when the cou-ple receive the child they want. For this the woman is given a cash payment. If the terms of the contract are not fulfilled, the cash is not given, or, for example, in the event of a miscarriage a partial payment is made. The exchange of cash is dependent upon the couple's obtaining the child they want.

The prosurrogacy camp argues that this is nothing but reimbursement for services provided. There is a partial truth here in that the biological father typically pays for the health care services utilized by the genetic-nurturing mother. The untested issue—fortunately—is whether the biological father could sue for recovery of these costs in the event the contract were not fulfilled in some way.

The biological father does not pay the surrogate fee when the contract is not fulfilled either because of claims that the child was not his or because the surrogate refused to relinquish the child. Assumedly, most people would think this is reasonable since the contract was not fulfilled.

The fulfillment of the surrogate contract essentially consists in the production by the genetic-nurturing mother of an acceptable child who is then taken by the biological father. When this occurs, a fee is exchanged. This is exchanging cash for a baby. In a debate on surrogacy, Angela Holder [counsel for Yale–New Haven Hospital] captured this point well when she argued that when you go into a store, ask for an item, and pay for it when the clerk hands it to you, you have bought it and it is yours. You have not purchased the services of the clerk, though to be sure some of the payment is the basis of his or her salary. You have purchased the item and you have it and a receipt saying you paid for it. If someone would try to take it away from you, this would be an act of theft for which that individual could be arrested and prosecuted. In surrogacy, cash changes hands and the baby changes families.[7]

If there is some relevant difference between fulfilling the terms of a contract by receiving some item when cash is exchanged upon receiving it and fulfilling the terms of a surrogacy contract by exchanging cash when the baby is relinquished, I truly fail to see it. In either case, money is exchanged for an object which then passes to a new owner when the terms of the contract are fulfilled. I even think Noel Keane [lawyer and surrogate motherhood broker] admits as much when he suggests that, even if surrogacy were a commercial exchange, fulfilling needs and wants in this way simply happens to be the way we do things in a commercialized society.[8] And surely he is correct. In our commercialized society we do indeed fulfill our needs and wants through commercial relations.

But from the fact that we buy and sell many—perhaps even most—things, it neither follows that we should sell everything nor that we are correct in selling what we already sell. If we accept the commercial model uncritically, we may fall into the danger of knowing the price of everything and the value of nothing. Additionally, by pricing babies in this fashion, we are making an explicit frontal assault on human dignity and the moral worth of an individual. Such pricing of an individual, by its nature reduces the individual to what he or she can be exchanged for on the market. The only worth, in this perspective, is economic worth. Any transcendental dimension of the person is diminished, if not disregarded, by such a pricing mechanism.

The surrogate contract is, in essence, a contract to buy or sell a child and should be prohibited. Such practices, as Angela Holder observes, are prohibited by the Thirteenth Amendment which outlaws the selling of humans.[9] Such a constitutional provision would, in my judgment, outweigh claims of rights to privacy and the right to reproduce derivative from the right to privacy. In addition to the Thirteenth Amendment's prohibition on selling persons, the state also has the right to restrict even constitutional rights when there is a compelling state interest to do so. Surely trafficking in babies would present such a compelling state interest.

FEMINIST PERSPECTIVES

...Surrogacy reinforces the still prevalent cultural stereotype that values women primarily, if not exclusively, for their reproductive function. This reduces the value of a woman to her physiology and specifically her reproductive capacity. Her person is lost and she has no dignity except that which accrues from the impersonality of biology.

The practice of surrogacy further denigrates the infertile woman. In essence, she is told that since she simply cannot meet her partner's need to have a child genetically related to him, he has to go out and rent a woman who can do this for him. Again, the primary value of the woman is reproductive capacity. Although many report that wives freely cooperate with this process, one has to wonder whether or not this is a survival mechanism. And even if the woman participates in the surrogacy situation to save the marriage or to keep her husband, what is this saying about the status of the woman, the dominance of the male, and the nature of this marriage?

Second, by agreeing to be a surrogate, a woman buys into the most narrow understanding of freedom: the freedom to buy and sell. While no one should dictate what women can and cannot do, we should attend to the understanding of freedom that women may literally be buying into in becoming surrogates. The freedom that money and access to it brings contributes enormously to our sense of well-being. Freedom from financial burdens and freedom to obtain one's needs and wants remove stress and allow one to have many of the advantages our culture provides. Yet if the freedom to buy or sell is the only or primary freedom, our lives would be poverty stricken. We would compromise, for example, our freedoms with respect to career choice, to participate in cultural activities, to relocate, to begin a new job, to be responsible for our actions.

Many of these freedoms require, obviously, an economic underpinning. But if the major or most desirable understanding of freedom is the ability to buy and sell, the majority of significant life experiences have been lost. To reduce freedom to only one aspect, and to such a narrow one at that, is to destroy freedom. . . .

Finally, and in a related context, surrogacy bears a close relation to prostitution. In prostitution the woman sells or rents a body part; the relation is impersonal; the woman does the man's bidding; her value is a function she performs; and she is to leave when the job is done. The surrogate mother does the same things. The only difference is that with the surrogate intercourse is typically technical, whereas with the prostitute both biological and technical means are used. And of course the surrogate is expected to become pregnant and the prostitute is not.

The context in which surrogacy is practiced seems to blunt the comparison with prostitution. After all, surrogacy is arranged in an attorney's office; the surrogate has been cleared with reference to her intelligence, appearance, and physical and psychological health; the motives are to help a couple to have what most other married couples have. Yet when this veneer is stripped away, the analogy with prostitution is right there. For the surrogate is selected essentially on the basis of desirable criteria, is paid to provide her body, and is then dumped. Many then complete the analogy by identifying the broker as the pimp. Many of the attorneys involved in this work understandably are unhappy with this label. But if the analogy between surrogacy and prostitution holds, then those associated with its practice must be expected to assume their proper position also.

Finally, surrogacy can contribute to the social stereotyping of women. Frequently in our culture, women are valued primarily because of their reproductive capacity and have social status through fulfilling social roles assumedly derived from that capacity. . . .

The responsibility for nurturing the young is an extremely important one. But the primary or main responsibility for this does not accrue to the woman because she has physically given birth. Surrogacy is in a paradoxical situation here. For it clearly affirms the split between reproduction and nurturing, but values the genetic-carrying mother only for that biological capacity, and it might suggest that the nurturing and socialization will be done primarily by the nurturing mother, the biological father having done his share by providing the sperm. Thus surrogacy functions to keep women in their place, a place frequently not chosen by them and, even if chosen, a place often devalued or rejected by the more market-driven values of our society. The ultimate irony is that while the practice of surrogacy may provide some women with the opportunity to achieve their desires and wants, it does this only through reducing other women to their biological functions and by reenforcing cultural stereotypes about women....

THE RIGHT TO HAVE CHILDREN

... Another contested issue is the claim of a right to have children.[10]... Legally and morally, the right to reproduce is a negative one. That is, the right is typically secured by the fact that *prima facie* no one may interfere with or prohibit one from seeking the exercise of that right. That is, given the fact that children are a good and that the individual has certain privacy rights, some restrictions on their actions are inappropriate. There is a liberty of action, a zone of privacy, and the inherent dignity of the person that must be respected. This is done by securing his or her liberty of action.

The right to reproduce does not include the right actually to *obtain* a child. What is protected legally and morally is the right to exercise a capacity, not the securing of the end of that capacity....

Similarly, the right to reproduce does not ensure those exercising that right that they will receive a child. Infertility, to borrow a phrase from [philosopher] H. Tristram Engelhardt, is unfortunate, but not unfair.[11] For individuals wishing a child, infertility is frequently a crushing blow. Yet no sense of justice has been violated because of this biological incapacity. Such an incapacity may be inconvenient, depressing, frustrating, and even destructive of a relationship, but the fact that a couple is infertile does not constitute a violation of justice. There is simply no argument which guarantees an individual even an average biological constitution in the natural lottery through which we are given our body.

Thus while there is a legally and morally protected right to procreate, there is no similar right which guarantees the obtaining of a child through the exercise of such a right. While unfortunate and tragic for the individuals involved, they have not been morally wronged by the fact of their infertility....

SUMMARY

In my judgment, these arguments constitute a strong case against the practice of surrogate motherhood. The practice is inherently problematic from a practical and moral perspective. Its utilization continues the social disenfranchisement of women, puts the child at the risk of existing in a compromised social and familial context, and simply encourages the commodification of women and children. I can only conclude that the practice of surrogate motherhood should be prohibited.

NOTES

1. William F. May, "Religion and the Donation of Body Parts," Hastings Center *Report* 15 (February 1985):38-42.

2. Marx Wartofsky, "On Doing It for Money," Thomas A. Mappes and Jane S. Zembaty, eds, *Biomedical Ethics* (New York: McGraw-Hill, 1981), pp. 186-94.

3. Thomas H. Murray, "Who Owns the Body? On the Ethics of Using Human Tissue for Commercial Purposes," *IRB: A Review of Human Subjects Research* 8 (January/February 1986):3.

4. Andrea Dworkin, *Right-Wing Women* (New York: Coward-McCann, Inc., 1983), pp. 176 and 182.

5. Judith Blake, "Coercive Pronatalism and American Population Policy," in E. Peck and J. Senderowitz, eds, *Pronatalism: The Myth of Mom and Apple Pie* (New York: Thomas Y. Crowell Company, 1974), pp. 29-67.

6. Philip Parker, M.D., "Motivation of Surrogate Mothers: Initial Findings," *American Journal of Psychiatry* 140 (January 1983): 117.

7. Angela Holder, quoted in Iver Peterson, "Ruling in Baby M Case is Due Today," *New York Times*, 31 March 1987, p. B2.

8. Noel Keane, "Legal Problems of Surrogate Motherhood," *Southern Illinois University Law Journal*, 1980, p. 156.

9. Angela Holder, "Surrogate Motherhood: Babies for Fun and Profit," *Law, Medicine, and Health Care* 12 (June 1984): 115-17.

10. Kathryn V. Lorio, "In Vitro Fertilization and Embryo Transfer: Fertile Areas for Litigation," *Southwest Law Journal* 35 (1982):1006ff. John Robertson, "Procreative Liberty and the Control of Conception, Pregnancy, and Childbirth," *Virginia Law Review* 69 (April 1983):405-63.

11. H. Tristram Engelhardt, Jr., M.D., Ph.D., "Allocating Scarce Medical Resources and the Availability of Organ Transplantation," *New England Journal of Medicine* 311 (5 July 1984):68.

NO

Carmel Shalev

BIRTH POWER

REPRODUCTIVE AGENCY

Reproduction, like all other human activities, takes place in a social context and can be conscious, rational, moral, and political. Reproductive "agency" denotes the human capacity, regardless of gender, to exercise reason and choice in making autonomous decisions and to bear responsibility for the consequences.... [W]hereas the legislative regulation of artificial insemination relations implicitly acknowledges the intention of the sperm donor to dissociate biological from social fatherhood, there is a reluctance to do so in the case of the surrogate mother. That the surrogate mother freely agrees to bear a child for another person does not apparently affect her right to keep the child after birth. Even though such change of mind may involve a breach of the initial agreement, her biological relation to the child is considered, in effect, to override any claim made by the other parties. The question is whether the disparate treatment of sperm donor and surrogate mother is justified.

The instinctive response is that whereas biological gender might not generally be material in determining individual merit and desert, when it comes to reproduction there is no avoiding the fact that the woman has the womb. The circumstances of the surrogate mother do appear to differ essentially from those of the sperm donor for she is involved in the process of reproduction continuously until the child's birth. It would seem further that pregnancy is an emotionally volatile condition and that some kind of instinctive maternal bonding to the fetus takes place in the process. It would be inhumane, therefore, to insist that the surrogate give up the child if it happens that against all her original good intentions she has become emotionally attached to the child.

This paternalistic refusal to force the surrogate mother to keep to her word denies the notion of female reproductive agency and reinforces the traditional perception of women as imprisoned in the subjectivity of their wombs. The benevolent protection of women from themselves places an inedible stamp of illegitimacy on the notion of a woman contracting to bear a child for another person. It implies that reproductive matters are not proper subjects for legal relations, reinforcing the public-private dichotomy that relegates women's reproductive activity to the shadow life of a male-dominated socioeconomic political order.

What prevents the surrogate mother from making a legally binding commitment toward the sponsoring parents? The only possible answer is: her biology. Her state of mind at the moment of agreement is not to be taken seriously because it is subject to change during the performance of her undertaking, due to the nature of pregnancy. The insinuation is that it is unreasonable to expect her to keep her promise because her faculty of reason is suspended by the emotional facets of her biological constituency.

Even though the pregnant woman appears to be physically possessed with a spirit not her own, she is an autonomous human being, no less in control of her human faculties than any other person. Without disregarding the physical incapacitation or emotional upheaval that she may experience in this unique womanly feat, she needs no more and no less excuse for her condition beyond those civilly accorded to any other human being in analogous creative situations. To deny this is to exclude women from full-fledged membership in human society. A woman pregnant with child is no less deserving of special treatment than an artist pregnant with inspiration. But her special condition in no way justifies the condescension that denies her autonomy as a human being.

The notion of female reproductive agency suggests an alternative perspective that perceives women as rational moral agents, competent to assess the emotional stakes of reproductive activity and to assume responsibility for its consequences, and frees us to examine the social construction of some self-evident truisms about our biological nature. Under the double standard of reproductive conduct, women normally rear the children they bear, and there has been little opportunity to explore the nonbiological aspects of the mother-fetus relationship. Certainly women have never been free to contemplate the significance of biological motherhood as such. The assumption that there is an instinctive mother-fetus attachment, regardless of the mother's intentions as to the child's rearing after birth, appears to be a matter of pure speculation at this point, given that women have been socially bound to take care of their children. Similarly, until fairly recently, the mother-infant relation was assumed to be a matter of natural instinct....

Moreover, the objection to commercial surrogacy, while tolerating altruistic engagements, smacks of the double standard of morally proper conduct. If a surrogacy for money arrangement is illegal, it should be noted, then a surrogate who performs her part in the agreement will have no legal remedy against a sponsoring parent who refuses to pay her as agreed. The rationale for the extension of the baby barter ban from the area of adoption—apart from the financial incentive that supposedly distorts the woman's decision-making process and renders her choice involuntary—is that it commercializes reproductive activity and "commodifies" human life. There is a tendency to overlook the considerable economic activity that accompanies the establishment of both biological and nonbiological parent-child relations, involving medical professionals, lawyers, and social workers, at the very least. Why is it that we balk precisely at paying women for their reproductive services? Is there anything special in the nature of childbearing that affects the volition of a woman negotiating the economic value of her reproductive labor, or is it merely that our moral sensibility is offended by the image of a rational woman controlling her bodily resources and selling her birth power?

RESPONSIBILITY

The cool-headed, detached attitude that informs deliberate reproductive activity goes against the grain of a patriarchal ideology that conceives of domestic relations as an insulated haven of emotion and affection amid a cold, impersonal economic-political world.[1] The normative upshot of this private-public dichotomy is to extol values of love and altruism in personal relations, as opposed to the market forces of power and self-interest. At the same time, however, the cushioned private realm of woman is deprecated in relation to the abrasive public realm of man. This is the "pedestal-cage" in which woman is first captured, then protected, and finally respected to the extent that "man aspires to clothe in his own dignity whatever he conquers and possesses."[2] Woman is confined to the noble domestic destiny of wife and mother by virtue of her supposedly natural timidity and delicacy; and the very same nature renders her inferior as a moral creature, incompetent and unfit to participate in the public world.[3]

Women have not only suffered inferior legal status because of their biology but have also been considered incapable of attaining the highest levels of moral development. [Psychologist] Carol Gilligan, however, suggests that women do not meet the standards of theories of moral maturity simply because these standards are based on studies of men, whereas women tend to exercise a different mode of moral reasoning and decision making.[4] The male point of view is that moral problems arise from competing rights and are resolved by a formal and abstract mode of thinking. If we bother to study women as moral agents in the process of making decisions, as Gilligan has done, we discover a different point of view—the female voice—according to which moral problems arise from conflicting responsibilities and are resolved by a contextual and narrative mode of thinking. Neither mode is the exclusive possession of one or the other biological sex; on the contrary, both modes interplay in each individual. They depict the very poles of the human tension that lie at the root of any moral problem—between attachment and separation, connection and individuation....

The concept of responsibility in the [female] ethic of passion and care correlates to that of right in the [male] ethic of justice and fairness. In our current normative system (which expresses the male voice) a concept of responsibility already exists as a derivative of right.[5] What I am suggesting here within an ethic of passion and care is that responsibility is a primary concept from which rights may derive. This normative concept draws from the perception that the human condition is essentially social, in that a person always exists within a network of relations. It is most apposite to an analysis of human reproduction, which is the origin of all existence and fundamentally social. In the simplest terms, some form of collaboration between persons (at least one male and one female) is a necessary condition of reproduction. The connection of woman and embryo/fetus, and then of parent and infant, moreover, is the primary experience of every human being and precedes all social interaction. The concept of right fails to take into account this human connectedness, which is elementary in all forms of social reproductive relations. Indeed, the language of rights appears to reach its limits in this context. In the abortion controversy, for example, it leads to a moral stalemate between the competing rights of two supposedly separate subjects (woman and fetus), whereas the reality is a oneness of woman-with-child.[6] ...

PRIVACY

... The United States Constitution mentions neither reproduction nor the marital family. These matters were probably not thought to have political significance when this document was drafted—if the biological family was "natural" it would not merit attention in a document that dealt with the distribution of political power. The states thus retained jurisdiction over the body of family law that developed during the nineteenth century, along with the social changes in domestic relations and the legal position of women and children. But state regulation of the family reached its constitutional limitations at the beginning of the twentieth century, when the U.S. Supreme Court enunciated the principle that parental autonomy protected the child-rearing function from undue state intervention.[7]

Reproduction as such was first recognized as a subject of constitutional protection when a male offender challenged a state law imposing sterilization as a criminal sanction. The court held that the law violated a fundamental "right to procreate."[8] Then a statute prohibiting the use of contraceptives was struck down as violating a constitutionally guaranteed "zone of privacy" in marriage.[9] In *Roe v. Wade* (1973),[10] the Supreme Court

subsequently held that the constitutional right to personal privacy embraced a woman's abortion decision. Although the Constitution did not explicitly mention this right, the court had recognized it in relation to certain fundamental personal rights in the areas of marriage, family relations, procreation, contraception, and child rearing and education, and it would now extend it to include a woman's decision to terminate a pregnancy.

Privacy in contraception and abortion protects a decision *not* to reproduce. The new reproductive technology involves positive decisions to reproduce, which should also be regarded as lying within the realm of privacy as a matter of personal decision-making authority. First, autonomy in reproductive decisions provides a check against the technical control of reproduction by detached parties for economic or political ends. Second, idiosyncrasy and diversity in circumstances of birth guarantee the continuing enrichment of human experience. Third, given the novelty of the technological options and the general flux in social norms of family, the state should refrain at this point from imposing any one viewpoint as to the propriety of reproductive activity and allow norms to emerge case by case from the grass-roots level on the basis of experience.

Under current legal doctrine, privacy appears to consist in a right to be let alone. In the scheme proposed here, privacy denotes responsibility within a context of social relations for idiosyncratic decisions that are effectuated through contract. It contains two elements: the authority to make a decision, and the capacity to create an effective legal relationship with others to implement that decision. The meaningful exercise of private decision-making authority requires the state to acknowledge and enforce contractual relations that embody consensual reproductive collaboration. Privacy thus replaces norms of marriage and illegitimacy as a constitutional principle that defines legal parent-child relations in accord with autonomous contractual agreement. Any state-imposed restriction on access to reproductive technology beyond that of general contractual capacity[11] would be considered a ruling on parental eligibility that is an a priori violation of constitutional privacy (unless justified on independent grounds, such as reasonable criteria for distributing a scarce resource). In principle there would be no more legitimate or illegitimate reproduction—certainly there would be no more illegitimate children....

Custody

In a sense, the greatest risk is that the surrogate mother will refuse to relinquish the child after birth. The question then is whether the legal system will force her to do so. On the face of it the rule that contracts for personal services are not specifically enforced would seem to apply. The general remedy for breach of contract is monetary. A decree of specific performance ordering the breaching party to do the very thing she agreed upon will be granted only if damages would be an inadequate remedy. Even then a court will not normally decree specific performance where ongoing court supervision is necessary for the order to be effective, as in a contract for personal services.[12]

The reluctance to order a surrogate mother to relinquish her child cannot, however, be entirely explained in this way. After all, she has performed the reproductive services that she contracted to provide. The reluctance of the court is to force her to separate from the child to which she has become emotionally attached. Analogous instances of contractual relations exist involving a personal and emotionally loaded duty of performance, such as a sculptor working on commission. It is technically impossible to force the sculptor to create a piece of art, but once it is completed the sculptor cannot refuse to deliver it to the commissioning party merely because she or he wants to keep it. Similarly, it may be technically impossible to force a surrogate mother to conceive and carry a pregnancy to term, since these are personal services that depend ultimately on her continuing voluntary cooperation. But once the child has been born, why should her emotional involvement prevent the child's placement with the sponsoring parents?

The part of the surrogacy agreement that addresses the child's placement is akin to a custody agreement. Courts usually honor such agreements unless there has been a significant change in circumstances that justify modification of the agreement, having regard to the best interests of the child.[13] Assuming that both the surrogate mother and the sponsoring couple are more or less equally competent to care for the child, a commitment to freedom of contract would favor the sponsoring couple as custodians, whereas sympathy for the gestational bond between mother and child would favor the surrogate mother.

The biological relation as such appears to be immaterial. Both the surrogate and the sponsoring father typically have a biological interest in the child. But even if the sponsoring parent has no biological relation to the child—as, for example, where a single man or woman commissions the surrogate mother to conceive through artificial insemination with sperm from an anonymous donor—the contractual approach would favor the sponsoring party on the basis of the social relations of reproduction and the legitimate expectations that arise therefrom.[14] Likewise, even if the surrogate mother has no genetic relation to the child—as, for example, where she has carried the pregnancy of a child conceived from the egg of another woman—sympathy for the gestational bond would still favor her as custodian.

The perception of a mother-child gestational bond is not merely a matter of sympathy toward the mother. It also lays the ground for a best-interest-of-the-child argument. The in utero bonding of fetus with mother would seem to dictate that the child remain with the surrogate and to override the sponsoring parents' contractual claim. Thus, Britain's Warnock Committee stated that surrogate arrangements are, among other things, "potentially damaging to the child, whose bonds with the carrying mother, regardless of genetic connections, are held to be strong, and whose welfare must be considered of paramount importance." The psychological or emotional dimensions of fetal bonding are not, however, altogether clear. A dissenting minority on the committee pointed out that "as very little is actually known about the extent to which bonding occurs when the child is *in utero*, no great claims should be made in this respect."[15] Indeed, the generally accepted view of Goldstein, Freud, and Solnit is that a newborn child has no appreciation of biological relation as such and responds to any adult who provides for its needs and cares for its physical and emotional development.[16]

The contractual approach advocated here stems, among other things, from a critique of the idea that mothers bond instinctively with their children since this concept binds and confines women to a biological destiny and impedes their individuation as autonomous persons while excluding men from the role of social parent. Moreover, if responsibility—as opposed to right—is taken as the key concept in the regulation of interpersonal relations, then adult responsibility becomes the correlative of the interests of the child. From this point of view, a policy that renders a surrogacy agreement unenforceable in effect encourages the surrogate to act irresponsibly toward the other adults involved in the arrangement. If adult responsibility is the measure of the child's best interests, then one who demonstrates consistency in his or her initial commitment is surely more deserving of the title of legal parent....

WAGES FOR REPRODUCTION

The proposition of female agency in reproductive activity is analogous to that of sexual agency. The contractual scheme for reproductive relations that I propose is part of a feminism that supports women's experiments and encourages the acquisition of knowledge through individual experience. It insists that to overcome the psychological constraints of patriarchy women must regard themselves as subjects, actors, and agents of their individual sexual and reproductive activity.[17]

The idea of a free market in reproductive activity nevertheless contains a commercial element that could lead to what [historian] Linda Gordon called "a loss of mothering in a symbolic sense." The fear is of a completely individualized society in which all services are based on egoistic cash nexus relations without any forms from which children can learn about lasting nurturing human commitments. The problem is to reconcile a philosophy of personal agency with notions of constructive bonds between individuals.[18]

Although we do not want to sacrifice the value of altruism altogether for the sake of individuality, it is important to note the pathological aspects of the image of the nurturing woman. As much as women are connected with others, and particularly with their children, they also have difficulty with separation and individuation.

Although an economic analysis of reproduction uses a language that seems to reduce complex social relations to simplistic cold terms of commerce, or trade in commodities—a danger that must be duly apprehended—it brings to light a fact largely glossed over by patriarchal culture, that women's reproductive activity does have economic value. Indeed, the tendency to commodification is far greater when we focus on the child as "product" than when we focus on the birth mother as "producer."

It must be clear from the outset that the transaction under consideration is not for the sale of a baby but for the sale of reproductive services. Reproductive contracts are transactions in which custody of a child is transferred from one person to another, whereas the sale of a baby implies the transferal of property rights in a human being as a variation on slavery. The concept of custody does indeed contain an element of exclusive possession and control of the child. Certainly, property notions of exclusive ownership of women and their children form the historical source of our current law of parent-child relations. (Although contemporary family arrangements, specifically in open adoption or postdivorce situations involving visitation or even shared custody, indicate a relaxation in the possessive character of the exclusive parent-child relation.) There is, however, a difference between acquiring a position to exercise custodial control of a child and its abuse. A free market in reproduction—based on prior-to-conception agreements—does not involve the purchase of transferable rights or imply a right to resell a child. Rather, a childless couple is regarded as purchasing the reproductive labor of a birth mother so as to acquire the privilege of being responsible for the long-term care of a child. Once that responsibility is established, it cannot be relinquished except through the mechanism of statutory adoption.

The value of the reproductive services is determined by various factors of supply and demand. It may be reasonable to assume initially that remuneration for reproductive labor would be relatively low, as in the case of other transactions involving widely available bodily functions that require little training or expertise, such as manual labor. At the same time, the value of the personal services would reflect the costs directly related to pregnancy and childbirth, the costs of other economic opportunities the birth mother may forego while engaged in the reproductive project, and the emotional costs she may incur in giving birth to a child she will not keep. On the other side, the consumer demand would take into account the emotional costs of childlessness, the availability of adoptable newborns, and the economic costs of alternative forms of collaborative reproduction (for example, in vitro fertilization as compared to artificial insemination or open adoption). In addition, there are information costs involved in locating the parties and bringing them to a mutually satisfactory arrangement, having regard to individual preferences and tastes.[19]

Assuming an unsatisfied demand of childless couples, any legal restriction on permissible forms of reproductive collaboration would merely drive the activity underground, creating a black market. The risk of incurring criminal sanctions and the additional information costs of a clandestine market would result in artificially high prices. Moreover, intermediary exploitation and dishonesty is granted effective immunity where the activity is illegal, since the parties lack access to courts of law to enforce the terms of their transaction.[20] Beyond this, it appears generally that any policy prohibiting (rather than regulating) commercial activity in a given area of social interaction is premised ultimately on a denial of individual autonomy. As in the case of the war on drugs, the mentality of prohibition appears to treat people as objects to be controlled rather than as responsible actors. It is assumed that their behavior is not generated by an internalized value structure but by external forces. It follows that the individual's attempt to govern his or her own consciousness must be suppressed for fear of what that person may do or experience. The idea of individual responsibility or accountability is alien to this point of view.[21]

A free market would allow a new source of reproductive activity for women who presently have limited income-earning opportunities, with two positive distributive effects: a shift of wealth from the childless consumers to the presumably less advantaged reproducers, and a reallocation of economic returns away from the exploiting intermediaries to the birth mothers.

In spite of all this, the prospect of a market for reproductive services is disquiet-ing, if not grotesque. We have an intuitive reaction that there is something fundamentally indecent in the possibility of prices, advertising, credit, discounts, and like attributes of consumer transactions.[22] It is not improbable, for example, that price differences would reflect racist prejudices that we strive particularly hard to overcome through other social policies.[23] And there is concern that a free market scheme would relegate underprivileged women to a new oppressed and undignified occupation, like prostitutes and wet nurses. But it should be obvious that the idea of a free market in reproduction does not attempt as such to rectify existing social inequities, and legal regulation could conceivably provide certain protections, such as court approval of reproductive agreements and minimum wage legislation.

There is, of course, the further objection that even if we call the transaction a contract for reproductive services rather than for the sale of a baby, the result is still the same—to put a monetary value on a life that is considered priceless. Yet the problem of pricing life is confronted in many areas of social activity, such as torts law, motor vehicle design, medical research, and most of all military strategics. Indeed, a similar debate took place in the late nineteenth century with respect to life insurance, which was thought to represent a form of trafficking in human lives.[24] Our acceptance of these instances of pricing life and death appears to be part of a complex process of transition in the cultural values of a postindustrial society. This process seems now to have reached the boundaries of the sacred institution of sexual-reproductive relations: marriage.

"What is it about child-bearing that makes it somehow dishonorable when done for money but most honorable when done for other reasons? Why does paying for childbirth or engaging in child-bearing for the sake of money convert a dignified activity into a despised one?"[25] Furthermore, why do we not object to paying doctors for their services in collaborative reproduction? Is the notion of paying for human life distasteful only when the recipient is the mother?

The idea of wages for reproduction poses an essential challenge to the public-private/market-family division that is the patriarchal foundation of our postindustrial economy. Woman as conscious, moral, social, and political being is also woman as economic being. We cannot separate ourselves from our economic existence or ignore the value (as commonplace as it may be) of our reproductive powers. The attachment of monetary value need not in itself determine the manner in which we conduct ourselves in our reproductive relations. But the failure to acknowledge the economic value of female reproductive labor is blind folly for those who wish for equity in women's social situation. . . .

Responsibility or accountability are key to positions of power. If we are to transform our patriarchal reproductive consciousness, we cannot evade the burden of our personal human agency. Far from advocating a revolution, all I am suggesting is that responsibility for reproductive decisions—both "right" and "wrong" ones—be left to the discretion of the individual, regardless of gender. Knowledge is the sum of our experience. We need not fear our experiments so long as we hold ourselves personally accountable for their consequences.

NOTES

1. Actually, the legal demarcation of family-market is not at all clearcut. For a comprehensive description of its blending, see Olsen, The Family and the Market: A Study of Ideology and Legal Reform, 96 *Harv. L. Rev.* 1497 (1983).

2. S. de Beauvoir, *The Second Sex* 74 (1949; reprint 1968).

3. See *Bradwell v. Ill.* 83 U.S. (16 Wall) 130 (1873), per Bradley, J., for a classic legal restatement of the "pedestal-cage" attitude to the female sex.

4. C. Gilligan, *In a Different Voice* (1982).

5. The correlative of a right, in the existing system, is a duty in another person toward the holder of the right. See W. N. Hohfeld, *Fundamental Legal Conceptions* 35–38 (1919). Responsibility derives from a failure to perform one's duty. A person who is found to be responsible for the violation of a right (by an impartial judge) will be held liable to compensate the injured person (civil liability) or society at large (criminal liability).

6. Compare Churchill and Simon, Abortion and the Rhetoric of Individual Rights, 12 *Hastings Center Rep.* 9 (1982).

7. *Meyer v. Neb.* 262 U.S. 390 (1923); *Pierce v. Soc'y of Sisters* 268 U.S. 510 (1925); cf. *Moore v. Cleveland* 431 U.S. 494 (1977).

8. *Skinner v. Okla.* 316 U.S. 535 (1942).

9. *Griswold v. Conn.* 381 U.S. 479 (1965).

10. *Roe v. Wade* 410 U.S. 116 (1973).

11. The rules of general contractual capacity would exclude minors and other legal incompetents from binding themselves in reproductive agreements.

12. P. Atiyah, *An Introduction to the Law of Contract*, 2nd Edition, 274–5 (1971).

13. See, e.g., Wexler, Rethinking the Modification of Child Custody Decrees, 94 *Yale L.J.*, 757 (1985).

14. Compare Erickson, Contracts to Bear a Child, 65 *Cal. L. Rev.* 611, 621 (1978); Robertson, Surrogate Mothers: Not So Novel After All, 13 *Hastings Center Rep.* 28, 33 (1983).

15. 1984 Report of the Committee of Inquiry into Human Fertilisation and Embryology (chaired by Dame Mary Warnock) (London, HMSO, Cmnd. 9314), secs 8.11, 8.16.

16. On the central notion of the psychological parent, see J. Goldstein, A. Freud, and A. Solnit, *Beyond the Best Interests of the Child* 12–17 (1973).

17. Vance, Pleasure and Danger: Towards a Politics of Sexuality, in *Pleasure and Danger: Exploring Female Sexuality*, 1, 24.

18. See Gordon, Why Nineteenth-Century Feminists Did Not Support 'Birth Control' and Twentieth-Century Feminists Do: Feminism, Reproduction, and the Family, in *Rethinking the Family* 40, 51 (Thorne and Freeman, eds., 1978).

19. Compare Landes and Posner, The Economics of the Baby Shortage, 7 *J. Legal Studies* 323, 336–37 (1978).

20. Id., at 338.

21. Wisotksy, Exposing the War on Cocaine: The Futility and Destructiveness of Prohibition, 1983 *Wis. L. Rev.* 1305, 1424–25.

22. Pritchard, A Market for Babies, 34 *U. Toronto L. Rev.* 341, 347 (1984).

23. Id., at 351; Landes and Posner, at 344–45.

24. Pritchard, at 357.

25. Id., at 353.

POSTSCRIPT

Should Commercial Surrogate Motherhood Be Banned?

In the aftermath of the Baby M case, the Task Force on New Reproductive Practices of the New Jersey Bioethics Commission recommended that commercial surrogacy be outlawed. It did not, however, recommend criminalizing noncommercial surrogacy; that is, when a woman volunteers to bear a child for an infertile relative without a fee. In one such case a 42-year-old librarian became pregnant with her infertile daughter's twins, thus carrying her own grandchildren. According to the American Society for Reproductive Medicine, in 1992 there were 230 egg retrievals from women who could not become pregnant, 172 transfers of embryos into surrogate mothers, and 68 deliveries.

In May 1993 the California Supreme Court endorsed surrogacy arrangements by upholding a couple's contract with a woman who carried an embryo created by in vitro fertilization from the couple's egg and sperm. In this case the court adopted a novel legal theory of "intent," declaring that when the genetic mother and the birth mother are not the same woman, the mother who intended to bring about the birth of the child is the natural mother. California thus became the first state to approve this kind of surrogacy arrangement. At least 18 other states, including New York, have banned or restricted commercial surrogacy. The law in many states remains murky.

Concerned by the growth of surrogate motherhood, the American College of Obstetricians and Gynecologists has issued ethical guidelines for its members. It also cautions physicians to avoid any surrogate mother arrangement that is likely to lead to financial exploitation of any of the parties involved.

In *Surrogates and Other Mothers* (Temple University Press, 1994), Ruth Macklin presents many issues about assisted reproduction through the experiences of a hypothetical infertile couple. Larry Gostin is the editor of a diverse collection titled *Surrogate Motherhood: Politics and Privacy* (Indiana University Press, 1990). Helena Ragoné, an anthropologist, looks at experiences of participants in the Contract Pregnancy program in *Surrogate Motherhood: Conception in the Heart* (Westview Press, 1994). See also Diane M. Bartels et al., eds., *Beyond Baby M: Ethical Issues in New Reproductive Technologies* (Humana Press, 1990), and Scott B. Rae, *The Ethics of Commercial Surrogate Motherhood: Brave New Families* (Praeger, 1994). Sue A. Meinke's *Surrogate Motherhood: Ethical and Legal Issues* (Scope Note No. 6, Kennedy Institute of Ethics, 1987) offers a good bibliography.

PART 2

Decisions About Death

What are the ethical responsibilities associated with death? Doctors are sworn "to do no harm," but this proscription is open to many different interpretations. Death is a natural event that can, in some instances, be hastened to put an end to suffering. Is it ethically necessary to prolong life at all times under all circumstances? Medical personnel as well as families often face these agonizing questions. Even the question of whether or not to tell terminally ill patients the truth about their conditions has great ethical implications. The right of an individual to decide his or her own fate may conflict with society's interest in maintaining the value of human life. This conflict is apparent in the matter of physician-assisted suicide. This section examines some of these anguishing questions.

■ Is It Ethical to Withhold the Truth
   from Dying Patients?

■ Should Physicians Be Allowed to
   Assist in Patient Suicide?

■ Is It Ever Morally Right to Withhold
   Food and Water from Dying Patients?

ISSUE 5

Is It Ethical to Withhold the Truth from Dying Patients?

YES: Bernard C. Meyer, from "Truth and the Physician," in E. Fuller Torrey, ed., *Ethical Issues in Medicine* (Little, Brown, 1968)

NO: Sissela Bok, from *Lying: Moral Choice in Public and Private Life* (Pantheon Books, 1978)

ISSUE SUMMARY

YES: Physician Bernard C. Meyer argues that physicians must use discretion in communicating bad news to patients. Adherence to a rigid formula of truth telling fails to appreciate the differences in patients' readiness to hear and understand the information.

NO: Philosopher Sissela Bok challenges the traditional physician's view by arguing that the harm resulting from disclosure is less than they think and is outweighed by the benefits, including the important one of giving the patient the right to choose among treatments.

In his powerful short story "The Death of Ivan Ilych," Leo Tolstoy graphically portrays the physical agony and the social isolation of a dying man. However, "What tormented Ivan Ilych most was the deception, the lie, which for some reason they all accepted, that he was not dying but was simply ill, and that he only need keep quiet and undergo a treatment and then something very good would result." Instrumental in setting up the deception is Ivan's doctor, who reassures him to the very end that all will be well. Hearing the banal news from his doctor once again, "Ivan Ilych looks at him as much as to say: 'Are you really never ashamed of lying?' But the doctor does not wish to understand this question."

Unlike many of the ethical issues discussed in this volume, which have arisen as a result of modern scientific knowledge and technology, the question of whether to tell dying patients the truth is an old and persistent one. But this debate has been given a new urgency because medical practices today are so complex that it is often difficult to know just what the "truth" really is. A dying patient's life can often be prolonged, although at great financial and personal cost, and many people differ over the definition of a terminal illness.

What must be balanced in this decision are two significant principles of ethical conduct: the obligation to tell the truth and the obligation not to harm others. Moral philosophers, beginning with Aristotle, have regarded truth as either an absolute value or one that, at the very least, is preferable to deception. The great nineteenth-century German philosopher Immanuel Kant argued that there is no justification for lying (although some later commentators feel that his absolutist position has been overstated). Other philosophers have argued that deception is sometimes justified. For example, Henry Sidgwick, an early twentieth-century British philosopher, believed that it was entirely acceptable to lie to invalids and children to protect them from the shock of the truth. Although the question has been debated for centuries, no clear-cut answer has been reached. In fact, the case of a benevolent lie to a dying patient is often given as the prime example of an excusable deception.

If moral philosophers cannot agree, what guidance is there for the physician torn between the desire for truth and the desire to protect the patient from harm (and the admittedly paternalistic conviction that the doctor knows best what will harm the patient)? None of the early medical codes and oaths offered any advice to physicians on what to tell patients, although they were quite explicit about the physician's obligation to keep confidential whatever a patient revealed. The American Medical Association's (AMA) 1847 "Code of Ethics" did endorse some forms of deception by noting that the physician has a sacred duty "to avoid all things which have a tendency to discourage the patient and to depress his spirits." The most recent (1980) AMA "Principles of Medical Ethics" say only that "a physician shall deal honestly with patients and colleagues." However, the American Hospital Association's "Patient's Bill of Rights," adopted in 1972, is more specific: "The patient has the right to obtain from his physician complete current information concerning his diagnosis, treatment, and prognosis in terms the patient can reasonably be expected to understand. When it is not medically advisable to give such information to the patient, the information should be made available to an appropriate person in his behalf."

In the following selections, Bernard C. Meyer argues for an ethic that transcends the virtue of uttering truth for truth's sake. He believes that the physician's prime responsibility is contained in the Hippocratic Oath—"So far as possible, do no harm." Sissela Bok counters with evidence that physicians often misread patients' wishes and that withholding the truth can often harm them more than disclosure.

YES

Bernard C. Meyer

TRUTH AND THE PHYSICIAN

Truth does not do so much good in this world as the semblance of it does harm.

—La Rochefoucauld

Among the reminiscences of his Alsatian boyhood, my father related the story of the local functionary who was berated for the crude and blunt manner in which he went from house to house announcing to wives and mothers news of battle casualties befalling men from the village. On the next occasion, mindful of the injunctions to be more tactful and to soften the impact of his doleful message, he rapped gently on the door and, when it opened, inquired, "Is the widow Schmidt at home?"

Insofar as this essay is concerned with the subject of truth it is only proper to add that when I told this story to a colleague, he already knew it and claimed that it concerned a woman named Braun who lived in a small town in Austria. By this time it would not surprise me to learn that the episode is a well-known vignette in the folklore of Tennessee where it is attributed to a woman named Smith or Brown whose husband was killed at the battle of Shiloh. Ultimately, we may find that all three versions are plagiarized accounts of an occurrence during the Trojan War.

COMMUNICATION BETWEEN PHYSICIAN AND PATIENT

Apocryphal or not, the story illustrates a few of the vexing aspects of the problem of conveying unpalatable news, notably the difficulty of doing so in a manner that causes a minimum amount of pain, and also the realization that not everyone is capable of learning how to do it. Both aspects find their application in the field of medicine where the imparting of the grim facts of diagnosis and prognosis is a constant and recurring issue. Nor does it seem likely that for all our learning we doctors are particularly endowed with superior talents and techniques for coping with these problems. On the contrary, for reasons to be given later, there is cause to believe that in not a few instances, elements in his own psychological makeup may cause the physician to be singularly ill-equipped to be the bearer of bad tidings. It should be observed, moreover, that until comparatively recent times, the subject of communication between physician and patient received little attention in medical curriculum and medical literature.

Within the past decade or so, coincident with an expanded recognition of the significance of emotional factors in all medical practice, an impressive number of books and articles by physicians, paramedical personnel, and others have been published, attesting to both the growing awareness of the importance of the subject and an apparent willingness to face it. An especially noteworthy example of this trend was provided by a three-day meeting in February, 1967, sponsored by the New York Academy of Sciences, on the subject of *The Care of Patients with Fatal Illness.* The problem of communicating with such patients and their families was a recurring theme in most of the papers presented.

Both at this conference and in the literature, particular emphasis has been focused on the patient with cancer, which is hardly surprising in light of its frequency and of the extraordinary emotional reactions that it unleashes not only in the patient and in his kinsmen but in the physician himself. At the same time, it should be noted that the accent on the cancer patient or the dying patient may foster the impression that in less grave conditions this dialogue between patient and physician hardly warrants much concern or discussion. Such a view is unfounded, however, and could only be espoused by someone who has had the good fortune to escape the experience of being ill and hospitalized. Those less fortunate will recall the emotional stresses induced by hospitalization, even when the condition requiring it is relatively banal.

A striking example of such stress may sometimes be seen when the patient who is hospitalized, say, for repair of an inguinal hernia, happens to be a physician. All the usual anxieties confronting a prospective surgical subject tend to become greatly amplified and garnished with a generous sprinkling of hypochondriasis in the physician-turned-patient. Wavering unsteadily between these two roles, he conjures up visions of all the complications of anesthesia, of wound dehiscence or infection, of embolization, cardiac arrest, and whatnot that he has ever heard or read about. To him, lying between hospital sheets, clad in impersonal hospital clothes, divested of his watch and the keys to his car, the hospital suddenly takes on a different appearance from the place he may have known in a professional capacity. Even his colleagues—the anesthetist who will put him to sleep or cause a temporary motor and sensory paralysis of the lower half of his body, and the surgeon who will incise it—appear different. He would like to have a little talk with them, a very professional talk to be sure, although in his heart he may know that the talk will also be different. And if they are in tune with the situation, they too know that it will be different, that beneath the restrained tones of sober and factual conversation is the thumping anxiety of a man who seeks words of reassurance. With some embarrassment he may introduce his anxieties with the phrase, "I suppose this is going to seem a little silly, but..."; and from this point on he may sound like any other individual confronted by the ordeal of surgical experience.[1] Indeed, it would appear that under these circumstances, to say nothing of more ominous ones, most people, regardless of their experience, knowledge, maturity or sophistication, are assailed by more or less similar psychological pressures, from which they seek relief not through pharmacological sedation, but through the more calming influence of the spoken word.

Seen in this light the question of what to tell the patient about his illness is but one facet of the practice of medicine as an art, a particular example of that spoken and mute dialogue between patient and physician which has always been and will always be an indispensable ingredient in the therapeutic process. How to carry on this dialogue, what to say and when to say it, and what not to say, are questions not unlike those posed by an awkward suitor; like him, those not naturally versed in this art may find themselves discomfited and needful of the promptings of some Cyrano who will whisper those words and phrases that ultimately will wing their way to soothe an anguished heart.

EMOTIONAL REACTIONS OF PHYSICIAN

The difficulties besetting the physician under these circumstances, however, cannot be ascribed simply to his mere lack of experience or innate eloquence. For like the stammering suitor, the doctor seeking to communicate with his patient may have an emotional stake in his message. When that message contains an ominous significance, he may find himself too troubled to use words wisely, too ridden with anxiety to be kind, and too depressed to convey hope. An understanding of such reactions touches upon a recognition of some of the several psychological motivations that have

led some individuals to choose a medical career. There is evidence that at times that choice has been dictated by what might be viewed as counterphobic forces. Having in childhood experienced recurring brushes with illness and having encountered a deep and abiding fear of death and dying, such persons may embrace a medical career as if it will confer upon them a magical immunity from a repetition of those dreaded eventualities; for them the letters M.D. constitute a talisman bestowing upon the wearer a sense of invulnerability and a pass of safe conduct through the perilous frontiers of life. There are others for whom the choice of a career dedicated to helping and healing appears to have arisen as a reaction formation against earlier impulses to wound and to destroy.[2] For still others among us, the practice of medicine serves as the professional enactment of a long-standing rescue fantasy.

It is readily apparent in these examples (which by no means exhaust the catalogue of motives leading to the choice of a medical career) that confrontation by the failure of one's efforts and by the need to announce it may unloose a variety of inner psychological disturbances: faced by the gravely ill or dying patient the "counterphobic" doctor may feel personally vulnerable again; the "reaction-formation" doctor, evil and guilty; and the "rescuer," worthless and impotent. For such as these, words cannot come readily in their discourse with the seriously or perilously ill. Indeed, they may curtail their communications; and, what is no less meaningful to their patients, withdraw their physical presence. Thus the patient with inoperable cancer and his family may discover that the physician, who at a more hopeful moment in the course of the illness had been both articulate and supportive, has become remote both in his speech and in his behavior. Nor is the patient uncomprehending of the significance of the change in his doctor's attitude. Observers have recorded the verbal expressions of patients who sensed the feelings of futility and depression in their physicians. Seeking to account for their own reluctance to ask questions (a reluctance based partly upon their own disinclination to face a grim reality), one such patient said, "He looked so tired." Another stated, "I don't want to upset him because he has tried so hard to help me"; and another, "I know he feels so badly already and is doing his best" (Abrams, 1966). To paraphrase a celebrated utterance, one might suppose that these remarks were dictated by the maxim: "Ask not what your doctor can do for you; ask what you can do for your doctor."[3]

ADHERENCE TO A FORMULA

In the dilemma created both by a natural disinclination to be a bearer of bad news and by those other considerations already cited, many a physician is tempted to abandon personal judgment and authorship in his discourse with his patients, and to rely instead upon a set formula which he employs with dogged and indiscriminate consistency. Thus, in determining what to say to patients with cancer, there are exponents of standard policies that are applied routinely in seeming disregard of the overall clinical picture and of the personality or psychological makeup of the patient. In general, two such schools of thought prevail; i.e., those that always tell and those that never do. Each of these is amply supplied with statistical anecdotal evidence proving the correctness of the pol-

icy. Yet even if the figures were accurate —and not infrequently they are obtained via a questionnaire, itself a rather opaque window to the human mind—all they demonstrate is that more rather than less of a given proportion of the cancer population profited by the policy employed. This would provide small comfort, one might suppose, to the patients and their families that constitute the minority of the sample.

TRUTH AS ABSTRACT PRINCIPLE

At times adherence to such a rigid formula is dressed up in the vestments of slick and facile morality. Thus a theologian has insisted that the physician has a moral obligation to tell the truth and that his withholding it constitutes a deprivation of the patient's right; therefore it is "theft, therefore unjust, therefore immoral" (Fletcher, 1954). "Can it be," he asks, "that doctors who practice professional deception would, if the roles were reversed, want to be coddled or deceived?" To which, as many physicians can assert, the answer is distinctly *yes*. Indeed so adamant is this writer upon the right of the patient to know the facts of his illness that in the event he refuses to hear what the doctor is trying to say, the latter should "ask leave to withdraw from the case, urging that another physician be called in his place."[4] (Once there were three boy scouts who were sent away from a campfire and told not to return until each had done his good turn for the day. In 20 minutes all three had returned, and curiously each one reported that he had helped a little old lady to cross a street. The scoutmaster's surprise was even greater when he learned that in each case it was the same little old lady, prompting him to inquire why it took the three of them to perform this one simple good deed. "Well, sir," replied one of the boys, "you see she really didn't want to cross the street at all.")

In this casuistry wherein so much attention is focused upon abstract principle and so little upon humanity, one is reminded of the no less specious arguments of those who assert that the thwarting of suicide and the involuntary hospitalization of the mentally deranged constitute violations of personal freedom and human right.[5] It is surely irregular for a fire engine to travel in the wrong direction on a one-way street, but if one is not averse to putting out fires and saving lives, the traffic violation looms as a conspicuous irrelevancy. No less irrelevant is the obsessional concern with meticulous definitions of truth in an enterprise where kindness, charity, and the relief of human suffering are the ethical verities. "The letter killeth," say the Scriptures, "but the spirit giveth life."

Problem of Definition

Nor should it be forgotten that in the healing arts, the matter of truth is not always susceptible to easy definition. Consider for a moment the question of the hopeless diagnosis. It was not so long ago that such a designation was appropriate for subacute bacterial endocarditis, pneumococcal meningitis, pernicious anemia, and a number of other conditions which today are no longer incurable, while those diseases which today are deemed hopeless may cease to be so by tomorrow. Experience has proved, too, the unreliability of obdurate opinions concerning prognosis even in those conditions where all the clinical evidence and the known behavior of a given disease should leave no room for doubt. To paraphrase Clemenceau, to

insist that a patient is hopelessly ill may at times be worse than a crime; it may be a mistake.

Problem of Determining Patient's Desires

There are other pitfalls, moreover, that complicate the problem of telling patients the truth about their illness. There is the naive notion, for example, that when the patient asserts that what he is seeking is the plain truth he means just that. But as more than one observer has noted, this is sometimes the last thing the patient really wants. Such assertions may be voiced with particular emphasis by patients who happen to be physicians and who strive to display a professional and scientifically objective attitude toward their own condition. Yet to accept such assertions at their face value may sometimes lead to tragic consequences, as in the following incident.

> A distinguished urological surgeon was hospitalized for a hypernephroma, which diagnosis had been withheld from him. One day he summoned the intern into his room, and after appealing to the latter on the basis of we're-both-doctors-and-grown-up-men, succeeded in getting the unwary younger man to divulge the facts. Not long afterward, while the nurse was momentarily absent from the room, the patient opened a window and leaped to his death.

Role of Secrecy in Creating Anxiety

Another common error is the assumption that until someone has been formally told the truth he doesn't know it. Such self-deception is often present when parents feel moved to supply their pubertal children with the sexual facts of life. With much embarrassment and a good deal of backing and filling on the subjects of eggs, bees, and babies, sexual information is imparted to a child who often not only already knows it but is uncomfortable in hearing it from that particular source. There is indeed a general tendency to underestimate the perceptiveness of children not only about such matters but where graver issues, notably illness and death, are concerned. As a consequence, attitudes of secrecy and overprotection designed to shield children from painful realities may result paradoxically in creating an atmosphere that is saturated with suspicion, distrust, perplexity, and intolerable anxiety. Caught between trust in their own intuitive perceptions and the deceptions practiced by the adults about them, such children may suffer greatly from a lack of opportunity of coming to terms emotionally with some of the vicissitudes of existence that in the end are inescapable. A refreshing contrast to this approach has been presented in a paper entitled "Who's Afraid of Death on a Leukemia Ward?" (Vernick and Karon, 1965). Recognizing that most of the children afflicted with this disease had some knowledge of its seriousness, and that all were worried about it, the hospital staff abandoned the traditional custom of protection and secrecy, providing instead an atmosphere in which the children could feel free to express their fears and their concerns and could openly acknowledge the fact of death when one of the group passed away. The result of this measure was immensely salutary.

Similar miscalculations of the accuracy of inner perceptions may be noted in dealing with adults. Thus, in a study entitled "Mongolism: When Should Parents Be Told?" (Drillien and Wilkinson, 1964), it was found that in nearly half the cases the mothers declared they had realized

before being told that something was seriously wrong with the child's development, a figure which obviously excludes the mothers who refused consciously to acknowledge their suspicions. On the basis of their findings the authors concluded that a full explanation given in the early months, coupled with regular support thereafter, appeared to facilitate the mother's acceptance of and adjustment to her child's handicap.

A pointless and sometimes deleterious withholding of truth is a common practice in dealing with elderly people. "Don't tell Mother" often seems to be an almost reflex maxim among some adults in the face of any misfortune, large or small. Here, too, elaborate efforts at camouflage may backfire, for, sensing that he is being shielded from some ostensibly intolerable secret, not only is the elderly one deprived of the opportunity of reacting appropriately to it, but he is being tacitly encouraged to conjure up something in his imagination that may be infinitely worse.

Discussion of Known Truth

Still another misconception is the belief that if it is certain that the truth is known it is all right to discuss it. How mistaken such an assumption may be was illustrated by the violent rage which a recent widow continued to harbor toward a friend for having alluded to cancer in the presence of her late husband. Hearing her outburst one would have concluded that until the ominous word had been uttered, her husband had been ignorant of the nature of his condition. The facts, however, were different, as the unhappy woman knew, for it had been her husband who originally had told the friend what the diagnosis was.

DENIAL AND REPRESSION

The psychological devices that make such seeming inconsistencies of thought and knowledge possible are the mechanisms of repression and denial. It is indeed the remarkable capacity to bury or conceal more or less transparent truth that makes the problem of telling it so sticky and difficult a matter, and one that is so unsusceptible to simple rule-of-thumb formulas. For while in some instances the maintenance of denial may lead to severe emotional distress, in others it may serve as a merciful shield. For example,

A physician with a reputation for considerable diagnostic acumen developed a painless jaundice. When, not surprisingly, a laparotomy revealed a carcinoma of the head of the pancreas, the surgeon relocated the biliary outflow so that postoperatively the jaundice subsided. This seeming improvement was consistent with the surgeon's explanation to the patient that the operation had revealed a hepatitis. Immensely relieved, the patient chided himself for not having anticipated the "correct" diagnosis. "What a fool I was!" he declared, obviously alluding to an earlier, albeit unspoken, fear of cancer.

Among less sophisticated persons the play of denial may assume a more primitive expression. Thus a woman who had ignored the growth of a breast cancer to a point where it had produced spinal metastases and paraplegia, attributed the latter to "arthritis" and asked whether the breast would grow back again. The same mental mechanism allowed another woman to ignore dangerous rectal bleeding by ascribing it to menstruation, although she was well beyond the menopause.

In contrast to these examples is a case reported by Winkelstein and Blacher of a man who, awaiting the report of a cervical node biopsy, asserted that if it showed cancer he wouldn't want to live, and that if it didn't he wouldn't believe it (Winkelstein and Blacher, 1967). Yet despite this seemingly unambiguous willingness to deal with raw reality, when the chips were down, as will be described later, this man too was able to protect himself through the use of denial.

From the foregoing it should be self-evident that what is imparted to a patient about his illness should be planned with the same care and executed with the same skill that are demanded by any potentially therapeutic measure. Like the transfusion of blood, the dispensing of certain information must be distinctly indicated, the amount given consonant with the needs of the recipient, and the type chosen with the view of avoiding untoward reactions. This means that only in selected instances is there any justification for telling a patient the precise figures of his blood pressure, and that the question of revealing interesting but asymptomatic congenital anomalies should be considered in light of the possibility of evoking either hypochondriacal ruminations or narcissistic gratification.

Under graver circumstances the choices of confronting the physician rest upon more crucial psychological issues. In principle, we should strive to make the patient sufficiently aware of the facts of his condition to facilitate his participation in the treatment without at the same time giving him cause to believe that such participation is futile. "The indispensable ingredient of this therapeutic approach," write Stehlin and Beach, "is free communication between [physician] and patient, in which the latter is sustained by hope within a framework of reality" (Stehlin and Beach, 1966). What this may mean in many instances is neither outright truth nor outright falsehood but a carefully modulated formulation that neither overtaxes human credulity nor invites despair. Thus a sophisticated woman might be expected to reject with complete disbelief the notion that she has had to undergo mastectomy for a benign cyst, but she may at the same time accept postoperative radiation as a prophylactic measure rather than as evidence of metastasis.

A doctor's wife was found to have ovarian carcinoma with widespread metastases. Although the surgeon was convinced she would not survive for more than three or four months, he wished to try the effects of radiotherapy and chemotherapy. After some discussion of the problem with a psychiatrist, he addressed himself to the patient as follows: to his surprise, when examined under the microscope the tumor in her abdomen proved to be cancerous; he fully believed he had removed it entirely; to feel perfectly safe, however, he intended to give her radiation and chemical therapies over an indeterminate period of time. The patient was highly gratified by his frankness and proceeded to live for nearly three more *years*, during which time she enjoyed an active and a productive life.

A rather similar approach was utilized in the case of Winkelstein and Blacher previously mentioned (Winkelstein and Blacher, 1967). In the presence of his wife the patient was told by the resident surgeon, upon the advice of the psychiatrist, that the biopsy of the cervical node showed cancer; that he had a cancerous growth in the abdomen; that it was the type of cancer that responds well to chemotherapy; that if the latter produced any discomfort he would receive medi-

cation for its relief; and finally that the doctors were very hopeful for a successful outcome. The patient, who, it will be recalled, had declared he wouldn't want to live if the doctors found cancer, was obviously gratified. Immediately he telephoned members of his family to tell them the news, gratuitously adding that the tumor was of low-grade malignancy. That night he slept well for the first time since entering the hospital and he continued to do so during the balance of his stay. Just before leaving he confessed that he had known all along about the existence of the abdominal mass but that he had concealed his knowledge to see what the doctors would tell him. Upon arriving home he wrote a warm letter of thanks and admiration to the resident surgeon.

It should be emphasized that although in both of these instances the advice of a psychiatrist was instrumental in formulating the discussion of the facts of the illness, it was the surgeon, not the psychiatrist, who did the talking. The importance of this point cannot be exaggerated, for since it is the surgeon who plays the central and crucial role in such cases, it is to him, and not to some substitute mouthpiece, that the patient looks for enlightenment and for hope. As noted earlier, it is not every surgeon who can bring himself to speak in this fashion to his patient; and for some there may be a strong temptation to take refuge in a sterotyped formula, or to pass the buck altogether. The surgical resident, in the last case cited, for example, was both appalled and distressed when he was advised what to do. Yet he steeled himself, looked the patient straight in the eye and spoke with conviction. When he saw the result, he was both relieved and gratified. Indeed, he emerged from the experience a far wiser man and a better physician.

THE DYING PATIENT

The general point of view expressed in the foregoing pages has been espoused by others in considering the problem of communicating with the dying patient. Aldrich stresses the importance of providing such persons with an appropriately timed opportunity of selecting acceptance or denial of the truth in their efforts to cope with their plight (Aldrich, 1963). Weisman and Hackett believe that for the majority of patients it is likely that there is neither complete acceptance nor total repudiation of the imminence of death (Weismann and Hackett, 1961). "To deny this 'middle knowledge' of approaching death," they assert,

> ... is to deny the responsiveness of the mind to both internal perceptions and external information. There is always a psychological sampling of the physiological stream; fever, weakness, anorexia, weight loss and pain are subjective counterparts of homeostatic alteration.... If to this are added changes in those close to the patient, the knowledge of approaching death is confirmed.

Other observers agree that a patient who is sick enough to die often knows it without being told, and that what he seeks from his physician are no longer statements concerning diagnosis and prognosis, but earnest manifestations of his unwavering concern and devotion. As noted earlier, it is at such times that for reason of their own psychological makeup some physicians become deeply troubled and are most prone to drift away, thereby adding, to the dying patient's physical suffering, the suffering that is caused by a sense of abandonment, isolation, and emotional deprivation.

In contrast, it should be stressed that no less potent than morphine nor less effective than an array of tranquilizers is the steadfast and serious concern of the physician for those often numerous and relatively minor complaints of the dying patient. To this beneficent manifestation of psychological denial, which may at times attain hypochondriacal proportions, the physician ideally should respond in kind, shifting his gaze from the lethal process he is now helpless to arrest to the living being whose discomfort and distress he is still able to assuage. In these, the final measures of the dance of life, it may then appear as if both partners had reached a tacit and a mutual understanding, an unspoken pledge to ignore the dark shadow of impending death and to resume those turns and rhythms that were familiar figures in a more felicitious past. If in this he is possessed of enough grace and elegance to play his part the doctor may well succeed in fulfilling the assertion of Oliver Wendell Holmes that if one of the functions of the physician is to assist at the coming in, another is to assist at the going out.

If what has been set down here should prove uncongenial to some strict moralists, one can only observe that there is a hierarchy of morality, and that ours is a profession which traditionally has been guided by a precept that transends the virtue of uttering truth for truth's sake; that is, "So far as possible, do no harm." Where it concerns the communication between the physician and his patient, the attainment of this goal demands an ear that is sensitive to both what is said and what is not said, a mind that is capable of understanding what has been heard, and a heart that can respond to what has been understood. Here, as in many difficult human enterprises, it may prove easier to learn the words than to sing the tune.

We did not dare to breathe a prayer

Or give our anguish scope!

Something was dead in each of us,

And what was dead was Hope!

—Oscar Wilde,

The Ballad of Reading Gaol

NOTES

1. It should be observed, however, that while the emotional conflicts of the sick doctor may contribute to the ambiguity of his position, that ambiguity may be abetted by the treating physician, who in turn may experience difficulty in assigning to his ailing colleague the unequivocal status of patient. Indeed the latter may be more or less tacitly invited to share the responsibility in the diagnosis and care of his own illness to a degree that in some instances he is virtually a consultant on his own case.

A similar lack of a clear-cut definition of role is not uncommon when members of a doctor's family are ill. Here a further muddying of the waters may be caused by the time-honored practice of extending so-called courtesy—i.e., free care—to physicians and their families, a custom which, however well intentioned, may place its presumed beneficiaries in a moral straitjacket that discourages them from making rather ordinary demands on the treating physician, to say nothing of discharging him. It is not surprising that the care of physicians and their families occasionally evokes an atmosphere of bitterness and rancor.

2. The notion that at heart some doctors are killers is a common theme in literature. It is claimed that when in a fit of despondency Napoleon Bonaparte declared he should have been a physician, Talleyrand commented: *"Toujours assassin."*

3. This aspect of the patient-doctor relationship has not received the attention it deserves. Moreover, aside from being a therapeutic success, there are other ways in which his patients may support the doctor's psychological needs. His self-esteem, no less than his economic well-being, may be nourished by an ever-growing roster of devoted patients, particularly when the latter include celebrities and other persons of prominence. How important this can be may be judged by the not too uncommon indiscretions perpetrated by some physicians (and sometimes by their wives) in leaking confidential matters pertaining to their practice, notably the identity of their patients.

4. The same writer relaxes his position when it concerns psychiatric patients. Here he would sanction the withholding of knowledge "precisely because he may prevent the patient's recovery by revealing it." But in this, too, the writer is in error, in double error, it would seem, for, first, it is artificial and inexact to make a sharp distinction between psychiatric and nonpsychiatric patterns— the seriously sick and the dying are not infrequently conspicuously emotionally disturbed: and second, because it may at times be therapeutically advisable to acquaint the psychiatric patient with the facts of his illness.

5. Proponents of these views have seemingly overlooked the unconscious elements in human behavior and thought. Paradoxical though it may seem, the would-be suicide may wish to live: what he seeks to destroy may be restricted to that part of the self that has become burdensome or hateful. By the same token, despite his manifest combativeness, a psychotic individual is often inwardly grateful for the restraints imposed upon his dangerous aggression. There can be no logical objection to designating such persons as "prisoners," as Szasz would have it, provided we apply the same term to breathless individuals who are "incarcerated" in oxygen tents.

REFERENCES

Abrams, R.D. The patient with cancer—His changing pattern of communication. *New Eng. J. Med.* 274:317, 1966.

Aldrich, C.K. The dying patient's grief. *J.A.M.A.* 184:329, 1963.

Drillien, C.M., and Wilkinson, E.M. Mongolism: When should parents be told? *Brit. Med. J.* 2:1306, 1964.

Fletcher, J. *Morals and Medicine.* Princeton: Princeton University Press, 1954.

Stehlin, J.S., and Beach, K.A. Psychological aspects of cancer therapy. *J.A.M.A.* 197:100, 1966.

Vernick, J., and Karon, M. Who's afraid of death on a leukemia ward? *Amer. J. Dis. Child,* 109:393, 1965.

Weisman, A.D., and Hackett, T. Predilection to death: Death and dying as a psychiatric problem. *Psychosom. Med.* 23:232, 1961.

Winkelstein, C., and Blacher, R. Personal communication, 1967.

NO

Sissela Bok

LIES TO THE SICK AND DYING

DECEPTION AS THERAPY

A forty-six-year-old man, coming to a clinic for a routine physical check-up needed for insurance purposes, is diagnosed as having a form of cancer likely to cause him to die within six months. No known cure exists for it. Chemotherapy may prolong life by a few extra months, but will have side effects the physician does not think warranted in this case. In addition, he believes that such therapy should be reserved for patients with a chance for recovery or remission. The patient has no symptoms giving him any reason to believe that he is not perfectly healthy. He expects to take a short vacation in a week.

For the physician, there are now several choices involving truthfulness. Ought he to tell the patient what he has learned, or conceal it? If asked, should he deny it? If he decides to reveal the diagnosis, should he delay doing so until after the patient returns from his vacation? Finally, even if he does reveal the serious nature of the diagnosis, should he mention the possibility of chemotherapy and his reasons for not recommending it in this case? Or should he encourage every last effort to postpone death?

In this particular case, the physician chose to inform the patient of his diagnosis right away. He did not, however, mention the possibility of chemotherapy. A medical student working under him disagreed; several nurses also thought that the patient should have been informed of this possibility. They tried, unsuccessfully, to persuade the physician that this was the patient's right. When persuasion had failed, the student elected to disobey the doctor by informing the patient of the alternative of chemotherapy. After consultation with family members, the patient chose to ask for the treatment.

Doctors confront such choices often and urgently. What they reveal, hold back, or distort will matter profoundly to their patients. Doctors stress with corresponding vehemence their reasons for the distortion or concealment: not to confuse the sick person needlessly, or cause what may well be unnecessary pain or discomfort, as in the case of the cancer patient; not to leave a patient without hope, as in those many cases where the dying are not told the truth about their condition; or to improve the chances of cure, as where unwarranted optimism is expressed about some form of therapy. Doctors use information as part of the therapeutic regimen; it is given out in amounts, in admixtures, and according to timing believed best for patients. Accuracy, by comparison, matters far less.

Lying to patients has, therefore, seemed an especially excusable act. Some would argue that doctors, and *only* doctors, should be granted the right to manipulate the truth in ways so undesirable for politicians, lawyers, and others. Doctors are trained to help patients; their relationship to patients carries special obligations, and they know much more than laymen about what helps and hinders recovery and survival.

Even the most conscientious doctors, then, who hold themselves at a distance from the quacks and the purveyors of false remedies, hesitate to forswear all lying. Lying is usually wrong, they argue, but less so than allowing the truth to harm patients. B. C. Meyer echoes this very common view:

> [O]urs is a profession which traditionally has been guided by a precept that transcends the virtue of uttering truth for truth's sake, and that is, "so far as possible, do no harm."

Truth, for Meyer, may be important, but not when it endangers the health and well-being of patients. This has seemed self-evident to many physicians in the past—so much so that we find very few mentions of veracity in the codes and oaths and writings by physicians through the centuries. This absence is all the more striking as other principles of ethics have been consistently and movingly expressed in the same documents....

Given such freedom, a physician can decide to tell as much or as little as he wants the patient to know, so long as he breaks no law. In the case of the man mentioned at the beginning of this chapter, some physicians might feel justified in lying for the good of the patient, others might be truthful. Some may conceal alternatives to the treatment they recommend; others not. In each case, they could appeal to the A.M.A. Principles of Ethics. A great many would choose to be able to lie. They would claim that not only can a lie avoid harm for the patient, but that it is also hard to know whether they have been right in the first place in making their pessimistic diagnosis; a "truthful" statement could therefore turn out to hurt patients unnecessarily. The concern for curing and for supporting those who cannot be cured then runs counter to the desire to be completely open. This concern is especially strong where the prognosis is bleak; even more so when patients are so affected by their illness or their medication that they are more dependent than usual, perhaps more easily depressed or irrational.

Physicians know only too well how uncertain a diagnosis or prognosis can be. They know how hard it is to give meaningful and correct answers regarding health and illness. They also know that disclosing their own uncertainty or fears can reduce those benefits that depend upon faith in recovery. They fear, too, that revealing grave risks, no matter how unlikely it is that these will come about, may exercise the pull of the "self-fulfilling prophecy." They dislike being the bearers of uncertain or bad news as much as anyone else. And last, but not least, sitting down to discuss an illness truthfully and sensitively may take much-needed time away from other patients.

These reasons help explain why nurses and physicians and relatives of the sick and dying prefer not to be bound by rules that might limit their ability to suppress, delay, or distort information. This is not to say that they necessarily plan to lie much of the time. They merely want to have the freedom to do so when they believe it wise. And the reluctance to see lying prohibited explains, in turn, the failure of the codes and oaths to come to grips with the problems of truth-telling and lying.

But sharp conflicts are now arising. Doctors no longer work alone with patients. They have to consult with others much more than before; if they choose to lie, the choice may not be met with approval by all who take part in the care of the patient. A nurse expresses the difficulty which results as follows:

> From personal experience I would say that the patients who aren't told about their terminal illness have so many verbal and mental questions unanswered that many will begin to realize that their illness is more serious than they're being told. . . .

The doctor's choice to lie increasingly involves coworkers in acting a part they find neither humane nor wise. The fact that these problems have not been carefully thought through within the medical profession, nor seriously addressed in medical education, merely serves to intensify the conflicts. Different doctors then respond very differently to patients in exactly similar predicaments. The friction is increased by the fact that relatives often disagree even where those giving medical care to a patient are in accord on how to approach the patient. Here again, because physicians have not worked out to common satisfaction the question of whether relatives have the right to make such requests, the problems are allowed to be haphazardly resolved by each physician as he sees fit.

THE PATIENT'S PERSPECTIVE

The turmoil in the medical profession regarding truth-telling is further augmented by the pressures that patients themselves now bring to bear and by empirical data coming to light. Challenges are growing to the three major arguments for lying to patients: that truthfulness is impossible; that patients do not want bad news; and that truthful information harms them.

The first of these arguments. . . confuses "truth" and "truthfulness" so as to clear the way for occasional lying on grounds supported by the second and third arguments. At this point, we can see more clearly that it is a strategic move intended to discourage the question of truthfulness from carrying much weight in the first place, and thus to leave the choice of what to say and how to say it up to the physician. To claim that "since telling the truth is impossible, there can be no sharp distinction between what is true and what is false" is to try to defeat objections to lying before even discussing them. One need only imagine how such an argument would be received, were it made by a car salesman or a real estate dealer, to see how fallacious it is.

In medicine, however, the argument is supported by a subsidiary point: even if people might ordinarily understand what is spoken to them, patients are often not in a position to do so. This is where paternalism enters in. When we buy cars or houses, the paternalist will argue, we need to have all our wits about us; but when we are ill, we cannot always do so. We need help in making choices, even if help can be given only by keeping us in the dark. And the physician is trained and willing to provide such help.

It is certainly true that some patients cannot make the best choices for themselves when weakened by illness or drugs. But most still can. And even those who are incompetent have a right to have someone—their guardian or spouse perhaps—receive the correct information.

The paternalistic assumption of superiority to patients also carries great dangers for physicians themselves—it risks turning to contempt. The following view was recently expressed in a letter to a medical journal:

> As a radiologist who has been sued, I have reflected earnestly on advice to obtain Informed Consent but have decided to "take the risks without informing the patient" and trust to "God, judge, and jury" rather than evade responsibility through a legal gimmick....
>
> [I]n a general radiologic practice many of our patients are uninformable and we would never get through the day if we had to obtain their consent to every potentially harmful study....

The argument which rejects informing patients because adequate truthful information is impossible in itself or because patients are lacking in understanding, must itself be rejected when looked at from the point of view of patients. They know that liberties granted to the most conscientious and altruistic doctors will be exercised also in the "Medicaid Mills"; that the choices thus kept from patients will be exercised by not only competent but incompetent physicians; and that even the best doctors can make choices patients would want to make differently for themselves.

The second argument for deceiving patients refers specifically to giving them news of a frightening or depressing kind. It holds that patients do not, in fact, generally want such information, that they prefer not to have to face up to serious illness and death. On the basis of such a belief, most doctors in a number of surveys stated that they do not, as a rule, inform patients that they have an illness such as cancer.

When studies are made of what patients desire to know, on the other hand, a large majority say that they *would* like to be told of such a diagnosis. All these studies need updating and should be done with larger numbers of patients and non-patients. But they do show that there is generally a dramatic divergence between physicians and patients on the factual question of whether patients want to know what ails them in cases of serious illness such as cancer. In most of the studies, over 80 percent of the persons asked indicated that they would want to be told.

Sometimes this discrepancy is set aside by doctors who want to retain the view that patients do not want unhappy news. In reality, they claim, the fact that patients say they want it has to be discounted. The more someone asks to know, the more he suffers from fear which will lead to the denial of the information even if it is given. Informing patients is, therefore, useless; they resist and deny having been told what they cannot assimilate. According to this view, empirical studies of what patients say they want are worthless since they do not probe deeply enough to uncover this universal resistance to the contemplation of one's own death.

This view is only partially correct. For some patients, denial is indeed well established in medical experience. A number of patients (estimated at between 15 percent and 25 percent) will give evidence of denial of having been told about their illness, even when they repeatedly ask and are repeatedly informed. And nearly everyone experiences a period of denial at some point in the course of approaching death. Elisabeth Kübler-Ross sees denial as resulting often from premature and abrupt information by a stranger who goes through the process quickly to "get it over with." She holds that denial functions as a buffer after unexpected shocking news, permitting individuals to collect themselves and to mobilize other defenses. She describes prolonged denial in one patient as follows:

> She was convinced that the X-rays were "mixed up"; she asked for reassurance that her pathology report could not possibly be back so soon and that another patient's report must have been marked with her name. When none of this could be confirmed, she quickly asked to leave the hospital, looking for another physician in the vain hope "to get a better explanation for my troubles." This patient went "shopping around" for many doctors, some of whom gave her reassuring answers, other of whom confirmed the previous suspicion. Whether confirmed or not, she reacted in the same manner; she asked for examination and reexamination....

But to say that denial is universal flies in the face of all evidence. And to take any claim to the contrary as "symptomatic" of deeper denial leaves no room for reasoned discourse. There is no way that such universal denial can be proved true or false. To believe in it is a metaphysical belief about man's condition, not a statement about what patients do and do not want. It is true that we can never completely understand the possibility of our own death, any more than being alive in the first place. But people certainly differ in the degree to which they can approach such knowledge, take it into account in their plans, and make their peace with it.

Montaigne claimed that in order to learn both to live and to die, men have to think about death and be prepared to accept it. To stick one's head in the sand, or to be prevented by lies from trying to discern what is to come, hampers freedom—freedom to consider one's life as a whole, with a beginning, a duration, an end. Some may request to be deceived rather than to see their lives as thus finite; others reject the information which would require them to do so; but most say that they want to know. Their concern for knowing about their condition goes far beyond mere curiosity or the wish to make isolated personal choices in the short time left to them; their stance toward the entire life they have lived, and their ability to give it meaning and completion, are at stake. In lying or withholding the facts which permit such discernment, doctors may reflect their own fears (which, according to one study, are much stronger than those of laymen) of facing questions about the meaning of one's life and the inevitability of death.

Beyond the fundamental deprivation that can result from deception, we are also becoming increasingly aware of all that can befall patients in the course of their illness when information is denied or distorted. Lies place them in a position where they no longer participate in choices concerning their own health, including the choice of whether to be a "patient" in the first place. A terminally ill person who is not informed that his illness is incurable and that he is near death cannot make decisions about the end of his life: about whether or not to enter a hospital, or to have surgery; where and with whom to spend his last days; how to put his affairs in order—these most personal choices cannot be made if he is kept in the dark, or given contradictory hints and clues.

It has always been especially easy to keep knowledge from terminally ill patients. They are most vulnerable, least able to take action to learn what they need to know, or to protect their autonomy. The very fact of being so ill greatly increases the likelihood of control by others. And the fear of being helpless in the face of such control is growing. At the same time, the period of dependency and slow deterioration of health and strength that people undergo has lengthened. There has been a dramatic shift toward institutionalization of the aged and those near death. (Over 80 percent of Americans now die in a hospital or other institution.)

Patients who are severely ill often suffer a further distancing and loss of control over their most basic functions. Electrical wiring, machines, intravenous administration of liquids, all create new dependency and at the same time new distance between the patient and all who come near. Curable patients are often willing to undergo such procedures; but when no cure is possible, these procedures merely intensify the sense of distance and uncertainty and can even become a substitute for comforting human acts. Yet those who suffer in this way often fear to seem troublesome by complaining. Lying to them, perhaps for the most charitable of purposes, can then cause them to slip unwittingly into subjection to new procedures, perhaps new surgery, where death is held at bay through transfusions, respirators, even resuscitation far beyond what most would wish.

Seeing relatives in such predicaments has caused a great upsurge of worrying about death and dying. At the root of this fear is not a growing terror of the *moment* of death, or even the instants before it. Nor is there greater fear of *being* dead. In contrast to the centuries of lives lived in dread of the punishments to be inflicted after death, many would now accept the view expressed by Epicurus, who died in 270 B.C.:

> Death, therefore, the most awful of evils, is nothing to us, seeing that, when we are, death is not come, and, when death is come, we are not.

The growing fear, if it is not of the moment of dying nor of being dead, is of all that which now precedes dying for so many: the possibility of prolonged pain, the increasing weakness, the uncertainty, the loss of powers and chance of senility, the sense of being a burden. This fear is further nourished by the loss of trust in health professionals. In part, the loss of trust results from the abuses which have been exposed—the Medicaid scandals, the old-age home profiteering, the commercial exploitation of those who seek remedies for their ailments; in part also because of the deceptive practices patients suspect, having seen how friends and relatives were kept in the dark; in part, finally, because of the sheer numbers of persons, often strangers, participating in the care of any one patient. Trust which might have gone to a doctor long known to the patient goes less easily to a team of strangers, no matter how expert or well-meaning.

It is with the working out of all that *informed consent*[1] implies and the information it presupposes that truth-telling is coming to be discussed in a serious way for the first time in the health professions. Informed consent is a farce if the information provided is distorted or withheld. And even complete information regarding surgical procedures or medication is obviously useless unless the patient also knows what the condition is that these are supposed to correct.

Bills of rights for patients, similarly stressing the right to be informed, are now gaining acceptance. This right is not new, but the effort to implement it is. Nevertheless, even where patients are handed the most elegantly phrased Bill of Rights, their right to a truthful diagnosis and prognosis is by no means always respected.

The reason why even doctors who recognize a patient's right to have information might still not provide it brings us to the third argument against telling all patients the truth. It holds that the information given might hurt the patient and that the concern for the right to such information is therefore a threat to proper health care. A patient, these doctors argue, may wish to commit suicide after being given discouraging news, or suffer a cardiac arrest, or simply cease to struggle, and thus not grasp the small remaining chance for recovery. And even where the outlook for a patient is very good, the disclosure of a minute risk can shock some patients or cause them to reject needed protection such as a vaccination or antibiotics.

The factual basis for this argument has been challenged from two points of view. The damages associated with the disclosure of sad news or risks are rarer than physicians believe; and the *benefits* which result from being informed are more substantial, even measurably so. Pain is tolerated more easily, recovery from surgery is quicker, and cooperation with therapy is greatly improved. The attitude that "what you don't know won't hurt you" is proving unrealistic; it is what patients do not know but vaguely suspect that causes them corrosive worry.

It is certain that no answers to this question of harm from information are the same for all patients. If we look, first, at the fear expressed by physicians that informing patients of even remote or unlikely risks connected with a drug prescription or operation might shock some and make others refuse the treatment that would have been best for them, it appears to be unfounded for the great majority of patients. Studies show that very few patients respond to being told of such risks by withdrawing their consent to the procedure and that those who do withdraw are the very ones who might well have been upset enough to sue the physician had they not been asked to consent before hand. It is possible that on even rarer occasions especially susceptible persons might manifest physical deterioration from shock; some physicians have even asked whether patients who die after giving informed consent to an operation, but before it actually takes place, somehow expire because of the information given to them. While such questions are unanswerable in any one case, they certainly argue in favor of caution, a real concern for the person to whom one is recounting the risks he or she will face, and sensitivity to all signs of distress.

The situation is quite different when persons who are already ill, perhaps already quite weak and discouraged, are told of a very serious prognosis. Physicians fear that such knowledge may cause the patients to commit suicide, or to be frightened or depressed to the point that their illness takes a downward turn. The fear that great numbers of patients will commit suicide appears to be unfounded. And if some do, is that a response so unreasonable, so much against the patient's best interest that physicians ought to make it a reason for concealment or lies? Many societies have allowed suicide in the past; our own has decriminalized it; and some are coming to make distinctions among the many suicides which ought to be prevented if at all possible, and those which ought to be respected.

Another possible response to very bleak news is the triggering of physiological mechanisms which allow death to come more quickly—a form of giving up or of preparing for the inevitable, depending on one's outlook. Lewis Thomas, studying responses in humans and animals, holds it not unlikely that:

> ... there is a pivotal movement at some stage in the body's reaction to injury or disease, maybe in aging as well, when the organism concedes that it is finished and the time for dying is at hand, and at this moment the events that lead to death are launched, as a coordinated mechanism. Functions are then shut off, in sequence, irreversibly, and, while this is going on, a neural mechanism, held ready for this occasion, is switched on. ...

Such a response may be appropriate, in which case it makes the moments of dying as peaceful as those who have died and been resuscitated so often testify. But it may also be brought on inappropriately, when the organism could have lived on, perhaps even induced malevolently, by external acts intended to kill. Thomas speculates that some of the deaths resulting from "hexing" are due to such responses. Levi-Strauss describes deaths from exorcism and the casting of spells in ways which suggest that the same process may then be brought on by the community.

It is not inconceivable that unhappy news abruptly conveyed, or a great shock given to someone unable to tolerate it, could also bring on such a "dying response," quite unintended by the speaker. There is every reason to be cautious and to try to know ahead of time how susceptible a patient might be to the accidental triggering—however rare—of such a response. One has to assume, however, that most of those who have survived long enough to be in a situation where their informed consent is asked have a very robust resistance to such accidental triggering of processes leading to death.

When, on the other hand, one considers those who are already near death, the "dying response" may be much less inappropriate, much less accidental, much less unreasonable. In most societies, long before the advent of modern medicine, human beings have made themselves ready for death once they felt its approach. Philippe Aries describes how many in the Middle Ages prepared themselves for death when they "felt the end approach." They awaited death lying down, surrounded by friends and relatives. They recollected all they had lived through and done, pardoning all who stood near their deathbed, calling on God to bless them, and finally praying. "After the final prayer all that remained was to wait for death, and there was no reason for death to tarry."

Modern medicine, in its valiant efforts to defeat disease and to save lives, may be dislocating the conscious as well as the purely organic responses allowing death to come when it is inevitable, thus denying those who are dying the benefits of the traditional approach to death. In lying to them, and in pressing medical efforts to cure them long past the point of possible recovery, physicians may thus rob individuals of an autonomy few would choose to give up.

Sometimes, then, the "dying response" is a natural organic reaction at the time when the body has no further defense. Sometimes it is inappropriately brought on by news too shocking or given in too abrupt a manner. We need to learn a great deal more about this last category, no matter how small. But there is no evidence that patients in general will be debilitated by truthful information about their condition.

Apart from the possible harm from information, we are coming to learn much more about the benefits it can bring patients. People follow instructions more carefully if they know what their disease is and why they are asked to take medication; any benefits from those procedures are therefore much more likely to come about.[2] Similarly, people recover faster from surgery and tolerate pain with less medication if they understand what ails them and what can be done for them.[3]

RESPECT AND TRUTHFULNESS

Taken all together, the three arguments defending lies to patients stand on much shakier ground as a counterweight to the right to be informed than is often thought. The common view that many patients cannot understand, do not want, and may be harmed by, knowledge of their condition, and that lying to them is either morally neutral or even to be recommended, must be set aside. Instead, we have to make a more complex comparison. Over against the right of patients to knowledge concerning themselves, the medical and psychological benefits to them from this knowledge, the unnecessary and sometimes harmful treatment to which they can be subjected if ignorant, and the harm to physicians, their profession, and other patients from deceptive practices, we have to set a severely restricted and narrowed paternalistic view—that *some* patients cannot understand, *some* do not want, and *some* may be harmed by, knowledge of their condition, and that they ought not to have to be treated like everyone else if this is not in their best interest.

Such a view is persuasive. A few patients openly request not to be given bad news. Others give clear signals to that effect, or are demonstrably vulnerable to the shock or anguish such news might call forth. Can one not in such cases infer implied consent to being deceived?

Concealment, evasion, withholding of information may at times be necessary. But if someone contemplates lying to a patient or concealing the truth, the burden of proof must shift. It must rest, here, as with all deception, on those who advocate it in any one instance. They must show why they fear a patient may be harmed or how they know that another cannot cope with the truthful knowledge. A decision to deceive must be seen as a very unusual step, to be talked over with colleagues and others who participate in the care of the patient. Reasons must be set forth and debated, alternatives weighed carefully. At all times, the correct information must go to *someone* closely related to the patient.

NOTES

1. The law requires that inroads made upon a person's body take place only with the informed voluntary consent of that person. The term "informed consent" came into common use only after 1960, when it was used by the Kansas Supreme Court in Nathanson vs. Kline, 186 Kan. 393, 350, p. 2d, 1093 (1960). The patient is now entitled to full disclosure of risks, benefits, and alternative treatments to any proposed procedure, both in therapy and in medical experimentation, except in emergencies or when the patient is incompetent, in which case proxy consent is required.

2. Barbara S. Hulka, J. C. Cassel, et al. "Communication, Compliance, and Concordance between Physicians and Patients with Prescribed Medications," *American Journal of Public Health*, Sept. 1976, pp. 847–53. The study shows that of the nearly half of all patients who do not follow the prescriptions of the doctors (thus foregoing the intended effect of these prescriptions), many will follow them if adequately informed about the nature of their illness and what the proposed medication will do.

3. See Lawrence D. Egbert, George E. Batitt, et al., "Reduction of Postoperative Pain by Encouragement and Instruction of Patients," *New England Journal of Medicine*, 270, pp. 825–27, 1964.

See also: Howard Waitzskin and John D. Stoeckle, "The Communication of Information about Illness," *Advances in Psychosomatic Medicine*, Vol. 8, 1972, pp. 185–215.

POSTSCRIPT

Is It Ethical to Withhold the Truth from Dying Patients?

In its 1983 report, *Making Health Care Decisions*, the President's Commission for the Study of Ethical Problems in Medicine and Biomedical and Behavioral Research cited evidence from a survey it conducted indicating that 94 percent of the public would "want to know everything" about a diagnosis and prognosis, and 96 percent would want to know specifically about a diagnosis of cancer. To the question, "If you had a type of cancer that usually leads to death in less than a year, would you want your doctor to give you a realistic estimate of how long you had to live, or would you prefer that he not tell you?" 85 percent said that they would want the realistic estimate. However, when physicians were asked a similar question about what they would disclose to a patient, only 13 percent would give a "straight, statistical prognosis," and a third said that they would not give a definite time period but would stress that it would not be a long one. Physicians, it appears, are more reluctant to tell the truth than the public (at least when faced with a hypothetical choice) is to hear it. Dennis H. Novack et al., "Physicians' Attitudes Toward Using Deception to Resolve Difficult Ethical Problems," *Journal of the American Medical Association* (May 26, 1989), reports on a survey conducted by a group from the Brown University Program in Medicine. Researchers found that 87 percent of 109 physicians "indicated that deception is acceptable on rare occasions."

An important, recent legal case concerning truth telling and informed consent is *Arcato v. Avedon*. Mr. Arcato, a California electrical contractor, was operated on in 1980 to remove a kidney that was not functioning. The surgeons also removed a tumor from his pancreas, but neither they nor the oncologist to whom they referred Arcato told him that approximately 95 percent of people with pancreatic cancer die within a year. Arcato died one year after the cancer had been diagnosed. His wife and children sued the doctors, claiming that California's informed-consent doctrine required the disclosure of the withheld information. If he had been told the truth, his family argued, he might not have undergone the difficult and unsuccessful experimental treatment his oncologist offered. The case ultimately went to the California Supreme Court, which in 1993 upheld the trial court's ruling in favor of the physicians. For more on the case, see George Annas, "Informed Consent, Cancer, and Truth in Prognosis," *The New England Journal of Medicine* (January 20, 1994), in which the author argues that the real issue was not the statistics on life expectancy but the impact of the proposed treatment in terms of prospects for long-term survival and quality of life.

For a strong defense of the patient's right to know the truth, see Robert M. Veatch, *Death, Dying, and the Biological Revolution* (Yale University Press, 1976), chapter 6. A philosophical argument with a different view is Donald Van DeVeer's article "The Contractual Argument for Withholding Information," *Philosophy and Public Affairs* (Winter 1980). See also Mark Sheldon, "Truth Telling in Medicine," *Journal of the American Medical Association* (February 5, 1982), and Thurstan B. Brewin, "Truth, Trust, and Paternalism," *The Lancet* (August 31, 1985).

Two books that stress the importance of communication in the doctor-patient relationship are Jay Katz, *The Silent World of Doctor and Patient* (Free Press, 1984) and Eric J. Cassell, *Talking with Patients*, 2 vols. (MIT Press, 1985). Susan J. Barnes edited a symposium called "Perspectives on J. Katz, *The Silent World of Doctor and Patient*," which appeared in the *Western New England Law Review* (vol. 9, no. 1, 1987).

Most of the literature on withholding the truth from patients concerns cancer. Drs. Margaret A. Drickamer and Mark S. Lachs address a different disease in their essay "Should Patients With Alzheimer's Disease Be Told Their Diagnosis?" *The New England Journal of Medicine* (April 2, 1992). Although they favor truth telling, they present the case for not telling, including such factors as the difficulty of conclusive diagnosis, the impaired decision-making capacity and competence of patients with Alzheimer's, and the limited therapeutic options. A cultural difference can be seen in Antonella Surbone's "Truth Telling to the Patient," *Journal of the American Medical Association* (October 7, 1992), in which she describes the practice of withholding information from seriously ill patients in Italy. The same issue contains an accompanying editorial by Edmund D. Pellegrino.

ISSUE 6

Should Physicians Be Allowed to Assist in Patient Suicide?

YES: Franklin G. Miller et al., from "Regulating Physician-Assisted Death," *The New England Journal of Medicine* (July 14, 1994)

NO: David Orentlicher, from "Physician-Assisted Dying: The Conflict With Fundamental Principles of American Law," in Robert H. Blank and Andrea L. Bonnicksen, eds., *Medicine Unbound: The Human Body and the Limitations of Medical Intervention* (Columbia University Press, 1994)

ISSUE SUMMARY

YES: Bioethicist Franklin G. Miller and his colleagues believe that voluntary physician-assisted suicide serves the moral goals of relief of suffering and patient self-determination in the relatively infrequent but troubling cases in which comfort care is inadequate. This option of last resort should, however, be carefully regulated.

NO: Physician and lawyer David Orentlicher argues that physician-assisted dying brings two fundamental principles into conflict. Assisted suicide violates the principle of the inalienable right to life, which at the very least means that a person should not have his life taken by another. Restrictions on the availability of physician-assisted suicide only to certain persons violates another fundamental principle—the equal status of each person under the law.

Since the early 1980s physicians, lawyers, philosophers, and judges have examined questions about withholding life-sustaining treatment. Their deliberations have resulted in a broad consensus that competent adults have the right to make decisions about their medical care, even if those decisions seem unjustifiable to others and even if they result in death. Furthermore, the right of individuals to name others to carry out their prior wishes or to make decisions if they should become incompetent is now well established. Thirty-eight states now have legislation allowing advance directives (commonly known as "living wills").

The debate in specific cases continues (see, for example, the issue on withholding food and nutrition), but on the whole, patients' rights to self-determination have been bolstered by 80 or more legal cases, dozens of reports, and statements made by medical societies and other organizations.

As often occurs in bioethical debate, the resolution of one issue only highlights the lack of resolution about another. There is clearly no consensus about either euthanasia or physician-assisted suicide.

Like truth telling, euthanasia is an old problem given new dimensions by the ability of modern medical technology to prolong life. The word itself is Greek (literally, *happy death*) and the Greeks wrestled with the question of whether, in some cases, people would be better off dead. But the Hippocratic Oath in this instance was clear: "I will neither give a deadly drug to anybody if asked for it, nor will I make a suggestion to that effect." On the other hand, if the goal of medicine is not simply to prolong life but to reduce suffering, at some point the question of what measures should be taken or withdrawn will inevitably arise. The problem is: When death is inevitable, how far should one go in hastening it?

The majority of cases in which euthanasia is raised as a possibility are among the most difficult ethical issues to resolve, for they involve the conflict between a physician's duty to preserve life and the burden on the patient and the family that is created by fulfilling that duty. One common distinction is between *active* euthanasia (that is, some positive act such as administering a lethal injection) and *passive* euthanasia (that is, an inaction such as deciding not to administer antibiotics when the patient has a severe infection). Another common distinction is between *voluntary* euthanasia (that is, the patient wishes to die and consents to the action that will make it happen) and *involuntary*—or better, *nonvoluntary*—euthanasia (that is, the patient is unable to consent, perhaps because he or she is in a coma).

The two selections that follow take up one aspect of this large issue: the question of whether physicians may ethically assist in a hopelessly ill patient's suicide. A multidisciplinary group headed by Franklin G. Miller proposes legalizing physician-assisted suicide as a treatment of last resort, an option to be used only after standard measures of comfort care have been found unsatisfactory by competent patients. David Orentlicher asserts that the ambivalence among Americans on this issue reflects an irreconcilable tension between two of the most important philosophies underlying American law and ethics. The right not to be killed is an inalienable right, he says. Proposals that legalize physician-assisted suicide violate this right. Yet proposals that include safeguards limiting the exercise of physician-assisted suicide to certain individuals violate the equally fundamental principle of egalitarianism—that each person is treated equally under the law. Logically, then, physician-assisted suicide should be legal for anyone or none.

YES

Franklin G. Miller et al.

REGULATING PHYSICIAN-ASSISTED DEATH

Voluntary physician-assisted death serves the moral goals of relief of suffering and self-determination on the part of patients.[1-3] It becomes a permissible option when comfort care ceases to be effective for the terminally or incurably ill. ("Comfort care" refers to palliative and supportive treatment used in hospice programs and elsewhere.) Comfort care ought to be the standard medical treatment for patients who are suffering from a terminal illness or who have refused curative or life-sustaining treatment.[1] It is aimed at relieving symptoms, enhancing the quality and meaning of the patient's remaining life, and easing the process of dying. As a treatment of last resort, physician-assisted death becomes a legitimate option only after standard measures for comfort care have been found unsatisfactory by competent patients in the context of their own situation and values. Accordingly, the policy we recommend aims to promote comfort care and to permit voluntary physician-assisted death only in the relatively infrequent but troubling cases in which comfort care is inadequate.

THE LEGAL STATUS OF PHYSICIAN-ASSISTED DEATH

Acts that intentionally cause the death of a person or induce a person to take his or her own life (for example, by force, duress, or deception) are unlawful throughout the United States. A physician is prohibited from knowingly and directly causing death irrespective of the patient's wishes, quality of life, or prognosis. In contrast, no national consensus exists about the legality of assisting suffering patients to commit suicide by providing medical advice about effective and painless ways to end life or by prescribing the means....

Because it exists in a legal limbo, physician-assisted suicide currently occurs in secret, without publicly sanctioned criteria and guidelines and without any independent scrutiny. A physician's willingness to assist in the death of a patient may depend as much on his or her attitude toward legal risk and authority as on the compelling nature of the patient's request. Accordingly, the legal status quo regarding physician-assisted death does not adequately

Adapted with permission from Franklin G. Miller, Timothy E. Quill, Howard Brody, John C. Fletcher, Lawrence O. Gostin, and Diane E. Meier, "Regulating Physician-Assisted Death," *The New England Journal of Medicine*, vol. 331, no. 2 (July 14, 1994), pp. 119–123. Copyright © 1994 by The Massachusetts Medical Society. All rights reserved.

serve the needs of patients with unrelievable suffering; rather, it compromises the professional integrity of physicians and undermines respect for the law.

THE RATIONALE FOR REGULATION

Decisions about medical treatment are normally made in the privacy of the doctor–patient relationship.[4] Yet regulatory safeguards providing independent monitoring of medical decisions that involve physician-assisted death are necessary for two reasons. First, any treatment whose purpose is to cause death lies outside standard medical practice, which is defined here as medically indicated interventions aimed at promoting health and healing and alleviating the suffering of patients. Currently accepted standards of comfort care allow for the use of aggressive palliative treatment that may indirectly and unintentionally contribute to a patient's death.[1] However, standards of comfort care stop short of permitting death to be caused intentionally as a means of ending unrelievable suffering.

We regard physician-assisted death as a nonstandard medical practice reserved for extraordinary circumstances, when it is requested voluntarily by a patient whose suffering has become intolerable and who has no other satisfactory options. Although we argue that physician-assisted death should be permitted as a treatment of last resort, we do not claim that patients have a right to physician-assisted death, as they do to standard medical care. Physicians must carefully assess patients' requests for assistance in dying and thoroughly explore alternatives for comfort care.[5] In addition, they must consider their own values and willingness to participate in physician-assisted death. Because of the nonstandard nature of physician-assisted death, even when patients and physicians agree that there are no acceptable alternatives, regulatory oversight should be required.

The second reason for regulating physician-assisted death is the risk of abuse of vulnerable patients. In addition to the highly publicized and problematic assisted suicides in which Jack Kevorkian has participated, there is evidence of a relatively widespread secret practice of physician-assisted death in the United States, which is completely unregulated.[6] Voluntary physician-assisted death has been widely practiced in the Netherlands in recent years, although it remains technically illegal.[7] Studies indicate that Dutch physicians have provided lethal treatment to some suffering incompetent patients who have made no request to die.[8-10] The Dutch practice of physician-assisted death is carried out mainly in the privacy of the doctor–patient relationship, subject to guidelines that are not independently monitored.

The risks of abuse in the absence of regulatory safeguards might be greater in the United States than in the Netherlands because of the pressures for cost containment in our health care system, the burdens imposed on family members by the responsibility of caring for dying patients, and our cultural penchant for seeking technological solutions to complex medical and social problems. Therefore, an acceptable policy of legalized physician-assisted death must include independent monitoring to ensure that it is used only as a treatment of last resort in response to the voluntary requests of competent patients who are suffering from terminal or incurable illnesses....

OBJECTIVES OF REGULATORY POLICY

We believe a policy regulating physician-assisted death should be designed with the following objectives: (1) to promote comfort care as standard treatment for dying patients; (2) to permit physician-assisted death only for competent patients suffering from terminal or incurable debilitating illnesses who voluntarily and repeatedly request to die; (3) to develop and promote practice guidelines for voluntary physician-assisted death aimed at making lethal treatment available only as a last resort for unrelievable suffering; (4) to provide independent and impartial oversight of decisions to pursue voluntary physician-assisted death without undue disruption of the doctor–patient relationship; (5) to provide a mechanism for prospective committee review of difficult or disputed cases; and (6) to ensure public accountability.

THE SCOPE OF LEGALIZED PHYSICIAN-ASSISTED DEATH

Our recommended policy reflects choices concerning two difficult issues: whether physician-assisted death should be limited to physician-assisted suicide, thus excluding voluntary, active euthanasia, and whether eligible patients must be only those for whom death is imminent or whether those who are not terminally ill but who suffer from incurable and debilitating conditions such as amyotrophic lateral sclerosis may also be considered eligible. We have opted for a liberal, inclusive policy with respect to these issues. To confine legalized physician-assisted death to assisted suicide unfairly discriminates against patients with unrelievable suffering who resolve to end their lives but are physically unable to do so. The method chosen is less important than the careful assessment that precedes assisted death. Limiting physician-assisted death to patients with terminal illness would deny this option of last resort to incurably, but not terminally, ill patients who make a rational decision to end their lives because of unremitting suffering. Physician-assisted death would be appropriate only after thorough consideration of potential ways to improve the patient's quality of life. We believe that the regulatory safeguards described below would minimize the risks associated with the legalization of physician-assisted death for patients who are not terminally ill and with the possibility of voluntary, active euthanasia.

OVERVIEW OF POLICY

The general responsibility for regulating physician-assisted death would be lodged with regional palliative-care committees. Case-specific oversight of decisions to undertake physician-assisted death would be provided by physicians certified as palliative-care consultants, who would report to the palliative-care committees. Treating physicians would be prohibited from providing lethal treatment without prior consultation and review by an independent, certified palliative-care consultant. The palliative-care committee would be available for prospective review in difficult or disputed cases.

In order to ensure that physician-assisted death is voluntary, which is the inviolable cornerstone of this policy, only adults with decision-making capacity should be eligible for physician-assisted death. Written or witnessed oral consent by the patient must be obtained. No physician would be obligated to participate in physician assisted death. Treating physicians would be required to report death by assisted suicide or the administration of lethal treatment to the proper public authority. Physicians who provided lethal treatment without compliance with the legal requirements would be liable to professional sanctions and criminal penalties.

PALLIATIVE-CARE CONSULTANTS

Independent and impartial oversight by a certified palliative-care consultant is a vital safeguard in this proposed policy of legalized physician-assisted death. Palliative-care consultants would be physicians with experience in treating dying patients, who were knowledgeable about and committed to comfort care, skilled in the assessment of the decision-making capacity of patients suffering from terminal or incurable conditions, and well educated about the ethics of end-of-life decision making....

PALLIATIVE-CARE COMMITTEES

Regional palliative-care committees, made up of professional and lay members, would perform a variety of functions. The committees would develop, issue, and revise practice guidelines for physicians to supplement the legal requirements for physician-assisted death. For example, in order to avoid undue influence on vulnerable patients, the request for the consideration of lethal treatment must come from patients, and physicians should accede only after fully exploring the meaning of the patients' request to die and the available alternatives.[5]

The palliative-care committees would be responsible for educating clinicians and the public about methods of comfort care (including pain management), ethical standards of informed refusal and discontinuation of life-sustaining treatment, and the option of physician-assisted death....

BALANCING THE BENEFITS AND BURDENS OF REGULATION

The process of regulation should be aimed at striking a balance between competing imperatives. On the one hand, physician-assisted death should not be an easy way out for suffering patients and their physicians. On the other hand, oversight should not be so restrictive and onerous as to deprive patients of an adequate response to intolerable suffering.

It might be objected that the policy we recommend is unworkable because it is too cumbersome and intrusive. Such an objection might be justified in the case of a policy requiring mandatory prior committee review or a court hearing to authorize physician-assisted death. Review by a certified palliative-care consultant, however, seems comparable to other consultations by specialists. For a decision of this magnitude, an independent expert opinion is clearly desirable. Some patients and physicians might still feel burdened by such oversight, especially in difficult cases referred or appealed to the palliative-care committee. We believe that this is a price worth paying to protect vulnerable patients and to ensure public accountability. Critical to the success of this policy, however, would be the timely availability of palliative-care consultants, education that emphasized the sensitive nature of the oversight function, and scrupulous protection of confidentiality. . . .

mits voluntary physician-assisted death as a last resort.

CONCLUSIONS

The ethical norms of relieving suffering and respecting patients' rights to self-determination support the permissibility of voluntary physician-assisted death as a last resort for terminally or incurably ill patients. The availability of the extraordinary option of lethal treatment, however, must be accompanied by careful regulation to minimize the risk of abuse. We recommend that physician-assisted death be legalized with adequate safeguards to protect vulnerable patients, preserve the professional integrity of physicians, and ensure accountability to the public. The policy we have outlined would ensure independent and impartial review of decisions to provide physician-assisted death in response to unrelievable suffering, without undue disruption of the doctor–patient relationship. We hope one or more states will decide democratically to expand the options for dying or incurably ill patients by implementing a policy that both promotes comfort care and per-

REFERENCES

1. Quill TE. Death and dignity. New York: W. W. Norton, 1993.
2. Brody H. Assisted death—a compassionate response to a medical failure. N Engl J Med 1992;327:1384–8.
3. Miller FG, Fletcher JC. The case for legalized euthanasia. Perspect Biol Med 1993;36:159–76.
4. Annas GJ, Glantz LH, Mariner WK. The right of privacy protects the doctor–patient relationship. JAMA 1990;263:858–61.
5. Quill TE. Doctor, I want to die. Will you help me? JAMA 1993;270:870–3.
6. Meier DE. Doctors' attitudes and experiences with physician-assisted death: a review of the literature. In: Humber JM, Almeder RF, Kasting GA, eds. Physician-assisted death. Totowa, N.J.: Humana Press, 1994:5–24.
7. van der Maas PJ, van Delden JJM, Pijnenborg L, Looman CWN. Euthanasia and other medical decisions concerning the end of life. Lancet 1991;338:669–74.
8. Gomez CF. Regulating death. New York: Free Press, 1991.
9. ten Have HA, Welie JV. Euthanasia: normal medical practice? Hastings Cent Rep 1992; 22:34–8.
10. Pijnenborg L, van der Maas PJ, van Delden JJM, Looman CWN. Life-terminating acts without explicit request of patient. Lancet 1993; 341:1196–9.

NO

David Orentlicher

PHYSICIAN-ASSISTED DYING: THE CONFLICT WITH FUNDAMENTAL PRINCIPLES OF AMERICAN LAW

On the issue of physician-assisted dying (i.e., physician-assisted suicide and euthanasia), people express considerable ambivalence.... Members of the medical profession are also divided....

The ambivalence toward physician-assisted dying reflects the complexity of the issue and the strength of the arguments both in favor and against its use (Brock 1992; Callahan 1992; Kass 1989; Orentlicher 1989; Pellegrino 1993; Weir 1992; Wolf 1989). In addition, the ambivalence may reflect an irreconcilable tension between two of the important philosophies that animate American law: the inalienability of certain rights and egalitarianism. Inalienable rights are rights that are so fundamental that they cannot be bought, sold, or otherwise transferred voluntarily from one person to another (Black, Nolan, and Nolan-Haley 1990). Egalitarianism refers to the equal status of each person under the law.

Physician-assisted dying is resisted in large part, both ethically and legally, because it violates the sense that the right to life is an inalienable right. Proposals for physician-assisted dying include safeguards that respond to concerns about inalienability, but these safeguards create a conflict with the principle that we have an egalitarian system of government. Efforts to reconcile physician-assisted dying with egalitarianism, in turn, exacerbate the conflict with inalienability. The more we deal with one concern, the greater the problems with the other. As I will explain, prohibiting physician-assisted dying may be necessary to avoid problems with either inalienability or egalitarianism.

To better understand the tension between inalienability and egalitarianism, it is useful to consider these two principles in some depth. As a prelude, it is interesting to note that the two principles were enunciated in the same passage of the American Declaration of Independence: "We hold these truths to be self-evident, that all men are created equal, they are endowed by their

From David Orentlicher, "Physician-Assisted Dying: The Conflict With Fundamental Principles of American Law," in Robert H. Blank and Andrea L. Bonnicksen, eds., *Medicine Unbound: The Human Body and the Limitations of Medical Intervention* (Columbia University Press, 1994). Copyright © 1994 by Columbia University Press. Reprinted by permission.

creator with certain unalienable rights, that among these are life, liberty and the pursuit of happiness."

DEFINING INALIENABLE RIGHTS

... I will identify four important characteristics of inalienable rights. First, a person cannot waive or give up an inalienable right, even if there is fully voluntary consent to do so (Kuflik 1986; McConnell 1984). For example, if I were to ask a friend to kill me, and he did so, he would still be subject to prosecution for homicide. My consent would not be a defense to the murder. The right to vote is another example of an inalienable right; I cannot sell my right to vote nor can I have someone else appear at the polling precinct in my place. I also cannot agree to become an indentured servant or go into slavery, nor can I agree to be battered by a family member (Kuflik 1986).

The second feature of an inalienable right is that it defines a person's relationships with others. An inalienable right cannot be transferred or waived with respect to someone else (McConnell 1984). This characteristic of inalienability may explain why the states that make assisted suicide a crime nevertheless do not make suicide a crime. Although most states prohibit assisted suicide (Quill, Cassel, and Meier 1992), suicide is no longer a crime in any state ("Physician-Assisted Suicide" 1992). Voting provides another example of how inalienability exists with respect to others. In the United States, unlike some other countries, I do not have to vote in public elections; I can decline to exercise my right. However, if I sell my vote to someone else, I will be violating the law.

As a corollary to the inability to waive or give up the right with respect to someone else, an agreement to give up the right is unenforceable. If I promise to sell my vote to a friend and I renege, the friend cannot obtain a court order to enforce my promise. In addition to being unenforceable, an agreement to give up the right may even result in legal liability. For example, it is against federal law to sell or buy a vote (18 U.S.C. 597). It is also against federal law to have an indentured servant (18 U.S.C. 1584).

A third important point about inalienable rights is that they are not necessarily absolute rights. For example, while I may not be able to voluntarily give up my right to life, I may still lose the right involuntarily by forfeiture (McConnell 1984). People who commit murders are subject to capital punishment; people who attack another may be killed by the other person in self-defense.

The fourth feature of inalienability is that it can be a broad or a narrow concept (McConnell 1984). If inalienability is conceived broadly, then a person can never waive an inalienable right through consent. The right might be lost for other reasons, as by forfeiture, but consent is never a basis for losing the right. Historically, the United States has treated euthanasia that way; euthanasia is not made acceptable because the patient agrees to its performance. If inalienability is conceived narrowly, then consent alone is not sufficient to give up the right, but consent plus other factors may make waiver of the right acceptable. Advocates of assisted suicide have implicitly defined the inalienability of the right to life narrowly. In their view, consent by the patient alone is not sufficient to justify assisted suicide; rather, there must be consent, *and* there must be terminal or incurable illness, suffering without prospect of relief, and other qualifying conditions (Quill, Cassel, and Meier 1992; Wanzer et al. 1989). Similarly, consent to indentured servitude is not sufficient to waive the right to be free of indentured servitude. Yet if there is consent plus national security concerns, then the right may be waived. Accordingly, people who volunteered to serve in the military were not free to withhold their services during the Persian Gulf War.

In order to discuss the concept of inalienable rights with respect to the right to life, it is necessary to give a definition of the right to life. Here, too, there are different understandings; for example, people disagree whether the right to life includes the right to medical treatment, irrespective of income (Annas et al. 1990). For the purposes of this discussion, it will be sufficient to conclude that, at the very least, the right to life includes the right of one person not to have his/her life taken by another. Accordingly, while euthanasia or physician-assisted suicide might violate this aspect of the right to life, a refusal of life-sustaining treatment would not. In addition, because another person participates more deeply in an individual's decision to die by euthanasia than by assisted suicide, euthanasia is more problematic than assisted suicide from the perspective of inalienability. This distinction may in part explain why euthanasia is prohibited by law in all states, but assisted suicide is not prohibited in every state.

CATEGORIZING RIGHTS AS INALIENABLE

To understand how proposals for legalizing physician-assisted dying respond to the inalienability of the right to life, it is useful to examine the reasons certain rights are considered inalienable....

Perhaps the most important concern is the ideal of preserving the moral worth of society. Permitting physician-assisted dying may undermine the high value that society places on life. If people can be killed simply because they consent, there is a serious risk that society will have less respect for human life and will become less troubled when there are actual violations of a person's right to life (McConnell 1984). That is, people may become less troubled when killing occurs without consent. Prohibiting physician-assisted dying prevents us from beginning the process of weakening the moral fibers of society. For many people, the concern about moral worth has religious aspects—people hold their bodies in a stewardship for some greater being or purpose. Because individuals do not own their bodies, they therefore have an obligation not to shorten their lifespan....

Second, inalienable rights preserve freedom of choice in areas of profound consequence to happiness (Kuflik 1986). The irreversibility of death explains why many people object to physician-assisted dying....

Inalienable rights serve the third purpose of avoiding the creation or perpetuation of hierarchies (Kuflik 1986). Inalienability helps prevent the domination of one group by another.... Concern about domination is particularly relevant to the right to life. One of the important arguments against physician-assisted dying is the fear that the handicapped and other vulnerable groups will be victimized if assisted suicide or euthanasia is permitted.

Authenticity is a fourth concern underlying inalienable rights (Kuflik 1986; McConnell 1984). If I report that I assisted someone's suicide, there may be no way to determine whether I am telling the truth; the other person can no longer serve as a witness. One of Dr. Jack Kevorkian's cases of assisted suicide, in October 1991, illustrates just this concern. The prosecutor charged that Marjorie Wantz died by euthanasia, rather than by assisted suicide, but there was no reliable way to distinguish between the two, and the charges were dismissed by the court (*State v. Kevorkian*, No. CR-92-115190-FC, slip op. at 17-19 [Mich. Cir. Ct. July 21, 1992]). In other cases, there may be legitimate doubt whether the dead person had a truly competent intent to end his/her life. The person's competence may have been compromised by a treatable depression or by the effects of the underlying disease or its treatment (Conwell and Caine 1991; Wanzer et al. 1989)....

LIMITING PHYSICIAN-ASSISTED DYING TO AVOID PROBLEMS WITH INALIENABILITY

Supporters of physician-assisted dying have generally advanced proposals that respond to the concerns of inalienability. In the Netherlands, strict criteria have to be satisfied before a person can undergo euthanasia. The patient must be experiencing intolerable and irreversible suffering, the patient must make repeated, competent, and consistent requests for euthanasia, and two physicians must determine that euthanasia is appropriate (de Wachter 1992). Similarly, when a group of distinguished physicians endorsed physician-assisted suicide, it was in the context of terminally ill, competent patients whose suffering is intolerable and unresponsive to therapeutic intervention (Wanzer et al. 1989). In both cases, the criteria are designed to respond to the concerns that have made the right to life inalienable.

The protective measures used in the Netherlands, and included in many domestic proposals for physician-assisted dying, can be characterized as either substantive or procedural protections. Substantive criteria set limits on who can seek physician-assisted dying; procedural criteria regulate the manner in which physician-assisted dying is carried out. As examples of procedural criteria, there are the requirements that a) the patient must make repeated, competent requests over a reasonable period of time; b) the request must be well documented in the record; and c) a second physician must agree that the physician-assisted dying is appropriate (Quill, Cassel, and Meier 1992). These procedural criteria respond to the concern about authenticity. We can minimize the possibility that the person's death was involuntary if all of these procedural hurdles are satisfied.

The substantive criteria respond to the other concerns underlying inalienability. Examples of substantive restrictions include the requirements that a) the patient must be terminally ill; and b) the patient must be suffering intolerably with no prospect of relief. These restrictions limit physician-assisted dying to the people who are truly suffering and whose prognosis is hopeless, people who therefore are truly in need of assistance in dying. For these patients, assisted suicide or euthanasia may be the most compassionate response possible. Proponents of physician-assisted dying contend that, by permitting the most compassionate response, we can enhance, rather than compromise, the moral worth of society.

The substantive criteria also respond to the concern that the powerless will be victimized. By restricting physician-assisted dying to the very narrow group of people who are terminally ill and suffering intolerably with no prospect of relief, we ensure that people's lives are not ended simply because of age and infirmity.

Finally, the substantive criteria respond to the concern about limiting freedom of choice in important areas. When a patient becomes terminally ill with intolerable suffering, there is already very little freedom to make choices about the way life will be lived (Rubenfeld 1989).

PROBLEMS WITH EGALITARIANISM

Although the substantive criteria for physician-assisted dying respond to concerns about inalienability, they may create serious problems with egalitarianism, the principle that people are entitled to equal treatment under the law. In an egalitarian society, each person is entitled to be treated with equality and evenhandedness by the government (Tribe 1988). However, if the state permits physician-assisted dying only for patients who meet a specific level of terminal illness and suffering, then it will be granting a right to certain persons that it denies to other persons. In terms of physician-assisted dying, there would not be equal treatment of all individuals under the law.

Of course, egalitarianism does not require that people always be treated in the same way. Because there are important differences among individuals, they may need to be treated differently in order to be treated as equals. As the U.S. Supreme Court has observed, "Sometimes the greatest discrimination can lie in treating things that are different as

though they were exactly alike" (*Jenness v. Fortson*, 403 U.S. 431, 442 [1971]). . . .

The difficult question for an egalitarian society is deciding when variations among individuals are relevant for purposes of drawing legal distinctions (Beauchamp and Childress 1989). A considerable body of law has developed to interpret the Fourteenth Amendment's guarantee of equal protection under the law. It is not critical for the purposes of this paper to define precisely the limits of egalitarianism. The important point is to highlight the egalitarian concerns that would arise from laws permitting physician-assisted dying.

As the development of equal-protection law has recognized, certain kinds of distinctions among individuals are less acceptable than others. For example, when the government draws distinctions on the basis of race, courts subject the distinctions to the most exacting scrutiny and, almost without fail, conclude that the distinctions are unconstitutional (Tribe 1988). On the other hand, governments have considerable freedom to draw distinctions between individuals on the basis of their occupation (*Williamson v. Lee Optical*, 348 U.S. 483 [1955]). If the state permits physician-assisted dying only for patients who meet a specific level of terminal illness and suffering, then it will be responding to concerns about inalienability but it will be making the kinds of distinctions among its citizens that are particularly troublesome on egalitarian grounds: distinctions that are based on judgments about the value of people's lives.

The reluctance to make such judgments has influenced the development of legal doctrine or public policy in other contexts. The evolution of the law in withdrawal-of-life-support cases illustrates this influence. When the right to refuse life-sustaining treatment was first recognized, it was often viewed as a right of terminally ill patients to refuse particularly burdensome, or "extraordinary," care. Living-will statutes typically restricted their coverage to terminally ill patients (many still do) (Orentlicher 1990a), and the early court cases focused on the patient's impending death and the invasiveness of the medical treatment. For example, in *In re Quinlan* (355 A.2d 647 [1976]), the New Jersey Supreme Court concluded that the right to refuse treatment depends upon the seriousness of the patient's prognosis and the degree of bodily invasion from medical treatment. Thus, at one time, the state drew an important distinction among its citizens: while there was a right to refuse life-sustaining treatment, the right belonged only to patients who were sufficiently sick and who were dependent upon burdensome treatment.

Recent cases have made it clear that the right to refuse life-sustaining treatment is not limited by the patient's prognosis or the medical treatment being provided. For example, the right may be exercised by patients who still can live for decades in a fully conscious state. In *Georgia v. McAfee* (385 S.E.2d 651 [Ga. 1989]), and *McKay v. Bergstedt* (801 P.2d 617 [Nev. 1990]), the right was recognized for two young men who had become quadraplegic and ventilator-dependent as a result of severe spinal cord injuries, but who had not suffered any loss of mental competence. The right to refuse life-sustaining treatment has also been expanded to include any medical treatment, including artificial nutrition and hydration (*Cruzan v. Director, Missouri Department of Health,* 110 S. Ct. 2481 [1990]). In short, over time, courts have gradually

eliminated their reliance on substantive criteria when making decisions about the right to refuse treatment. The right is no longer denied to patients because they do not have a severe enough prognosis or because the medical treatment upon which they depend is not unduly burdensome. If the government were to require treatment based upon substantive criteria, it would be saying that some lives still had sufficient value that they must be maintained. It would also be taking the position that other lives were so devoid of value that they did not have to be maintained. As the court in *Bouvia v. Superior Court* (225 Cal. Rptr. 297, 305 [Cal. Ct. App. 1986]) observed, however:

> Who shall say what the minimum amount of available life must be? Does it matter if it be 15 to 20 years, 15 to 20 months, or 15 to 20 days, if such life has been physically destroyed and its quality, dignity, and purpose gone? As in all matters lines must be drawn at some point, somewhere, but that decision must ultimately belong to the one whose life is in issue.

This abandonment of substantive criteria in withdrawal-of-treatment cases ensures that the government will not be making the worst kind of value judgments for a government to make—judgments about the value of a person's life (Tribe 1988).

To be sure, procedural criteria continue to play an important role in cases about the withdrawal of life-sustaining treatment. States may require clear and convincing evidence of an incompetent patient's wishes before treatment is withdrawn or, when such evidence is absent, states may permit family members to decide whether treatment should be discontinued (Orentlicher 1990b). Similarly, living-will statutes may require that two witnesses co-sign a living-will document and that the patient's diagnosis be confirmed by two physicians before the living will is carried out. As already noted, procedural criteria are designed to ensure authenticity; in the context of withdrawal-of-treatment cases, they are designed to ensure that treatment is withdrawn only if the patient would have wanted treatment withdrawn. By ensuring authenticity, the procedural criteria protect the ability of patients to make their own decisions about the value of their lives, thereby serving the goals of both egalitarianism and inalienability....

RESOLVING THE CONFLICT BETWEEN EGALITARIANISM AND INALIENABILITY

Concerns about egalitarianism in physician-assisted dying can be resolved by eliminating a role for substantive criteria. If the government does not limit the option of physician-assisted dying to only certain people, concerns about value-of-life judgments would not arise. In other words, from an egalitarian perspective, it may make sense to permit physician-assisted dying for everyone or no one, thereby removing from the government the task of deciding when life becomes intolerable. Indeed, some states, such as Michigan, do not have criminal prohibitions against assisted suicide at all (*State v. Kevorkian*, No. CR-92-115190-FC, slip op. at 5-16 [Mich. Cir. Ct. July 21, 1992]), and in the states that prohibit assisted suicide, the laws apply to all people (e.g., Ariz. Rev. Stat. Ann. 13-1103 [1989]); Fla. Stat. Ann. 782.08 [West 1992]; N.Y. Penal Law 125.15 [McKinney 1987]). As discussed previously, however, the principle of inalienability indicates that physician-assisted dying should be permitted for

only certain people or no one. Accordingly, to satisfy both inalienability and egalitarianism, it may be necessary to prohibit physician-assisted dying altogether.

The author gratefully acknowledges the helpful comments of Teri Randall.

REFERENCES

Annas, George J., Sylvia A. Law, Rand E. Rosenblatt, and Kenneth R. Wing. 1990. *American Health Law.* Boston: Little, Brown.

Beauchamp, Tom L., and James F. Childress. 1989. *Principles of Biomedical Ethics.* 3d ed. New York: Oxford University Press.

Black, Henry C., Joseph R. Nolan, and Jacqueline M. Nolan-Haley. 1990. *West's Law Dictionary.* 6th ed. St. Paul, Minn.: West.

Brock, Dan W. 1992. "Voluntary Active Euthanasia." *Hastings Center Report* 22(2):10–22.

Callahan, Daniel. 1992. "When Self-Determination Runs Amok." *Hastings Center Report* 22(2):52–55.

Conwell, Yeates, and Eric D. Caine. 1991. "Rational Suicide and the Right to Die: Reality and Myth." *New England Journal of Medicine* 325(15):1100–1103.

de Wachter, Maurice A. M. 1992. "Euthanasia in the Netherlands." *Hastings Center Report* 22(2):23–30.

Kass, Leon R. 1989. "Neither for Love nor Money: Why Doctors Must Not Kill." *Public Interest* 94 (Winter):25–46.

Kuflik, Arthur. 1986. "The Utilitarian Logic of Inalienable Rights." *Ethics* 97 (October):75–87.

McConnell, Terrance. 1984. "The Nature and Basis of Inalienable Rights." *Law and Philosophy* 3(1):25–59.

Orentlicher, David. 1989. "Physician Participation in Assisted Suicide." *Journal of the American Medical Association* 262(13):1844–1845.

Orentlicher, David. 1990a. "Advance Medical Directives." *Journal of the American Medical Association* 263(17):2365–2367.

Orentlicher, David. 1990b. "The Right to Die after *Cruzan.*" *Journal of the American Medical Association* 264(18):2444–2446.

Pellegrino, Edmund D. 1993. "Compassion Needs Reason Too." *Journal of the American Medical Association* 270(7):874–875.

"Physician-Assisted Suicide and the Right to Die with Assistance." 1992. *Harvard Law Review* 105(8):2021–2040.

Quill, Timothy E., Christine K. Cassel, and Diane E. Meier. 1992. "Care of the Hopelessly Ill: Proposed Clinical Criteria for Physician-Assisted Suicide."

New England Journal of Medicine 327(19):1380–1384.

Rubenfeld, Jed. 1989. "The Right to Privacy." *Harvard Law Review* 102(4):737–807.

Tribe, Laurence H. 1988. *American Constitutional Law.* 2d ed. Mineola, N.Y.: Foundation Press.

Wanzer, Sidney H., Daniel D. Federman, S. James Adelstein, Christine K. Cassel et al. 1989. "The Physician's Responsibility Toward Hopelessly Ill Patients: A Second Look." *New England Journal of Medicine* 320(13):844–849.

Weir, Robert F. 1992. "The Morality of Physician-Assisted Suicide." *Law, Medicine, and Health Care* 20(1-2):116–126.

Wolf, Susan M. 1989. "Holding the Line on Euthanasia." *Hastings Center Report* 19(1)(Supp.):13–15.

POSTSCRIPT

Should Physicians Be Allowed to Assist in Patient Suicide?

In November 1994 voters in Oregon voted by a small majority to decriminalize assisted suicide. This makes the state the first place in America to allow physicians to assist patients in suicide. Assistance, however, is limited to prescribing, but not administering, lethal doses of drugs to terminally ill patients.

The law is being challenged by a group of patients and doctors who say it violates the Constitution's equal protection and due process clauses, as well as the federal Americans with Disabilities Act of 1990. Similar initiatives in the states of Washington and California failed to win approval.

In May 1994 Judge Barbara Rothstein, a federal judge in Seattle, Washington, struck down a law banning assisted suicide. In her ruling, the judge held that the right of terminally ill people to end their suffering is guaranteed by the constitutional right of privacy.

On May 2, 1994, a Michigan jury cleared retired pathologist Jack Kevorkian of charges that he had violated a state law against assisted suicide by helping Thomas W. Hyde, Jr., kill himself in 1993. Hyde suffered from a rapidly progressing case of multiple sclerosis. Kevorkian's method involves specially constructed devices that inject lethal drugs. Michigan passed a law in 1992 that made it a felony to assist in a suicide. The jury decided that Kevorkian as not guilty because he was relieving a patient's pain. So far Kevorkian has assisted 21 people in suicide.

For more analysis on the ethics of physician-assisted suicide, see *Suicide and Euthanasia: Historical and Contemporary Themes,* edited by Baruch A. Brody (Kluwer, 1989); Gilbert Meilaender, "Human Equality and Assistance in Suicide," *Second Opinion* (volume 19, no. 4, 1994); and James M. Humber et al., eds., *Biomedical Ethics Reviews, 1993—Physician-Assisted Death* (Humana Press, 1994).

The New York State Task Force on Life and the Law opposes physician-assisted suicide and favors instead improved public policy around treating terminally ill persons; see *When Death Is Sought: Assisted Suicide and Euthanasia in the Medical Context* (N.Y. State Task Force on Life and the Law, 1994). Analyses of physician attitudes toward helping dying patients to kill themselves can be found in Robyn Shapiro's "Willingness to Perform Euthanasia," *Archives of Internal Medicine* (March 14, 1994), and Thomas A. Preston's "Professional Norms and Physician Attitudes Toward Euthanasia," *The Journal of Law, Medicine & Ethics* (Spring 1994).

ISSUE 7

Is It Ever Morally Right to Withhold Food and Water from Dying Patients?

YES: Joanne Lynn and James F. Childress, from "Must Patients Always Be Given Food and Water?" *Hastings Center Report* (October 1983)

NO: Gilbert Meilaender, from "On Removing Food and Water: Against the Stream," *Hastings Center Report* (December 1984)

ISSUE SUMMARY

YES: Physician Joanne Lynn and professor of religious studies James F. Childress claim that nutrition and hydration are not morally different from other life-sustaining medical treatments that may be withheld or withdrawn, according to the patient's best interest.

NO: Professor of religion Gilbert Meilaender asserts that removing the ordinary human care of feeding aims to kill and is morally wrong.

The landmark *Quinlan* decision in 1976 affirmed the right of a patient to refuse life-sustaining treatment and the right of a parent or guardian to make that same decision for an incompetent patient. But Karen Ann Quinlan's parents wanted only to remove her from a respirator; they did not even consider the removal of a nasogastric tube through which she was artificially fed for the next 10 years until her death.

The question of whether food and water must always be provided reached the public arena in a series of legal cases that began in 1981. In that year Robert Nejdl and Neil Barber, two Los Angeles physicians, were charged with murder for taking Clarence Herbert, their patient who had suffered severe brain damage after an operation, off a respirator and then, when he continued to breathe, removing all artificial nutrition. The charges were dropped, and the court ruled in 1983 that artificial feeding was like any other medical treatment and could be withheld with consent of the patient or family.

Also in 1981 in Danville, Illinois, the parents and physician of newborn conjoined twins (often called Siamese twins) decided not to feed the infants. The courts disagreed and feeding and other treatments were given. But in 1982, in Bloomington, Indiana, another newborn—with Down's syndrome, a genetic disease that results in mild to severe mental retardation—was not given surgery to correct a defect of his esophagus and was not fed. The baby's death led to a series of governmental regulations.

In a series of other cases, the courts have grappled with the same problem but have come up with different answers. In New Jersey, in the 1983 case of Claire Conroy, the court ruled, after her death, that food and nutrition could be withheld from a nursing home patient as long as a series of complicated procedures were followed to prevent abuse. In Massachusetts, in the 1986 case of Paul Brophy, a firefighter in a persistent vegetative state, the court ruled that feeding could not be withdrawn, despite the unanimous wishes of the family and the judgment of several physicians that he would never recover. A New Jersey court also held, in the case of Nancy Jobes, a 31-year-old woman in a persistent vegetative state, that feeding tubes could not be removed in the nursing home if the staff disagreed, but could be removed at home.

The most groundbreaking decision since *Quinlan* is the case of Nancy Cruzan, a 33-year-old Missouri woman who remained in a persistent vegetative state after an automobile accident in 1983. State courts refused to honor her parents' request to remove artificial nutrition and hydration, so they appealed to the Supreme Court. In June 1990 the Court ruled that it was not unconstitutional for Missouri to require very high standards of evidence that Nancy herself would have refused this treatment. Since those standards had not been met, the parents' request could be denied. In this case the Supreme Court sent a clear message that individuals' prior decisions to refuse treatment could be honored but that these decisions had to be "clear and convincing."

The ethical question centers on whether artificial nutrition and hydration is ordinary care, which must be provided for every patient, or a medical treatment like antibiotics or a respirator, which can be withheld if it is not in the patient's best interests. The symbolic value of feeding a dying patient must be weighed against the likely benefit to the patient.

In the following selections, Joanne Lynn and James F. Childress provide three circumstances when, in their view, it would be ethical to withhold fluids and nutrition: when the procedures would be futile in achieving improved nutritional and fluid levels; when the improvement, though achievable, would not benefit the patient; and when the burden of receiving the treatment outweights the benefits. Gilbert Meilaender sees a willingness to provide food and drink "even when the struggle against death has been lost" as "the last evidence we can offer that . . . we are willing to love to the very point of death."

YES

Joanne Lynn and James F. Childress

MUST PATIENTS ALWAYS BE GIVEN FOOD AND WATER?

Many people die from the lack of food or water. For some, this lack is the result of poverty or famine, but for others it is the result of disease or deliberate decision. In the past, malnutrition and dehydration must have accompanied nearly every death that followed an illness of more than a few days. Most dying patients do not eat much on their own, and nothing could be done for them until the first flexible tubing for instilling food or other liquid into the stomach was developed about a hundred years ago. Even then, the procedure was so scarce, so costly in physician and nursing time, and so poorly tolerated that it was used only for patients who clearly could benefit. With the advent of more reliable and efficient procedures in the past few decades, these conditions can be corrected or ameliorated in nearly every patient who would otherwise be malnourished or dehydrated. In fact, intravenous lines and nasogastric tubes have become common images of hospital care.

Providing adequate nutrition and fluids is a high priority for most patients, both because they suffer directly from inadequacies and because these deficiencies hinder their ability to overcome other diseases. But are there some patients who need not receive these treatments? ...

The answer in any real case should acknowledge the psychological contiguity between feeding and loving and between nutritional satisfaction and emotional satisfaction. Yet this acknowledgement does not resolve the core question. ...

[W]e will concentrate upon the care of patients who are incompetent to make choices for themselves. Patients who are competent to determine the course of their therapy may refuse any and all interventions proposed by others, as long as their refusals do not seriously harm or impose unfair burdens upon others.[1] A competent patient's decision regarding whether or not to accept the provision of food and water by medical means such as tube feeding or intravenous alimentation is unlikely to raise questions of harm or burden to others.

What then should guide those who must decide about nutrition for a patient who cannot decide? As a start, consider the standard by which other medical

From Joanne Lynn and James F. Childress, "Must Patients Always Be Given Food and Water?" *Hastings Center Report*, vol. 13, no. 5 (October 1983). Copyright © 1983 by The Hastings Center. Reprinted by permission.

decisions are made: one should decide as the incompetent person would have if he or she were competent, when that is possible to determine, and advance that person's interests in a more generalized sense when individual preferences cannot be known.

THE MEDICAL PROCEDURES

There is no reason to apply a different standard to feeding and hydration. Surely, when one inserts a feeding tube, or creates a gastrostomy opening, or inserts a needle into a vein, one intends to benefit the patient. Ideally, one should provide what the patient believes to be of benefit, but at least the effect should be beneficial in the opinions of surrogates and caregivers.

Thus, the question becomes: is it ever in the patient's interest to become malnourished and dehydrated, rather than to receive treatment? Posing the question so starkly points to our need to know what is entailed in treating these conditions and what benefits the treatments offer.

The medical interventions that provide food and fluids are of two basic types. First, liquids can be delivered by a tube that is inserted into a functioning gastrointestinal tract, most commonly through the nose and esophagus into the stomach or through a surgical incision in the abdominal wall and directly into the stomach. The liquids used can be specially prepared solutions of nutrients or a blenderized version of an ordinary diet. The nasogastric tube is cheap; it may lead to pneumonia and often annoys the patient and family, sometimes even requiring that the patient be restrained to prevent its removal.

Creating a gastrostomy is usually a simple surgical procedure, and, once the wound is healed, care is very simple. Since it is out of sight, it is aesthetically more acceptable and restraints are needed less often. Also, the gastrostomy creates no additional risk of pneumonia. However, while elimination of a nasogastric tube requires only removing the tube, a gastrostomy is fairly permanent, and can be closed only by surgery.

The second type of medical intervention is intravenous feeding and hydration, which also has two major forms. The ordinary hospital or peripheral IV, in which fluid is delivered directly to the bloodstream through a small needle, is useful only for temporary efforts to improve hydration and electrolyte concentrations. One cannot provide a balanced diet through the veins in the limbs: to do that requires a central line, or a special catheter placed into one of the major veins in the chest. The latter procedure is much more risky and vulnerable to infections and technical errors, and it is much more costly than any of the other procedures. Both forms of intravenous nutrition and hydration commonly require restraining the patient, cause minor infections and other ill effects, and are costly, especially since they ordinarily require the patient to be in a hospital.

None of these procedures, then, is ideal; each entails some distress, some medical limitations, and some costs. When may a procedure be foregone that might improve nutrition and hydration for a given patient? Only when the procedure and the resulting improvement in nutrition and hydration do not offer the patient a net benefit over what he or she would otherwise have faced.

Are there such circumstances? We believe that there are; but they are few and limited to the following three kinds of situations: 1. The procedures that would be required are so unlikely to achieve improved nutritional and fluid levels that they could be correctly considered futile; 2. The improvement in nutritional and fluid balance, though achievable, could be of no benefit to the patient; 3. The burdens of receiving the treatment may outweigh the benefit.

WHEN FOOD AND WATER MAY BE WITHHELD

Futile Treatment. Sometimes even providing "food and water" to a patient becomes a monumental task. Consider a patient with a severe clotting deficiency and a nearly total body burn. Gaining access to the central veins is likely to cause hemorrhage or infection, nasogastric tube placement may be quite painful, and there may be no skin to which to suture the stomach for a gastrostomy tube. Or consider a patient with severe congestive heart failure who develops cancer of the stomach with a fistula that delivers foods from the stomach to the colon without passing through the intestine and being absorbed. Feeding the patient may be possible, but little is absorbed. Intravenous feeding cannot be tolerated because the fluid would be too much for the weakened heart. Or consider the infant with infarction of all but a short segment of bowel. Again, the infant can be fed, but little if anything is absorbed. Intravenous methods can be used, but only for a short time (weeks or months) until their complications, including thrombosis, hemorrhage, infections, and malnutrition, cause death.

In these circumstances, the patient is going to die soon, no matter what is done. The ineffective efforts to provide nutrition and hydration may well directly cause suffering that offers no counterbalancing benefit for the patient. Although the procedures might be tried, especially if the competent patient wanted them or the incompetent patient's surrogate had reason to believe that this incompetent patient would have wanted them, they cannot be considered obligatory. To hold that a patient must be subjected to this predictably futile sort of intervention just because protein balance is negative or the blood serum is concentrated is to lose sight of the moral warrant for medical care and to reduce the patient to an array of measurable variables.

No Possibility of Benefit. Some patients can be reliably diagnosed to have permanently lost consciousness. This unusual group of patients includes those with anencephaly, persistent vegetative state, and some preterminal comas. In these cases, it is very difficult to discern how any medical intervention can benefit or harm the patient. These patients cannot and never will be able to experience any of the events occurring in the world or in their bodies. When the diagnosis is exceedingly clear, we sustain their lives vigorously mainly for their loved ones and the community at large.

While these considerations probably indicate that continued artificial feeding is best in most cases, there may be some cases in which the family and the caregivers are convinced that artificial feeding is offensive and unreasonable. In such cases, there seems to be no adequate reason to claim that withholding food and water violates any obligations that these parties or the general society have with regard to permanently unconscious patients. Thus, if the parents of an anencephalic infant or of a patient like Karen Quinlan in a persistent vegetative state feel strongly that no medical procedures should be applied to provide nutrition and hydration, and the caregivers are willing to comply, there should be no barrier in law or public policy to thwart the plan.[2]

Disproportionate Burden. The most difficult cases are those in which normal nutritional status or fluid balance could be restored, but only with a severe burden for the patient. In these cases, the treatment is futile in a broader sense— the patient will not actually benefit from the improved nutrition and hydration. A patient who is competent can decide the relative merits of the treatment being provided, knowing the probable consequences, and weighing the merits of life under various sets of constrained circumstances. But a surrogate decision maker for a patient who is incompetent to decide will have a difficult task. When the situation is irremediably ambiguous, erring on the side of continued life and improved nutrition and hydration seems the less grievous error. But are there situations that would warrant a determination that this patient, whose nutrition and hydration could surely be improved, is not thereby well served?

Though they are rare, we believe there are such cases. The treatments entailed are not benign. Their effects are far short of ideal. Furthermore, many of the patients most likely to have inadequate food and fluid intake are also likely to suffer the most serious side effects of these therapies.

Patients who are allowed to die without artificial hydration and nutrition may well die more comfortably than patients who receive conventional amounts of intravenous hydration.[3] Terminal pulmonary edema, nausea, and mental confusion are more likely when patients have been treated to maintain fluid and nutrition until close to the time of death.

Thus, those patients whose "need" for artificial nutrition and hydration arises only near the time of death may be harmed by its provision. It is not at all clear that they receive any benefit in having a slightly prolonged life, and it does seem reasonable to allow a surrogate to decide that, for this patient at this time, slight prolongation of life is not warranted if it involves measures that will probably increase the patient's suffering as he or she dies.

Even patients who might live much longer might not be well served by artificial means to provide fluid and food. Such patients might include those with fairly severe dementia for whom the restraints required could be a constant source of fear, discomfort, and struggle. For such a patient, sedation to tolerate the feeding mechanisms might preclude any of the pleasant experiences that might otherwise have been available. Thus, a decision not to intervene, except perhaps briefly to ascertain that there are no treatable causes, might allow such a patient to live out a shorter life with fair freedom of movement and freedom from fear, while a decision to maintain artificial nutrition and hydration might consign the patient to end his or her life in unremitting anguish. If this were the case a surrogate decision maker would seem to be well justified in refusing the treatment.

INAPPROPRIATE MORAL CONSTRAINTS

Four considerations are frequently proposed as moral constraints on foregoing medical feeding and hydration. We find none of these to dictate that artificial nutrition and hydration must always be provided.

The Obligation to Provide "Ordinary" Care. Debates about appropriate medical treatment are often couched in terms of "ordinary" and "extraordinary" means of treatment. Historically, this distinction emerged in the Roman Catholic tradition to differentiate optional treatment from treatment that was obligatory for medical professionals to offer and for patients to accept.[4] These terms also appear in many secular contexts, such as court decisions and medical codes. The recent debates about ordinary and extraordinary means of treatment have been interminable and often unfruitful, in part because of a lack of clarity about what the terms mean. Do they represent the premises of an argument or the conclusion, and what features of a situation are relevant to the categorization as "ordinary" or "extraordinary"?[5]

Several criteria have been implicit in debates about ordinary and extraordinary means of treatment; some of them may be relevant to determining whether and which treatments are obligatory and which are optional. Treatments have been distinguished according to their simplicity (simple/complex), their naturalness (natural/artificial), their customariness (usual/unusual), their invasiveness (noninvasive/invasive), their chance of success (reasonable chance/futile), their balance of benefits and burdens (proportionate/disproportionate), and their expense (inexpensive/costly). Each set of paired terms or phrases in the parentheses suggests a continuum: as the treatment moves from the first of the paired terms to the second, it is said to become less obligatory and more optional.

However, when these various criteria, widely used in discussions about medical treatment, are carefully examined, most of them are not morally relevant in distinguishing optional from obligatory medical treatments. For example, if a rare, complex, artificial, and invasive treatment offers a patient a reasonable chance of nearly painless cure, then one would have to offer a substantial justification not to provide that treatment to an incompetent patient.

What matters, then, in determining whether to provide a treatment to a competent patient is not a prior determination that this treatment is "ordinary" per se, but rather a determination that the treatment is likely to provide this patient benefits that are sufficient to make it worthwhile to endure the burdens that accompany the treatment. To this end, some of the considerations listed above are irrelevant: whether a treatment is likely to succeed is an obvious example. But such considerations taken in isolation are inconclusive. Rather, the surrogate decision maker is obliged to assess the desirability to this patient of each of the options presented, including nontreatment. For most people at most times, this assessment would lead to a clear obligation to provide food and fluids.

But sometimes, as we have indicated, providing food and fluids through medical interventions may fail to benefit and may even harm some patients. Then the treatment cannot be said to be obligatory, no matter how usual and simple its provisions may be. If "ordinary" and "extraordinary" are used to convey the conclusion about the obligation to treat, providing nutrition and fluids would have become, in these cases, "extraordinary." Since this phrasing is misleading, it is probably better to use "proportionate" and "disproportionate," as the Vatican now suggests,[6] or "obligatory" and "optional."

Obviously, providing nutrition and hydration may sometimes be necessary to keep patients comfortable while they are dying even though it may temporarily prolong their dying. In such cases, food and fluids constitute warranted palliative care. But in other cases, such as a patient in a deep and irreversible coma, nutrition and hydration do not appear to be needed or helpful, except perhaps to comfort the state and family.[7] And sometimes the interventions needed for nutrition and hydration are so burdensome that they are harmful and best not utilized.

The Obligation to Continue Treatments Once Started. Once having started a mode of treatment, many caregivers find it very difficult to discontinue it. While this strongly felt difference between the ease of withholding a treatment and the difficulty of withdrawing it provides a psychological explanation of certain actions, it does not justify them. It sometimes even leads to a thoroughly irrational decision process. For example, in caring for a dying, comatose patient, many physicians apparently find it harder to stop a functioning peripheral IV than not to restart one that has infiltrated (that is, has broken through the blood vessel and is leaking fluid into surrounding tissue), especially if the only way to reestablish an IV would be to insert a central line into the heart or to do a cutdown (make an incision to gain access to the deep large blood vessels).[8]

What factors might make withdrawing medical treatment morally worse than withholding it? Withdrawing a treatment seems to be an action, which, when it is likely to end in death, initially seems more serious than an omission that ends in death. However, this view is fraught with errors. Withdrawing is not always an act: failing to put the next infusion into a tube could be correctly described as an omission, for example. Even when withdrawing is an act, it may well be morally correct and even morally obligatory. Discontinuing intravenous lines in a patient now permanently unconscious in accord with that patient's well-informed advance directive would certainly be such a case. Furthermore, the caregiver's obligation to serve the patient's interests through both acts and omissions rules out the exculpation that accompanies omissions in the usual course of social life. An omission that is not warranted by the patient's interests is culpable.

Sometimes initiating a treatment creates expectations in the minds of caregivers, patients, and family that the treatment will be continued indefinitely or until the patient is cured. Such expectations may provide a reason to continue the treatment as a way to keep a promise. However, as with all promises, caregivers could be very careful when initiating a treatment to explain the indications for its discontinuation, and they could modify preconceptions with continuing reevaluation and education during treatment. Though all patients are entitled to expect the continuation of care in the patient's best interests, they are not and should not be entitled to the continuation of a particular mode of care.

Accepting the distinction between withholding and withdrawing medical treatment as morally significant also has a very unfortunate implication: caregivers may become unduly reluctant to begin some treatments precisely because they fear that they will be locked into continuing treatments that are no longer of value to the patient. For example, the physician who had been unwilling to stop the respirator while the infant, Andrew Stinson, died over several months is reportedly "less eager to attach babies to respirators now." But if it were easier to ignore malnutrition and dehydration and to withhold treatments for these problems than to discontinue the same treatments when they have become especially burdensome and insufficiently beneficial for this patient, then the incentives would be perverse. Once a treatment has been tried, it is often much clearer whether it is of value to this patient, and the decision to stop it can be made more reliably.

The same considerations should apply to starting as to stopping a treatment, and whatever assessment warrants withholding should also warrant withdrawing.

The Obligation to Avoid Being the Unambiguous Cause of Death. Many physicians will agree with all that we have said and still refuse to allow a choice to forego food and fluid because such a course seems to be a "death sentence." In this view death seems to be more certain from malnutrition and dehydration than from foregoing other forms of medical therapy. This implies that it is acceptable to act in ways that are likely to cause death, as in not operating on a gangrenous leg, only if there remains a chance that the patient will survive. This is a comforting formulation for caregivers, to be sure, since they can thereby avoid feeling the full weight of the responsibility for the time and manner of a patient's death. However, it is not a persuasive moral argument.

First, in appropriate cases discontinuing certain medical treatments is generally accepted despite the fact that death is as certain as with nonfeeding. Dialysis in a patient without kidney function or transfusions in a patient with severe aplastic anemia are obvious examples. The dying that awaits such patients often is not greatly different from dying of dehydration and malnutrition.

Second, the certainty of a generally undesirable outcome such as death is always relevant to a decision, but it does not foreclose the possibility that this course is better than others available to this patient.[10] Ambiguity and uncertainty are so common in medical decision making that caregivers are tempted to use them in distancing themselves from direct responsibility. However, caregivers are in fact responsible for the time and manner of death for many patients. Their distaste for this fact should not constrain otherwise morally justified decisions.

The Obligation to Provide Symbolically Significant Treatment. One of the most common arguments for always providing nutrition and hydration is that it symbolizes, expresses, or conveys the essence of care and compassion. Some actions not only aim at goals, they also express values. Such expressive actions should not simply be viewed as means to ends; they should also be viewed in light of what they communicate. From this perspective food and water are not only goods that preserve life and provide comfort; they are also symbols of care and compassion. To withhold or withdraw them—to "starve" a patient—can never express or convey care.

Why is providing food and water a central symbol of care and compassion? Feeding is the first response of the community to the needs of newborns and remains a central mode of nurture and comfort. Eating is associated with social interchange and community, and providing food for someone else is a way to create and maintain bonds of sharing and expressing concern. Furthermore, even the relatively low levels of hunger and thirst that most people have experienced are decidedly uncomfortable, and the common image of severe malnutrition or dehydration is one of unremitting agony. Thus, people are rightly eager to provide food and water. Such provision is essential to minimally tolerable existence and a powerful symbol of our concern for each other.

However, *medical* nutrition and hydration, we have argued, may not always provide net benefits to patients. Medical procedures to provide nutrition and hydration are more similar to other medical procedures than to typical human ways of providing nutrition and hydration, for example, a sip of water. It should be possible to evaluate their benefits and burdens, as we evaluate any other medical procedure. Of course, if family, friends, and caregivers feel that such procedures affirm important values even when they do not benefit the patient, their feelings should not be ignored. We do not contend that there is an obligation to withhold or to withdraw such procedures (unless consideration of the patient's advance directives or current best interest unambiguously dictates that conclusion); we only contend that nutrition and hydration may be foregone in some cases.

The symbolic connection between care and nutrition or hydration adds useful caution to decision making. If decision makers worry over withholding or withdrawing medical nutrition and hydration, they may inquire more seriously into the circumstances that putatively justify their decisions. This is generally salutary for health care decision making. The critical inquiry may well yield the sad but justified conclusion that the patient will be served best by not using medical procedures to provide food and fluids.

ACKNOWLEDGMENTS

We are grateful to Haavi Morreim and Steven DalleMura for their helpful comments on an earlier version of this paper. We are also grateful for the instruction provided Dr. Lynn by the staff and patients of The Washington Home and its Hospice.

REFERENCES

1. See e.g., the President's Commission for the Study of Ethical Problems in Medicine and Biomedical and Behavioral Research, *Making Health Care Decisions* (Washington, D.C.: Government Printing Office, 1982).
2. President's Commission, *Deciding to Forego Life-Sustaining Treatment*, pp. 171–96.
3. Joyce V. Zerwekh, "The Dehydration Question," *Nursing83* (January 1983), 47–51, with comments by Judith R. Brown and Marion B. Dolan.
4. James J. McCartney, "The Development of the Doctrine of Ordinary and Extraordinary Means of Preserving Life in Catholic Moral Theology before the Karen Quinlan Case," *Linacre Quarterly* 47 (1980), 215ff.
5. President's Commission, *Deciding to Forego Life-Sustaining Treatment*, pp. 82–90. For an argument that fluids and electrolytes can be "extraordinary," see Carson Strong, "Can Fluids and Electrolytes be 'Extraordinary' Treatment?" *Journal of Medical Ethics* 7 (1981), 83–85.
6. The Sacred Congregation for the Doctrine of the Faith, *Declaration on Euthanasia*, Vatican City, May 5, 1980.
7. Paul Ramsey contends that "when a man is irreversibly in the process of dying, to feed him and to give him drink, to ease him and keep him comfortable—these are no longer given as means of preserving life. The use of a glucose drip should often be understood in this way. This keeps a patient who cannot swallow from feeling dehydrated and is often the only remaining 'means' by which we can express our

present faithfulness to him during his dying." Ramsey, *The Patient as Person* (New Haven: Yale University Press, 1970), pp. 128–29. But Ramsey's suggestion would not apply to a patient in a deep irreversible coma, and he would be willing to disconnect the IV in the Quinlan case; see Ramsey, *Ethics at the Edges of Life: Medical and Legal Intersections* (New Haven: Yale University Press, 1978), p. 275. Bernard Towers describes an appropriate approach to comfort and dignity: "When a patient is conscious to even the smallest degree, and if he appears to be thirsty and to have a swallowing reflex, and if there is no contraindication to oral fluids, his comfort and dignity would surely demand that he be given nourishing liquids, or at least water. If he lapses into coma, good nursing practice has traditionally required sponging out the mouth and moistening the lips. Now, if he lapses into deep coma and is on a dying trajectory, would we then try to 'push' fluids by mouth or nasogastric tube? If we did, dignity would surely suffer. The 'comfort' of the patient would, of course, be unaffected if the coma were deep enough and irreversible." Towers, "Irreversible Coma and Withdrawal of Life Support: Is It Murder If the IV Line Is Disconnected?" *Journal of Medical Ethics* 8 (1982), 205.

8. See Kenneth C. Micetich, Patricia H. Steinecker, and David C. Thomasma, "Are Intravenous Fluids Morally Required for a Dying Patient?" *Archives of Internal Medicine* 143 (May 1983), 975–78.

9. Robert and Peggy Stinson, *The Long Dying of Baby Andrew* (Boston: Little, Brown and Company, 1983), p. 355.

10. A recent article discussed a hypothetical case of maintaining a dying, comatose patient on a respirator while withdrawing IV fluids. The authors contend that this approach is not ironic because withdrawal of the respirator "creates the immediate consequence of death for which we must take responsibility. It represents an extreme form of abandonment." Nevertheless, they were willing to stop IV fluids, knowing that death would occur before long. As the article's survey reported, other physicians would have provided nutrition and fluids. See Micetich, Steinecker, and Thomasma, "Are Intravenous Fluids Morally Required for a Dying Patient?"

NO

Gilbert Meilaender

ON REMOVING FOOD AND WATER: AGAINST THE STREAM

As infants we were given food and drink when we were too helpless to nourish ourselves. And for many of us a day will come before we die when we are once again too helpless to feed ourselves. If there is any way in which the living can stand by those who are not yet dead, it would seem to be through the continued provision of food and drink even when the struggle against disease has been lost. To continue to nourish the life of one who has been defeated in that battle is the last evidence we can offer that we are more than frontrunners, that we are willing to love to the very point of death.

Today this intuitive reaction is being challenged. The President's Commission for the Study of Ethical Problems in Medicine and Biomedical and Behavioral Research has suggested that for patients with permanent loss of consciousness artificial feeding interventions need not be continued.[1] A group of physicians writing in the *New England Journal of Medicine* has counseled doctors that for irreversibly ill patients whose condition warrants nothing more aggressive than general nursing care, "naturally or artificially administered hydration and nutrition may be given or withheld, depending on the patient's comfort."[2]

Court decisions ... are contradictory,[3] but a consensus is gradually building toward the day when what we have already done in the case of some nondying infants with birth defects who were "allowed to die" by not being fed will become standard "treatment" for all patients who are permanently unconscious or suffering from severe and irreversible dementia. Those who defend this view stand ready with ethical arguments that nutrition and hydration are not "in the best interests" of such patients, but Daniel Callahan may have isolated the energizing force that is driving this consensus: "A denial of nutrition," he says, "may in the long run become the only effective way to make certain that a large number of biologically tenacious patients actually die."[4]

To the degree that this is true, however, the policy toward which we are moving is not merely one of "allowing to die": it is one of aiming to kill. *If* we are in fact heading in this direction, we should turn back before this policy

From Gilbert Meilaender, "On Removing Food and Water: Against the Stream," *Hastings Center Report*, vol. 14, no. 6 (December 1984). Copyright © 1984 by The Hastings Center. Reprinted by permission.

corrupts our intellect and emotions and our capacity for moral reasoning. That stance I take to be a given, for which I shall not attempt to argue. Here I will consider only whether removal of artificial nutrition and hydration really does amount to no more than "allowing to die."

WHY FEEDING IS NOT MEDICAL CARE

The argument for ceasing to feed seems strongest in cases of people suffering from a "persistent vegetative state," those (like Karen Quinlan) who have suffered an irreversible loss of consciousness. Sidney Wanzer and his physician colleagues suggest that in such circumstances "it is morally justifiable to withhold antibiotics and artificial nutrition and hydration, as well as other forms of life-sustaining treatment, allowing the patient to die." The President's Commission advises: "Since permanently unconscious patients will never be aware of nutrition, the only benefit to the patient of providing such increasingly burdensome interventions is sustaining the body to allow for a remote possibility of recovery. The sensitivities of the family and of care giving professionals ought to determine whether such interventions are made." Joanne Lynn, a physician at George Washington University, and James Childress, a professor of religious studies at the University of Virginia, believe that "in these cases, it is very difficult to discern how any medical intervention can benefit or harm the patient."[5] But we need to ask whether the physicians are right to suggest that they seek only to allow the patient to die; whether the President's Commission has used language carefully enough in saying that nutri-

tion and hydration of such persons is merely sustaining a *body*; whether Lynn and Childress may too readily have assumed that providing food and drink is *medical* treatment.

Should the provision of food and drink be regarded as *medical* care? It seems, rather, to be the sort of care that all human beings owe each other. All living beings need food and water in order to live, but such nourishment does not itself heal or cure disease. When we stop feeding the permanently unconscious patient, we are not withdrawing from the battle against any illness or disease; we are withholding the nourishment that sustains all life.

The President's Commission does suggest that certain kinds of care remain mandatory for the permanently unconscious patient: "The awkward posture and lack of motion of unconscious patients often lead to pressure sores, and skin lesions are a major complication. Treatment and prevention of these problems is standard nursing care and should be provided." Yet it is hard to see why such services (turning the person regularly, giving alcohol rubs, and the like) are standard nursing care when feeding is not. Moreover, if feeding cannot benefit these patients, it is far from clear how they could experience bed sores as harm.

If this is true, we may have good reason to question whether the withdrawal of nutrition and hydration in such cases is properly characterized as stopping medical treatment in order to allow a patient to die. There are circumstances in which a plausible and helpful distinction can be made between killing and allowing to die, between an aim and a foreseen but unintended consequence. And sometimes it may make excellent moral sense to hold that we should cease to provide a now useless treatment, foreseeing but not intending that death will result. Such reasoning is also useful in the ethics of warfare, but there its use must be strictly controlled lest we simply unleash the bombs while "directing our intention" to a military target that could be attacked with far less firepower. Careful use of language is also necessary lest we talk about unconscious patients in ways that obscure our true aim.

Challenging those who have argued that it is no longer possible to distinguish between combatants and noncombatants in war, Michael Walzer has pointed out that "the relevant distinction is not between those who work for the war effort and those who do not, but between those who make what soldiers need to fight and those who make what they need to live, like the rest of us."[6]

Hence, farmers are not legitimate targets in war simply because they grow the food that soldiers need to live (and then to fight). The soldiers would need the food to live, even if there were no war. Thus, as Paul Ramsey has observed, though an army may march upon its belly, bellies are not the target. It is an abuse of double-effect reasoning to justify cutting off the food supply of a nation as a way of stopping its soldiers. We could not properly say that we were aiming at the soldiers while merely foreseeing the deaths of the civilian population.

Nor can we, when withdrawing food from the permanently unconscious person, properly claim that our intention is to cease useless treatment for a dying patient. These patients are not dying, and we cease no treatment aimed at disease; rather, we withdraw the nourishment that sustains all human beings whether healthy or ill, and we do so when the only result of our action can be death.

At what, other than that death, could we be aiming?

One might argue that the same could be said of turning off a respirator, but the situations are somewhat different. Remove a person from a respirator and he may die—but, then, he may also surprise us and continue to breathe spontaneously. We test to see if the patient can breathe. If he does, it is not our task—unless we are aiming at his death—now to smother him (or to stop feeding him). But deprive a person of food and water and she will die as surely as if we had administered a lethal drug, and it is hard to claim that we did not aim at her death.

I am unable—and this is a lack of insight, not of space—to say more about the analogy between eating and breathing. Clearly, air is as essential to life as food. We might wonder, therefore, whether provision of air is not also more than medical treatment. What justification could there be, then for turning off a respirator? If the person's death, due to the progress of a disease, is irreversibly and imminently at hand, then continued assistance with respiration may now be useless. But if the person is not going to die from any disease but, instead, simply needs assistance with breathing because of some injury, it is less clear to me why such assistance should not be given. More than this I am unable to say. I repeat, however, that to remove a respirator is not necessarily to aim at death; one will not go on to kill the patient who manages to breathe spontaneously. But it is difficult for me to construe removal of nutrition for permanently unconscious patients in any other way. Perhaps we only wish them dead or think they would be better off dead. There are circumstances in which such a thought is understandable.

But it would still be wrong to enact that wish by aiming at their death.

SEPARATING PERSONHOOD AND BODY

Suppose that we accept the view that provision of food and water is properly termed medical treatment. Is there good reason to withhold this treatment from permanently unconscious patients? A treatment refusal needs to be justified either on the ground that the treatment is (or has now become) useless, or that the treatment (though perhaps still useful) is excessively burdensome for the patient. Still taking as our focus the permanently unconscious patient, we can consider, first, whether feeding is useless. There could be occasions on which artificial feeding would be futile. Lynn and Childress offer instances of patients who simply cannot be fed effectively, but they are not cases of permanently unconscious patients.

Yet for many people the uselessness of feeding the permanently unconscious seems self-evident. Why? Probably because they suppose that the nourishment we provide is, in the words of the President's Commission, doing no more than "sustaining the body." But we should pause before separating personhood and body so decisively. When considering other topics (care of the environment, for example) we are eager to criticize a dualism that divorces human reason and consciousness from the larger world of nature. Why not here? We can know people—of all ranges of cognitive capacity —only as they are embodied; there is no other "person" for whom we might care. Such care is not useless if it "only" preserves bodily life but does not restore cognitive capacities. Even if it is less than we

wish could be accomplished, it remains care for the embodied person.

Some will object to characterizing as persons those who lack the capacity or, even, the potential for self-awareness, for envisioning a future for themselves, for relating to other selves. I am not fully persuaded that speaking of "persons" in such contexts is mistaken, but the point can be made without using that language. Human nature has a capacity to know, to be self-aware, and to relate to others. We can share in that human nature even though we may not yet or no longer exercise all the functions of which it is capable. We share in it simply by virtue of being born into the human species. We could describe as persons all individuals sharing our common nature, all members of the species. Or we could ascribe personhood only to those human beings presently capable of exercising the characteristic human functions.

I think it better—primarily because it is far less dualistic—to understand personhood as an endowment that comes with our nature, even if at some stages of life we are unable to exercise characteristic human capacities. But the point can be made, if anyone wishes, by talking of embodied human beings rather than embodied persons. To be a human being one need not presently be exercising or be capable of exercising the functions characteristic of consciousness. Those are capacities of human nature; they are not functions that all human beings exercise. It is human beings, not just persons in that more restricted sense, whose death should not be our aim. And if this view is characterized as an objectionable "speciesism," I can only reply that at least it is not one more way by which the strong and gifted in our world rid themselves of the weak, and it does not fall prey to that abstraction by which we reify consciousness and separate it from the body.

The permanently unconscious are not dying subjects who should simply be allowed to die. But they will, of course, die if we aim at their death by ceasing to feed them. If we are not going to feed them because that would be nothing more than sustaining a body, why not bury them at once? No one, I think, recommends that. But if, then, they are still living beings who ought not be buried, the nourishment that all human beings need to live ought not be denied them. When we permit ourselves to think that care is useless if it preserves the life of the embodied human being without restoring cognitive capacity, we fall victim to the old delusion that we have failed if we cannot *cure* and that there is, then, little point to continued *care*. David Smith, a professor of religious studies at the University of Indiana, has suggested that I might be mistaken in describing the comatose person as a "nondying" patient. At least in some cases, he believes lapsing into permanent coma might be a sign that a person is trying to die. Thus, though a comatose state would not itself be sufficient reason to characterize someone as dying, it might be one of several conditions which, taken together, would be sufficient. This is a reasonable suggestion, and it might enable us to distinguish different sorts of comatose patients—the dying, for whom feeding might be useless; the nondying, for whom it would not. Even then, however, I would still be troubled by the worry I raised earlier: whether food and drink are really medical treatment that should be withdrawn when it becomes useless.

Even when care is not useless it may be so burdensome that it should be dispensed with. When that is the case, we can honestly say—and it makes good moral sense to say—that our aim is to relieve the person of a burden, with the foreseen but unintended effect of a hastened death. We should note, however, that this line of argument *cannot* be applied to the cases of the permanently unconscious. Other patients—those, for example, with fairly severe dementia—may be made afraid and uncomfortable by artificial nutrition and hydration. But this can hardly be true of the permanently unconscious. It seems unlikely that they experience the care involved in feeding them as burdensome.

Even for severely demented patients who retain some consciousness, we should be certain that we are considering the burden of the treatment, not the burden of continued existence itself.... That is a judgment, I think, that no one should make for another; indeed, it is hard to know exactly how one would do so. Besides, it seems evident that if the burden involved is her continued life, the point of ceasing to feed is that we aim at relieving her of that burden—that is, we aim to kill.

Having said that, I am quite ready to grant that the burden of the feeding itself may sometimes be so excessive that it is not warranted. Lynn and Childress offer examples, some of which seem persuasive. If, however, we want to assess the burden of the treatment, we should certainly not dispense with nutrition and hydration until a reasonable trial period has demonstrated that the person truly finds such care excessively burdensome.

In short, if we focus our attention on irreversibly ill adults for whom general nursing care but no more seems appropriate, we can say the following: First, when the person is permanently unconscious, the care involved in feeding can hardly be experienced as burdensome. Neither can such care be described as useless, since it preserves the life of the embodied human being (who is not a dying patient). Second, when the person is conscious but severely and irreversibly demented, the care involved in feeding, though not useless, *may* be so burdensome that it should cease. This requires demonstration during a trial period, however, and the judgment is quite different from concluding that the person's life has become too burdensome to preserve. Third, for both sorts of patients the care involved in feeding is not, in any strict sense, medical treatment, even if provided in a hospital. It gives what all need to live; it is treatment of no particular disease; and its cessation means certain death, a death at which we can only be said to aim, whatever our motive.

That we should continue to feed the permanently unconscious still seems obvious to some people, even as it was to Karen Quinlan's father at the time he sought removal of her respirator. It has not always seemed so to me, but it does now. For the permanently unconscious person, feeding is neither useless nor excessively burdensome. It is ordinary human care and is not given as treatment for any life-threatening disease. Since this is true, a decision not to offer such care can enact only one intention: to take the life of the unconscious person.

I have offered no arguments here to prove that such a life-taking intention and aim would be morally wrong, though I believe it is and that to embrace such an aim would be corrupting. If we can face the fact that withdrawing the nourishment of such persons is, indeed, aiming to kill, I am hopeful (though not altogether confident) that the more fundamental principle will not need to be argued. Let us hope that this is the case, since that more basic principle is not one that can be argued *to;* rather, all useful moral arguments must proceed *from* the conviction that it is wrong to aim to kill the innocent.

REFERENCES

1. The President's Commission for the Study of Ethical Problems in Medicine and Biomedical and Behavioral Research, *Deciding to Forego Life-Sustaining Treatment* (Washington, DC: Government Printing Office, 1982), p. 190.
2. Sidney H. Wanzer, M.D., et al., "The Physician's Responsibility Toward Hopelessly Ill Patients," *New England Journal of Medicine*, 310 (April 12, 1984) 958.
3. See a discussion of the first two cases in Bonnie Steinbock, "The Removal of Mr. Herbert's Feeding Tube," *Hastings Center Report*, 13 (October 1983) 13–16; also see George J. Annas, "The Case of Mary Hier: When Substituted Judgment Becomes Sleight of Hand," *Hastings Center Report* 14 (August 1984), 23–25.
4. Daniel Callahan, "On Feeding the Dying," *Hastings Center Report*, 13 (October 1983) 22.
5. Joanne Lynn and James Childress, "Must Patients Always Be Given Food and Water?" *Hastings Center Report*, 13 (October 1983) 18.
6. Michael Walzer, *Just and Unjust Wars* (New York: Basic Books, Inc., 1977), p. 146.

POSTSCRIPT

Is It Ever Morally Right to Withhold Food and Water from Dying Patients?

In November 1990, four months after the Supreme Court *Cruzan* decision, Nancy Cruzan's parents went back to court with new witnesses who testified that Nancy had clearly indicated that she would not want to live in a vegetative state. The state of Missouri, which had opposed the parents' decision to withdraw her feeding tube, asked to be dismissed from the case, satisified that guidelines were established to protect the patient's interests.

Following the *Cruzan* decision, a Florida Supreme Court ruled that dying people had a right to refuse food and that guardians could make the decision for incompetent people. The case they considered involved Estelle Browning, an elderly woman who spent the last two and a half years of her life in a nursing home fed by tube even though she had signed a "living will" affirming that she did not want to be kept alive under these circumstances.

A study of terminally ill patients found that administering food and fluids beyond the patients' specific requests may play a minimal role in providing comfort care. The authors concluded that artificial feeding is often initiated to alleviate concerns of families but that it does not reduce suffering (see Robert M. McCann et al., "Comfort Care for Terminally Ill Patients," *Journal of the American Medical Association*, October 26, 1994). In "A Conversation With My Mother," *Journal of the American Medical Association* (July 20, 1994), Dr. David Eddy describes his elderly mother's "happy" death when she decided to forgo continuing medical treatment and to stop eating.

Considerations of the removal of food and water from a dying patient are part of the more general issue of advance directives, commonly called "living wills." In December 1991 the federal Patient Self-Determination Act (PSDA) went into effect, requiring health care providers in facilities receiving Medicare or Medicaid to inform competent patients of their existing rights under state law to refuse treatments and to prepare advance directives. Although most commentators favor the use of advance directives, some are concerned about their implementation. See, for example, John A. Robertson, "Second Thought on Living Wills," *Hastings Center Report* (November/December 1991). "Practicing the PSDA," a *Hastings Center Report* special supplement (September/October 1991), presents several views on the PSDA. Joan M. Teno et al. report that a relatively minor provision of the PSDA has had a positive impact in "The Impact of the Patient Self-Determination Act's Requirement That States Describe Law Concerning Patient's Rights," *Journal of Law, Medicine and Ethics* (Spring 1993).

PART 3

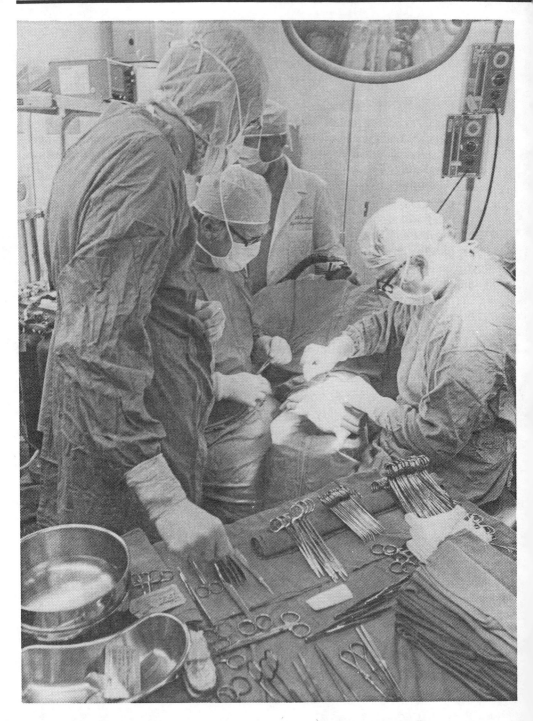

The Doctor-Patient Relationship

While the most publicized issues in bioethics concern dramatic, life-and-death decisions or the uses of high-technology medicine, the ordinary encounters between doctors and patients also create ethical dilemmas. The relationships between patients and practitioners are often unequal, with physicians controlling the terms. Nevertheless, physicians are obligated to serve their patients' interests. In most cases both parties share an understanding of the patient's needs and the most appropriate ways to meet them. Sometimes, however, conflicts arise, and physicians are forced to choose between their patients' interests and their own or others' interests. The issues in this section confront some of these situations.

- Are There Limits to Confidentiality?
- Is It Ethical to Treat Short Children With Human Growth Hormone?
- Should HIV-Infected Surgeons Be Allowed to Operate?
- Should Doctors Be Able to Refuse Demands for "Futile" Treatment?

145

ISSUE 8

Are There Limits to Confidentiality?

YES: Mark Siegler, from "Confidentiality in Medicine: A Decrepit Concept," *The New England Journal of Medicine* (December 9, 1982)

NO: Michael H. Kottow, from "Medical Confidentiality: An Intransigent and Absolute Obligation," *Journal of Medical Ethics* (vol. 12, 1986)

ISSUE SUMMARY

YES: Physician Mark Siegler argues that confidentiality is necessarily compromised in order to ensure complete and proper medical treatment.

NO: Physician Michael H. Kottow argues that any kind of breach of patient confidentiality causes harms that are more serious than hypothetical benefits.

"If I tell you a secret, will you promise not to tell anyone?" This simple question, familiar from childhood, captures two important features of human relationships: the need to confide one's fears and hopes to another person and the need to trust that person not to reveal the secret. If the person who receives the confidence agrees not to reveal it, he or she has made a promise. All ethical systems place a high value on promise keeping.

When this exchange occurs in a professional relationship—between patient and physician or therapist, client and attorney, or priest and confessor—there is even more at stake. The professional, as part of achieving that status, has accepted an ethical code that states that confidentiality will be maintained. One of the earliest formulations of this concept is found in the Hippocratic Oath, which is still sworn to by all physicians: "What I may see or hear in the course of the treatment or even outside of the treatment in regard to the life of men, which on no account one must spread abroad, I will keep to myself." More recently numerous codes of professional ethics, such as those of the American Medical Association, have reaffirmed the principle of medical confidentiality. The traditions of religious ethics and the patients' rights movement have also strongly supported medical confidentiality.

But no value is absolute, and some exceptions to the rule of confidentiality are well established. For example, considerations of public health underlie laws that require physicians to report certain contagious diseases such as syphilis, measles, meningitis, and (most recently) acquired immunodeficiency syndrome (AIDS). Similarly, a physician must report cases of gunshot wounds to the authorities, since a crime may have been committed. Physicians and social workers are required by law to report suspected cases of child abuse, so that a child who is being harmed physically or mentally can be protected.

In recent years two situations have raised questions about the limits of confidentiality. As Sissela Bok, a philosopher who has written extensively on secrets, puts it: "Does a professional owe confidentiality to clients who reveal plans or acts that endanger others directly?" The question, she says, arises equally for the lawyer whose client lets it be known that he plans a bank robbery, for the pediatrician who suspects that a mother drugs her children to keep them quiet, and for the psychiatrist whose patient reveals his violent jealousy of his wife. This last situation arose in the celebrated case of Tatiana Tarasoff, a student who was killed by a suitor she had spurned after he told a psychiatrist of his plans. The legal resolution of the case in 1976 resulted in the establishment of a "duty to protect" on the part of therapists in the state of California.

Another challenge to confidentiality arises when a person with AIDS or infection with the human immunodeficiency virus (HIV) refuses to inform his or her sexual partner of the potential risk of transmission. Is the physician or other professional who knows of this situation obligated to protect the third party and, by so doing, breach his or her primary obligation to maintain the confidentiality of the patient?

The following two selections provide the context for discussing these specific instances. Although Mark Siegler believes that confidentiality can be defended as a principle, in modern medical practice it is a matter of expediency and has inherent limits. Michael H. Kottow takes a strong stand in favor of absolute adherence to confidentiality. Confidentiality, he says, is a "brittle arrangement" that disintegrates if misdirected to pursue other goals.

YES

Mark Siegler

CONFIDENTIALITY IN MEDICINE: A DECREPIT CONCEPT

Medical confidentiality, as it has traditionally been understood by patients and doctors, no longer exists. This ancient medical principle, which has been included in every physician's oath and code of ethics since Hippocratic times, has become old, worn-out, and useless; it is a decrepit concept. Efforts to preserve it appear doomed to failure and often give rise to more problems than solutions. Psychiatrists have tacitly acknowledged the impossibility of ensuring the confidentiality of medical records by choosing to establish a separate, more secret record. The following case illustrates how the confidentiality principle is compromised systematically in the course of routine medical care.

A patient of mine . . . was transferred from the surgical intensive-care unit to a surgical nursing floor two days after . . . elective [surgery]. On the day of transfer, the patient saw a respiratory therapist writing in his medical chart . . . and became concerned about the confidentiality of his hospital records. The patient threatened to leave the hospital prematurely unless I could guarantee that the confidentiality of his hospital record would be respected.

This patient's complaint prompted me to enumerate the number of persons who had both access to his hospital record and a reason to examine it. I was amazed to learn that at least 25 and possibly as many as 100 health professionals and administrative personnel at our university hospital had access to the patient's record and that all of them had a legitimate need, indeed a professional responsibility, to open and use that chart. These persons included 6 attending physicians (the primary physician, the surgeon, the pulmonary consultant, and others); 12 house officers (medical, surgical, intensive-care unit, and "covering" house staff); 20 nursing personnel (on three shifts); 6 respiratory therapists; 3 nutritionists; 2 clinical pharmacists; 15 students (from medicine, nursing, respiratory therapy, and clinical pharmacy); 4 unit secretaries; 4 hospital financial officers; and 4 chart reviewers (utilization review, quality assurance review, tissue review, and insurance

From Mark Siegler, "Confidentiality in Medicine: A Decrepit Concept," *The New England Journal of Medicine*, vol. 307, no. 24 (December 9, 1982), pp. 1518–1521. Copyright © 1982 by The Massachusetts Medical Society. Reprinted by permission.

auditor). It is of interest that this patient's problem was straightforward, and he therefore did not require many other technical and support services that the modern hospital provides. For example, he did not need multiple consultants and fellows, such specialized procedures as dialysis, or social workers, chaplains, physical therapists, occupational therapists, and the like.

Upon completing my survey I reported to the patient that I estimated that at least 75 health professionals and hospital personnel had access to his medical record. I suggested to the patient that these people were all involved in providing or supporting his health-care services. They were, I assured him, working for him. Despite my reassurances the patient was obviously distressed and retorted, "I always believed that medical confidentiality was part of a doctor's code of ethics. Perhaps you should tell me just what you people mean by 'confidentiality'!"

TWO ASPECTS OF MEDICAL CONFIDENTIALITY

Confidentiality and Third-Party Interests

Previous discussions of medical confidentiality usually have focused on the tension between a physician's responsibility to keep information divulged by patients secret and a physician's legal and moral duty, on occasion, to reveal such confidences to third parties, such as families, employers, public-health authorities, or police authorities. In all these instances, the central question relates to the stringency of the physician's obligation to maintain patient confidentiality when the health, well-being, and safety of identifiable others or of society in general would be threatened by a failure to reveal information about the patient. The tension in such cases is between the good of the patient and the good of others.

Confidentiality and the Patient's Interest

As the example above illustrates, further challenges to confidentiality arise because the patient's personal interest in maintaining confidentiality comes into conflict with his personal interest in receiving the best possible health care. Modern high-technology health care is available principally in hospitals (often, teaching hospitals), requires many trained and specialized workers (a "health-care team"), and is very costly. The existence of such teams means that information that previously had been held in confidence by an individual physician will now necessarily be disseminated to many members of the team. Furthermore, since health-care teams are expensive and few patients can afford to pay such costs directly, it becomes essential to grant access to the patient's medical record to persons who are responsible for obtaining third-party payment. These persons include chart reviewers, financial officers, insurance auditors, and quality-of-care assessors. Finally, as medicine expands from a narrow, disease-based model to a model that encompasses psychological, social, and economic problems, not only will the size of the health-care team and medical costs increase, but more sensitive information (such as one's personal habits and financial condition) will now be included in the medical record and will no longer be confidential.

The point I wish to establish is that hospital medicine, the rise of health-care teams, the existence of third-party insurance programs, and the expanding limits of medicine all appear to be responses to the wishes of people for better and more comprehensive medical care. But each of these developments necessarily modifies our traditional understanding of medical confidentiality.

THE ROLE OF CONFIDENTIALITY IN MEDICINE

Confidentiality serves a dual purpose in medicine. In the first place, it acknowledges respect for the patient's sense of individuality and privacy. The patient's most personal physical and psychological secrets are kept confidential in order to decrease a sense of shame and vulnerability. Secondly, confidentiality is important in improving the patient's health care —a basic goal of medicine. The promise of confidentiality permits people to trust (i.e., have confidence) that information revealed to a physician in the course of a medical encounter will not be disseminated further. In this way patients are encouraged to communicate honestly and forthrightly with their doctors. This bond of trust between patient and doctor is vitally important both in the diagnostic process (which relies on an accurate history) and subsequently in the treatment phase, which often depends as much on the patient's trust in the physician as it does on medications and surgery. These two important functions of confidentiality are as important now as they were in the past. They will not be supplanted entirely either by improvements in medical technology or by recent changes in relations between some patients and doctors toward a rights-based, consumerist model.

POSSIBLE SOLUTIONS TO THE CONFIDENTIALITY PROBLEM

First of all, in all nonbureaucratic, noninstitutional medical encounters— that is, in the millions of doctor-patient encounters that take place in physicians' offices, where more privacy can be preserved—meticulous care should be taken to guarantee that patients' medical and personal information will be kept confidential.

Secondly, in such settings as hospitals or large-scale group practices, where many persons have opportunities to examine the medical record, we should aim to provide access only to those who have "a need to know." This could be accomplished through such administrative changes as dividing the entire record into several sections—for example, a medical and financial section—and permitting only health professionals access to the medical information.

The approach favored by many psychiatrists—that of keeping a psychiatric record separate from the general medical record—is an understandable strategy but one that is not entirely satisfactory and that should not be generalized. The keeping of separate psychiatric records implies that psychiatry and medicine are different undertakings and thus drives deeper the wedge between them and between physical and psychological illness. Furthermore, it is often vitally important for internists or surgeons to know that a patient is being seen by a psychiatrist or is taking a particular medication. When separate records are kept, this information may not be available. Finally, if generalized, the practice of keeping a separate psychiatric record could lead to the unacceptable consequence of having a separate record for each type of medical problem.

Patients should be informed about what is meant by "medical confidentiality." We should establish the distinction between information about the patient that generally will be kept confidential regardless of the interest of third parties and information that will be exchanged among members of the health-care team in order to provide care for the patient. Patients should be made aware of the large number of persons in the modern hospital who require access to the medical record in order to serve the patient's medical and financial interests.

Finally, at some point most patients should have an opportunity to review their medical record and to make informed choices about whether their entire record is to be available to everyone or whether certain portions of the record are privileged and should be accessible only to their principal physician or to others designated explicitly by the patient. This approach would rely on traditional informed-consent procedural standards and might permit the patient to balance the personal value of medical confidentiality against the personal value of high-technology, team health care. There is no reason that the same procedure should not be used with psychiatric records instead of the arbitrary system now employed, in which everything related to psychiatry is kept secret.

AFTERTHOUGHT: CONFIDENTIALITY AND INDISCRETION

There is one additional aspect of confidentiality that is rarely included in discussions of the subject. I am referring here to the wanton, often inadvertent, but avoidable exchanges of confidential information that occur frequently in hospital rooms, elevators, cafeterias, doctors' offices, and at cocktail parties. Of course, as more people have access to medical information about the patient the potential for this irresponsible abuse of confidentiality increases geometrically.

Such mundane breaches of confidentiality are probably of greater concern to most patients than the broader issue of whether their medical records may be entered into a computerized data bank or whether a respiratory therapist is reviewing the results of an arterial blood gas determination. Somehow, privacy is violated and a sense of shame is heightened when intimate secrets are revealed to people one knows or is close to—friends, neighbors, acquaintances, or hospital roommates—rather than when they are disclosed to an anonymous bureaucrat sitting at a computer terminal in a distant city or to a health professional who is acting in an official capacity.

I suspect that the principles of medical confidentiality, particularly those reflected in most medical codes of ethics, were designed principally to prevent just this sort of embarrassing personal indiscretion rather than to maintain (for social, political, or economic reasons) the absolute secrecy of doctor-patient communications. In this regard, it is worth noting that Percival's Code of Medical Ethics (1803) includes the following admonition: "Patients should be interrogated concerning their complaint in a tone of voice which cannot be overheard." We in the medical profession frequently neglect these simple courtesies.

CONCLUSION

The principle of medical confidentiality described in medical codes of ethics and still believed in by patients no longer exists. In this respect, it is a decrepit concept. Rather than perpetuate the myth of confidentiality and invest energy vainly to preserve it, the public and the profession would be better served if they devoted their attention to determining which aspects of the original principle of confidentiality are worth retaining. Efforts could then be directed to salvaging those.

NO

Michael H. Kottow

MEDICAL CONFIDENTIALITY: AN INTRANSIGENT AND ABSOLUTE OBLIGATION

AUTHOR'S ABSTRACT

Clinicians' work depends on sincere and complete disclosures from their patients; they honour this candidness by confidentially safeguarding the information received. Breaching confidentiality causes harms that are not commensurable with the possible benefits gained. Limitations or exceptions put on confidentiality would destroy it, for the confider would become suspicious and un-co-operative, the confidant would become untrustworthy and the whole climate of the clinical encounter would suffer irreversible erosion. Excusing breaches of confidence on grounds of superior moral values introduces arbitrariness and ethical unreliability into the medical context. Physicians who breach the agreement of confidentiality are being unfair, thus opening the way for, and becoming vulnerable to, the morally obtuse conduct of others.

Confidentiality should not be seen as the cosy but dispensable atmosphere of clinical settings; rather, it constitutes a guarantee of fairness in medical actions. Possible perils that might accrue to society are no greater than those accepted when granting inviolable custody of information to priests, lawyers and bankers. To jeopardise the integrity of confidential medical relationships is too high a price to pay for the hypothetical benefits this might bring to the prevailing social order.

The contemporary expansion of ethics in general and medical ethics in particular harbours the danger of increasing scholasticism to the point where not even pressing practical problems are being offered workable solutions. People involved in health care may end up by distrusting the discipline of ethics, thus increasing the improbability of agreement between pragmatists and analysts (1). Even traditionally straightforward practices, such as confidentiality, have been subject to extensive review and analysis which have proved incapable of offering committed stances or unequivocal guidelines for action (2, 3). In an effort to illustrate that more stringency is desirable and possible, the status of confidentiality as an exceptionless or absolute commitment is here defended. It should be stated at the outset that I share general scepticism about absolute ethical propositions (4), and that confidentiality is here not defended as an inviolable moral value—a position that would be self-defeating—but as an interpersonal communications strategy that ceases to function unless strictly adhered to. Confidentiality is a brittle arrangement that disintegrates if misdirected in pursuance of other goals and, since it is a necessary component of medical practice, care should be taken to safeguard its integrity.

DEFINING CONFIDENTIALITY

The following definition of confidentiality is used: a situation is confidential when information revealing that harmful acts have been or possibly will be performed is consciously or voluntarily passed from one rationally competent person (confider) to another (confidant) in the understanding that this information shall not be further disclosed without the confider's explicit consent. The harm alluded to may be physical, but moral damage alone may also be the subject matter of a confidential exchange. When this sort of communication occurs in a medical setting it constitutes medical confidentiality.

WHAT IS AT ISSUE IN CONFIDENTIALITY CONFLICTS?

The main ethical controversy around confidentiality concerns the assessment of whether more harm is done by occasionally breaching confidentiality or by always respecting it regardless of the consequences. As long as the physician gathers private information, that is information that only concerns the confider and harbours no element of past or potential harm, confidentiality will concern exclusively the patient and any disclosure would be nothing but a malicious or at the very least gratuitous act of the physician, of little or no moral significance. It seems redundant to discuss other instances of confidentiality than those involving either the possibility of impending harm or testimonial of past injury, for these are the fundamental cases where dilemmas arise and a breach of confidence must seek justification.

Breaching is defended on the ground that the harm announced in the confidence is severe and can possibly only be averted by the confidant's disclosure (5, 6, 7). Exceptionless confidentiality, on the other hand, is upheld by the idea that breaching will relentlessly harm the confider, subjecting her or him to precautionary investigations and constraints of some sort, perhaps even with unavoidable defamatory consequences. The harm purportedly averted is merely potential and all the less likely to occur, the more exorbitant and preposterous the threatener's claims are. After all, excessively vicious menaces may well be uttered by psychotics who are rationally incompetent and therefore not protected by a pledge to confidentiality they can neither honour nor demand. Furthermore, the practice of confidentiality is in itself damaged by breaching because its trust-worthiness is disqualified. Ultimately, de-grees and probability of harm are so dif-ficult to assess (8), that they will hardly deliver an intersubjectively acceptable ar-gument for or against confidentiality, ex-cept for one: breaching confidentiality can not be a significant and enduring contribution against harmful actions, for these are no more than potential, whereas the damages caused to the confidant, to the practice of confidentiality and to the honesty of clinical relationships are un-avoidable.

Perhaps less elusive is the conflict of rights—and their correlative obligations —which ensue in confidential situations. Confidentiality is an agreement bound by the principle of fairness (9); it gives the confider the right to expect discre-tion whereas the confidant has the right to hear the truth, but also the obliga-tion to ensure guardianship of the in-formation received. It could be argued against this right that past victims might be vindicated or potential ones helped by divulging confidential information that seems critical, and that these victims also have a right, namely to vindication or protection. In order for the victim's right to prevail, the confider must involuntar-ily forfeit her or his right to secrecy, which the confidant will forcefully violate by divulging information against the con-fider's will. This forfeiture of the con-fider's right can only occur subsequently to the confidence, for it is triggered by the contents of the confider's disclosure. To avoid the risk of losing the right to secrecy, confiders would have to con-fide falsely or not at all, a strategy that would erode their legitimate and initially granted right to be impunibly outspoken, distort or reduce confidentiality to lies and irrelevancies, and destroy both the confidant's right to hear the truth and the institution of confidentiality.

MEDICAL CONFIDENTIALITY

Physicians would appear to be under the *prima facie* obligation to respect the right to secrecy, but also to abide by the right of potential victims to be protected. In cases involving moral conflict they must necessarily override one of these rights. Infringing certain rights for the sake of other rights may be justifiable, but it leaves a sediment of negative feelings of regret, shame or guilt (10, 11). It is an un-healthy and paralysing notion to know that the relationship one enters into with patients may unexpectedly turn into a sit-uation of conflict, infringement of rights, and guilt. This guilt may be compounded by the awareness that breaching relates to a family of dubious practices that mis-use information obtained by resorting to deception or even duress. Of course, con-fidentiality is enacted in the unfettered environment of medical encounters, but its breaching infringes the rights of the confiders, harms them, and abrades con-fidentiality as an institution, all this in the name of elusive values and hard-to-specify protective and vindicative func-tions.

In the case where a physician believes the patient's exorbitant threats and alerts the police, a morally questionable prin-ciple becomes involved. The patient has sought the clinical encounter and prof-fered information on the understanding that this is necessary for an efficient ther-apy and also that the relationship with the physician is protected by a mantle of confidentiality. Confidence is offered and accepted in medical acts, and known to be an indispensable component of the clini-cal encounter, thus enticing the patient to deliver unbiased, unfiltered, uncensored and sincerely presented information (12).

Consequently, it appears contradictory and perverse first to offer confidentiality as an enticement to sincerity, only subsequently to breach it because the information elicited is so terrible it cannot remain unpublicised. Confidence is understood as an unconditional offer, otherwise it would not be accepted, and it appears profoundly unfair to disown the initial conditions once the act of confiding has occurred.

Should one decide to introduce exception clauses, it would only be fair to promulgate them beforehand, allowing every potential confider to know what to expect. But officially sanctioned exceptions would have the undesirable side-effect of creating a second-class kind of medicine for those cases where the patient considers it too risky to assume confidentiality. The communication between patient and physician would in these cases be hampered and would thus render the patient's medical care less than optimal.

GATHERING CONFIDENTIAL MATERIAL

The covenant of confidentiality only obtains if information is voluntarily and consciously given. No question of confidence arises unless the relationship involves rational, conscious and free individuals. But subtleties arise in the medical context when incriminating information reaches the physician unintentionally. Does this information fall within the confidence pact in virtue of being part of the clinical encounter? Or does it obey independent rules because it occurred marginally to the intended doctor/patient relationship?

During the clinical encounter a perspicacious physician may find tell-tale signs of matters the patient did not intend to disclose (skin blemishes perhaps caused by alcohol excess, suspiciously pin-point pupils, injection marks). This involuntary information transfer might not seem at first to fall under any confidentiality agreement according to the above presented definition. Nevertheless, it is the product of a conscious interaction between patient and physician. In consulting a doctor, a person implicitly accepts the risk of surrendering more information than intended but at the same time understands herself or himself to be under the protection of confidentiality. Information fortuitously gained within the freely chosen association of the clinical encounter is to be considered confidential and treated in the same way as information voluntarily disclosed by the patient. Everything that happens in the interpersonal relationship of a clinical encounter is confidential.

ARE THERE EXCEPTIONS TO CONFIDENTIALITY?

Exceptions to unrelenting confidentiality (6) have been invoked for the sake of the confider (paternalistic breaching in general and medical consultations as a special case thereof), in the name of potentially endangered innocent others, in the name of institutional or public interests, and less explicitly, in cases where the confidant is potentially in danger.

CONFIDENTIALITY THROUGHOUT TIME

Confidants may consider the potential harm of divulging information they have had in custody eventually to diffuse after the confider's death, so that a posthumous revelation will not be injurious. The contrary position that harm after death is possible is too weak to support obligations to the dead (13). A more convincing approach suggests that posthumous disclosures may be harmful to surviving persons. If the death of a famous politician should prompt a physician to uncover his knowledge about the deceased's homosexual inclination, still living patients of the same physician might register with distaste and fear the possibility that private information about them could eventually be disclosed after they died. This suspicion may well be unsettling and therefore harmful to them, especially if they happen to believe in some form of 'after-life', the quality of which would be polluted by indiscretions occurring after their biological death. Also to be considered are the negative effects a disparaging disclosure might have upon surviving family members as well as groups of individuals with whom the deceased had a commonality of interests. Death does not cancel the obligation of confidentiality which remains of import to all survivors within the radius of interests of the deceased.

PATERNALISTIC BREACHING

A commonly suggested exemption to confidentiality is that some patients' interests might be better served by physicians' indiscretion (14). Harming confiders for their own purported good is like forcing therapeutic decisions on patients for the sake of their health care. Such stern paternalism has nothing to recommend it, for it is generally agreed that autonomous individuals are not to be compelled into undergoing medical procedures they have explicitly rejected. If rationally competent patients refuse a medical procedure that would do them good, the physician is not authorised to insist, let alone proceed. Rationally competent individuals are allowed to take decisions against their own interests and this does not make them irrational, as some have misleadingly suggested (15). Why, then, should confidentiality function differently? If patients wish certain knowledge to be kept confidential even if this course of action injures their own interests, they are entitled to do so and no one, not even the physician, has the right to breach confidentiality in the name of patients' welfare.

MEDICAL CONSULTATIONS

Multi-professional care seems to offer plausible alibis to breach confidentiality for the sake of the confider (16). It has been argued that patients negotiate confidentiality with their primary-care physician and that if additional professionals are involved in the patient's care they are to report to the confidant physician. This position is discarded by those who believe that patients, in as much as their autonomy is respected, are to re-negotiate— or count upon—confidentiality with every physician involved. Such a line of thought has much to recommend it since every physician/patient encounter may unveil unedited information which the patient is willing to discuss in a certain setting but is reluctant to have brought to the attention of the primary-care physician. Consultations and other expansions of a medical care programme do not serve as an excuse to exchange information about patients against their will. If they did, they would be supporting double morality and possibly double-quality medicine, where primary health-care would have a paternalistic format embedded in trust and confidence whilst secondary and tertiary services would operate in a contractual setting. This would not be acceptable, it being preferable that each act of confidence be equally and non-transmittably entrenched in all medical encounters.

HARM TO INNOCENT OTHERS

Another major exception invoked against absolute confidentiality concerns the aversion of damage to uninvolved and innocent third parties. These are the oft-quoted cases of the doctor telling the bride that her fiancé is homosexual, or calling the wife because he is treating the husband for venereal disease. Escalating examples include informing authorities about a confider's intention to kill someone, as well as encounters with terrorists at large.

This postulated exemption to confidentiality is self-defeating. Firstly, if physicians become known as confidence-violators, problem-ridden patients will try to lie, accommodate facts to their advantage or, if this does not work, avoid physicians altogether (17). Physicians would then be unable to give optimal advice or treatment to the detriment of both the reluctant patients and their threatened environment. It is better to treat and advise the syphilitic husband without informing the wife than not have him come at all for fear of undesired revelations.

Physicians who believe themselves in possession of information that must be disclosed in order to safeguard public interests are contemplating preventive action against the putative malefactor. Like all preventive policies, breaching confidentiality is difficult to analyse in terms of costs/benefits: is the danger real, potential or fictitious? what preventive measure will appear justified? how much harm may these measures cause before they lose justification? Since physicians will rarely be instrumental in deciding or carrying out preventive actions, they have no way of knowing in advance whether taking the risk of honouring confidentiality will eventually prove more or less harmful than breaching it.

If physicians play it safe and commit frequent breaches of confidentiality they will unleash overreacting preventive programmes, at the same time progressively losing credibility as reliable informers. On the other hand, should they remain critical and carefully decide each case on its own merits, they will be equally suspect and unreliable informers, for their conscientiousness and judgement might well deviate from what other authorities, notably the police, consider adequate.

In apparently more delicate cases it could be argued that physicians might subject their co-operation with the authorities to some conditions in order to defuse the dramatic moment. They may suggest that violence be refrained from, that their own intervention be kept secret, that the preventive action be discreet. But certainly, if physicians accept that their confidential relationship with patients is conditional, they must consequently expect authorities to handle their own role as informants in a similarly unpredictable and contingent way. Physicians who breach confidentiality cannot expect to be protected by it just because they have exchanged the confidant for the confider role. Physicians who are known to take confidentiality as a *prima facie* value cannot demand that the authorities they are serving by disclosing information should honour their request for discretion. For similar reasons they must expect some patients to become increasingly inconsiderate or even vicious. By breaking confidentiality, physicians are helping sustain a language of dishonesty and they cannot expect violence-prone patients to refrain from blackmailing, threatening or otherwise molesting them. As a physician, I would be most unsettled if it became a matter of policy that my colleagues violated confidentiality for the public good, for it would leave me defenceless when confronted with a public offender. No amount of promising would help, since physicians would already have a reputation as unpredictable violators of agreements.

Who should control the policy of confidentiality in medicine anyhow? If public interest demands a catalogue of situations where the physician would be under obligation to inform, medicine becomes subaltern to political design and starts down a treacherous path. Should one prefer to leave the management of confidentiality to the physician's conscience and moral judgement, public interest would not be relying on a consistent and trustworthy source of information. Fear of either political misuse or personal arbitrariness should make us wary of opening the doors of confidentiality for the sake of public interest.

What about possible conflicts between the frailties of public figures and the purported interests of society? National leaders from time to time suffer from disabilities due to old age and the question is raised whether the attending medical team are under an obligation to publish full-fledged clinical reports. It must again be brought to mind that the medical team have been commissioned not to safeguard the public interest but to care for the health of this individual who happens to be influential. Consequently, the medical team's duties remain in the clinical realm, not in the political arena. Furthermore, if the leader in question were in such a precarious situation as to constitute a public danger, his political mismanagement would become obvious to other individuals more qualified to take public decisions and would not require the physicians to play the role of enlightening figures. Observers of the political scene have preferred to suggest constitutional amendments and political measures to cope with this problem, being aware that cajoling physicians out of their commitment to confidentiality is no solution (18).

COMPETING CLAIMS TO CONFIDENTIAL MATERIAL

This issue refers to conflicts arising from individual interests colliding with those of groups or institutions. It differs from those previously discussed in that here physicians do not necessarily engage in active disclosure but restrict themselves to a one-sided co-operation. The emphasis here is not so much on harm being prevented—although this also plays a major role—but on conflicting parties claiming the physician's loyalty.

Company doctors doing routine examinations of employees are under obligation to report even disparaging findings, for their duty is to the commissioning company. By failing to report an epileptic bus driver or a hypertensive pilot, the doctor is deceiving the company and hindering its efforts to secure safe transportation. If, on the contrary, the same bus driver or pilot goes to the private office of a doctor unconnected with his employer, there would be no excuse for unauthorisedly reporting any findings to the company, for the physician is now being commissioned by the individual, not by the institution, to perform a medical act under the mantle of confidentiality. If this results in the bus driver continuing to work under precarious conditions it means that the company has not established an efficient medical service to check its drivers and is negligent. Physicians are to declare themselves explicitly and unmistakably loyal to those who engage their services, for, again, the legitimate claim to confidentiality is in the act of entering an agreement, not in the contents of the confided material.

Not even these competing claims of loyalty can be settled unless a robust and relentless position in favour of exceptionless confidentiality is upheld. If a physician owes loyalty to an institution, he has no right to misuse the confidence of his employer in order to honour any personal desire for confidentiality. Conversely, when physicians are committed to the confidential situations that arise in their consulting rooms, they lack the right to infringe this agreement to the benefit of other interests.

DOES RISK TO THE CONFIDANT JUSTIFY BREACHING?

The situation could arise where the patient's revelations contain threats of harm or disclosure of damage already done directly to the confidant physician, his or her family members or their interests. Can the physician disclaim the obligation to confidentiality in the name of self-defence? If physicians were morally allowed to breach confidentiality in defence of their own interests, it would mean accepting the principle that one can inflict harm upon others for self-interested reasons. It has already been stated that in disclosing confidential information there is no adequate way of comparing amounts of harm inflicted with harm prevented, so it might well occur that a person brought about severe harm to others in an effort to avert a fairly trivial or improbable harm to her or his own interests, comparable to killing a burglar who is running away with some property—perhaps no more than a loaf of bread. Since an unbiased view can hardly be expected from someone who believes his interests to be in jeopardy, legal systems do not tolerate self-administered justice and condemn, albeit with leniency, injuring others in the face of putative menace to self-interests. Physicians may not safeguard their own interests by mishandling patients, so why should they be allowed to cause harm by breaching confidentiality only because they believe or fear their interests to be imperilled?

Although imaginary situations can be concocted that make it awkward to insist on not breaching, the basic attitude should still be to respect confidentiality to the utmost. Admittedly, if the patient's disclosure implies impending harm to the confidant, the moral obligation to the confidential relationship is weakened in its core, but this admission requires a double qualification: firstly, such situations are highly improbable and therefore of little paradigmatic interest; secondly, even if they should obtain, breaching confidentiality should be used as a last, certainly not first, resort to resolve the conflict, precisely because there is no suasive justification for employing confidentiality as a weapon to avert harm.

CONCLUDING REMARKS

Confidentiality is a widely recognised implicit warranty of fairness in clinical situations and thus constitutes a technically and morally essential element of efficient medical care. If breaches of confidentiality occur, they do so necessarily after the communication and therefore retroactively introduce unfairness into the clinical encounter. A situation that is potentially, even if only occasionally, unfair can no longer be described as fair, especially if breaching occurs unpredictably. All possible exceptions to an attitude of unrelenting confidentiality lead to morally untenable situations where harm avoided v harm inflicted is incommensurable, and rights preserved are less convincing than rights eroded. Confidentiality collapses unless strictly adhered to, for even occasional, exceptional or otherwise limited leaks are sufficient to discredit confidentiality into inefficiency.

The clinical encounter is consistently described as a confidential relationship. If this statement is adhered to, there can be no room for violation without making the initial statement untrue. Nor can the description be qualified—'usually confidential'—or made into a conditional—'confidential unless'—statement, for these half-hearted commitments are, from the confider's point of view, as worthless as no guarantee of confidentiality at all. Confidentiality cannot but be, factually and morally, an all or none proposition. It might perhaps be easier to present a plausible defence of conditional confidentiality, but the ethical atmosphere of the clinical encounter, the autonomy of patients and the sovereignty of the medical profession are all better served by making confidentiality an unexceptionable element of medicine.

REFERENCES

1. MacIntyre A. Moral philosophy: what next? In: Hauerwas S, MacIntyre A, eds. *Revisions: changing perspectives in moral philosophy.* Notre Dame/London: University of Notre Dame Press, 1983: 1–15.
2. Thompson I E. The nature of confidentiality. *Journal of medical ethics* 1979; 5: 57–64.
3. Pheby D F H. Changing practice on confidentiality: a cause for concern. *Journal of medical ethics* 1982; 8: 12–18.
4. Anscombe G E M. Modern moral philosophy. In: Anscombe G E M. *Ethics, religion and politics.* Oxford: Blackwell, 1981: 26–42.
5. Walters L. Confidentiality. In: Beauchamp T L, Walters L, eds. *Contemporary issues in bioethics.* Encino/Belmont: Dickenson, 1978: 169–175.
6. *Handbook of medical ethics.* London: British Medical Association 1981.
7. Anonymous. Medical confidentiality [editorial]. *Journal of medical ethics* 1984; 10: 3–4.
8. Carli T. Confidentiality and privileged communication: a psychiatrist's perspective. In: Basson M D, ed. *Ethics, humanism, and medicine.* New York: Liss, 1980: 245–251.
9. Rawls J. *A theory of justice.* Cambridge, Mass: Belknap Press, 1971: 342–350.
10. Melden A I. *Rights and persons.* Oxford: Blackwell, 1977: 47–48.
11. Morris H. The status of rights. *Ethics* 1981; 92: 40–56.
12. Veatch R M. *A theory of medical ethics.* New York: Basic Books, 1981: 184–189.
13. Levenbook B B. Harming someone after his death. *Ethics* 1984; 94: 407–419.
14. Veatch R M. *Case studies in medical ethics.* Cambridge/London: Harvard University Press, 1977: 131–135.
15. Culver C M, Gert B. *Philosophy in medicine.* New York: Oxford, 1983: 26–28.
16. Siegler M. Medical consultations in the context of the physician-patient relationship. In: Agich G J, ed. *Responsibility in health care.* Dordrecht: Reidel, 1982: 141–162.
17. Havard J. Medical confidence. *Journal of medical ethics* 1985; 11: 8–11.
18. Robins R S, Rothschild H. Hidden health disabilities and the presidency: medical management and political consideration. *Perspectives in biology and medicine* 1981; 24: 240–253.

POSTSCRIPT

Are There Limits to Confidentiality?

The decision in *Tarasoff* was widely criticized by lawyers and mental health professionals. Nevertheless, the doctrine that therapists have a duty to protect potential victims has been endorsed by several other state and federal courts, for example, in New Jersey, Nebraska, Indiana, Georgia, Michigan, Washington, and Kansas. In one New Jersey case, a court held a psychiatrist liable for failing to protect a patient's former girlfriend who was killed by the adolescent patient—even though the patient had never expressed any intent to harm her and had only talked about his jealous feelings. However, some courts have limited the duty to protect to known, identifiable victims. In 1990, for example, a Pennsylvania appeals court upheld a lower court decision that a psychiatrist had no duty to protect the live-in girlfriend of a patient who decided she was a Russian spy and strangled her in a shopping mall. The patient had never threatened to harm her, the court said, adding that the fact that they lived together created no special situation requiring a warning of the patient's schizophrenic condition. A 1986 decision of the Vermont Supreme Court, on the other hand, in a case involving a barn burning, creates liability for property damage as well as for personal injury.

Prosenjit Poddar, the man who killed Tatiana Tarasoff, was convicted of second-degree murder, but the conviction was overturned on appeal because the jury had been incorrectly instructed. Since more than five years had elapsed since the crime, the state decided not to retry Poddar but to release him if he would promise to return to India, which he did. For the aftermath of the decision, see "Protecting Third Parties: A Decade After *Tarasoff*," by Mark J. Mills, Greer Sullivan, and Spencer Eth, *American Journal of Psychiatry* (January 1987); Vanessa Merton, "Confidentiality and the 'Dangerous' Patient: Implications of *Tarasoff* for Psychiatrists and Lawyers," *Emory Law Journal* (vol. 31, 1982); Paul S. Appelbaum, "Tarasoff and the Clinician: Problems in Fulfilling the Duty to Protect," *American Journal of Psychiatry* (April 1985); and Alan A. Stone, "Vermont Adopts Tarasoff: A Real Barn-Burner," *American Journal of Psychiatry* (March 1986). See also Alan R. Felthous, *The Psychotherapist's Duty to Warn or Protect* (Charles C. Thomas, 1989) and *Confidentiality Versus the Duty to Protect: Forseeable Harm in the Practice of Psychiatry* edited by James C. Beck (American Psychiatric Association, 1990).

A consensus is developing concerning appropriate exceptions to confidentiality in the case of an HIV-infected person who refuses to notify a third party at risk because of sexual contact. In July 1988 the American Medical Association stated, "Ideally, a physician should attempt to persuade the infected party to cease endangering the third party; if persuasion fails, the authorities should be notified; and if the authorities take no action, the physician should notify and counsel the endangered third party." New York has passed AIDS confidentiality protection legislation that allows for this sort of exception. Four articles addressing this issue are Kenneth E. Labowitz, "Beyond *Tarasoff*: AIDS and the Obligation to Breach Confidentiality," *Saint Louis University Public Law Review* (1990); Bernard M. Dickens, "Confidentiality and the Duty to Warn," in Lawrence O. Gostin, ed., *AIDS and the Health Care System* (Yale University Press, 1990); Benjamin Freedman, "Violating Confidentiality to Warn of a Risk of HIV Infection: Ethical Work in Progress," *Theoretical Medicine* (vol. 12, 1991); and Sherry K. Lynch, "AIDS: Balancing Confidentiality and the Duty to Protect," *Journal of College Student Development* (March 1993).

The computerization of medical records, the complexity of health care, and the trend toward large managed-care group practices have created new threats to privacy as well as new opportunities to maximize benefits. For proposals to protect patient confidentiality in these circumstances, see Sheri Alpert, "Smart Cards, Smarter Policy: Medical Records, Privacy, and Health Care Reform," *Hastings Center Report* (November–December 1993); Lawrence O. Gostin et al., "Privacy and Security of personal Information in a New Health Care System," *Journal of theAmerican Medical Association* (November 24, 1993); and M. S. Donaldson and K. N. Lohr, eds., *Health Data in the Information Age: Use, Disclosure, and Privacy* (National Academy Press, 1994).

A rare glimpse of a physician's decision-making process about keeping secrets from patients (for example, when a family member reveals some information about the patient's hidden behavior or mental incapacity and asks the doctor not to tell its source) is found in John F. Burnum, "Secrets About Patients," *The New England Journal of Medicine* (April 18, 1991). In general, Dr. Burnum advised the family members to discuss the problem openly with the patient, but on some occasions he simply kept silent. On confidentiality in general, see *Secrets* by Sissela Bok (Pantheon Books, 1982). See also Robert M. Veatch, *Case Studies in Medical Ethics* (Harvard University Press, 1977), chapter 5; Louis Everstine et al., "Threats to Confidentiality," *American Psychologist* (September 1980); the chapter on "Confidentiality," by David Joseph and Joseph Onek, in *Psychiatric Ethics*, 2d ed. edited by Sidney Bloch and Paul Chodoff, (Oxford University Press, 1991); Terrence McConnell, "Confidentiality and the Law," *Journal of Medical Ethics* (March 1994); and Bernard Friedland, "Physician-Patient Confidentiality: Time to Re-examine a Venerable Concept in Light of Contemporary Society and Advances in Medicine," *Journal of Legal Medicine* (vol. 15, no. 2, 1994).

ISSUE 9

Is It Ethical to Treat Short Children With Human Growth Hormone?

YES: David B. Allen, from "Growth Hormone Therapy for the Disability of Short Stature," *Growth, Genetics, and Hormones* (May 1992)

NO: John D. Lantos, from "Why Growth Hormone Should Not Be Used for Non-Growth Hormone Deficient Children," *Growth, Genetics, and Hormones* (May 1992)

ISSUE SUMMARY

YES: Pediatrician David B. Allen argues that short stature is a disability in American society and that it is ethical to use growth hormone to bring short children into the normal range for height.

NO: Pediatrician John D. Lantos asserts that short children are healthy and that widespread use of growth hormone will increase the gap between short and tall, thus conferring benefits to some children at the expense of other, untreated children.

Americans generally look up to tall people. George Washington, the first president of the United States, was extremely tall (6 ft., 2 in.) for his time. All but two succeeding presidents were also taller than the average men of their time. Tall men have advantages in business, in the professions, in choosing mates, in most sports, and in just about every aspect of contemporary society. Tall women set standards for beauty and sex appeal in fashion and have similar advantages in the business and professional world. Although average height has been increasing because of better nutrition, there is still nothing one can do to gain a height advantage for one's child, beyond choosing a tall mate and hoping for the best.

The advent of genetic engineering has expanded the options. Human growth hormone, produced naturally by the pituitary gland, can be manufactured synthetically. The first attempts to produce this growth hormone were made by utilizing the pituitary glands of human cadavers. The drug was extremely rare and expensive. Furthermore, early versions carried a virus that caused a lethal neurological disease called Cruetzfeld-Jacob disease.

The use of recombinant DNA technology made it possible to produce this drug more efficiently and safely. There are now two growth hormone drugs on the market—Protropin, produced by Genentech, Inc., and Humatrope, produced by Eli Lilly Company. Both have been approved by the Food and

Drug Administration only to treat children whose bodies do not produce adequate levels of growth hormone. These "pituitary dwarfs"—of whom there are approximately 20,000 in the United States—have a documented hormone deficiency, although there is some disagreement about how to measure this deficiency. It soon became apparent, however, that the drugs might be used to treat short children who do not have clear evidence of growth hormone deficiency. Some of these children have genetic conditions, such as Turner's syndrome (a growth disorder in girls), or other illnesses, such as kidney disease, that have stunted their growth. Some, however, are just short children with short parents. Although the drugs are not approved for these purposes, licensed physicians can prescribe them. Such "off label" uses of approved drugs are common.

A child who is prescribed a growth hormone is injected with the drug daily, or at least three times a week, for a period of 10 years. The cost ranges from $15,000 to $20,000 a year, paid for by some insurance companies and by Medicaid. The price may soon drop because, as of March 1994, biosynthetic human growth hormone has been approved for production by other companies under a generic label.

The short-term medical risks of this treatment appears to be rare, although there has been concern about a reported increased risk of leukemia in children treated with growth hormone. Long-term risks are still unknown. There are, however, significant psychosocial risks. A child who undergoes such intensive therapy may believe that his body is unacceptable to his parents and physicians. The treatment itself may reinforce the view that short is bad, a belief that can be especially harmful if the treatment is not fully successful.

Based on results seen to date, it appears that the drug works in the short term (one year) in some children who do not have a growth hormone deficiency but not in others. No one can predict whether a specific child will grow taller or how much taller the child will get. The positive effect on growth rate appears to wane with time. There is no good evidence that a child treated with human growth hormone will become a much taller adult.

The following two selections grapple with the issue of whether or not to treat short children who do not have a growth hormone deficiency. David B. Allen believes that growth hormone therapy is justified because extreme short stature interferes with normal activities and is therefore a handicap. Whatever the cause of their disability, all very short children are entitled to the same treatment to enhance their potential. John D. Lantos, on the other hand, declares that any bad outcomes associated with short stature are not related to disease but to social attitudes. If the treatment works, treating some short children will only make the situation worse for the least well-off—the shortest children who do not receive treatment.

YES

David B. Allen

GROWTH HORMONE THERAPY FOR THE DISABILITY OF SHORT STATURE

INTRODUCTION AND CONCEPTUAL GUIDELINES

Limited availability of human growth hormone (GH) once provided a barrier to expanding its use beyond children who were unequivocally GH deficient (GHD). By necessity, strict arbitrary criteria were established to identify classic GHD children entitled to GH. Today, increased availability of recombinant DNA-derived GH has allowed investigation of its growth-promoting effect in short children who do not fit traditional definitions of GHD. Increased supply has created increased demand; more than twice as many children received GH therapy in 1989 and 1990 than in 1985 and 1986 at an average annual cost per child of $10,000.

Advantages conferred by increased height in social, economic, professional, and political realms of Western society are well-documented. Stigmatization and discrimination are shared by *all* extremely short children, whether GHD or not. *If* GH is shown to have growth-promoting effects in non-GHD children and *if* treatment of such children can be accomplished without toxicity, then what ethical criteria should determine entitlement to long-term, invasive, and (currently) expensive therapy? Would it be justified to restrict access to GH based on the diagnosis of GHD? And whatever the indication for GH therapy, to what attained height should GH therapy be considered an entitlement?

Answering these questions requires rethinking of the medical indications for GH therapy. Toward the goal of achieving both controlled but fair access to GH, the following conceptual guidelines are proposed: (1) GH be viewed as a treatment for the disability of short stature (SS) and not for the diagnosis of GHD; (2) GH-responsiveness, not GHD, be the central criterion for GH treatment; and (3) entitlement to (and reimbursement for) GH therapy be guided by the degree of disability and the degree of GH-responsiveness rather than by a child's diagnosis.[1]

THE CONTINUUM OF GROWTH HORMONE SECRETION: DISEASE, POTENTIAL, AND HANDICAP

The once clear boundary between GHD and GH sufficiency has become blurred. Traditional criteria for the diagnosis of GHD do not identify all children who are GH-responsive. A continuum of "inadequate" GH secretion likely spans classic and partially GHD children,[2] children with delayed growth and puberty, and other poorly growing short children who pass provocative tests but still secrete less GH than their peers.[3] Furthermore, GH *augmentation* therapy in short children with no detectable abnormalities of GH secretion increases growth velocity and, if given for sufficient time prior to puberty, may increase eventual adult height.[4,5]

Arguments emphasizing proven GHD as the primary criterion for GH therapy are often rooted in notions of disease, handicap, or potential. The treatment of disease, "an abnormal condition of an organism that impairs normal physiologic functioning" (*American Heritage Dictionary*, 1985), is one function of medicine. One might argue that GH therapy be confined to those with the "disease" of GHD. Restoration of hormonal equilibrium by supplementing deficient or suppressing excessive levels of hormones is a justifiable, time-honored principle in endocrinology. The GHD child is viewed as more entitled to therapy because something has been taken away that needs to be restored. The American Academy of Pediatrics statement recommending GH therapy only for GHD children concludes with the old adage, "If it ain't broke, don't fix it."[6] But what exactly is "broke" when it comes to SS and GH therapy? This view ignores both the likely, though yet unrecognized, physiologic "defects" that lead to genetic SS and its accompanying psychosocial impairment. Both GHD and non-GHD short children, if they have a disease at all, have the disease of SS.

If the legitimate function of medicine includes the alleviation of handicap, "a disadvantage or deficiency, especially a physical or mental disability that prevents or restricts normal achievement," then the short child's well-being is viewed in the context of his or her interaction with the environment. GH therapy is justified by recognition that extreme SS interferes with normal activities such as driving a car and reaching shelves, as well as competition for jobs, schools, incomes, and mates. After all, preventing handicapping SS is the primary impetus for treating GHD children. Other beneficial physiologic effects occur with GH therapy, but these are of secondary importance. Growth rate and final adult height are the measures by which we judge therapeutic success. Whether burdens associated with SS of a given degree qualify for designation as a handicap is not the central question. The point is that short children of equal height have the same handicap regardless of the cause.

The concept of potential is also invoked to distinguish treatment of GHD and non-GHD children. For some, a GHD child with parents of normal height is "meant," by virtue of genetic endowment, to be taller than the child with familial SS. He or she is entitled to treatment with GH until a height appropriate for the genetic endowment is attained. GH supplementation of the familial short child who appears to be GH-sufficient is "tampering with nature" and outside the proper province of medicine. But this analysis fails, since both children (given an equal height prognosis) are equally unlucky, one by virtue of having GHD and the other by virtue of having short parents. For both, attaining maximum adult height requires "tampering with nature" by providing exogenous GH.

EQUITABLE RESTRICTION OF GROWTH HORMONE THERAPY

While concepts of disease, handicap, and potential do not distinguish GHD from GH-responsive children with regard to entitlement to GH therapy, it does not follow that *all* GH-responsive short children are entitled to therapy. Resolving that question requires consideration of balancing benefits and risks and asking further questions about allocation of health-care resources.

Response to GH is not an "all or none" phenomenon. GHD children are likely to be *more* responsive than non-GHD children, justifying their preferential treatment as a class. Possible GH toxicity in non-GHD children, while apparently rare, still requires further study. Risks of psychosocial stigmatization also require careful consideration; short, otherwise normal children exposed to injections to promote growth may conclude (with some accuracy) that their bodies are unacceptable in the eyes of their parents and physicians.[7] Statistically significant increments in final adult height may not actually improve psychosocial adaptation, failing a primary objective of GH therapy. Finally, unrestricted access to GH would shift the bell-shaped curve of height upward without changing the handicap for those at the lower percentiles in competing for social, professional, and athletic status.

Assuming that clinical trials of GH in non-GHD children show efficacy with acceptable risk, how might access to GH therapy be equitably restricted? First, the goals in treating SS must be clarified. If the goal is to achieve each child's maximum height potential, GH therapy would (ethically) need to be offered to any potentially responsive short child. Providing GH therapy only to those with documented GHD and treating them until maximal adult stature is reached would be unfair to equally short, non-GHD children who could grow with GH supplementation. On the other hand, if the goal is to alleviate the disability of extreme SS (from any cause), GH-responsive short children should have equal access to treatment until they reach a height no longer considered a handicap.

This latter goal, bringing short children into the normal opportunity range for height, coincides with society's duty to provide basic needs to its citizens. There is no duty to provide the *very best* opportunity for all, and an insistence on equal access to GH by those who have already achieved a normal final height compromises this goal. To improve opportunities for those truly disabled by height, GH must be selectively available to them. The challenge is to define this group, and to apply criteria of disability consistently in deciding when to commence and when to *discontinue therapy*. The diagnosis of GHD should not be rewarded with unlimited access to GH while access is denied to equally handicapped non-GHD but potentially GH-responsive children.

TOWARD RESPONSIBLE USE OF GROWTH HORMONE

Any definition of "handicapping height" would be arbitrary, but the difficulty in defining boundaries precisely should not be an obstacle to making distinctions. Decisions about treatment are always based on probability, not certainty. While

Figure 1
Allocation of Growth Hormone to Children

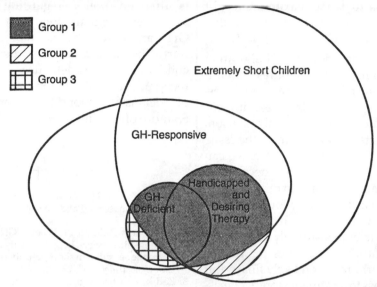

(Group 1) Equitable, but restricted entitlement to GH therapy based upon preferential allocation to children *disabled* by height who demonstrate GH-responsiveness. (Group 2) Children unresponsive to GH or (Group 3) GH-responsive but not sufficiently disabled by small stature, including GH-deficient children who have achieved *non-handicapping adult stature* would not receive public or privately subsidized therapy.

current methods for height prediction remain suboptimal, *some* determination of a height considered a handicap needs to be made if GH allocation in the future is to be both controlled and fair.

Emphasizing degree of disability and GH-responsiveness as selection criteria for therapy equitably fulfills reasonable goals of growth-promoting therapy. (See Figure 1.) Children disadvantaged by stature, regardless of pathogenesis, would be brought closer to or within the normal opportunity range for height. The attainment of maximum height potential would not be a valid treatment goal, and the use of GH to make normal-statured children taller would be opposed. The normal range of height would not be altered, but rather the disparity between percentiles—for example, between the 0.1th and 1st percentiles—would be lessened. By restricting GH therapy to those seeking only to achieve the normal opportunity range for height, we would not exploit the perception that taller is better.

Widespread distribution of GH has been deterred in part by high drug prices[8] and concern about toxicity. Assuming efficacy of GH in increasing final adult height, the relevant question is not how much should be spent on GHD versus non-GHD children but rather how should health-care resources by responsibly and fairly expended on the treatment of SS in general.[9] Resources for this endeavor may in fact be limited, but treatment of severely SS individuals can still be approached with *consistency*. If our goal is to help (all) children attain a height closer to the normal opportunity range, the cause of the SS really should not matter. The central question about allocation of GH is this: To what maximum height should any GH-treated child be entitled to receive private or public support?

Moreover, the crisis in GH allocation will expand not with its failures but with its successes, and not as the cost of therapy rises but as it falls. These impediments, which may be resolved soon, have distracted attention from the issue of responsible use of GH. What we can do with GH therapy is not necessarily what we *should* do. We who prescribe GH should now ask how we would respond if families who do not require insurance reimbursement strongly request GH therapy. Without guidelines for restriction based arbitrarily on likely final adult height, access to treatment would increasingly reflect ability to pay, providing yet another societal advantage to those already well-off. Rather, a consistent goal of growth-promoting therapy should be to lessen the burden for those who are so short as to be handicapped; that is, to provide GH therapy to those disabled by height only until a height within the normal opportunity range is attained. Consideration of degree of disability, rather than diagnosis, both when commencing and when discontinuing GH therapy, will most responsibly contain an expanding cohort of candidates for GH treatment.

The physician's duty to respond to the needs of each child does not necessarily extend to parental aspirations or hopes for the child. In an era of plentiful GH, child advocacy requires consideration of the needs of all children, bringing as many as possible into the normal opportunity range of height without deliberately trying to make some taller than others.[10] The paradox of GH therapy is that no policy regarding its use will ever eliminate the 1st percentile. GH cannot replace parental love and nurturing of a child, regardless of the child's height. Prudent use of GH will recognize these limitations, encouraging physicians to respond to concerns about SS more often with counseling than with injections.

REFERENCES

1. Allen DB, Fost NC. Growth hormone for short stature: panacea or Pandora's box. *J Pediatr* 1990; 117: 16–21.
2. Hindmarsh P, Smith PJ, Brook CGD, et al. The relationship between height velocity and growth hormone secretion in short prepubertal children. *Clin Endocrinol* 1987; 27: 581–591.
3. Zadik, A, Chalew SA, Raiti S, et al. Do short children secrete insufficient growth hormone? *Pediatrics* 1985; 76: 355–360.
4. Rosenfeld GH, Hintz RL, Johanson AF, et al. Three-year results of a randomized prospective trial of methionyl human growth hormone and oxandrolone in Turner syndrome. *J Pediatr* 1988; 113: 393.
5. Lesage C, Walker J, Landier F, et al. Near normalization of adolescent height with growth hormone therapy in very short children without growth hormone deficiency. *J Pediatr* 1991; 119: 29–34.
6. Ad Hoc Committee on Growth Hormone Usage, The Lawson Wilkins Pediatric Endocrine Society, and Committee on Drugs, American Academy of Pediatrics. Growth hormone in the treatment of children with short stature. *Pediatrics* 1983; 72: 891–894.
7. Diekema DS. Is taller really better? Growth hormone therapy in short children. *Persp Biol Med* 1990; 34: 109–123.
8. Schoen EJ. More on growth hormone therapy for otherwise normal short children. *J Pediatr* 1991; 119: 341. Letter.
9. Allen DB, Fost NC. More on growth hormone therapy for otherwise normal short children. *J. Pediatr* 1991; 119: 341–342. Reply.
10. Allen DB. Determining who needs growth hormone. *Medical Ethics for the Pediatrician* 1991; 6: 6–7.

NO
John D. Lantos

WHY GROWTH HORMONE SHOULD NOT BE USED FOR NON-GROWTH HORMONE DEFICIENT CHILDREN

INTRODUCTION AND ASSUMPTIONS

Much of the discussion about the indications for growth hormone (GH) has focused on criteria for the initiation of therapy. While this is a difficult problem, it may be more difficult to determine the endpoint of therapy. Indications for the initiation of therapy may be arbitrary, but at least they can be consistently applied: we can say, for example, that everybody with a predicted adult height below the 1st percentile ought to be treated. Once treatment is begun, however, variations in response to GH therapy and different therapeutic goals will make decisions about when to stop treatment even more contentious than decisions to initiate treatment. I will argue that certain features of GH therapy will make it impossible to limit the use of GH to the shortest children. Instead, we are moving towards a world in which GH will be allocated based primarily on parental preferences. Furthermore, I will argue that pediatricians should resist this trend.

For the purposes of this discussion, I will make 4 assumptions. First, I will assume that there are no long-term side effects of GH therapy. If any major side effect of GH is discovered, it will make treatment of even GH-deficient (GHD) children (and certainly non-GHD children) morally questionable. At present, the practical question is whether, or at what point, we are willing to say that GH is safe. I will assume that evidence of GH safety will continue to accumulate.

My second assumption is that GH will increase final adult height of many non-GHD children. Again, if the data show that this is not the case, there will be no real argument in favor of treatment (except, perhaps, the more limited argument that certain children with growth delay would benefit psychologically by reaching their predicted adult height faster, but I will ignore that issue). The moral argument will center on the use of treatment that is effective.

I will assume that money is not a factor. The money issue too easily cuts both ways. If GH is good for children, it should be provided regardless of cost. If it is not good for children, it should not be provided even if it is free. An intermediate position would be to view GH as a consumer good, rather than a medical treatment, and its allocation based on ability to pay. To do this is essentially to assume that there is no compelling argument for the use of GH in short children and so no serious concerns about injustice. Furthermore, questions of economics and justice must fix a price for GH in order to compare its value with other goods. But the price is both relative and variable. Therefore, it is justifiable, for the sake of argument, to set it very low, so that it drops out of the moral equation. By ignoring economics, I will better focus on the primary question of whether GH is good or bad for children. Only after that question is answered can we discuss its relative worth.

Finally, I will assume that GH therapy will require daily injections for years. In the final part of the paper, I will discuss the implications of any change that would allow oral or transdermal administration of GH.

SHORT CHILDREN ARE HEALTHY

Arguments about whether short stature (SS) is or is not a disease generally focus on the difference between social and biologic conceptions of disease. Such arguments turn on whether something must have a biologic substrate or explanation before it can be classified as a disease. Generally, arguments about the relative contributions of biology and sociology to the classification of an entity as a disease ignore or abjure the idea that there is a thing called health. I believe that health is a nonarbitrary quality that may be present or absent in all living things. Although I cannot define health in a way that is precise and inclusive, I believe, along with Kass, that health is not relative but that it is "a state or condition unrelated to, and prior to, both illness and physicians."[1] Health is not social or cultural, and is not defined in relation to others. It is a property of biologic entities.

In spite of the fact that people who are short may suffer as a result of their stature, just as amputees may suffer as a result of their disability, they are generally healthy. Most of the bad outcomes associated with SS, such as poor self-esteem, poor school performance, lower earning potential, etc, may lead to poor health but are not themselves inconsistent with health. Healthy people may not do well in school or may be poor, but this does not indicate that they are diseased. We generally do not give otherwise healthy children shots to improve their school performance or improve their earning potential; we give them better teachers and a better education.

The lack of association between stature and health has important implications for the role of pediatricians in dealing with SS. Because stature is not associated with health, there is no height below which we can call someone intrinsically unhealthy, and no height above which we can define someone as being healthy enough. Whatever goods come from height are relative. Generally speaking, the more height one gains, the more such goods will come. Thus, anybody who would want treatment to achieve some gain in height would likely want as much such treatment as possible.

TREATMENT OF SHORT STATURE: THE END POINT DILEMMA

Suppose we see 2 sisters in a clinic—one has a predicted adult height of 152 cm (5 feet 0 inches; just below the 5th percentile) and a growth rate of <4 cm/yr. The other has a predicted adult height of 155 cm (5 feet 2 inches). We treat the first but not the second. At the end of a year of therapy, the first has responded with a growth spurt and now has a predicted adult height of 156 cm. The second still has a predicted height of 155 cm. Do we continue to treat the first, in order to make her 165 cm? Do we stop treatment, since her predicted adult height is now in the normal range? If we continue to treat the first child, do we offer treatment to the second child, since her predicted height is now less than the child whom we are treating? Suppose GH works even better, and after 3 years, our treated child now has a predicted height of 168 cm. Do we continue treatment, or do we say that it has been too successful and so is no longer justifiable?

Such decisions will be manageable if GH hardly works at all, so that the first child moves only from a predicted adult height of 152 cm to 155 cm. If it works well, so that we can titrate doses to allow almost anyone to reach almost any height, we will create unavoidable inconsistency in our treatment. We will inevitably care for children who are too tall to meet eligibility criteria for the initiation of GH treatment but whose predicted adult height is shorter than that of children who are being treated and who are responding. If these children are not candidates for GH therapy, their SS will be relatively more significant, and any psychosocial sequelae of SS will be worsened. If they are treated, it will create

a continuously sliding scale of eligibility that will eventually include children of any height....

The question, then, is whether pediatricians should prescribe GH for any child whose parents want the child to have GH. The stakes for pediatricians in this debate are high. We ask society to recognize us as having the moral authority to speak about what is in the best interests of children. As our part of the bargain, we agree to be so careful and conservative in our assessments of the interests of children that our views and our opinions will be allowed to override the decisions that parents make for their children.

We are granted such power primarily because we have earned a reputation as the guardians of and spokespersons for the well-being of children. The moral regard in which we are held, and society's willingness to respect our views, is conditional. We cannot say whatever we want. We need to base our views on knowledgeable statements about the health of children. I don't think that we can now make knowledgeable and unambiguous statements that the treatment of non-GHD children with GH is in the best interest of any particular child. Furthermore, I think we can say that widespread use of GH will be detrimental to the interest of children as a whole.

The benefits of GH are necessarily relative. Whether SS is conceived of as disease, disability, or normal variant, GH can alleviate the sequelae of SS only by changing the relative height of some children in relation to others. This highlights the difference between SS and ill health. Stature is relative in a way that health is not, and interventions that preserve or protect health are generally beneficial in a way that GH is not.

If all children are immunized against polio or pertussis, they are all better off. If everybody is screened for and treated for anemia or lead poisoning, then everybody will be better off. The general health of the population will improve. But if everybody was treated with GH and if they all responded, then nobody would be better off. The shortest people would still be relatively short. In fact, everybody would be worse off, since in order to maintain their relative state of well-being, everyone would require a daily injection. If only some people are treated or only some people respond, they will be better off in relation to others, who will be relatively worse off.

Seen in this way, pediatricians who administer GH will be either increasing the net burden of medical treatment for children without any compensatory benefit or selectively conferring benefits on some children by creating detriments for others. GH therapy could be unique among pediatric therapies in that it can confer benefits to some children only at the expense of other children....

CONCLUSIONS

... I have argued against GH therapy for non-GHD children assuming research results that would be most favorable to children—that it is safe, effective, and afford-able. Even under those circumstances, I argue that it should not be used for non-GHD children. Any data indicating that it is ineffective and/or has side effects, and certainly any consideration of social justice, would only strengthen these arguments.

Two lines of research might change my conclusions. One would be the discovery of a method of administering GH by mouth. This would minimize the burden of therapy. If, as I've assumed and as research shows, GH remains safe and effective, an orally administered version should probably be sold over the counter, like vitamins. Parents could then decide for themselves whether they wanted to alter their children's height. Another line of research that might change my conclusions would be research delineating a clear-cut association between SS and psychiatric conditions, and a convincing demonstration that GH not only alleviates those problems but also alleviates them more effectively than alternative psychiatric interventions, such as counseling. Such research is not currently being done.

REFERENCES

1. Kass L. The end of medicine and the pursuit of health. In: Kass L. *Toward a More Natural Science.* New York, NY: Free Press; 1985: 170.

POSTSCRIPT

Is It Ethical to Treat Short Children With Human Growth Hormone?

In May 1993 the National Institutes of Health resumed recruiting very short children for two clinical trials of biosynthetic growth hormone. One study involved very short, healthy children; the other involved girls with Turner's syndrome. The studies had been stopped because of injunctions filed by two advocacy groups that claimed the trials violated federal reserach regulations on experimentation with children. Special panels convened to review the protocols recommended some modifications.

In August 1994 a federal grand jury in Minneapolis indicted Dr. David Brown on charges that he received $1.1 million in kickbacks from Genentech, Inc., the company that produces the growth hormone Protropin. Officials at Genentech and at Caremark, the company that distributes the drug, were also indicted. A House of Representatives subcommittee, chaired by Representative Ron Wyden (D-Oregon) is also investigating these companies' marketing practices, which purportedly included paying private foundations for school surveys to identify short children in schools. These children would then, it is alleged, be referred to pediatricians who would prescribe the drug. The companies and Dr. Brown have denied any wrongdoing.

Human growth hormone is also being used by adolescents who believe it will improve their athletic performance by building muscle and tendon strength. One study of tenth-grade boys at two suburban Chicago high schools indicated that 5 percent reported past or present use of growth hormone and that 78 percent had heard of the substance. The survey sample was poorly informed about possible long-term side effects. Since the drug is very expensive, it is possible that they were using another substance that claimed to enhance athletic performance (see Vaughn I. Rickert, et al., "Human Growth Hormone: A New Substance of Abuse Among Adolescents?" *Clinical Pediatrics,* December 1992).

Other views on the use of human growth hormone are: Gladys B. White, "Human Growth Hormone: The Dilemma of Expanded Use in Children," *Kennedy Institute of Ethics Journal* (vol. 3, no. 4, 1993); Barry Werth, "How Short Is Too Short? Marketing the Human Growth Hormone" *The New York Times Magazine* (June 16, 1991); and John D. Lantos, Mark Siegler, and Leona Cuttler, "Ethical Issues in Growth Hormone Therapy" *Journal of the American Medical Association* (February 17, 1989). An article that discusses clinical trials of human growth hormone is Carol A. Tauer, "The NIH Trials of Growth Hormone for Short Stature," *IRB: A Review of Human Subjects Research* (May-June 1994).

ISSUE 10

Should HIV-Infected Surgeons Be Allowed to Operate?

YES: Inge B. Corless, from "Much Ado About Something: The Restriction of HIV-Infected Health-Care Providers," *AIDS and Public Policy Journal* (Summer 1992)

NO: Carson Strong, from "Should Physicians Infected With Human Immunodeficiency Virus Be Allowed to Perform Surgery?" *American Journal of Obstetrics and Gynecology* (May 1993)

ISSUE SUMMARY

YES: Nursing professor Inge B. Corless asserts that a single-minded emphasis on restricting the practice of an HIV-infected health care worker rather than insistence on universal protections to prevent infection actually puts patients at greater risk for transmission of infection.

NO: Philosopher Carson Strong believes that physicians infected with HIV should be restricted from procedures involving risks of patient exposure great enough to require informed consent or, at the least, procedures involving an open wound.

Among the more than 400,000 cases of AIDS reported in the United States to date, only six have been documented as cases of HIV transmission from a health care practitioner to a patient. And of these six—all patients of one dentist, Dr. David Acer—only one has come to symbolize public fears about this mode of transmission. That patient was Kimberly Bergalis, a 23-year-old Florida woman who died in 1991 of her disease after making impassioned pleas to legislators and public health officials to take action to prevent another case like hers. By the end of 1994 three other patients had died.

Despite extensive investigations, the Centers for Disease Control and Prevention (CDC), the federal agency responsible for monitoring disease spread and transmission in the United States, has not been able to determine definitively just what it was about Dr. Acer or the way he practiced dentistry that resulted in HIV transmission. Nevertheless, what had before been just a theoretical risk became a reality.

The CDC estimates the risk that a patient will contract HIV infection from an HIV-infected surgeon during an operation as between 1 in 42,000 and 1 in 420,000. This is less than the risk of dying because of the general anesthesia used in the operation (1 in 10,000) and about the same as the risk of contracting

HIV infection after the transfusion of blood that has been screened for the virus (1 in 60,000).

Although extensive "look-back" studies conducted among 19,000 former patients of 57 physicians who have died of AIDS (as of March 1993) have not shown any cases of transmission from doctor to patient, these studies may have missed some cases of transmission. The CDC estimates that by 1991 between 3 and 28 patients had been infected by surgeons and between 10 and 100 by dentists. Transmission from HIV-infected patients to health care practitioners is much more likely to occur. That risk is about 1 in 330.

Public opinion responded swiftly to the news about the dentist's HIV transmission and especially to the dramatic entreaties of Kimberly Bergalis. Public opinion polls showed strong support for mandatory testing of health care professionals, required disclosure of HIV infection status, and restrictions on professionals' practices.

In July 1991 the CDC recommended that "health care workers who perform exposure-prone invasive procedures should know their HIV antibody status." It rejected mandatory testing of health care professionals because the risk to patients was too low to justify this massive diversion of resources. Although some medical organizations, such as the American Medical Association, supported restrictions on HIV-infected professionals, many others rejected the CDC's recommendations. No professional group would agree to construct a list of "exposure-prone" invasive procedures because of the difficulty in defining this category in any scientific way.

The arguments for and against restricting the practice of HIV-infected professionals have several ethical dimensions: the basis of the doctor-patient relationship; the obligations of professionals to their patients to prevent harm; patients' rights of autonomy, including the right to full disclosure by the health care provider of relevant information; and the right of professionals to privacy and to be protected from discrimination based on prejudice and political pressure.

Inge B. Corless suggests that emphasis on a health care worker's HIV status is the wrong way to protect patients, who are much more at risk from other aspects of surgery. She stresses the importance of universal protections to prevent transmission of all infections as the most scientifically based method. Carson Strong, on the other hand, presents an ethical view that relies on the doctrine of informed consent. If the procedure is serious enough to require informed consent, an HIV-infected physician should be restricted from performing it. This would, in essence, bar HIV-infected surgeons from operating.

YES

Inge B. Corless

MUCH ADO ABOUT SOMETHING: THE RESTRICTION OF HIV-INFECTED HEALTH-CARE PROVIDERS

It is a relief to be able to say about some stressful event, "It was much ado about nothing." Such words, however, cannot be uttered in response to the putative transmission of the human immunodeficiency virus (HIV) to 5 patients by Dr. David Acer of Stuart, Florida.[1] The Acer case is indeed much ado about something; but it is the potential consequences of the way that "something" has been framed, the response to that "something," that are as dire as the events that precipitated the concern.

The facts as outlined by the Centers for Disease Control (CDC) are that 5 patients from 1 dental practice, with no other known risk factor apart from treatment by an HIV-infected dentist, became HIV-antibody positive.[2] State-of-the-art laboratory analysis by Gerald Myers of Los Alamos indicates an isomorphism in the proviral DNA sequences sampled from Dr. Acer and the 5 patients (notably in the C2-V3 region of gp 120 of the lymphocytes) —an isomorphism far greater than that observed between this group and 2 other patients from the practice with known risk factors, and 35 other HIV-antibody-positive persons residing within 90 miles.[3]

Questions have been raised about the methods employed in the CDC-Los Alamos analysis. The initial questions are about the representativeness of the local controls and the manner in which samples from these individuals were processed. Given Dr. Acer's reported penchant from privacy, should the control group also have included individuals outside the immediate area, such as individuals from Key West?[4] Time since initial infection may have been another important variable to be considered in selecting the local controls.[5] Variations in scientific method, notably the omission of the cloning step in the analysis of the samples from the local controls, introduced what may be an important source of variance.[6] Smith and Waterman also question the appropriateness of using the Wilcoxon rank-sum test, given that the date used failed to meet the assumptions of the test.[7]

From Inge B. Corless, "Much Ado About Something: The Restriction of HIV-Infected Health-Care Providers," *AIDS and Public Policy Journal*, vol. 7, no. 2 (Summer 1992). Copyright © 1992 by University Publishing Group, Inc. Reprinted by permission.

The scientists at Los Alamos and CDC used several approaches to examine these complex questions and did so under the pressure of time. The difficulty is that if the method used led to a failure to uncover similarities between the dentist, the 5 patients and the controls, that failure is very serious in that it would have led to the wrong conclusions.

What does seem certain at this time is that the viral strains infecting Dr. Acer and the 5 patients were closely related. What remains a matter for dispute, in addition to some of the methodological issues, is the mode of transmission. It is known that the disinfection technique used in the practice did not meet accepted standards; that is, among other breaks in technique including re-use of gloves, instruments were reported to have been immersed in an unspecified disinfectant for variable lengths of time.[8] It is also known that the instruments used for patients were employed as well in providing dental care to Dr. Acer.[9] A review of Dr. Acer's medical records revealed that he was diagnosed with Kaposi's sarcoma following a biopsy of the palate.[10] The significance of this particular diagnosis for HIV transmission, if any, has not been considered in the CDC's discussion of the case. Moreover, at least 1 of Dr. Acer's sexual partners was also a patient in the practice. So much is known.

What is not known is how the transmission occurred.[11] Dr. Jaffe of the CDC is dubious of ever being able to determine the mode of transmission in the Acer case.[12] Meanwhile, the debate over preventive efforts has formed the basis for unprecedented political harangue and policy formulation.

The American Medical Association and the American Dental Association have asked their HIV-antibody-positive members to refrain voluntarily from engaging in invasive exposure-prone procedures.[13] The Centers for Disease Control's response to the potential for transmission of the human immunodeficiency virus in the health–care setting was to ask professional organizations to identify exposure-prone practices during which viral transmission might occur if there were injury to an HIV-infected health-care worker (HCW).[14] ...

Although prevention of inadvertent HIV transmission to patients is professionally obligatory, the means proposed are questionable. In its most recent formulation, the conditions for practice for an HIV-antibody-positive HCW will be determined by a committee composed of the health-care worker's personal physician, a specialist in infectious diseases with experise in the epidemiology of HIV and HBV transmission, a health professional with expertise in the procedures performed by the health-care worker, and state or local public-health official(s).[15] In an earlier discussion of the management of HIV-infected workers, the CDC indicated that the infected worker's personal physician and the employer's medical advisors could make the decision as to the worker's scope of practice.[16]

Barring HIV-positive professionals from exposure-prone procedures as identified by health professionals with expertise in these procedures can be accomplished only if everyone is tested periodically or if everyone who suspects he or she is HIV-antibody positive obtains testing and, if positive or has reason to believe that he or she may be infected, voluntarily withdraws or is prohibited from engaging in invasive procedures, or both. That is, testing would be done repeatedly, and infected health-care workers would be mandated not to engage in exposure-prone invasive procedures.

There are numerous problems associated with the determination of HIV status and of conditions for practice. The American Nurses Association, the American Medical Association, and the World Health Organization have issued proclamations opposing mandatory HIV testing of nurses and physicians.[17] Another approach, self-exclusion from practice requires individual knowledge of antibody status. Moreover, even if each individual in the health-care profession who thought he or she might have been privy to even the smallest risk were to seek testing voluntarily, some HIV-infected professionals would still test antibody negative due to the window period (prior to the manifestation of HIV antibodies in the blood) or to problems with the test itself, or they would falsely test antibody positive, with a host of attendant problems.

The level of safety currently proposed for HIV-positive health-care providers who engage in invasive procedures is a standard, in some instances, that is greater than that for the screening of blood for transfusion. The CDC estimates the probability of HIV transmission as 1 in 263,158 to 1 in 2,631,579 during dental procedures in which bleeding may occur; and 1 in 41,667 to 1 in 416,667 during surgery performed by an HIV-infected surgeon.[18] Lowenfels and Wormser estimate the probability of HIV transmission from an HIV-infected surgeon to be 1 chance in 83,000 per hour of surgery with upper and lower bounds of 1 in 500,000 and 1 in 28,000.[19] When the HIV status of the surgeon is unknown, the risk is estimated to be 1 in 20 million.[20] The risk of becoming HIV "infected through blood or blood products is between 1 in 100,000 and 200,000," with

estimates as high as 1 in 60,000 per unit of transfused blood, even with prior negative screening results.[21] In either case, and with a clearer danger in the instance of the blood transfusion given the size of the potential inoculum, some persons who are HIV infected won't be detected for the previously mentioned reasons. A recent study by Conley and Holmberg found 15 persons who were infected through blood that had tested antibody negative.[22] To put these arguments regarding risks in perspective, the industry standard for manufacturing defects in condoms is 4 in 1,000![23]

The emphasis on conditions of practice, namely whether the practitioner engages in invasive exposure-prone procedures, avoids the question of fitness for practice. The occurrence of HIV-positive serostatus automatically assigns the health-care worker borderline status, wherein fitness for practice will be determined by the practice rather than the fitness. Were the emphasis given to functional capacity, the question would be similar to that for HIV testing; that is, how frequently should functional capacity be assessed? Although at first blush that may appear to be a thorny issue, an open and continuing dialogue among health-care worker, personal physician, and supervisor would allow for adjustments if and when they were appropriate.

The current emphasis on serostatus and invasive exposure-prone procedures, even without lists determined by professional organizations or the Centers for Disease Control, provides a simplistic solution that runs roughshod over the rights of health-care providers. This solution to a political problem will have multiple repercussions as organizations rush to comply with a legislative mandate that states adopt the CDC requirements or develop equivalent guidelines....

What is perplexing is that this rage to limit practice by HIV-antibody professionals is based on what is essentially one case—albeit a case involving transmission to 5 individuals. The grief of those individuals and their families and friends, however, will not be eliminated or assuaged by ill-considered actions. Douard argues that the "sloppy habits" of one health-care worker ought not to be used to develop policy for other HIV-infected health-care professionals.[24]

In other documented instances of HIV-antibody-positive health-care providers, no instances of provider-to-patient transmission have been uncovered.[25]... As stated in a special communication by a joint committee of the Association for Practitioners in Infection Control and the Society of Hospital Epidemiologists of America, "The occurrence of a single case, or even of rare epidemiologically unrelated cases, of HCW-to-patient transmission of HIV should not be the basis upon which policy is drawn.[26]...

Current calls for self-disclosure and withdrawal from invasive procedures will have more professional and personal consequences on health-care providers if such calls are not accompanied by opportunities for retraining. Moreover, various health-sciences disciplines may prohibit HIV-positive individuals from admission to their programs. Schools of medicine, dentistry, nursing, and perhaps even pharmacy may determine that seropositive status with regard to certain viruses constitutes ineligibility for admission. Such a determination may deprive society of highly motivated individuals interested in careers in health care.

An additional area for concern is that if HIV-positive individuals are prohibited from engaging in invasive procedures and perhaps even in health care in general, a negative message will be conveyed to all health-care professionals. Will those individuals who engage in professionally appropriate behavior by providing care to persons with HIV disease be concerned that occupationally sustained infection will be compounded by professionally imposed unemployment? Will health-care workers not seek health care, lest they discover they are, in fact, HIV seropositive? Will such delays result in more rapid downhill trajectories? Will concerns about unemployment lead to delays in obtaining health care?

The Federation of State Medical Boards considers it to be professional misconduct for those engaged in exposure-prone procedures not to know their HIV status.[27] Given that the federation represents licensing and disciplinary boards, health-care workers are threatened with a potential loss of license for failure to know their status. But how frequently will testing be necessary to avoid being out of compliance, and will the potential loss of employment pose the greater threat? If voluntary compliance is deemed desirable, then at the very least employment counseling and worker's compensation insurance must be provided for professionals in training as well as for professionally qualified practitioners who become disabled as a result of occupational practice. A similar program of counseling and retraining, minus the worker's compensation, would be helpful to all health-care providers who are HIV-antibody positive. Such counseling is provided to doctors and other health-care workers by the Medical Expertise Retention Program on a volunteer basis.[28]

But more is necessary. Science must be used as the basis for decision making in scientific issues. It is all too tempting to "play" to different audiences to achieve goals unrelated to the issue at hand. Unfortunately, a variety of agendas is being realized with this issue. Groups whose concerns are with individuals associated with various transmission groups may find an opportunity in the response to the Acer situation to enact programs of stigmatization and quarantine. HIV-infected individuals may consider these discussions to be yet one more instance of discrimination. While the discrimination may result from the political machinations associated with this situation, it is not inherent in the issue.

The issue is still what to do about something; after all, 5 people were infected with the human immunodeficiency virus in what appears to be professional negligence of some sort. As mentioned before, the emphasis needs to be on disinfection procedures and the use of universal precautions. Only such procedures will protect the public from fomite transmission, whether the source is a health-care providers or another patient. The current single-minded emphasis on the HIV-infected health-care provider actually puts patients at greater risk for transmission of infection from other patients. Adequate disinfection interrupts the chain of events that can result in patient-to-patient transmission; exclusion of seropositive health-care providers does not.

New York State's policy regarding the HIV-infected health-care worker incorporates this broader perspective by requiring training in infection control of all personnel who engage in invasive procedures as a condition for licensure, renewal of licensure, or certification.[29] The policy also contains a voluntary evaluation process that examines functional capacity and ability to comply with infection-control guidelines, among other factors.[30] This policy takes a constructive approach and appears to protect both health-care worker and patient.

The patient's right to know about conditions that could influence his or her decision making about certain health-care risks is vouchsafed by the notion of informed consent, although this concept has been applied to procedures rather than to conditions of practice. Just as the American Medical Association, as a matter of prudence (and ethics), advocates that the medical profession "err on the side of protecting patients,"[31] so too will patients as a matter of prudence err on the side of protecting themselves and their loved ones.[32] Ginzburg discusses the case of an HIV-infected surgeon whose patients, on learning of his HIV status, sought other health-care providers.[33] The effect for many health-care workers who are HIV positive and who are involved in invasive procedures, given the fear of HIV infection, will be the requirement to disclose their status to their patients or withdraw from invasive procedures (read practice) and possibly to engage in retraining.[34] A change in specialty occurs with other instances of health-care-worker impairment and is not limited to HIV disease. The argument here, however, is that HIV-antibody-positive serostatus is not necessarily equivalent to health-care-worker impairment. When health-care workers are truly impaired, it will be important to enhance employee support and retraining programs.

Focusing on a given professional's HIV status obfuscates other issues associated with illness care. The most important issues for the potential surgery patient are the numbers of persons who survive surgery, who develop iatrogenic conditions, or who survive six months after treatment by a given surgeon or physician in a given hospital. The patient clearly has the right to know about such relevant considerations for informed decision making, regardless of the practitioner's HIV status.

Daniels presents a cogent argument that the absence of practice restrictions on HIV-infected health-care workers results in fewer cases of provider-to-patient transmission than would occur if such restrictions were instituted.[35] The emphasis given by national political figures on protecting the patient from the HIV-infected health-care provider thus misdirects efforts and resources away from activities that would do the most to protect the health of the public—namely the procedures that emphasize good infection-control practice. The argument here is not intended to negate the rights of the patient nor to suggest that the health-care professional can do no wrong. Rather, this article stresses the importance of science in developing policy and abjures the mayhem and mischief of ill-considered action. Hippocrates, who is oft quoted for asserting that the doctor first and foremost do no harm, also said: "Science and opinion are two different things; science is the father of knowledge but opinion breeds ignorance."[36]

The responsibility of health-care professionals is to use science to benefit humanity. Pandering to what is politic rather than deriving policy from a foundation of science may accelerate careers, but it also betrays the trust of the public. The scientific evidence to date strongly suggests the importance of emphasizing effective disinfection practices and strict adherence to universal precautions lest we succumb to ignorance and ill-considered action.

NOTES

1. Centers for Disease Control (henceforth, CDC). "Possible Transmission of Human Immunodeficiency Virus to a Patient During an Invasive Dental Procedure," *Morbidity & Mortality Weekly Report* 39 (1990):489–93; G. Friedland, "HIV Transmission from Health Care Workers," *AIDS Clinical Care* 3, no. 4 (1991):29–30; "Changed Climate Clouds Debate," *AIDS Information Exchange* 3 (1991):5.

2. CDC, "Update: Transmission of HIV Infection During Invasive Dental Procedures—Florida," *Morbidity & Mortality Weekly Report* 40, no. 23 (1991):377–81.

3. CDC, "Update Transmission of HIV Infection"; C.Y. Ou, C.A. Ciesielski, G. Myers, et al., "Molecular Epidemiology of HIV Transmission in a Dental Practice," *Science* 256 (22 May 1992): 1165–71.

4. A. Novick. Private communication with author, 3 June 1992.

5. T. F. Smith and M. S. Waterman, "The Continuing Case of the Florida Dentist," *Science* 256 (22 May 1992): 1155–56.

6. *Ibid.*, 1156; J. Palca, "CDC Closes the Case of the Florida Dentist," *Science* 256 (22 May 1992); 1130–31.

7. Smith and Waterman, "The Continuing Case."

8. D. Marianos, B. Gooch, L. Furman, et al., "HIV Transmission and Infection Control in the Office of a Dentist with AIDS," in *Seventh International Conference on AIDS: Abstract Book*, vol. 1 (Florence, Italy: Seventh International Conference on AIDS, 1991), M.C. 3071; "Staff Unaware of Acer's Infection," *AIDS Alert* 6, no. 7 (July 1991):135–36.

9. "Portrait of the Infected Provider," *AIDS Alert* 6, no. 7 (July 1991):130–39.

10. C. Ciesielski, D. Marianos, and C. Y. Ou, "Transmission of Human Immunodeficiency Virus in a Dental Practice," *Annals of Internal Medicine*, 116, no. 10 (15 May 1992):798–805.

11. H. Jaffe, O. Cy, C. Ciesielski, et al., "HIV Transmission to Patients During Dental Care," In *Seventh International Conference on AIDS: Abstract Book*, vol. 2, no 84 (Florence, Italy: Seventh International Conference on AIDS, 1991), TH.D. 110; D. L. Breo, "The 'Slippery Slope': Handling HIV-infected Health Workers," *Journal of the American Medical Association* 264, no. 11 (1990):1464–65.

12. H. Jaffe, "Comment During Workshop on Health Care Workers Issues II," in *Seventh International Conference on AIDS: Abstract Book*, vol. 2 (Florence, Italy: Seventh International Conference on AIDS, 1991), D. 13.

13. American Medical Association, "AMA Statement on HIV Infected Physicians," *Newsletter: American Medical Association* 8, no. 3 (1991):1–2.

14. CDC, "Process for Identifying Exposure-prone Invasive Procedures," *Morbidity & Mortality Weekly Report* 40, no. 32 (1991):565; CDC, "Recommendations for Preventing Transmission of Human Immunodeficiency Virus and Hepatitis B Virus to Patients During Exposure-Prone Invasive Procedures," *Morbidity & Mortality Weekly Report* 40, no. RR-8 (1991):1–9.

15. CDC, "Recommendations for Preventing Transmission of Human Immunodeficiency Virus and Hepatitis B Virus to Patients During Exposure-prone Invasive Procedures," 5.

16. CDC, "Guidelines for Prevention of Transmission of Human Immunodeficiency Virus and Hepatitis B. Virus to Health-care and Public Safety Workers," *Morbibity & Mortality Weekly Report* 38, no. s-6 (1989): 9.

17. B. Russell, "Testimony of the American Nurses Association on Risks of Transmission of Bloodborne Pathogens to Patients during Invasive Procedures" (Paper delivered on behalf of the American Nurses Association, 21 February 1991, at the CDC); American Medical Association, "Ethical Issues Involved in the Growing AIDS Crisis: Council on Ethical and Judicial Affairs," *Journal of the American Medical Association* 259 (1988):1360–61; World Health Organization, *Report of a Consultation on the Prevention of HBV-HIV Transmission in the Health Care Setting* (Geneva: WHO/GPA/DIR/91.5, 11–12 April 1991), 9.

18. The US Conference of Mayors, "CDC Estimates Number of Patients Infected by HCW's," *AIDS Information Exchange* 8, no. 3 (June 1991):11; M. E. Chamberland and D. M. Bell, "HIV Transmission from Health Care Worker to Patient: What Is the Risk?" *Annals of Internal Medicine* 116, no. 10 (15 May 1992):871–73.

19. A. B. Lowenfels and G. Wormser, "Risk of Transmission of HIV From Surgeon to Patient," *New England Journal of Medicine* 325, no. 12 (1991):883–89.

20. N. Daniels, "HIV-Infected Professionals, Patient Rights, and the 'Switching Dilemma'," *Journal of the American Medical Association* 267, no. 10 (1992):1368–71.

21. T. H. Murray, "The Poisoned Gift," *Milbank Quarterly* 68, Supplement 2 (1990):205–25; B. Lo and R. Steinbrook, "Health Care Workers Infected with the Human Immunodeficiency Virus," *Journal of the American Medical Association* 267, no. 8 (1992): 1101.

22. L. J. Conley and S. D. Holmberg, "Transmission of AIDS from Blood Screened Negative for Antibody to the Human Immunodeficiency Virus," *New England Journal of Medicine* 326, no. 22 (28 May 1992): 1499–1500.

23. CDC, "Condoms for Prevention of Sexually Transmitted Diseases," *Morbidity & Mortality Weekly Report* 37, no. 9 (1988):134–35.

24. J. Douard, "HIV+ Health Care Workers: Ethical Problem or Social Problem?" *AIDS and Public Policy Journal* 6, no. 4 (Winter 1991):175–80.

25. B. Mishu, W. Schaffner, J. M. Horan, *et al.*, "A Surgeon with AIDS," *Journal of the American Medical Association* 264, no. 4 (1990):467–70; J. D. Porter, J. G. Cruickshank, P. H. Gentle, *et al.*, "Management of Patients Treated by Surgeon with HIV Infection," *Lancet* 335 (1990) 113–14; J. J. Sacks, "AIDS in a Surgeon," *New England Journal of Medicine* 313, no. 16 (1985):1017–18; F. P. Armstrong, J. C. Miner, and W. H. Wolfe, "Investigation of a Health Care Worker with Symptomatic Human Immunodeficiency Virus Infection: An Epidemiologic Approach," *Military Medicine* 152, no. 8 (1987):414–18; R. W. Comer, D. R. Myers, C. D. Steadman, *et al.*, "Management Considerations for an HIV Positive Dental Student," *Journal of Dental Education* 55, no. 3 (1991):187–91; CDC, "Investigations of Patients Who Have Been Treated by HIV-Infected Health-Care Workers," *Journal of the American Medical Association* 267, no. 21 (3 June 1992):2864–65.

26. Association of Practitioners in Infection Control and the Society of Hospital Epidemiologists of America, "Position Paper: The HIV-Infected Health Care Worker," *American Journal of Infection Control* 18 (1988):373.

27. Lo and Steinbrook, "Health Care Workers Infected," 1102.

28. Medical Expertise Retention Program, Ben Schatz, Director, 273 Church St., San Francisco, CA 94114, (415) 864–0408.

29. "States Oppose Automatic Restrictions," *AIDS Alert* 7, no. 1 (January 1992): 8.

30. "Infected Workers Evaluated on Several Factors," *AIDS Alert* 7, no. 1 (January 1992): 8.

31. American Medical Association, "AMA Statement," 1–2.

32. Daniels, "HIV-Infected Professionals," 1368–71.

33. H. M. Ginzburg, "The Right of an HIV-Infected Surgeon to Practice—The Behringer Case," *Pediatric AIDS and HIV Infection: Fetus to Adolescent* 2, no. 6 (1991):366–71.

34. D. I. Schulman, "Stigma, Risk and the Florida AIDS Dental Cases," *AIDS Patient Care* 6 no. 1 (February 1992):3–4.

35. Daniels, "HIV-Infected Professionals," 1368–71,

36. J. Chadwick and W. Mann, *The Medical Works of Hippocrates* (Oxford: Blackwell Scientific Publications, 1950.)

NO
Carson Strong

SHOULD PHYSICIANS INFECTED WITH HUMAN IMMUNODEFICIENCY VIRUS BE ALLOWED TO PERFORM SURGERY?

For physicians in surgical specialties, the possible effects of becoming infected with human immunodeficiency virus (HIV) during one's practice of medicine are illustrated by the case of Dr. William Behringer. He practiced otolaryngology and facial plastic surgery at a hospital in Princeton, New Jersey, and in 1987 was diagnosed as having acquired immunodeficiency syndrome (AIDS).[1,2] The administrators of the hospital where he practiced learned about this, and meetings of the hospital board of directors were held to determine what action to take. The board decided that Dr. Behringer could continue to treat patients but that he should not perform procedures posing any risk of HIV transmission to patients. Accordingly, the board revoked his surgical privileges, against his wishes. Dr. Behringer continued in an office practice, but his surgical privileges were never reinstated. Other cases involving practice restrictions on HIV-infected physicians have arisen, including cases involving obstetrician-gynecologists in residency[3] and private practice.[4] The Centers for Disease Control and Prevention (CDC) has estimated that in the United States > 300 physicians in surgical specialties might currently be HIV positive.[5] This number could increase as the AIDS epidemic continues, and the issue of practice restrictions is likely to remain important. Such restrictions can significantly interfere with a physician's freedom to practice, as in Dr. Behringer's case. A question that should be asked is whether this intrusion is justified by the degree of risk to patients.

An important aspect of this issue is the attitudes of the public toward HIV-positive physicians. In 1988 Gerbert et al.[6] surveyed a nationwide sample of American adults, asking whether they would switch physicians if their doctor were HIV positive. Although this survey occurred before the highly publicized case of Dr. David Acer, the Florida dentist who is believed to have transmitted HIV infection to five of his patients,[7] 56% of respondents stated that they would switch.[6] After the Acer case the percentage increased, according to a similar survey conducted by *Newsweek* and The Gallup Organization.[8]

From Carson Strong, "Should Physicians Infected With Human Immunodeficiency Virus Be Allowed to Perform Surgery?" *American Journal of Obstetrics and Gynecology*, vol. 168, no. 3 (May 1993). Copyright © 1993 by Mosby-Year Book, Inc. Reprinted by permission.

The number who would switch increased to 65%, and an additional 13% stated they would continue treatment but exclude surgery or other invasive procedures. Ninety-five percent of respondents indicated that they would want to be told if their surgeon were HIV positive.[8]

Patient switching also is illustrated by the case of Dr. Behringer. This arose from a failure of the hospital at which he practiced to adequately protect this confidentiality.[1] Dr. Behringer himself had been a patient at the hospital, and his positive HIV test result was recorded in his chart. Word quickly spread among hospital staff that he was HIV positive. From there, word spread to the local community. Physician acquaintances and other friends he had not told about this condition began calling his home to express their condolences. Soon patients began calling his office to cancel appointments and request transfer of medical records. Dr. Behringer lost many patients.[1]

The attitudes of the public toward HIV-positive physicians have been described as irrational[6] and "occasionally hysterical."[9] The public is perceived to have overreacted, given the actual level of risk to patients.[10] However, even if these characterizations are true, they do not preclude the possibility that it is reasonable to restrict surgical procedures by HIV-infected physicians. This can be ascertained only after examining all sides of the issue. . . .

ETHICAL VIEWS

Suppose an HIV-positive physician performs surgery and an accident results in patient exposure to the physician's blood. A question that arises is whether the patient should be told about this after surgery. The answer clearly is yes because the patient needs to know, to be tested and to prevent possible transmission to loved ones. Therefore consideration must be given to the patient's experiences on being told. After receiving the news, the patient will need baseline and periodic follow-up testing. All of this likely will involve considerable anxiety for the patient and the patient's family. Probably, changes in life-style will be needed, such as modifications in sexual activity. For patients of reproductive age, changes in reproductive plans might be considered. This scenario shows that the risks to patients are not limited to the risks of transmission. What often has been overlooked in discussions of this issue is the significant impact of exposure to the physician's blood on the patient's life. The likelihood that such exposure will occur can be estimated with the CDC's probability figures... $(25/1000 \times 32/100)$, yielding a probability of 8 per 1000 surgical cases.

Although the risk of transmission might arguably be so low that it need not be revealed for informed consent, several considerations support the claim that the risk of exposure is great enough to require informed consent. Patient self-determination is supported by a legal standard of informed consent referred to as the "reasonable person" standard.[11] According to this standard, information should be provided if a reasonable person in the patient's position would find the information relevant to the decision to consent to the proposed treatment.[11] The relevance of information about risks depends on the likelihood that the risk will materialize and the seriousness of the harm that would occur.[11] A risk having a low probability can be relevant when the degree of harm is substantial. Those who have been exposed to HIV-infected blood in the health care setting have attested that the anxiety can be great.[12] Exposure has been described as an "emotional crisis" having a profound impact because of fear of AIDS and uncertainty about HIV infection.[12] A reasonably prudent patient would regard information that the surgeon is infected with HIV relevant to the decision to consent to an invasive surgical procedure because the harms associated with exposure are substantial and a probability of exposure of 8 per 1000 surgical cases, while low, is not negligible. With this information the patient has the option of avoiding this risk while obtaining the therapeutic benefit of the surgery by seeking another physician.

To push the above scenario further, suppose the patient is not told about the physician's seropositivity in advance and then learns that he or she has been exposed to the physician's blood. It seems likely that in a high percentage of such situations a lawsuit will arise. In a recent legal case, damages were awarded for emotional distress for fear of contracting AIDS after exposure to HIV-infected blood.[13] Although that case did not involve a physician, it would be a precedent for cases involving patient exposure to blood of HIV-positive physicians. Thus it is reasonable for hospitals to be concerned about liability involving HIV-positive physicians.

These considerations suggest that revealing a seropositive status is not feasible because the physician's practice likely would be disrupted, but not revealing seropositive status and performing surgery are not acceptable because the patient's right to informed consent would be violated. The only alternative is to restrict the surgical practice of HIV-positive physicians. This suggests that an ethically justifiable view is in the middle ground between the two views discussed here.

A third view, which is in the middle ground, holds that HIV-positive physicians should be restricted from performing some subset of invasive procedures involving a relatively higher risk of transmission. Several commentators have advocated this view,[2,4] and the CDC's July 12, 1991, recommendations[14] are a version of it. The shortcoming of this view is its focus on the risk of transmission rather than exposure. As discussed, it is the risk of exposure that triggers the need to reveal for purposes of informed consent. Because revealing is not feasible and operating without telling is not ethically acceptable, the risk of exposure also triggers the need for restrictions.

Therefore another middle-ground view such as the following seems indicated. HIV-infected physicians should refrain from performing procedures in which the risk of patient exposure to the physician's blood is great enough to require informed consent. If we accept the CDC exposure risk estimate as reasonable given current information, this view implies that HIV-positive physicians should refrain, at the least, from performing surgical procedures involving an open wound. Examples of procedures that the CDC study identified as involving patient exposures include abdominal and vaginal hysterectomy, ovarian cystectomy, and salpingo-oophorectomy.[15] Although cesarean sections were not observed in the CDC study, reports of hepatitis B virus transmission from infected obstetricians to patients during cesarean sections[16] suggest that there is a risk of exposure from HIV-positive physicians during such procedures. Because procedures involving small incisions such as laparoscopy were not observed in the CDC study, exposure risks associated with such procedures remain to be defined. This raises the possibility of exempting procedures involving small incisions from practice restrictions, pending availability of more data. Future empiric studies might help define more precisely those procedures in which the probability of exposure is high enough to trigger restrictions. . . .

COMMENT

If practice restrictions are to be imposed on HIV-infected physicians in surgical specialties, it is necessary to consider what can be done to ameliorate harms to physicians whose practices are restricted. One area needing greater attention is disability insurance. Every physician at risk of acquiring HIV infection should have the opportunity to obtain disability insurance that explicitly covers HIV. Moreover, the amount of compensation should be sufficient to avoid significant loss of income. Another area needing improvement is accommodation and support by coworkers and hospitals. For physicians who are employees, reassignment to job duties not posing risks to patients should be offered by employers, rather than firing physicians because they are seropositive. Although such accommodation is required of employers by the Americans with Disabilities Act,[17] it is less clear that HIV-positive physicians in group practices have such legal protections. In one reported case an HIV-infected gynecologist was forced out of a group practice.[4] A group's desire to protect its practice provides a strong incentive for such action. Unfortunately, accommodation such as permitting an infected group member to continue in an office practice may be difficult given current public attitudes. This underscores the need for public education concerning the risks of exposure and transmission. Finally, greater attention should be given to improving surgical instruments and techniques[18] to reduce the risks of injury to patients and physicians, where possible.

REFERENCES

1. *Estate of Behringer v Medical Center at Princeton*, 592 A2d 1251 (NJ Super Ct Law Div 1991).
2. Orentlicher D. HIV-infected surgeons: Behringer v Medical Center. JAMA 1991;266:1134–7.
3. *Application of Milton S. Hershey Medical Center*, 595 A2d 1290 (Pa Super Ct 1991).
4. Gostin L. The HIV-infected health care professional: public policy, discrimination, and patient safety. Law Med Health Care 1990;18:303–10.
5. Centers for Disease Control. Estimates of the risk of endemic transmission of hepatitis B virus and human immunodeficiency virus to patients by the percutaneous route during invasive surgical and dental procedures. Atlanta: Centers for Disease Control, 1991.
6. Gerbert B, Maguire BT, Hulley SB, Coates TJ. Physicians and acquired immunodeficiency syndrome: what patients think about human immunodeficiency virus in medical practice. JAMA 1989;262:1969–72.
7. Ciesielski C, Marianos D, Ou C-Y, et al. Transmission of human immunodeficiency virus in a dental practice. Ann Intern Med 1992;116:798–805.
8. Kantrowitz B, Springer K, McCormick J, et al. Doctors and AIDS. Newsweek 1991 July 1:48–57.
9. Dickey NW. Physicians and acquired immunodeficiency syndrome: a reply to patients. JAMA 1989;262:2002.
10. Barondess JA. Working Group Convened by the New York Academy of Medicine. The risk of contracting HIV infection in the course of health care. JAMA 1991;265:1872–3.
11. *Henderson v Milobsky*, 595 F2d 654 (DC Cir 1978).
12. Henry K, Thurn J. HIV infection in healthcare workers. Postgrad Med 1991;89:30–8.
13. *Johnson v West Virginia University Hospitals, Inc.*, 413 SE2d 889 (W Va 1991).
14. Centers for Disease Control. Recommendations for preventing transmission of human immunodeficiency virus and hepatitis B virus to patients during exposure-prone invasive procedures. MMWR 1991;40:1–9.

15. Tokars JI, Bell DM, Culver DH, et al. Percutaneous injuries during surgical procedures. JAMA 1992;267:2899–904.
16. Lettau LA, Smith JD, Williams D, et al. Transmission of hepatitis B with resultant restriction of surgical practice. JAMA 1986;255:934–7.

17. Americans with Disabilities Act of 1990. Pub L No. 101–336, 104 Stat 327.
18. Burget GC, Orane AM, Teplica D. HIV-infected surgeons. JAMA 1992;267:803.

POSTSCRIPT

Should HIV-Infected Surgeons Be Allowed to Operate?

In December 1993 an Australian case was reported in which four patients were infected with HIV in a doctor's office. The doctor was not HIV-infected, but one of his patients was and he failed to sterilize his instruments. This case reemphasized the need for infection control measures to prevent patient-to-patient transmission.

In June 1992 the CDC backed away from its earlier proposals to establish a list of "exposure-prone" invasive procedures, although it did not withdraw the plan. Instead it deferred to state and local health departments in deciding on a case-by-case basis what types of care can be provided by HIV-infected health care professionals. This decision was also criticized because it left open the possibility of widely divergent policies being adopted and because it abdicated the CDC's national leadership role. Some states, such as New York, have developed policies that emphasize mandatory infection control training as a condition of licensing and relicensing and voluntary counseling and testing.

Florida has enacted legislation that allows health care professionals whose practices have been restricted because of their HIV status to be covered by disability health insurance if they have lost income. Laws in Iowa, Alabama, and Oklahoma establish review panels to determine what procedures an individual HIV-infected professional may not perform. Illinois law allows the State Health Department to notify the former patients of health care workers who have been diagnosed with AIDS.

In April 1991, in the case of *Behringer v. Medical Center,* a New Jersey trial court upheld a hospital's decision to restrict the surgical privileges of a doctor with AIDS. At the same time it ruled that the hospital had violated Dr. Behringer's confidentiality by failing to take reasonable precautions to prevent his AIDS diagnosis from becoming publicly known. This case is discussed in David Orentlicher, "HIV-Infected Surgeons: *Behringer v. Medical Center," Journal of the American Medical Association* (August 28, 1991).

One "look-back" study of the patients of an HIV-infected surgeon concluded that "the risk of HIV transmission during surgery may be so small that it will be quantified only by pooling data from multiple, methodologically similar investigations" (Audrey Smith Rogers et al., "Investigation of Potential HIV Transmission to the Patients of an HIV-Infected Surgeon," *Journal of the American Medical Association,* April 14, 1993). The controversy has produced a flood of articles, most of them opposing mandatory restrictions on HIV-infected health care workers. See Norman Daniels, "HIV-Infected Professionals, Patient Rights, and the 'Switching Dilemma,' *Journal of the American Medical Association* (March 11, 1992) for an ethical analysis concluding that all patients would be worse off if they switched to uninfected practitioners. See Leonard H. Glantz, Wendy K. Mariner, and George J. Annas, "Risky Business: Setting Public Health Policy for HIV-Infected Health Care Professionals," *The Milbank Quarterly* (vol. 70, no. 1, 1992); Bernard Lo and Robert Steinbrook, "Health Care Workers Infected With the Human Immunodeficiency Virus," *Journal of the American Medical Association* (February 26, 1992); and Mark Barnes et al., "The HIV-Infected Health Care Professional: Employment Policies and Public Health," *Law, Medicine and Health Care* (Winter 1990).

For arguments supporting at least some level of restriction, see Larry Gostin's "The HIV-Infected Health Care Professional: Public Policy, Discrimination, and Patient Safety," *Law, Medicine and Health Care* (Winter 1990) and "HIV-Infected Physicians and the Practice of Seriously Invasive Procedures," *Hastings Center Report* (January–February 1989), and Albert R. Jonsen, "Is Individual Responsibility a Sufficient Basis for Public Confidence?" *Archives of Internal Medicine* (April 1991). See also Gordon G. Keyes, "Health Care Professionals With AIDS: The Risk of Transmission Balanced Against the Interests of Professionals and Institutions," *Journal of College and University Law* (Spring 1990).

See also Mary E. Chamberland et al., "Health Care Workers With AIDS: National Surveillance Update," *Journal of the American Medical Association* (December 25, 1991); Richard N. Danila et al., "A Look-Back Investigation of Patients of an HIV-Infected Physician," *The New England Journal of Medicine* (November 14, 1991); and Troyen Brennan, "Transmission of the Human Immunodeficiency Virus in the Health Care Setting—Time for Action," *The New England Journal of Medicine* (May 21, 1991). For another debate on the issue, see Kenneth A. De Ville, "Nothing to Fear But Fear Itself: HIV-Infected Physicians and the Law of Informed Consent," *The Journal of Law, Medicine & Ethics* (Summer 1994); and in the same issue, Donald H. J. Hermann, "Commentary: A Call for Authoritative CDC Guidelines for HIV-Infected Health Care Workers."

ISSUE 11

Should Doctors Be Able to Refuse Demands for "Futile" Treatment?

YES: Steven H. Miles, from "Informed Demand for 'Non-Beneficial' Medical Treatment," *The New England Journal of Medicine* (August 15, 1991)

NO: Felicia Ackerman, from "The Significance of a Wish," *Hastings Center Report* (July/August 1991)

ISSUE SUMMARY

YES: Physician Steven H. Miles believes that physicians' duty to follow patients' wishes ends when the requests are inconsistent with what medical care can reasonably be expected to achieve, when they violate community standards of care, and when they consume an unfair share of collective resources.

NO: Philosopher Felicia Ackerman contends that it is ethically inappropriate for physicians to decide what kind of life is worth prolonging and that decisions involving personal values should be made by the patient or family.

In the typical controversy involving life-prolonging treatment, it is the patient or patient's family who wants to stop treatment and the doctor or hospital administrator who wants to continue it. That line of cases began, most prominently, with the *Quinlan* case (1976) and was most recently decided in the *Cruzan* case (1990). Another scenario, however, is emerging. What happens when the patient or family demands that treatment be continued past the point that doctors or hospital administrators feel it is warranted? Families may hope for a miracle and want "everything possible" done to preserve life. In the case of "Baby L," described by John Paris, Robert K. Crone, and Frank Reardon in *The New England Journal of Medicine* (April 5, 1990), pediatricians refused a mother's request to start ventilator treatment for a severely compromised, blind, deaf, and neurologically impaired child who had spent all 28 months of her life in intensive care.

In other cases, patients or families may act out of religious convictions that life is a God-given gift that must be preserved at all costs. In her book *Ethics on Call* (Crown Publishers, 1992), Nancy Dubler describes the case of "Joseph," a devoutly religious man who interpreted Jewish law to mean that life can be taken only by God, and that he must take whatever measures are available to sustain his life, no matter what suffering was entailed. There may even be cases in which a criminal prosecution may hinge on whether a patient dies or not, or there may be financial motivations to preserving life.

These cases stretch the limits of patient autonomy and come to a full stop when they reach the boundaries of professional responsibility. Just as patients are moral agents, so too are physicians. Their professional ethic begins with the Hippocratic injunction "First, do no harm." Beyond avoiding harm, they are guided by the obligation to do good—to provide benefit to patients within the limits of their expertise. Since ancient times physicians have felt it is their prerogative to determine whether or not treatment is justified. The writings of Hippocrates and Plato warn physicians to acknowledge when their art is doomed to fail.

In modern times the Vatican's 1980 *Declaration on Euthanasia* places a strong emphasis on physician judgment, pointing out that "[doctors] may ... judge that the investment in instruments and personnel is disproportionate to the results foreseen; they may also judge that the techniques applied impose on the patient strain or suffering out of proportion with the benefits." The U.S. President's Commission for the Study of Bioethical Problems in Medicine concluded in 1983 that "health care professionals or institutions may decline to provide a particular option because that choice may violate their conscience or professional judgement, though, in doing so they may not abandon a patient." Even more recently (December 1990), the Society of Critical Care Medicine declared that "treatments that offer no benefit and serve to prolong the dying process should not be employed."

As frequently happens in bioethics, one case—not necessarily the first to arise—serves to focus the arguments. In the area of demands for "nonbeneficial" treatment, that case involved the treatment of Helga Wanglie, an elderly Minnesota woman who suffered a series of medical problems, culminating in a year and a half spent unconscious on a respirator in a persistent vegetative state. Her physicians asked her husband to consent to withdrawing treatment; his refusal set off a chain of events described in the following selections.

Steven H. Miles, a gerontologist and ethics consultant to Mrs. Wanglie's physicians, believes that Mrs. Wanglie was "overmastered" by her disease and that continued intensive care was inappropriate and inconsistent with reasonable medical expectations of benefit. Felicia Ackerman maintains that decisions about what lives are worth living properly fall to those who share the values of the patient—in this case, the family.

YES

Steven H. Miles

INFORMED DEMAND FOR "NON-BENEFICIAL" MEDICAL TREATMENT

An 85-year-old woman was taken from a nursing home to Hennepin County Medical Center on January 1, 1990, for emergency treatment of dyspnea [shortness of breath] from chronic bronchiectasis [widening of the air passages]. The patient, Mrs. Helga Wanglie, required emergency intubation [insertion of a tube] and was placed on a respirator. She occasionally acknowledged discomfort and recognized her family but could not communicate clearly. In May, after attempts to wean her from the respirator failed, she was discharged to a chronic care hospital. One week later, her heart stopped during a weaning attempt; she was resuscitated and taken to another hospital for intensive care. She remained unconscious, and a physician suggested that it would be appropriate to consider withdrawing life support. In response, the family transferred her back to the medical center on May 31. Two weeks later, physicians concluded that she was in a persistent vegetative state.... She was maintained on a respirator, with repeated courses of antibiotics, frequent airway suctioning, tube feedings, an air flotation bed, and biochemical monitoring.

In June and July of 1990, physicians suggested that life-sustaining treatment be withdrawn since it was not benefiting the patient. Her husband, daughter, and son insisted on continued treatment. They stated their view that physicians should not play God, that the patient would not be better off dead, that removing life support showed moral decay in our civilization, and that a miracle could occur. Her husband told a physician that his wife had never stated her preferences concerning life-sustaining treatment. He believed that the cardiac arrest would not have occurred if she had not been transferred from Hennepin County Medical Center in May. The family reluctantly accepted a do-not-resuscitate order based on the improbability of Mrs. Wanglie's surviving a cardiac arrest. In June, an ethics committee consultant recommended continued counseling for the family. The family declined counseling, including the counsel of their own pastor, and in late July asked

From Steven H. Miles, "Informed Demand for 'Non-Beneficial' Medical Treatment," *The New England Journal of Medicine*, vol. 325, no. 7 (August 15, 1991), pp. 512–515. Copyright © 1991 by The Massachusetts Medical Society. Reprinted by permission.

that the respirator not be discussed again. In August, nurses expressed their consensus that continued life support did not seem appropriate, and I, as the newly appointed ethics consultant, counseled them.

In October 1990, a new attending physician consulted with specialists and confirmed the permanence of the patient's cerebral and pulmonary conditions. He concluded that she was at the end of her life and that the respirator was "non-beneficial," in that it could not heal her lungs, palliate her suffering, or enable this unconscious and permanently respirator-dependent woman to experience the benefit of the life afforded by respirator support. Because the respirator could prolong life, it was not characterized as "futile."[1] In November, the physician, with my concurrence, told the family that he was not willing to continue to prescribe the respirator. The husband, an attorney, rejected proposals to transfer the patient to another facility or to seek a court order mandating this unusual treatment. The hospital told the family that it would ask a court to decide whether members of its staff were obliged to continue treatment. A second conference two weeks later, after the family had hired an attorney, confirmed these positions, and the husband asserted that the patient had consistently said she wanted respirator support for such a condition.

In December, the medical director and hospital administrator asked the Hennepin County Board of Commissioners (the medical center's board of directors) to allow the hospital to go to court to resolve the dispute. In January, the county board gave permission by a 4-to-3 vote. Neither the hospital nor the county had a financial interest in terminating treatment. Medicare largely financed the $200,000 for the first hospitalization at Hennepin County; a private insurer would pay the $500,000 bill for the second. From February through May of 1991, the family and its attorney unsuccessfully searched for another health care facility that would admit Mrs. Wanglie. Facilities with empty beds cited her poor potential for rehabilitation.

The hospital chose a two-step legal procedure, first asking for the appointment of an independent conservator to decide whether the respirator was beneficial to the patient and second, if the conservator found it was not, for a second hearing on whether it was obliged to provide the respirator. The husband cross-filed, requesting to be appointed conservator. After a hearing in late May, the trial court on July 1, 1991, appointed the husband, as best able to represent the patient's interests. It noted that no request to stop treatment had been made and declined to speculate on the legality of such an order.[2] The hospital said that it would continue to provide the respirator in the light of continuing uncertainty about its legal obligation to provide it....

DISCUSSION

This sad story illustrates the problem of what to do when a family demands medical treatment that the attending physician concludes cannot benefit the patient. Only 600 elderly people are treated with respirators for more than six months in the United States each year.[3] Presumably, most of these people are actually or potentially conscious. It is common practice to discontinue the use of a respirator before death when it can no longer benefit a patient.[4,5]

We do not know Mrs. Wanglie's treatment preferences. A large majority of elderly people prefer not to receive prolonged respirator support for irreversible unconsciousness.[6] Studies show that an older person's designated family proxy overestimates that person's preference for life-sustaining treatment in a hypothetical coma.[7-9] The implications of this research for clinical decision making have not been cogently analyzed.

A patient's request for a treatment does not necessarily oblige a provider or the health care system. Patients may not demand that physicians injure them (for example, by mutilation), or provide plausible but inappropriate therapies (for example, amphetamines for weight reduction), or therapies that have no value (such as laetrile for cancer). Physicians are not obliged to violate their personal moral views on medical care so long as patients' rights are served. Minnesota's Living Will law says that physicians are "legally bound to act consistently within my wishes within limits of reasonable medical practice" in acting on requests and refusals of treatment.[10] Minnesota's Bill of Patients' Rights says that patients "have the right to appropriate medical... care based on individual needs... [which is] limited where the service is not reimbursable."[11] Mrs. Wanglie also had aortic insufficiency. Had this condition worsened, a surgeon's refusal to perform a life-prolonging valve replacement as medically inappropriate would hardly occasion public controversy. As the Minneapolis *Star Tribune* said in an editorial on the eve of the trial,

> The hospital's plea is born of realism, not hubris.... It advances the claim that physicians should not be slaves to technology—any more than patients should be its prisoners. They should be free to deliver, and act on, an honest and

time-honored message: "Sorry, there's nothing more we can do."[12]

Disputes between physicians and patients about treatment plans are often handled by transferring patients to the care of other providers. In this case, every provider contacted by the hospital or the family refused to treat this patient with a respirator. These refusals occurred before and after this case became a matter of public controversy and despite the availability of third-party reimbursement. We believe they represent a medical consensus that respirator support is inappropriate in such a case.

The handling of this case is compatible with current practices regarding informed consent, respect for patients' autonomy, and the right to health care. Doctors should inform patients of all medically reasonable treatments, even those available from other providers. Patients can refuse any prescribed treatment or choose among any medical alternatives that physicians are willing to prescribe. Respect for autonomy does not empower patients to oblige physicians to prescribe treatments in ways that are fruitless or inappropriate. Previous "right to die" cases address the different situations of a patient's right to choose to be free of a prescribed therapy. This case is more about the nature of the patient's choice in using that entitlement.

The proposal that this family's preference for this unusual and costly treatment, which is commonly regarded as inappropriate, establishes a right to such treatment is ironic, given that preference does not create a right to other needed, efficacious, and widely desired treatments in the United States. We could not afford a universal health care system based on patients' demands. Such a system would irrationally allocate health care to socially powerful people with strong preferences for immediate treatment to the disadvantage of those with less power or less immediate needs.

After the conclusion was reached that the respirator was not benefiting the patient, the decision to seek a review of the duty to provide it was based on an ethic of "stewardship." Even though the insurer played no part in this case, physicians' discretion to prescribe requires responsible handling of requests for inappropriate treatment. Physicians exercise this stewardship by counseling against or denying such treatment or by submitting such requests to external review. This stewardship is not aimed at protecting the assets of insurance companies but rests on fairness to people who have pooled their resources to insure their collective access to appropriate health care. Several citizens complained to Hennepin County Medical Center that Mrs. Wanglie was receiving expensive treatment paid for by people who had not consented to underwrite a level of medical care whose appropriateness was defined by family demands.

Procedures for addressing this kind of dispute are at an early stage of development. Though the American Medical Association[13] and the Society of Critical Care Medicine[14] also support some decisions to withhold requested treatment, the medical center's reasoning most closely follows the guidelines of the American Thoracic Society.[15] The statements of these professional organizations do not clarify when or how a physician may legally withdraw or withhold demanded life-sustaining treatments. The request for a conservator to review the medical conclusion before considering the medical obligation was often miscon-

strued as implying that the husband was incompetent or ill motivated. The medical center intended to emphasize the desirability of an independent review of its medical conclusion before its obligation to provide the respirator was reviewed by the court. I believe that the grieving husband was simply mistaken about whether the respirator was benefiting his wife. A direct request to remove the respirator seems to center procedural oversight on the soundness of the medical decision making rather than on the nature of the patient's need. Clearly, the gravity of these decisions merits openness, due process, and meticulous accountability. The relative merits of various procedures need further study.

Ultimately, procedures for addressing requests for futile, marginally effective, or inappropriate therapies require a statutory framework, case law, professional standards, a social consensus, and the exercise of professional responsibility. Appropriate ends for medicine are defined by public and professional consensus. Laws can, and do, say that patients may choose only among medically appropriate options, but legislatures are ill suited to define medical appropriateness. Similarly, health-facility policies on this issue will be difficult to design and will focus on due process rather than on specific clinical situations. Public or private payers will ration according to cost and overall efficacy, a rationing that will become more onerous as therapies are misapplied in individual cases. I believe there is a social consensus that intensive care for a person as "overmastered" by disease as this woman was is inappropriate.

Each case must be evaluated individually. In this case, the husband's request seemed entirely inconsistent with what medical care could do for his wife, the standards of the community, and his fair share of resources that many people pooled for their collective medical care. This case is about limits to what can be achieved at the end of life.

REFERENCES

1. Tomlinson T. Brody H. Futility and the ethics of resuscitation. JAMA 1990; 264:1276–80.
2. In re Helga Wanglie, Fourth Judicial District (Dist. Ct., Probate Ct. Div.) PX-91-283. Minnesota, Hennepin County.
3. Office of Technology Assessment Task Force. Life-sustaining technologies and the elderly. Washington, D.C.: Government Printing Office, 1987.
4. Smedira NG, Evans BH, Grais LS, et al. Withholding and withdrawal of life support from the critically ill. N Engl J Med 1990; 322:309–15.
5. Lantos JD, Singer PA, Walker RM, et al. The illusion of futility in clinical practice. Am J Med 1989; 87:81–4.
6. Emanuel LL, Barry MJ, Stoeckle JD, Ettelson LM, Emanuel EJ. Advance directives for medical care —a case for greater use. N Engl J Med 1991; 324:889–95.
7. Zweibel NR, Cassel CK. Treatment choices at the end of life: a comparison of decisions by older patients and their physician-selected proxies. Gerontologist 1989; 29:615–21.
8. Tomlinson T, Howe K, Notman M, Rossmiller D. An empirical study of proxy consent for elderly persons. Gerontologist 1990; 30:54–64.
9. Danis M, Southerland LI, Garrett JM, et al. A prospective study of advance directives for life-sustaining care. N Engl J Med 1991; 324:882–8.
10. Minnesota Statutes. Adult Health Care Decisions Act. 145b.04.
11. Minnesota Statutes. Patients and residents of health care facilities: Bill of rights. 144.651:Subd. 6.
12. Helga Wanglie's life. Minneapolis Star Tribune. May 26, 1991:18A.
13. Council on Ethical and Judicial Affairs. American Medical Association. Guidelines for the appropriate use of do-not-resuscitate orders JAMA 1991; 265:1868–71.
14. Task Force on Ethics of the Society of Critical Care Medicine. Consensus report on the ethics of foregoing life-sustaining treatments in the critically ill. Crit Care Med 1990; 18:1435–9.
15. American Thoracic Society. Withholding and withdrawing life-sustaining therapy. Am Rev Respir Dis (in press).

NO
Felicia Ackerman

THE SIGNIFICANCE OF A WISH

The case of Helga Wanglie should be seen in the general context of conflicts that can arise over whether a patient should be maintained on life-support systems. Well-publicized conflicts of this sort usually involve an institution seeking to prolong the life of a patient diagnosed as terminally ill and/or permanently comatose, versus a family that claims, with varying degrees of substantiation, that the patient would not have wanted to be kept alive under these circumstances. But other sorts of conflicts about prolonging life also occur. Patients who have indicated a desire to stay alive may face opposition from family or medical staff who think these patients' lives are not worth prolonging. Such cases can go badly for patients, who may have difficulty getting their preferences even believed, let alone respected.[1]

Helga Wanglie's case is not as clear cut. But in view of the fact that keeping her on a respirator will prolong her life, that there is more reason to believe she would have wanted this than to believe she would not have wanted it, that medical diagnoses of irreversible unconsciousness are not infallible, and that her private health insurance plan has not objected to paying for her respirator support and in fact has publicly taken the position that cost should not be a factor in treatment decisions, I believe HCMC [Hennepin County Medical Center] should continue to maintain Mrs. Wanglie on a respirator. This respirator support is medically and economically feasible, and it serves a recognized medical goal—that of prolonging life and allowing a chance at a possible, albeit highly unlikely, return to consciousness.

THE SIGNIFICANCE OF MEDICAL EXPERTISE

Dr. Steven Miles, ethics consultant at HCMC, has argued that continued respirator support is "medically inappropriate" for Mrs. Wanglie. The argument is based on a criterion of medical appropriateness that allows doctors to prescribe respirators for any of three purposes: to allow healing, to alleviate suffering, and to enable otherwise disabled persons to continue to enjoy life. Since keeping Mrs. Wanglie on a respirator serves none of these ends, it is argued, such treatment is medically inappropriate.

From Felicia Ackerman, "The Significance of a Wish," *Hastings Center Report*, vol. 21, no. 4 (July/August 1991). Copyright © 1991 by The Hastings Center. Reprinted by permission.

But just what does "medically inappropriate" mean here? A clear case of medical inappropriateness would be an attempt to cure cancer with laetrile, since medicine has presumably shown that laetrile cannot cure cancer. Moreover, since laetrile's clinical ineffectiveness is a technical medical fact about which doctors are supposed to have professional expertise, it is professionally appropriate for doctors to refuse to grant a patient's request to have laetrile prescribed for cancer. But HCMC's disagreement with Mrs. Wanglie's family is not a technical dispute about a matter where doctors can be presumed to have greater expertise than laymen. The parties to the dispute do not disagree about whether maintaining Mrs. Wanglie on a respirator is likely to prolong her life; they disagree about whether her life is worth prolonging. This is not a medical question, but a question of values. Hence the term "medically inappropriate," with its implication of the relevance of technical medical expertise, is itself inappropriate in this context. It is as presumptuous and *ethically* inappropriate for doctors to suppose that their professional expertise qualifies them to know what kind of life is worth prolonging as it would be for meteorologists to suppose their professional expertise qualifies them to know what kind of destination is worth a long drive in the rain.

It has also been argued that continued respirator support does not serve Mrs. Wanglie's interests since a permanently unconscious person cannot "enjoy any realization of the quality of life."[2] Yet were this approach to be applied consistently, it would undermine the idea frequently advanced in other life-support cases that it is in the interests of the irreversibly comatose to be "allowed" to die "with dignity." Such people are not suffering or even conscious, so how can death benefit them or serve their interests? The obvious reply in both cases is that there is a sense in which it is in a permanently comatose person's interests to have his or her previous wishes and values respected. And there is some evidence that Mrs. Wanglie would want to be kept alive.

But why suppose doctors are any more obliged to serve this want than they would be to help gratify some nonmedical desire such as a desire to be remembered in a certain way? An obvious answer is that prolonging life is a medical function, as is allowing a possible return to consciousness. Medical diagnoses of irreversible coma are not infallible, as the recent case of Carrie Coons clearly demonstrates. The court order to remove her feeding tube, requested by her family, was rescinded after Mrs. Coons regained consciousness following five and a half months in what was diagnosed as an irreversible vegetative state.[3] Such cases cast additional light on the claim that respirator support is medically inappropriate and not in Mrs. Wanglie's interests. When the alternative is death, the question of whether going for a long-shot chance of recovering consciousness is worth it is quite obviously a question of values, rather than a technical medical question doctors are especially professionally qualified to decide.

THE SIGNIFICANCE OF QUALITY OF LIFE

Medical ethicists who take into account the possibility that seemingly irreversibly comatose patients might regain consciousness have offered further general arguments against maintaining such patients on life-support systems. One such argument relies on the fact that "the few

patients who have recovered consciousness after a prolonged period of unconsciousness were severely disabled,"[4] with
disabilities including blindness, inability
to speak, permanent distortion of limbs,
and paralysis. Since many blind, mute,
and/or paralyzed people seem to find
their lives well worth living, however,
the assumption that disability is a fate
worse than death seems highly questionable. Moreover, when the patient's views
on the matter are unknown, maintaining
him on a respirator to give him a chance
to regain consciousness and then decide
whether to continue his disabled existence seems preferable to denying him
even the possibility of a choice by deciding in advance that he would be better off dead. Keeping alive someone who
would want to die and "allowing" to die
someone who would want a chance of
regained consciousness are not parallel
wrongs. While both obviously go against
the patient's values, only the latter has the
additional flaw of doing this in a way that
could actually affect his conscious experience.

The other argument asserts that since
long-term treatment imposes emotional
and often financial burdens on the comatose patient's family and most patients, before losing consciousness, place
a high value on their families' welfare,
presumably these patients would rather
die than be a burden to their loved ones.[5]
Though very popular nowadays, this latter sort of argument is cruel because it attributes extreme self-abnegation to those
unable to speak for themselves. It is also
biased because it assumes great sacrificial
love on the part of the patient, but not
the family. Why not argue instead that
a loving family will not want to deny a
beloved member a last chance at regained
consciousness and hence that it is *not* in

the interest of the patient's loved ones to
withdraw life supports? Mrs. Wanglie's
family clearly wants her kept alive.[6]

THE SIGNIFICANCE OF A GESTURE

Mrs. Wanglie's family claims that she
would want to be kept alive. Yet Dr.
Cranford suggests that her family at first
denied having previously discussed the
matter with her, and that it was only
after the HCMC committed itself to going
to court that the family claimed Mrs.
Wanglie had said she would want to
be kept alive. Dr. Miles mentions that
during the months when she was on a
respirator before becoming unconscious,
Mrs. Wanglie at times pulled at her
respirator tubing.

I agree that Mrs. Wanglie's views are
less than certain. Yet for reasons given
above and also because death is irrevo-
cable, there should be a presumption in
favor of life when a patient's views are
unclear or unknown. Pulling at a respirator tube is obviously insufficient evidence of even a fleeting desire to die; it
may simply be a semi-automatic attempt
to relieve discomfort, like pulling away
in a dentist's chair even when one has
an overriding desire that the dental work
be performed. Basically, although the circumstances of the family's claim about
Mrs. Wanglie's statement of her views
make the claim questionable, it is their
word against nobody's. No one claims
that she ever said she would prefer *not*
to be kept alive, despite her months of
conscious existence on a respirator.

It has also been argued that we should
not allow patients to demand medically
inappropriate care when the costs of that
care are borne by others who have not
consented to do so. I have already discussed the question of medical appropri-

ateness. And a private health plan is paying for Mrs. Wanglie's care, a plan whose officials have publicly stated that cost should not be a factor in treatment decisions. The pool of subscribers to the plan, whose premiums are what indirectly subsidize Mrs. Wanglie's care, have, by being members of this plan, committed themselves to a practice of medicine that does not take cost into account. It would be unfair to make cost a factor in Mrs. Wanglie's treatment decision now. Public statements by health insurance plan officials are expected to be taken into account by consumers selecting health insurance and must not be reneged upon. Mrs. Wanglie's insurer is not seeking to renege. Instead, it is her *doctors* who have decided that her life is not worth prolonging.

Moreover, to say it would be the underlying disease rather than the act of removing the respirator that would cause Helga Wanglie's death is not helpful. If Mrs. Wanglie is, as the HCMC staff claims, irreversibly respirator-dependent, then saying that removing the respirator would cause her death is just as logical as saying that withdrawing a rope from a drowning man would cause his death, even if his death is to be "attributed" to his drowning. If the person in either case has an interest in living, one violates his interest by withdrawing the necessary means. This is what HCMC is seeking court permission to do to Mrs. Wanglie.

REFERENCES

1. For example, consider the case of seventy-eight-year-old Earl Spring, whose mental deterioration did not prevent him from saying that he did not want to die. The statement of this preference was not considered conclusive reason to keep him on dialysis over his family's objections. Similarly, the *New York Times Magazine* recently described the situation of a severely disabled, elderly woman whose explicit advance directive that she wanted everything possible done to keep her alive was apparently ignored by both her husband and the hospital's ethics committee (K. Bouton, "Painful Decisions: The Role of the Medical Ethicist," 5 August 1990).

2. This argument comes from an unpublished letter from Dr. Steven Miles, made available to me by the *Hastings Center Report* at his request.

3. The Coons case was widely reported in newspapers. For example, see C. DeMare, "'Hopeless' Hospital Patient, 86, Comes Out of Coma," *Albany Times Union*, 12 April 1989. Additional cases of this sort are cited in President's Commission for the Study of Ethical Problems in Medicine and Biomedical and Behavioral Research, *Deciding to Forego Life-Sustaining Treatment* (Washington, D.C.: U.S. Government Printing Office, 1983).

4. President's Commission, *Deciding to Forego Life-Sustaining Treatment*, p. 182.

5. President's Commission, *Deciding to Forego Life-Sustaining Treatment*, p. 183.

6. I have given this sort of argument in a letter to the *New York Times*, 4 November 1987, as well as in a short story about terminal illness, "The Forecasting Game, in *Prize Stories 1990: The O. Henry Awards*, ed. W. Abrahams (New York: Doubleday, 1990), pp. 315–35, and in an op-ed "No Thanks, I Don't Want to Die with Dignity," *Providence Journal-Bulletin*, 19 April 1990 (reprinted in other newspapers under various different titles).

POSTSCRIPT

Should Doctors Be Able to Refuse Demands for "Futile" Treatment?

Three days after the Minnesota court named Oliver Wanglie as his wife's legal conservator, thus preserving his right to make decisions about her treatment, Helga Wanglie died of multisystem organ failure. Her aggressive treatment had been continued throughout. Mr. Wanglie said, "We felt that when she was ready to go that the good Lord would call her, and I would say that's what happened." Her daughter said that her mother's care had been excellent; "We just had a disagreement on ethics."

A series of cases involving infants has extended the debate on medical futility. The most publicized case is that of "Baby K," who was born with most of her brain missing. In most cases of this condition (anencephaly), babies die within a few days. Baby K's mother, however, insisted that Fairfax Hospital in Falls Church, VA, provide ventilator support to help the baby breathe, which has kept her alive in a nursing home for almost two years. In February 1994 the hospital's request to stop this treatment was denied by a federal appeals court, which extended to this case a federal law requiring hospitals to treat emergency patients even if they cannot pay. Payment is not an issue here, however, because the mother is a member of a Health Maintenance Organization, which is paying the bills.

E. Haavi Morreim addresses the issue of how to preserve respect for moral diversity while preventing patients, families, physicians, and society from coercing one another into providing costly ineffective treatments in "Profoundly Diminished Life: The Casualties of Coercion," *Hastings Center Report* (January/February 1994).

In an article titled "Autonomy and the Common Weal," *Hastings Center Report* (January/February 1991), philosopher Larry Churchill calls for a vision of patient autonomy that includes citizenship. He says, "The patient as citizen has rights within health care, but also duties to make judicious and proportionate choices." Physician Marcia Angell argues that only Helga Wanglie's family, not her doctors, has the right to decide on the continued use of her respirator in "The Case of Helga Wanglie: A New Kind of 'Right to Die' Case," *The New England Journal of Medicine* (August 15, 1991).

John S. Paris and Frank E. Reardon provide a comprehensive overview of the cases in this area in "Physician Refusal of Requests for Futile or Ineffective Treatments," a chapter in *Emerging Issues in Biomedical Policy, vol. 2,* edited by Robert H. Blank and Andrea L. Bonnicksen (Columbia University Press, 1993).

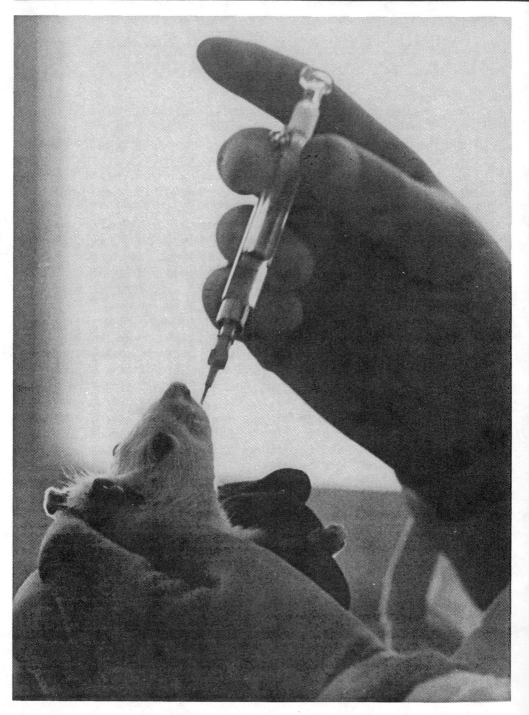

PART 4

Human and Animal Experimentation

The goal of scientific research is knowledge that will benefit society. But achieving that goal may subject humans and animals to some risks. Questions arise not only about how research should be conducted but whether or not it should be conducted at all, such as in the use of animals or fetal tissue. Another question concerns whether or not research is carried out equitably among men and women. These questions transcend national boundaries and raise questions of whether or not research can be "ethical" in one country and not in another. This section contends with issues that will shape the future of experimental science.

- Should Animal Experimentation Be Permitted?

- Will Fetal Tissue Research Encourage Abortions?

- Is There a Gender Bias in Medicine and Research?

ISSUE 12

Should Animal Experimentation Be Permitted?

YES: Jerod M. Loeb et al., from "Human vs. Animal Rights: In Defense of Animal Research," *Journal of the American Medical Association* (November 17, 1989)

NO: Tom Regan, from "Ill-Gotten Gains," in Donald Van DeVeer and Tom Regan, eds., *Health Care Ethics: An Introduction* (Temple University Press, 1987)

ISSUE SUMMARY

YES: Jerod M. Loeb and his colleagues, representing the American Medical Society's Group on Science and Technology, assert that concern for animals, admirable in itself, cannot impede the development of methods to improve the welfare of humans.

NO: Philosopher Tom Regan argues that conducting research on animals exacts the grave moral price of failing to show proper respect for animals' inherent value, whatever the benefits of the research.

In 1865 the great French physiologist Claude Bernard wrote, "Physicians already make too many dangerous experiments on man before carefully studying them in animals." In his insistence on adequate animal research before trying a new therapy on human beings, Bernard established a principle of research ethics that is still considered valid. But in the past few decades this principle has been challenged by another view—one that sees animals not as tools for human use and consumption but as moral agents in their own right. Animal experimentation, according to this theory, cannot be taken for granted but must be justified by ethical criteria at least as stringent as those that apply to research involving humans.

Philosophers traditionally have not ascribed any moral status to animals. Like St. Thomas Aquinas before him, René Descartes, a seventeenth-century French physiologist and philosopher, saw no ethical problem in experimentation on animals. Descartes approved of cutting open a fully conscious animal because it was, he said, a machine more complex than a clock but no more capable of feeling pain. Immanuel Kant argued that animals need not be treated as ends in themselves because they lacked rationality.

Beginning in England in the nineteenth century, antivivisectionists (people who advocate the abolition of animal experimentation) campaigned, with varying success, for laws to control scientific research. But the internal dissensions in the movement and its frequent lapses into sentimentality made it only partially effective. At best the antivivisectionists achieved some legislation that mandated more humane treatment of animals used for research, but they never succeeded in abolishing animal research or even in establishing the need for justification of particular research projects.

The more recent movement to ban animal research, however, is both better organized politically and more rigorously philosophical. The movement, often called animal liberation or animal rights, is similar in principle to the civil rights movement of the 1960s. Just as blacks, women, and other minorities sought recognition of their equal status, animal advocates have built a case for the equal status of animals.

Peter Singer, one of the leaders of this movement, has presented an eloquent case that we practice not only racism and sexism in our society but also "speciesism." That is, we assume that human beings are superior to other animals; we are prejudiced in favor of our own kind. Experimenting on animals and eating their flesh are the two major forms of speciesism in our society. Singer points out that some categories of human beings—infants and mentally retarded people—rate lower on a scale of intelligence, awareness, and self-consciousness than some animals. Yet we would not treat these individuals in the way we do animals. He argues that "all animals are equal" and that the suffering of an animal is morally equal to the suffering of a human being.

Proponents of animal research counter that such views are fundamentally misguided, that human beings, with the capacity for rational thought and action, are indeed a superior species. They contend that, while animals deserve humane treatment, the good consequences of animal research (i.e., knowledge that will benefit human beings) outweigh the suffering of individual animals. No other research techniques can substitute for the reactions of live animals, they declare.

In the selections that follow, Jerod M. Loeb and his colleagues reaffirm the American Medical Association's defense of animal research because it is essential for medical progress and it would be unethical to deprive humans and animals of advances in medicine that result from this research. Tom Regan disputes the view that benefit to humans justifies research on animals. Pointing to their inherent value, he says that "whatever our gains, they are ill-gotten," and he calls for an end to such research.

YES

Jerod M. Loeb et al.

HUMAN VS. ANIMAL RIGHTS: IN DEFENSE OF ANIMAL RESEARCH

Research with animals is a highly controversial topic in our society. Animal rights groups that intend to stop all experimentation with animals are in the vanguard of this controversy. Their methods range from educational efforts directed in large measure to the young and uninformed, to promotion of restrictive legislation, filing lawsuits, and violence that includes raids on laboratories and death threats to investigators. Their rhetoric is emotionally charged and their information is frequently distorted and pejorative. Their tactics vary but have a single objective—to stop scientific research with animals.

The resources of the animal rights groups are extensive, in part because less militant organizations of animal activists, including some humane societies, have been infiltrated or taken over by animal rights groups to gain access to their fiscal and physical holdings. Through bizarre tactics, extravagant claims, and gruesome myths, animal rights groups have captured the attention of the media and a sizable segment of the public. Nevertheless, people invariably support the use of animals in research when they understand both sides of the issue and the contributions of animal research to relief of human suffering. However, all too often they do not understand both sides because information about the need for animal research is not presented. When this need is explained, the presentation often reveals an arrogance of the scientific community and an unwillingness to be accountable to public opinion.

The use of animals in research is fundamentally an ethical question: is it more ethical to ban all research with animals or to use a limited number of animals in research under humane conditions when no alternatives exist to achieve medical advances that reduce substantial human suffering and misery?...

ANIMALS IN SCIENTIFIC RESEARCH

Animals have been used in research for more than 2000 years. In the third century BC, the natural philosopher Erisistratus of Alexandria used animals

From Jerod M. Loeb, William R. Hendee, Steven J. Smith, and M. Roy Schwarz, "Human vs. Animal Rights: In Defense of Animal Research," *Journal of the American Medical Association*, vol. 262, no. 19 (November 17, 1989), pp. 2716–2720. Copyright © 1989 by The American Medical Association. Reprinted by permission.

to study bodily function. In all likelihood, Aristotle performed vivisection on animals. The Roman physician Galen used apes and pigs to prove his theory that veins carry blood rather than air. In succeeding centuries, animals were employed to confirm theories about physiology developed through observation. Advances in knowledge from these experiments include demonstration of the circulation of blood by Harvey in 1622, documentation of the effects of anesthesia on the body in 1846, and elucidation of the relationship between bacteria and disease in 1878.[1] In his book *An Introduction to the Study of Experimental Medicine* published in 1865, Bernard[2] described the importance of animal research to advances in knowledge about the human body and justified the continued use of animals for this purpose.

In this century, many medical advances have been achieved through research with animals.[3] Infectious diseases such as pertussis, rubella, measles, and poliomyelitis have been brought under control with vaccines developed in animals. The development of immunization techniques against today's infectious diseases, including human immunodeficiency virus disease, depends entirely on experiments in animals. Antibiotics that control infection are always tested in animals before use in humans. Physiological disorders such as diabetes and epilepsy are treatable today through knowledge and products gained by animal research. Surgical procedures such as coronary artery bypass grafts, cerebrospinal fluid shunts, and retinal reattachments have evolved from experiments with animals. Transplantation procedures for persons with failed liver, heart, lung, and kidney function are products of animal research.

Animals have been essential to the evolution of modern medicine and the conquest of many illnesses. However, many medical challenges remain to be solved. Cancer, heart disease, cerebrovascular disease, dementia, depression, arthritis, and a variety of inherited disorders are yet to be understood and controlled. Until they are, human pain and suffering will endure, and society will continue to expend its emotional and fiscal resources in efforts to alleviate or at least reduce them.

Animal research has not only benefited humans. Procedures and products developed through this process have also helped animals.[4,5] Vaccines against rabies, distemper, and parvovirus in dogs are a spin-off of animal research, as are immunization techniques against cholera in hogs, encephalitis in horses, and brucellosis in cattle. Drugs to combat heartworm, intestinal parasites, and mastitis were developed in animals used for experimental purposes. Surgical procedures developed in animals help animals as well as humans.

Research with animals has yielded immeasurable benefits to both humans and animals. However, this research raises fundamental philosophical issues concerning the rights of humans to use animals to benefit humans and other animals. If these rights are granted (and many people are loath to do so), additional questions arise concerning the way that research should be performed, the accountability of researchers to public sentiment, the nature of an ethical code for animal research, and who should compose and approve the code. Today, some animal activists are asking whether humans have the right to exercise dominion over animals for any purpose, including research. Others suggest that because humans have dominion over other forms of life, they are obligated to protect and preserve animals and ensure that they are not exploited. Still others agree that animals can be used to help people, but only under circumstances that are so structured as to be unattainable by most researchers. These attitudes may all differ, but their consequences are similar. They all threaten to diminish or stop animal research.

CHALLENGE TO ANIMAL RESEARCH

Challenges to the use of animals to benefit humans are not new—their origins can be traced back several centuries. With respect to animal research, opposition has been vocal in Europe for more than 400 years and in the United States for at least 100 years.[6]

Most of the current arguments against research with animals have historic precedents that must be grasped to understand the current debate. These precedents originated in the controversy between Cartesian and utilitarian philosophers that extended from the 16th to the 18th centuries.

The Cartesian-utilitarian debate was opened by the French philosopher Descartes, who defended the use of animals in experiments by insisting the animals respond to stimuli in only one way —"according to the arrangement of their organs."[7] He stated that animals lack the ability to reason and think and are, therefore, similar to a machine. Humans, on the other hand, can think, talk, and respond to stimuli in various ways. These differences, Descartes argued, make animals inferior to humans and justify their use as a machine, including as experimental subjects. He proposed that animals learn only by experience, whereas

humans learn by "teaching-learning." Humans do not always have to experience something to know that it is true.

Descartes' arguments were countered by the utilitarian philosopher Bentham of England. "The question," said Bentham, "is not can they reason? nor can they talk? but can they suffer?"[8] In utilitarian terms, humans and animals are linked by their common ability to suffer and their common right not to suffer and die at the hands of others. This utilitarian thesis has rippled through various groups opposed to research with animals for more than a century.

In the 1970s, the antivivisectionist movement was influenced by three books that clarified the issues and introduced the rationale for increased militancy against animal research. In 1971, the anthology *Animals, Men and Morals,* by Godlovitch et al,[9] raised the concept of animal rights and analyzed the relationships between humans and animals. Four years later, *Victims of Science,* by Ryder,[10] introduced the concept of "speciesism" as equivalent to fascism. Also in 1975, Singer[11] published *Animal Liberation: A New Ethic for Our Treatment of Animals.* This book is generally considered the progenitor of the modern animal rights movement. Invoking Ryder's concept of speciesism, Singer deplored the historic attitude of humans toward nonhumans as a "form of prejudice no less objectionable than racism or sexism." He urged that the liberation of animals should become the next great cause after civil rights and the women's movement.

Singer's book not only was a philosophical treatise; it also was a call to action. It provided an intellectual foundation and a moral focus for the animal rights movement. These features attracted many who were indifferent to the emotional appeal based on a love of animals that had characterized antivivisectionist efforts for the past century. Singer's book swelled the ranks of the antivivisectionist movement and transformed it into a movement for animal rights. It also has been used to justify illegal activities intended to impede animal research and instill fear and intimidation in those engaged in it....

DEFENSE OF ANIMAL RESEARCH

The issue of animal research is fundamentally an issue of the dominion of humans over animals. This issue is rooted in the Judeo-Christian religion of western culture, including the ancient tradition of animal sacrifice described in the Old Testament and the practice of using animals as surrogates for suffering humans described in the New Testament. The sacredness of human life is a central theme of biblical morality, and the dominion of humans over other forms of life is a natural consequence of this theme.[12] The issue of dominion is not, however, unique to animal research. It is applicable to every situation where animals are subservient to humans. It applies to the use of animals for food and clothing; the application of animals as beasts of burden and transportation; the holding of animals in captivity such as in zoos and as household pets; the use of animals as entertainment, such as in sea parks and circuses; the exploitation of animals in sports that employ animals, including hunting, racing, and animal shows; and the eradication of pests such as rats and mice from homes and farms. Even provision of food and shelter to animals reflects an attitude of dominion of humans over animals. A person who truly does not believe in human dominance over animals would be forced to oppose all of these practices, including keeping animals as household pets or in any form of physical or psychological captivity. Such a posture would defy tradition evolved over the entire course of human existence.

Some animal advocates do not take issue with the right of humans to exercise dominion over animals. They agree that animals are inferior to humans because they do not possess attributes such as a moral sense and concepts of past and future. However, they also claim that it is precisely because of these differences that humans are obligated to protect animals and not exploit them for the selfish betterment of humans.[13] In their view, animals are like infants and the mentally incompetent, who must be nurtured and protected from exploitation. This view shifts the issues of dominion from one of rights claimed by animals to one of responsibilities exercised by humans.

Neither of these philosophical positions addresses the issue of animal research from the perspective of the immorality of not using animals in research. From this perspective, depriving humans (and animals) of advances in medicine that result from research with animals is inhumane and fundamentally unethical. Spokespersons for this perspective suggest that patients with dementia, stroke, disabling injuries, heart disease, and cancer deserve relief from suffering and that depriving them of hope and relief by eliminating animal research is an immoral and unconscionable act. Defenders of animal research claim that animals sometimes must be sacrificed in the development of methods to relieve pain and suffering of humans (and animals) and to affect treatments and cures of a variety of human maladies.

The immeasurable benefits of animal research to humans are undeniable. One example is the development of a vaccine for poliomyelitis, with the result that the number of cases of poliomyelitis in the United States alone declined from 58,000 in 1952 to 4 in 1984. Benefits of this vaccine worldwide are even more impressive.

Every year, hundreds of thousands of humans are spared the braces, wheelchairs, and iron lungs required for the victims of poliomyelitis who survive this infectious disease. The research that led to a poliomyelitis vaccine required the sacrifice of hundreds of primates. Without this sacrifice, development of the vaccine would have been impossible, and in all likelihood the poliomyelitis epidemic would have continued unabated. Depriving humanity of this medical advance is unthinkable to almost all persons. Other diseases that are curable or treatable today as a result of animal research include diphtheria, scarlet fever, tuberculosis, diabetes, and appendicitis.[3] Human suffering would be much more stark today if these diseases, and many others as well, had not been amendable to treatment and cure through advances obtained by animal research.

ISSUES IN ANIMAL RESEARCH

Animal rights groups have several stock arguments against animal research. Some of these issues are described and refuted herein.

The Clinical Value of Basic Research
Persons opposed to research with animals often claim that basic biomedical research has no clinical value and therefore does not justify the use of animals. However, basic research is the foundation for most medical advances and consequently for progress in clinical medicine. Without basic research, including that with animals, chemotherapeutic advances against cancer (including childhood leukemia and breast malignancy), beta-blockers for cardiac patients, and electrolyte infusions for patients with dysfunctional metabolism would never have been achieved.

Duplication of Experiments
Opponents of animal research frequently claim that experiments are needlessly duplicated. However, the duplication of results is an essential part of the confirmation process in science. The generalization of results from one laboratory to another prevents anomalous results in one laboratory from being interpreted as scientific truth. The cost of research animals, the need to publish the results of experiments, and the desire to conduct meaningful research all function to reduce the likelihood of unnecessary experiments. Furthermore, the intense competition of research funds and the peer review process lessen the probability of obtaining funds for unnecessary research. Most scientists are unlikely to waste valuable time and resources conducting unnecessary experiments when opportunities for performing important research are so plentiful....

The Use of Primates in Research
Animal activists often make a special plea on behalf of nonhuman primates, and many of the sit-ins, demonstrations, and break-ins have been directed at primate research centers. Efforts to justify these activities invoke the premise that primates are much like humans because they exhibit suffering and other emotions.

Keeping primates in cages and isolating them from others of their kind is considered by activists as cruel and destructive of their "psychological well-being." However, the opinion that animals that resemble humans most closely and deserve the most protection and care reflects an attitude of speciesism (i.e., a hierarchical scheme of relative importance) that most activists purportedly abhor. This logical fallacy in the drive for special protection of primates apparently escapes most of its adherents.

Some scientific experiments require primates exactly because they simulate human physiology so closely. Primates are susceptible to many of the same diseases as humans and have similar immune systems. They also possess intellectual, cognitive, and social skills above those of other animals. These characteristics make primates invaluable in research related to language, perception, and visual and spatial skills.[14] Although primates constitute only 0.5% of all animals used in research, their contributions have been essential to the continued acquisition of knowledge in the biological and behavioral sciences.[15]

Do Animals Suffer Needless Pain and Abuse?

Animal activists frequently assert that research with animals causes severe pain and that many research animals are abused either deliberately or through indifference. Actually, experiments today involve pain only when relief from pain would interfere with the purpose of the experiments. In any experiment in which an animal might experience pain, federal law requires that a veterinarian must be consulted in planning the experiment, and anesthesia, tranquilizers, and analgesics must be used except when they

would compromise the results of the experiment.[16]

In 1984, the Department of Agriculture reported that 61% of research animals were not subjected to painful procedures, and another 31% received anesthesia or pain-relieving drugs. The remaining 8% did experience pain, often because improved understanding and treatment of pain, including chronic pain, were the purpose of the experiment.[14] Chronic pain is a challenging health problem that costs the United States about $50 billion a year in direct medical expenses, lost productivity, and income.[15]

Alternatives to the Use of Animals

One of the most frequent objections to animal research is the claim that alternative research models obviate the need for research with animals. The concept of alternatives was first raised in 1959 by Russell and Burch[17] in their book, *The Principles of Humane Experimental Technique.* These authors exhorted scientists to reduce the pain of experimental animals, decrease the number of animals used in research, and replace animals with nonanimal models whenever possible.

However, more often than not, alternatives to research animals are not available. In certain research investigations, cell, tissue, and organ cultures and computer models can be used as adjuncts to experiments with animals, and occasionally as substitutes for animals, at least in preliminary phases of the investigations. However, in many experimental situations, culture techniques and computer models are wholly inadequate because they do not encompass the physiological complexity of the whole animal. Examples where animals are essential to research include development of a vaccine against human immunodeficiency virus, refinement of organ transplantation techniques, investigation of mechanical devices as replacements for and adjuncts to physiological organs, identification of target-specific pharmaceuticals for cancer diagnosis and treatment, restoration of infarcted myocardium in patients with cardiac disease, evolution of new diagnostic imaging technologies, improvement of methods to relieve mental stress and anxiety, and evaluation of approaches to define and treat chronic pain. These challenges can only be addressed by research with animals as an essential step in the evolution of knowledge that leads to solutions. Humans are the only alternatives to animals for this step. When faced with this alternative, most people prefer the use of animals as the research model.

COMMENT

Love of animals and concern for their welfare are admirable characteristics that distinguish humans from other species of animals. Most humans, scientists as well as laypersons, share these attributes. However, when the concern for animals impedes the development of methods to improve the welfare of humans through amelioration and elimination of pain and suffering, a fundamental choice must be made. This choice is present today in the conflict between animal rights activism and scientific research. The American Medical Association made this choice more than a century ago and continues to stand squarely in defense of the use of animals for scientific research. In this position, the Association is supported by opinion polls that reveal strong endorsement of the American public for the use of animals in research and testing.[18] ...

The American Medical Association believes that research involving animals is absolutely essential to maintaining and improving the health of people in America and worldwide.[6] Animal research is required to develop solutions to human tragedies such as human immunodeficiency virus disease, cancer, heart disease, dementia, stroke, and congenital and developmental abnormalities. The American Medical Association recognizes the moral obligation of investigators to use alternatives to animals whenever possible, and to conduct their research with animals as humanely as possible. However, it is convinced that depriving humans of medical advances by preventing research with animals is philosophically and morally a fundamentally indefensible position. Consequently, the American Medical Association is committed to the preservation of animal research and to the conduct of this research under the most humane conditions possible.[19,20]

REFERENCES

1. Rowan AN, Rollin BE. Animal research—for and against: a philosophical, social, and historical perspective. *Perspect Biol Med.* 1983; 27:1–17.
2. Bernard C; Green HC, trans. *An Introduction to the Study of Experimental Medicine.* New York, NY: Dover Publications Inc; 1957.
3. Council on Scientific Affairs. Animals in research. *JAMA*, 1989; 261:3602–3606.
4. Leader RW, Stark D. The importance of animals in biomedical research. *Perspect Biol Med.* 1987; 30:470–485.
5. Kransney JA. Some thoughts on the value of life. *Buffalo Physician*, 1984: 18:6–13.
6. Smith SJ, Evans RM, Sullivan-Fowler M, Hendee WR. Use of animals in biomedical research: historical role of the American Medical Association and the American physician. *Arch Intern Med.* 1988; 148:1849–1853.

7. Descartes R. *'Principles of Philosophy,' Descartes: Philosophical Writings*. Anscombe E. Geach PT, eds. London, England: Nelson & Sons; 1969.

8. Bentham J. *Introduction to the Principles of Morals and Legislation*. London, England: Athlone Press; 1970.

9. Godlovitch S, Godlovitch, Harris J. *Animals, Men and Morals*. New York, NY: Taplinger Publishing Co Inc; 1971.

10. Ryder R. *Victims of Science*. London, England: Davis-Poynter; 1975.

11. Singer P. *Animal Liberation: A New Ethic for Our Treatment of Animals*. New York, NY: Random House Inc; 1975.

12. Morowitz HJ, Jesus, Moses, Aristotle and laboratory animals. *Hosp Pract*. 1988; 23:23–25.

13. Cohen C. The case for the use of animals in biomedical research. *N Engl J Med*. 1986; 315: 865–870.

14. *Alternatives to Animal Use in Research, Testing, and Education*. Washington, DC: Office of Technology Assessment; 1986. Publication OTA-BA-273.

15. Committee on the Use of Laboratory Animals in Biomedical and Behavioral Research. *Use of Laboratory Animals in Biomedical and Behavioral Research*. Washington, DC: National Academy Press; 1988.

16. *Biomedical Investigator's Handbook*. Washington, DC: Foundation for Biomedical Research; 1987.

17. Russell WMS, Burch RL. *The Principles of Humane Experimental Technique*. Springfield, Ill: Charles C Thomas Publisher; 1959.

18. Harvey LK, Shubat SC. *AMA Survey of Physician and Public Opinion on Health Care Issues*. Chicago, Ill: American Medical Association; 1989.

19. Smith SJ, Hendee WR. Animals in research. *JAMA* 1988; 259:2007–2008.

20. Smith SJ, Loeb JM, Evans RM, Hendee WR. Animals in research and testing; who pays the price for medical progress? *Arch Ophthalmol*. 1988; 106:1184–1187.

NO

Tom Regan

ILL-GOTTEN GAINS

THE STORY

Late in 1981 a reporter for a large metropolitan newspaper (we'll call her Karen to protect her interest in remaining anonymous) gained access to some previously classified government files. Using the Freedom of Information Act, Karen was investigating the federal government's funding of research into the short- and long-term effects of exposure to radioactive waste. It was with understandable surprise that, included in these files, she discovered the records of a series of experiments involving the induction and treatment of coronary thrombosis (heart attack). Conducted over a period of fifteen years by a renowned heart specialist (we'll call him Dr. Ventricle) and financed with federal funds, the experiments in all likelihood would have remained unknown to anyone outside Dr. Ventricle's sphere of power and influence had not Karen chanced upon them.

Karen's surprise soon gave way to shock and disbelief. In case after case she read of how Ventricle and his associates took otherwise healthy individuals, with no previous record of heart disease, and intentionally caused their heart to fail. The methods used to occasion the "attack" were a veritable shopping list of experimental techniques, from massive doses of stimulants (adrenaline was a favorite) to electrical damage of the coronary artery, which, in its weakened state, yielded the desired thrombosis. Members of Ventricle's team then set to work testing the efficacy of various drugs developed in the hope that they would help the heart withstand a second "attack." Dosages varied, and there were the usual control groups. In some cases, certain drugs administered to "patients" proved more efficacious than cases in which others received no medication or smaller amounts of the same drugs. The research came to an abrupt end in the fall of 1981, but not because the project was judged unpromising or because someone raised a hue and cry about the ethics involved. Like so much else in the world at that time, Ventricle's project was a casualty of austere economic times. There simply wasn't enough federal money available to renew the grant application.

One would have to forsake all the instincts of a reporter to let the story end there. Karen persevered and, under false pretenses, secured an interview with Ventricle. When she revealed that she had gained access to the file, knew in detail the largely fruitless research conducted over fifteen years, and was incensed about his work, Ventricle was dumbfounded. But not because Karen had unearthed the file. And not even because it was filed where it was (a "clerical error," he assured her). What surprised Ventricle was that anyone would think there was a serious ethical question to be raised about what he had done. Karen's notes of their conversation include the following:

VENTRICLE: But I don't understand what you're getting at. Surely you know that heart disease is the leading cause of death. How can there be any ethical question about developing drugs which *literally* promise to be life-saving?

KAREN: Some people might agree that the goal—to save life—is a good, a noble end, and still question the means used to achieve it. Your "patients," after all, had no previous history of heart disease. *They* were healthy before you got your hands on them.

VENTRICLE: But medical progress simply isn't possible if we wait for people to get sick and then see what works. There are too many variables, too much beyond our control and comprehension, if we try to do our medical research in a clinical setting. The history of medicine shows how hopeless that approach is.

KAREN: And I read, too, that upon completion of the experiment, assuming that the "patient" didn't die in the process—it says that those who survived were "sacrificed." You mean killed?

VENTRICLE: Yes, that's right. But always painlessly, always painlessly. And

the body went immediately to the lab, where further tests were done. Nothing was wasted.

KAREN: And it didn't bother you—I mean, you didn't ever ask yourself whether what you were doing was wrong? I mean...

VENTRICLE: (interrupting): My dear young lady, you make it seem as if I'm some kind of moral monster. I work for the benefit of humanity, and I have achieved some small success, I hope you will agree. Those who raise cries of wrongdoing about what I've done are well intentioned but misguided. After all, I use animals in my research—chimpanzees, to be more precise—not human beings.

THE POINT

The story about Karen and Dr. Ventricle is just that—a story, a small piece of fiction. There is no real Dr. Ventricle, no real Karen, and so on. But there *is* widespread use of animals in scientific research, including research like our imaginary Dr. Ventricle's. So the story, while its details are imaginary—while it is, let it be clear, a literary device, not a factual account—is a story with a point. Most people reading it would be morally outraged if there actually were a Dr. Ventricle who did coronary research of the sort described on otherwise healthy human beings. Considerably fewer would raise a morally quizzical eyebrow when informed of such research done on animals, chimpanzees, or whatever. The story has a point, or so I hope, because, catching us off-guard, it brings this difference home to us, gives it life in our experience, and, in doing so, reveals something about ourselves, something about our own constellation of values. If we think what Ventricle did would be wrong if done to human beings but all right if done to chimpanzees, then we must believe that there are different moral standards that apply to how we may treat the two—human beings and chimpanzees. But to acknowledge this difference, if acknowledge it we do, is only the beginning, not the end, of our moral thinking. We can meet the challenge to think well from the moral point of view only if we are able to cite a *morally relevant difference* between humans and chimpanzees, one that illuminates in a clear, coherent, and rationally defensible way why it would be wrong to use humans, but not chimpanzees, in research like Dr. Ventricle's....

THE LAW

Among the difference between chimps and humans, one concerns their legal standing. It is against the law to do to human beings what Ventricle did to his chimpanzees. It is not against the law to do this to chimps. So, here we have a difference. But a morally relevant one?

The difference in the legal status of chimps and humans would be morally relevant if we had good reason to believe that what is legal and what is moral go hand in glove: where we have the former, there we have the latter (and maybe vice versa too). But a moment's reflection shows how bad the fit between legality and morality sometimes is. A century and a half ago, the legal status of black people in the United States was similar to the legal status of a house, corn, a barn: they were property, other people's property, and could legally be bought and sold without regard to their personal interests. But the legality of the slave trade did not make it moral, any more than the law against drinking, during the era of that "great experiment" of Prohibition,

made it immoral to drink. Sometimes, it is true, what the law declares illegal (for example, murder and rape) is immoral, and vice versa. But there is no necessary connection, no pre-established harmony between morality and the law. So, yes, the legal status of chimps and humans differs; but that does not show that their moral status does. Their difference in legal status, in other words, is not a morally relevant difference and will not morally justify using these animals, but not humans, in Ventricle's research.

THE VALUE OF THE INDIVIDUAL

[An] alternative vision [to utilitarian value] consists in viewing certain individuals as themselves having a distinctive kind of value, what we will call "inherent value." This kind of value is not the same as, is not reducible to, and is not commensurate either with such values as preference satisfaction or frustration (that is, mental states) or with such values as artistic or intellectual talents (that is, mental and other kinds of excellences or virtues). We cannot, that is, equate or reduce the inherent value of an individual to his or her mental states or virtues, and neither can we intelligibly compare the two. In this respect, the three kinds of value (mental states, virtues, and the inherent value of the individual) are like proverbial apples and oranges.

They are also like water and oil: they don't mix. It is not only that [a man's] inherent value is not the same as, not reducible to, and not commensurate with *his* satisfaction, pleasures, intellectual and artistic skills, etc. In addition, *his* inherent value is not the same as, is not reducible to, and is not commensurate with the valuable mental states or talents of *other* individuals, whether taken singly or collectively. Moreover, and as a corollary of the preceding, the individual's inherent value is in all ways independent both of his or her usefulness relative to the interest of others and of how others feel about the individual (for example, whether one is liked or admired, despised or merely tolerated). A prince and a pauper, a streetwalker and a nun, those who are loved and those who are forsaken, the genius and the retarded child, the artist and the philistine, the most generous philanthropist and the most unscrupulous used car salesman— all have inherent value, according to the view recommended here, and all have it equally....

WHAT DIFFERENCE DOES IT MAKE?

To view the value of individuals in this way is not an empty abstraction. To the question, "What difference does it make whether we view individuals as having equal inherent value, or as utilitarians do, as lacking such value, or, as perfectionists do, as having such value but to varying degree?"—our response to this question must be, "It makes all the moral difference in the world!" Morally, we are *always* required to treat those who have inherent value in ways that display proper respect for their distinctive kind of value, and though we cannot on this occasion either articulate or defend the full range of obligations tied to this fundamental duty, we can note that we fail to show proper respect for those who have such value whenever we treat them as if they were mere receptacles of value or as if their value was dependent on, or reducible to, their possible utility relative to the interests of others. In particular, therefore, Ventricle would fail to act as duty re-

quires—would, in other words, do what is morally wrong—if he conducted his coronary research on competent human beings, without their informed consent, on the grounds that this research just might lead to the development of drugs or surgical techniques that would benefit others. That would be to treat these human beings as mere receptacles or as mere medical resources for others, and though Ventricle might be able to do this and get away with it, and though others might benefit as a result, that would not alter the nature of the grievous wrong he would have done. And it would be wrong, not because (or only if) there were utilitarian considerations, or contractarian considerations, or perfectionist considerations against his doing his research on these human beings, but because it would mark a failure on his part to treat them with appropriate respect. To ascribe inherent value to competent human beings, then, provides us with the theoretical wherewithal to ground our moral case against using competent human beings, against their will, in research like Ventricle's.

WHO HAS INHERENT VALUE?

If inherent value could nonarbitrarily be limited to competent humans, then we would have to look elsewhere to resolve the ethical issues involved in using other individuals (for example, chimpanzees) in medical research. But inherent value can only be limited to competent human beings by having the recourse to one arbitrary maneuver or another. Once we recognize that we have direct duties to competent and incompetent humans as well as to animals such as chimpanzees; once we recognize the challenge to give a sound theoretical basis for these duties in the case of these humans and animals; once we recognize the failure of indirect duty, contractarian, and utilitarian theories of obligation; once we recognize that the inherent value of competent humans precludes using them as mere resources in such research; once we recognize that perfectionist vision of morality, one that assigns degrees of inherent value on the basis of possession of favored virtues, is unacceptable because of its inegalitarian implications, and once we recognize that morality simply will not tolerate double standards, then we cannot, except arbitrarily, withhold ascribing inherent value, to an equal degree, to incompetent humans and animals such as chimpanzees. All have this value, in short, and all have it equally. All considered, this is an essential part of the most adequate total vision of morality. Morally, none of those having inherent value may be used in Ventricle-like research (research that puts them at risk of significant harm in the name of securing benefits for others, whether those benefits are realized or not). And none may be used in such research because to do so is to treat them as if their value is somehow reducible to their possible utility relative to the interests of others, or as if their value is somehow reducible to their value as "receptacles." What contractarianism, utilitarianism, and the other "isms" discussed earlier will allow is not morally tolerable.

HURTING AND HARMING

The prohibition against research like Ventricle's, when conducted on animals such as chimps, cannot be avoided by the use of anesthetics or other palliatives used to eliminate or reduce suffering. Other things being equal, to cause an animal to suffer is to harm that animal—is, that is, to diminish that individual animal's welfare. But these two notions—harming on the one hand and suffering on the other —differ in important ways. An individual's welfare can be diminished independently of causing her to suffer, as when, for example, a young woman is reduced to a "vegetable" by painlessly administering a debilitating drug to her while she sleeps. We mince words if we deny that harm has been done to her, though she suffers not. More generally, harms, understood as reductions in an individual's welfare, can take the form either of *inflictions* (gross physical suffering is the clearest example of a harm of this type) or *deprivations* (prolonged loss of physical freedom is a clear example of a harm of this kind). Not all harms hurt, in other words, just as not all hurts harm.

Viewed against the background of these ideas, an untimely death is seen to be the ultimate harm for both humans and animals, such as chimpanzees, and it is the ultimate harm for both because it is their ultimate deprivation or loss —their loss of life itself. Let the means used to kill chimpanzees be as "humane" (a cruel word, this) as you like. That will not erase the harm that an untimely death is for these animals. True, the use of anesthetics and other "humane" steps lessens the wrong done to these animals, when they are "sacrificed" in Ventricle-type research. But a lesser wrong is not a right. To do research that culminates in the "sacrifice" of chimpanzees or that puts these and similar animals at risk of losing their life, in the hope that we might learn something that will benefit others, is morally to be condemned, however "humane" that research may be in other respects.

THE CRITERION OF
INHERENT VALUE

It remains to be asked, before concluding, what underlies the possession of inherent value. Some are tempted by the idea that life itself is inherently valuable. This view would authorize attributing inherent value to chimpanzees, for example, and so might find favor with some people who oppose using these animals in research. But this view would also authorize attributing inherent value to anything and everything that is alive, including, for example, crabgrass, lice, bacteria, and cancer cells. It is exceedingly unclear, to put the point as mildly as possible, either that we have a duty to treat these things with respect or that any clear sense can be given to the idea that we do.

More plausible by far is the view that those individuals have inherent value who are *the subjects of a life*—who are, that is, the experiencing subjects of a life that fares well or ill for them over time, those who have *an individual experiential welfare*, logically independent of their utility relative to the interests or welfare of others. Competent humans are subjects of a life in this sense. But so, too, are those incompetent humans who have concerned us. And so, too, and not unimportantly, are chimpanzees. Indeed, so too are the members of many species of animals: cats and dogs, monkeys and sheep, cetaceans and wolves, horses and cattle. Where one draws the line between those animals who are, and those who are not, subjects of a life is certain to be controversial. Still there is abundant reason to believe that the members of mammalian species of animals do have a psychophysical identity over time, do have an experiential life, do have an individual welfare. Common sense is on the side of viewing these animals in this way, and ordinary language is not strained in talking of them as individuals who have an experiential welfare. The behavior of these animals, moreover, is consistent with regarding them as subjects of a life, and the implications of evolutionary theory are that there are many species of animals whose members are, like the members of the species *Homo sapiens*, experiencing subjects of a life of their own, with an individual welfare. On these grounds, then, we have very strong reason to believe, even if we lack conclusive proof, that these animals meet the subject-of-a-life criterion.

If, then, those who meet this criterion have inherent value, and have it equally relative to all who meet it, chimpanzees and other animals who are subjects of a life, not just human beings, have this value *and* have neither more nor less of it than we do. (To hold that they have less than we do is to land oneself in the inegalitarian swamp of perfectionism). Moreover, if, as has been argued, having inherent value morally bars others from treating those who have it as mere receptacles or as mere resources for others, then any and all medical research like Ventricle's, done on these animals in the name of possibly benefitting others, stands morally condemned. And it is not only cases in which the benefits for others do not materialize that are condemnable; also to be condemned are cases, such as the research done on chimps regarding hepatitis, for example, in which the benefits for others are genuine. In these cases, as in others like them in the relevant respects, the ends do not justify the means. The *many millions* of mammalian animals used each year for scientific purposes, including medical research, bear mute, tragic testimony to the narrowness of our moral vision.

CONCLUSIONS

This condemnation of such research probably is at odds with the judgment that most people would make about this issue. If we had good reason to assume that the truth always lies with what most people think, then we could look approvingly on Ventricle-like research done on animals like chimps in the name of benefits for others. But we have no good reason to believe that the truth is to be measured plausibly by majority opinion, and what we know of the history of prejudice and bigotry speaks powerfully, if painfully, against this view. Only the cumulative force of informed, fair, rigorous argument can decide where the truth lies, or most likely lies, when we examine a controversial moral question. Although openly acknowledging and, indeed, insisting on the limitations of the arguments . . . , these arguments make the case, in broad outline, against using animals such as chimps in medical research such as Ventricle's. . . .

Those who oppose the use of animals such as chimps in research like Ventricle's and who accept the major themes advanced here, oppose it, then, not because they think that all such research is a waste of time and money, or because they think that it never leads to any benefits for others, or because they view those who do such research as, to use Ventricle's, words, "moral monsters," or even because they love animals. Those of us who condemn such research do so because this research is not possible except at the grave moral price of failing to show proper respect for the value of the animals who are used. Since, whatever our gains, they are ill-gotten, we must bring to an end research like Ventricle's, whatever our losses. A fair measure of our moral integrity will be the extent of our resolve to work against allowing our scientific, economic, health, and other interests to serve as a reason for the wrongful exploitation of members of species of animals other than our own.

POSTSCRIPT

Should Animal Experimentation Be Permitted?

In 1985 Congress passed the Health Research Extension Act, which directed the National Institutes of Health (NIH) to establish guidelines for the proper care of animals to be used in biomedical and behavioral research. The NIH regulations implementing the law require institutions that receive federal grants to establish Animal Care and Use Committees. The Office of Science and Technology Policies' "Principles for the Utilization and Care of Vertebrate Animals Used in Testing, Research and Training," *Federal Register* (May 20, 1985) serves as the basis for the U.S. government's policy. The NIH's *Guide for the Care and Use of Laboratory Animals*, rev. ed. (1985) offers explicit instructions.

In February 1993 a federal judge ruled that the Department of Agriculture's standards on the treatment of laboratory dogs and primates were not stringent enough and that the agency had failed to put into effect the 1985 law. Charles R. McCarthy, in "Improved Standards for Laboratory Animals?" *Kennedy Institute of Ethics* (vol. 3, no. 3, 1993), asserts that this ruling actually lowers the standard for the care of laboratory animals.

Although they do not recommend a complete ban on animal research, some authors have argued that current practices in animal research must be reevaluated and better regulated. See, for example, *Lives in the Balance: The Ethics of Using Animals in Biomedical Research* edited by Jane A. Smith and Kenneth M. Boyd (Oxford University Press, 1991) and *In the Name of Science: Issues in Responsible Animal Experimentation* by F. Barbara Orlans (Oxford University Press, 1993).

For an opposing view, see the Office of Technology Assessment's *Alternatives to Animal Use in Research, Testing, and Education* (Government Printing Office, 1986). Richard P. Vance analyzes what he believes are erroneous myths held by supporters of animal research in "An Introduciton to the Philosophical Presuppositions of the Animal Liberation/Rights Movement," *Journal of the American Medical Association* (October 7, 1992). Also see *Ethics and Animals* edited by Harlan B. Miller and William H. Williams (Humana Press, 1983); *Of Mice, Models, and Men: A Critical Evaluation of Animal Research* by Andrew Rowan (State University of New York Press, 1984); the Hastings Center's "Animals, Science, and Ethics," *Hastings Center Report* (May/June 1990); and the *Hastings Center Report* special supplement "The Brave New World of Animal Biotechnology" (January/February 1994). Also see the *Hastings Center Report* case study "New Creations?" (January–February 1991), which presents opposing views on research on manipulating genes to produce new animal strains.

ISSUE 13

Will Fetal Tissue Research Encourage Abortions?

YES: Douglas K. Martin, from "Abortion and Fetal Tissue Transplantation," *IRB: A Review of Human Subjects Research* (May/June 1993)

NO: Dorothy E. Vawter and Karen G. Gervais, from "Commentary on 'Abortion and Fetal Tissue Transplantation,'" *IRB: A Review of Human Subjects Research* (May/June 1993)

ISSUE SUMMARY

YES: Bioethicist Douglas K. Martin argues that the therapeutic use of fetal tissue cannot be separated from moral concerns over abortion and that the option to donate fetal tissue may well influence some women to choose abortion.

NO: Bioethicists Dorothy E. Vawter and Karen G. Gervais contend that knowledge of the option to donate tissue is not an incentive for a woman to abort a fetus she would otherwise carry to term as long as potential recipients remain anonymous and no financial gain is involved.

About 500,000 Americans suffer from Parkinson's disease, a progressively debilitating and incurable nerve disorder that leads to rigidity and tremors. No one knows what causes the disease, and current drug treatments have disturbing side effects. As the disease worsens, patients become incapacitated, unable to carry out even the simplest activities.

In 1987, Mexican surgeon Dr. Ignacio Madrazo Navarro reported success in treating five Parkinson's patients by transplanting fetal tissue into their brains. Previous attempts to transplant adrenal tissue had been disappointing. Transplantation of living tissue is intended to enhance the brain's production of dopamine, a chemical that is important for regulating movement and that is not secreted in normal quantities in Parkinson's patients.

Other potential uses of fetal tissue include the treatment of Alzheimer's disease, brain and spinal cord injuries, some forms of epilepsy, and other serious neurological conditions. It is even possible that fetal tissue might be beneficial in the treatment of diabetes or blood and metabolic disorders. Researchers in Sweden, the United States, China, Canada, and elsewhere are working with animal models and, in a few cases, with human subjects to determine whether or not these techniques will prove beneficial. Before any such use of fetal tissue transplantation can be considered a therapy with proven benefits, research involving human subjects must be conducted. But such studies raise serious ethical questions.

Concern about fetal research arose in the aftermath of the 1973 U.S. Supreme Court decision of *Roe v. Wade*, which legalized abortion. Before *Roe v. Wade*, fetal research had been conducted with little apparent public concern. But reports of research conducted by Scandinavian researchers using live, postabortion fetuses fueled a hot and emotional debate in this country and led to a moratorium imposed by the National Institutes of Health (NIH) on any research involving a living fetus before or after abortion. In 1975, spurred by public protests, Congress established the National Commission for the Protection of Human Subjects of Biomedical and Behavioral Research to examine the ethical issues surrounding experimentation. The first topic on its agenda was fetal research.

Research that would impose little or no risk to the fetus, or that was intended to benefit the fetus, posed few ethical difficulties for the commission. However, irreconcilable differences arose when abortion entered the picture. Research using about-to-be-aborted fetuses, for example, might be intended to determine the harmful or beneficial effects on the fetus of drugs given to the pregnant woman during pregnancy or labor. Other types of research might be harmful to the fetus and could not ethically be performed on a fetus that is destined to be delivered at term. The commission (with one dissent) approved minimal-risk research if abortion was anticipated, but they required the approval of a national ethical review body for research that involved more than minimal risk. The commission's recommendations, with some modifications, were incorporated into the federal regulations governing human subject research in 1975. The Reagan and Bush administrations opposed using aborted fetal tissue for research, and during most of the 1980s and early 1990s, there was a federal ban on funding fetal tissue research. In 1988 a National Institutes of Health Fetal Tissue Transplantation Research Panel concluded that funding such research is "acceptable public policy." In May 1992 Congress voted to overturn the ban, but President Bush vetoed it because, he said, it encouraged abortions.

When Bill Clinton became president in 1992, he lifted the ban. Accordingly the debate has shifted to the question of whether the procedural safeguards recommended by the NIH panel are sufficient to prevent women from aborting fetuses because they want to donate fetal tissue.

The following selections take up this debate. Douglas K. Martin believes that the NIH guidelines are unfeasible and unethical and that the therapeutic uses of aborted tissue cannot be separated from moral concerns about abortion. Dorothy E. Vawter and Karen G. Gervais believe that it is possible to prevent fetal tissue transplantation from leading a woman to abort a fetus she would otherwise carry to term. They argue that procedural safeguards such as timing, restricting the use of tissue to anonymous recipients, and banning payment would address those concerns.

YES

Douglas K. Martin

ABORTION AND FETAL TISSUE TRANSPLANTATION

Government moratoria on public funding for research in fetal tissue transplantation have been based on the concern that knowledge of fetal tissue transplantation, and the option to donate tissue for transplantation, may influence some women to have abortions. In response to this concern, in 1988 the director of the National Institutes of Health, James B. Wyngaarden, convened a research panel to examine the issue. At the conclusion of their deliberations, a majority of the panelists did not consider the concern compelling and recommended procedures they felt would be adequate to morally separate abortion from the use of the fetal tissue. Advocates of fetal tissue transplantation have repeatedly referred to these and similar guidelines as a means of ensuring the ethical acceptability of such therapy.

The NIH panel evaded the fundamental question of whether using tissue from electively aborted fetuses was itself ethically acceptable. The panel report skipped directly to recommending procedures that would enable fetal tissue research to advance. The panel side-stepped the ethical questions by resorting to legal and policy arguments upon which to base its chief recommendation, which was:

> It is of moral relevance that human fetal tissue for research has been obtained from induced abortions. However, in light of the fact that abortion is legal and that the research in question is intended to achieve significant medical goals, the panel concludes that the use of such tissue is acceptable public policy.[1, p. 1]

It is important to emphasize that in asserting that abortion is legal and the research well intended the panel did not comment on the ethical merit of fetal tissue transplantation.

A majority of the panel maintained that permitting research in fetal tissue transplantation was acceptable public policy "either because the source of the tissue posed no moral problem or because the immorality of its source could be ethically isolated from the morality of its use in research."[1, p. 2] To accommodate individuals who believe that abortion is immoral, or at least undesirable, the panel made several recommendations with the express intent of morally

From Douglas K. Martin, "Abortion and Fetal Tissue Transplantation," *IRB: A Review of Human Subjects Research*, vol. 15, no. 3 (May/June 1993). Copyright © 1993 by The Hastings Center. Reprinted by permission.

isolating fetal tissue transplantation from abortion. These recommendations included that:

- the decision to terminate a pregnancy be kept independent from the retrieval and use of fetal tissue;
- informed consent for the research be distinct from and subsequent to consent for the abortion; and
- even preliminary information about tissue donation be withheld from the pregnant woman before she consents to the abortion.

I contend that these and similar proposals, for example the recently considered U.S. federal legislation H.R. 2507, are both unfeasible and unethical, and therefore cannot achieve the stated goal of morally insulating fetal tissue research from abortion. I will address three points of argument: (1) the realities of consent as a process, which makes the recommended constraint on the timing of disclosure unfeasible; (2) the influence that publicized fetal tissue transplantation will have on women confronted with an unwanted pregnancy—an influence that morally and practically cannot be prevented by gag orders on health care professionals; and (3) the autonomy of women considering abortion, and the ethical obligation on professionals to fully inform a woman in the process of making any decision regarding her fetus.

THE CONSENT PROCESS

A simplistic and sometimes callous belief held by many, and implicit in the NIH panel report, is that informed consent is a bureaucratic/legalistic act in which information is disclosed and a consent form is signed at a particular moment in time.[2,3] However, it has been strongly argued that informed consent should be considered an essential part of the professional-patient relationship, a process occurring over a length of time. A metaphor that has been utilized to describe this process is the "conversation model" of informed consent employed by Jay Katz and others.[4,5] During an informed consent process, like a series of conversations, the bidirectional ebb and flow of information is unpredictable. As in conversation, one must go through each process before knowing its outcome.

Despite the fact that in the abortion scenario urgency may curtail the extent of an ongoing physician-patient relationship, a fully explored consent process is still possible and necessary. One could reasonably argue that an extended consent process should be mandatory in an abortion decision because of the emotional distress that often accompanies the circumstances promulgating the decision. Furthermore, as in all medical procedures, a woman contemplating an abortion may sign a consent form and even make an appointment for the procedure before she has fully resolved in her mind what her final decision will be. Her irreversible consent does not occur until she physically submits herself for the procedure. A woman may choose not to go through with the abortion at any time prior to procedure.

In empirical studies ambivalence and anxiety over the abortion are commonly documented characteristics of women facing this decision;[6] as many as 40 percent of women contemplating abortion reported changing their mind at least once before coming to a final decision, and those who aborted were significantly more likely to rethink their original choice and to regret their decision;[7-9] up to 37 percent of women who abort do not finally decide until just before the procedure.[6-10] Some women who have decided to abort will change their mind at the last minute. One study followed 505 women who went to a clinic and applied to have an abortion: after they filled out the background paperwork, were examined by a gynecologist, and were interviewed by a social worker and psychiatrist, 6 percent changed their minds and decided to continue the pregnancy.[11]

To be prepared to preserve the tissue, researchers must receive consent from the woman for the use of the tissue before the abortion. Therefore, the consent for tissue use will often precede the final consent for the abortion, and always precede the irreversible consent for the abortion. Yet the panel recommended that "the informed consent for the abortion should precede informed consent... for tissue donation.[1, p. 4] This is unfeasible.

THE INFLUENCE OF FETAL TISSUE TRANSPLANTATION ON WOMEN FACING AN UNWANTED PREGNANCY

Regarding the abortion decision, empirical evidence indicates that somewhat less than 10 percent of abortions are chosen for medical reasons. Upwards of 90 percent of abortions are chosen for a multiplicity of reasons (an average of 4) based predominantly on life-style preferences.[12] In one study, up to one-half of women who chose abortion found the decision difficult to make.[7,8] As previously stated, in another study 40 percent of women who contemplated abortion changed their minds at least once and found the decision difficult to make. For these women, it was reported that the "pros and cons of the decision were somewhat evenly balanced."[9] In other words,

women choose abortion because of a combination of many reasons, most often relating to personal preferences; and the decision is often difficult to make, with a close balance of pros and cons. It is reasonable to suggest that new factors which may be introduced into this decision may well contribute to tipping the balance one way or the other.

It is also reasonable to suggest that the knowledge that aborted fetal tissue might be used to benefit sick people might be an important consideration for some women. Arthur Caplan, an advocate of fetal tissue transplantation, has argued that such an option may provide "solace" to women having abortions.[13] Swedish scientists involved in fetal tissue research have testified that, in their experience, almost all women approached consent to donate the tissue and they do so because they are "glad something positive could come out of it."[14] In research currently underway at the Centre for Bioethics, women aged 18 to 40 were surveyed about their opinions regarding abortion and fetal tissue transplantation. Preliminary results show that 12 percent of these women indicated that, if they were pregnant, they would be more likely to choose abortion if they knew that they could donate tissue for transplantation.[15] Thus the knowledge that a woman may donate the tissue from her aborted fetus for therapeutic transplantation could be an important factor in the decision to abort, and may well be a decisive one.

In addition, it must be stressed that this evidence suggesting that women may be influenced by fetal tissue transplantation was obtained in a social climate where the efficacy of such therapy is not established. Researchers hope that in the near future fetal tissue transplantation might provide significant benefit for patients suffering from Parkinson's disease, Type I diabetes, or any of the more than 20 diseases currently being considered. If it is shown that fetal tissue transplantation would benefit at least some of these millions of patients, it must be presumed that the influence this knowledge will exert on women facing an unwanted pregnancy will be much greater, and that the influence society will exert on these women will be much greater—even in the absence of direct influence or information from a physician.

The NIH panel reported that they "regarded it highly unlikely that a woman would be encouraged to make this decision [the abortion decision] because of the knowledge that fetal remains might be used in research."[1, p. 3] This speculation is not in accord with present evidence and is naive to the future implications of fetal tissue transplantation. Contrary to this presumption, current evidence suggests that the option to donate fetal tissue for transplantation may well influence some women to choose abortion.

THE AUTONOMY OF WOMEN CONSIDERING ABORTION

The Belmont Report, which outlines guidelines for the conduct of biomedical research, states that "to withhold information necessary to make a considered judgment, when there are not compelling reasons to do so" shows lack of respect for autonomous agents. In the matter of clinical practice, consent to treatment is not currently addressed in legislation. However, Canadian case law has determined that, to obtain a valid informed consent, a health professional must explore and disclose all information "material" to the patient's decision.[16,3] Furthermore, the professional must not withhold

information nor present information such that it misleads the patient.[3] As I have argued, for a woman contemplating abortion information regarding the donation of aborted fetal tissue may reasonably constitute important, even decisive, information. Prohibiting disclosure of this information contradicts modern ethical and legal standards of disclosure based on the ethical principle of autonomy.

The NIH advisory committee held that "the decision and consent to abort must precede discussion of the possible use of the fetal tissue."[1, p. 3] and that "informed consent for abortion should precede... the provision of preliminary information for tissue donation."[1, p. 4] The panel also wrote that "in the consent process for termination of pregnancy, we believe there should be no mention at all of the possibility of fetal tissue use in transplantation and research."[1, p. 4] If these guidelines were followed, the consent for the abortion would not be ethically valid, and might not be legally valid, and the autonomy of the woman in question would be violated. Therefore, the guidelines are unfeasible and unethical.

REFERENCES

1. Consultants to the Advisory Committee to the Director, National Institutes of Health, *Report of the Human Fetal Tissue Transplantation Research Panel.* vol. 1. Bethesda, Md.: National Institutes of Health, 1988.
2. For critical discussion, see Faden, RR, and Beauchamp, TL: *A History and Theory of Informed Consent.* New York: Oxford University Press, 1986.
3. Rozovsky, LE, and Rozovsky, FA: *The Canadian Law of Consent to Treatment.* Toronto: Butterworths, 1990.
4. Katz, J: *The Silent World of Doctor and Patient.* New York: Free Press, 1984.
5. Brody, H: Transparency: Informed consent in primary care. *Hastings Center Report.* 1989; 19(5):5–9.

6. Reardon, DC: *Aborted Women*. Westchester, IL: Crossway, 1987; Nadleson, C: Abortion counseling: Focus on adolescent pregnancy. *Pediatrics* 1974; 54:768.
7. Kerenyi, TD, Glascock, EL, and Horowitz, ML: Reasons for delayed abortion: Results of four hundred interviews. *American Journal of Obstetrics and Gynecology* 1973; 117(3):299–311; at 307.
8. Bracken, MB: The stability of the decision to seek induced abortion. In *Report and Recommendations on Research on the Fetus*, National Commission for the Protection of Human Subjects of Biomedical and Behavioral Research, 1975, Appendix 16.
9. Bracken, MB, Klerman, LV, and Bracken, MA: Abortion, adoption, or motherhood: An empirical study of decision-making during pregnancy. *American Journal of Obstetrics and Gynecology* 1978; 130(3):251–62; at 256–57.
10. Diamond, M, et al.: Sexuality, birth control and abortion: A decision-making sequence. *Journal of Biosocial Science* 1973; 5:347.
11. Swigar, ME, Breslin, R, Pouzzner, MG, and Quinlan, D: Interview follow-up of abortion applicant dropouts. *Social Psychiatry* 1976; 11:135–43.
12. Torres, A, Forrest, JD: Why do women have abortions? *Family Planning Perspectives* 1988; 20:170–76.
13. Caplan, AL: Should foetuses or infants be utilized as organ donors? *Bioethics* 1987; 1(2):119–40.
14. Testimony of Lars Olson, 14 September 1988. Reported in J. Bopp and J. Burtchaell: Statement of dissent in consultants to the Advisory Committee to the Director, National Institutes of Health. *Report of the Human Fetal Tissue Transplantation Research Panel*, vol 1; at p. 57.
15. Martin, DK, Lowy, FH, Williams, JI, and Dunn, EV: Women's attitudes toward abortion and fetal tissue transplantation. Unpublished ms.
16. *Reibel v. Hughes*, (1980) 2 S.C.R. 880 (1980), 14 C.C.L.T.1; *Hopp v. Lepp*, (1980) 2 S.C.R. 192, 13 C.C.L.T. 66.

NO

Dorothy E. Vawter
and Karen G. Gervais

COMMENTARY ON "ABORTION AND FETAL TISSUE TRANSPLANTATION"

The former ban on the use of federal funds for fetal tissue transplantation research was based on the belief that it is impossible to prevent women from aborting fetuses for the purpose of donation if such transplants are permitted. One of the few points of agreement in the debate concerning fetal tissue transplantation is that it is wrong to use tissue from fetuses aborted specifically for donation. The major problem with abortion for donation is that it involves grave disrespect for the living fetus; the fetus is valued more for its parts and its usefulness to someone else than for being a potential human person. Whether it is possible to prevent fetal tissue transplants from leading to abortion for donation, and if so, how, remain subjects of contention. Those who believe it is possible to prevent abortion for donation have focused on a set of three policy recommendations to ensure that a woman's decision to abort is made separately from, and prior to, a decision to donate fetal tissue.

The two most important policy recommendations to prevent abortion for donation remove possible incentives, namely, the desire either to save the life of a relative or close friend or to obtain financial benefits. The NIH Human Fetal Tissue Transplantation Research Panel, Congress, and many other groups recommend that women be prohibited from designating the recipient of fetal tissue, and from benefiting financially from donation.[1] Since donating to anonymous recipients is not believed to provide a woman with an incentive to abort, these groups permit women to donate fetal tissue for this purpose. Their third recommendation is directed at preventing abortion clinic personnel from pressuring a pregnant woman to donate tissue before she has consented to an abortion, possibly thereby causing her to abort to donate. They recommend prohibiting abortion clinic personnel from raising the option of fetal tissue donation, and from seeking the woman's consent, until after she has consented to an abortion.

Martin criticizes this third policy recommendation on two grounds. First, restricting the timing of invitations to donate will not prevent women from knowing of the option to abort to donate and ultimately choosing to abort for this reason. Second, restricting the timing of invitations to donate is unethical because it requires the withholding of information material to women's abortion decisions. He concludes that it is impossible to prevent fetal tissue transplantation from encouraging women to abort for the purpose of donating tissue to anonymous recipients, and that it is impossible to insulate abortion and fetal tissue transplantation from one another. He stops short, however, of disclosing whether he believes abortion for donation is unethical or whether the transplantation of tissue from electively aborted fetuses should be prohibited.

We believe that it is permissible to transplant tissue from electively aborted fetuses if provisions are in place to adequately respect and protect fetuses as well as women. We support the policy recommendations made by the NIH panel, Congress, and other groups to prevent abortion for donation, including the restriction on when abortion clinic personnel may raise the option to donate. Contrary to Martin, we maintain that:

- It is possible to prevent fetal tissue transplantation from leading a woman to abort a fetus she would otherwise carry to term.
- A woman would not choose abortion in response to knowing there is a chance some of the fetal tissue may be suitable for transplantation in an anonymous recipient.
- If a woman is properly informed of the potential risks to her privacy and well-being from donating tissue for transplantation, she not only has no incentive to donate, but has disincentives as well.
- The primary purpose of restricting the timing of invitations to donate is to prevent abortion clinic personnel from pressuring women to abort to donate, not to prevent women from knowing of the option to donate.
- Restricting the timing of invitations to donate is ethically required because it is protective and respectful of women as well as fetuses.

There is no basis for assuming that a woman weighs the option to donate fetal tissue to anonymous recipients when considering an abortion. That a woman may be ambivalent about her abortion decision, and may change her mind, does not prove that information about donating to anonymous recipients or an invitation to donate would have any affect on the woman's ambivalence or abortion decision. That 40 to 50 percent of women find the abortion decision difficult does not mean that a woman does not have good reasons for and against it. The option to donate fetal tissue is at least equally irrelevant to a woman's decision to abort as the option to donate hip bone is to a patient considering a hip replacement. Knowledge of the option to donate fetal tissue to anonymous recipients neither generates a dilemma about whether to have an abortion nor assists a woman in resolving such a dilemma.

Believing otherwise rests on confusing the solace a woman may seek from donating fetal tissue with her reasons for having an abortion. A woman may agree to donate fetal tissue out of a desire to relieve some of her pain over her previous and independent decision to abort; she will not, however, choose to have an abortion as a means of obtaining solace. The desire for solace is not a reason to abort; it is a reason for deciding to donate subsequent to a separate decision to abort.

Finally, we have reservations about the preliminary results reported from a study of women's opinions about abortion and fetal tissue transplantation. Martin says that the study supports the claim that women will abort for the purpose of donating tissue (to anonymous others?). Until the details of the study are published it is clearly impossible to fully evaluate this information. However, given how situation-specific women's abortion decisions are, it is unclear what useful information can be obtained from asking women global hypothetical questions about whether they believe the option to donate would affect their decision to terminate a "generic" pregnancy sometime in the future.

It is especially important to know how the questions are framed. For example, might the response to a question about whether the opportunity to donate tissue to anonymous recipients would make the respondent feel better about her abortion be unjustifiably interpreted as evidence that women would abort for the purpose of donating tissue? It is also important to know whether the respondents were provided with the information that a woman should properly receive concerning the donation, procurement, and transplantation of fetal tissue, including the associated risks to her privacy and well-being.[2] Were the respondents informed of the low likelihood that the tissue they donate will be usable or used? Were they informed that they would not be permitted to designate the recipient or to receive financial compensation? The problems inherent in studies involving hypothetical questions are magnified if the respondents lack full understanding of the activity they are asked to imagine participating in.

Martin ends his critique with the startling suggestion that it is unethical not to inform a woman considering abortion of the option to abort to donate. He argues that because some women, in his view, will choose to abort to donate, information about the option to donate must be considered material to a woman's abortion decision and must, therefore, be disclosed to all women considering abortion. This suggests that a woman's decision to abort and her decision to donate should be allowed to be a single decision and that it is wrong for health professionals not to provide a woman the opportunity to abort to donate. By extension this implies that it is wrong for health care providers to fail to inform all patients of the ways they may serve as live donors of tissues and organs, perhaps even of unethical or illegal types of donation.[3]

First, disclosure requirements for therapeutic interventions do not require disclosing options unrelated to the health problem for which the patient is seeking assistance. Inviting a patient to be a live organ or tissue donor, or a human research subject, is never obligatory. Moreover, before making such a request or invitation it is necessary to have special protections in place to assure that the "patient" is respected, is not exposed to unreasonable risks, and is fully informed. Treating all pregnant women considering abortion as persons who must be given the opportunity to undergo an invasive procedure for the purpose of assisting anonymous recipients is disrespectful of, as well as potentially harmful to, the woman seeking medical assistance, the living fetus, and the special relationship between a pregnant woman and her fetus. Second, insofar as it is unethical (and illegal) for a woman to abort to donate, not only is there no obligation to disclose the option to donate, but health providers should be prohibited from inviting the woman to donate before she has consented to abortion.

In our view, the policy recommendation to restrict the timing of invitations to donate is ethically required to protect and respect women as well as fetuses.

- It prevents abortion clinic personnel from pressuring women to abort to donate.
- It protects women considering abortion from being treated merely as potential live tissue donors and from possibly being denied a genuinely therapeutic relationship with their physician.
- It protects living fetuses from being valued for their tissues and being treated as renewable, or optional, tissue specimens of women.
- It prevents any suggestion that it is permissible to abort to donate.

Once the incentives to abort to donate for financial gain or to save the life of a relative or friend are eliminated, there is no reason to be concerned about women knowing of the option to donate tissue. Knowledge of the option to donate tissue to anonymous recipients is not an incentive for a woman to abort a fetus she would otherwise carry to term. However, if clinic personnel are permitted to seek a woman's consent to donate prior to obtaining her consent to an abortion, there is reason to be concerned that women may be pressured to choose abortion. Taken together, the three policy recommendations—prohibiting designated donation, prohibiting the buying and selling of fetal tissue, and prohibiting invitations to donate before a woman has consented to an abortion—prevent abortion for donation, while permitting abortion and donation. Nevertheless, as the fetal tissue bill currently before Congress makes clear, these are only some of the provisions necessary to ensure that the transplantation of fetal tissue is adequately respectful and protective of fetuses and women.

NOTES

1. The National Organ Transplant ACT (NOTA) and most state Uniform Anatomical Gift Acts (UAGAs) already prohibit the buying and selling of fetal tissue.

2. Vawter, DE, Gervais, KG, and Caplan, AL: Risks of fetal tissue donation to women. *Journal of Neural Transplantation and Plasticity* 1992; 3(4), forthcoming.

3. In some jurisdictions abortion providers are legally prohibited from performing an abortion on a woman known to be seeking an abortion for donation.

POSTSCRIPT

Will Fetal Tissue Research Encourage Abortions?

In May 1990 a successful fetus-to-fetus transplant of liver cells was undertaken to block a genetic defect that causes Hurler's syndrome. This condition, also known as "gargoylism" because of its characteristic distortion of facial features, is lethal within the first few years of life. Although the father, Baptist minister Guy Walden, opposes abortion, he consented to the procedure.

Research on Parkinson's disease has continued, with encouraging results in small groups of patients. A Swedish study, reported in 1992, demonstrated that impaired brain tissue was repaired by implants of fetal brain tissue. In this study, two American heroin addicts damaged by tainted drugs improved considerably after the transplants, and brain scans revealed that their brains were producing chemicals that had been lacking since their injuries. Two American research groups, at the University of Colorado and at Yale University, also reported small but definite effects in 10 patients with Parkinson's disease who were treated with fetal brain tissue. These research projects were privately funded.

The first grant for fetal tissue research, after the government ban was lifted, was awarded by the National Institute of Neurological Disorders and Stroke in January 1994. The $4.5 million grant went to three institutions to study 40 patients with Parkinson's disease. However, patients will have to pay $40,000 to be in the study because insurance companies will generally not reimburse experimental procedures.

For an extensive review of the arguments and the conclusions of the 1988 NIH panel that addressed the use of aborted fetal tissue in research, see James F. Childress, "Ethics, Public Policy, and Human Fetal Tissue Transplantation Research," *Kennedy Institute of Ethics Journal* (June 1991). John Fletcher offers a critique of government policy in "Human Fetal and Embryo Research: Lysenkoism in Reverse—How and Why?" *Emerging Issues in Biomedical Policy, vol. 2*, edited by Robert H. Blank and Andrea L. Bonnicksen (Columbia University Press, 1993).

For further reading on fetal tissue and Parkinson's disease, see Jerome P. Kassirer and Marcia Angell, "The Use of Fetal Tissue in Research on Parkinson's Disease," *The New England Journal of Medicine* (November 26, 1992). For more analysis about the ethics of using materials from an elective abortion, see Michelle A. Mullen and Frederick H. Lowy, "Physician Attitudes Toward the Regulation of Fetal Tissue Therapies: Empirical Findings and Implications for Public Policy," *The Journal of Law, Medicine & Ethics* (Summer 1993).

ISSUE 14

Is There a Gender Bias in Medicine and Research?

YES: Ruth Macklin, from "Women's Health: An Ethical Perspective," *Law, Medicine, and Ethics* (Spring 1993)

NO: Andrew G. Kadar, from "The Sex-Bias Myth in Medicine," *The Atlantic Monthly* (August 1994)

ISSUE SUMMARY

YES: Philosopher and medical ethicist Ruth Macklin argues that the traditional focus on men—in both medicine and research—violates the principle of distributive justice, denying to women a fair allocation of society's burdens and benefits.

NO: Physician Andrew G. Kadar argues that women are not discriminated against in medicine and that, in fact, they receive more medical care and benefit more from medical research than men do.

In George Bernard Shaw's play *Pygmalion* (and its musical version, *My Fair Lady*), Professor Henry Higgins asks in exasperation, "Why can't a woman be more like a man?" With the exception of a few differences relating to reproduction, medical research has in fact been generally based on the assumption that women *are* like men. Until very recently, new drugs have been typically tested on men but marketed for both men and women. Moreover, until recently most doctors and researchers have been men; women's advocates have claimed that this has led to a bias in the diseases studied and the therapies offered.

Women have been excluded from some clinical trials on the grounds that they are a "vulnerable" population in need of special protections because they might become pregnant. The experience that has most shaped the exclusion of women from research is related to the drug thalidomide.

Thalidomide was synthesized in West Germany in 1954 and approved for marketing in that country in 1958. Its primary use was as a sedative and an antidote for nausea in early pregnancy. At least 20 countries approved the over-the-counter sale of thalidomide—including Canada, Great Britain, Australia, and Sweden—but not the United States.

During the period in which thalidomide was being widely distributed, physicians noted an alarming increase in the number of children being born with an unusual and extremely rare set of deformities. The most prominent feature was phocomelia, a condition in which the hands are attached to the shoulders and the feet to the hips, superficially resembling the flippers of a seal. By 1962, when sufficient statistical evidence had been accumulated to establish thalidomide as the agent causing these deformities, about 8,000 children had been affected. About a third of the women who received this drug in early pregnancy (even a single dose) bore deformed babies.

The harm done to women and their infants by thalidomide was not the result of their participation in research; it was the result of inadequate research (even by contemporary standards), corporate greed, and physicians' uncritical acceptance of promotional claims. In the United States, a cautious Food and Drug Administration (FDA) official, Dr. Frances Kelsey, delayed marketing approval of thalidomide as an antinausea agent, thus lessening the impact on American women. Nevertheless, over 1,200 U.S. physicians did give their patients thalidomide, which was made available to them by the drug company seeking approval. At least 18 thalidomide babies were born as a result, and many more women carrying affected fetuses miscarried.

As a result of the publicity received, amendments to the Food, Drug, and Cosmetic Act made in 1962 outlined a rigorous preapproval process. Equally important, the powerful impact of the thalidomide experience created an aversion among researchers and regulators to involving women—especially pregnant women or women of childbearing age—in drug research. In 1977 the FDA issued guidelines for drug development recommending that women of childbearing potential be excluded from early phases of drug development (except for life-threatening diseases).

In the 1980s women's groups began to challenge the status quo, not only in the inclusion of women in research but also in the choice of research areas and in the practice of medicine generally. A 1985 report of the U.S. Public Health Service's Task Force on Women's Health Issues concluded that "the historical lack of research focus on women's health concerns has compromised the quality of health information available to women as well as the health care they receive." In 1990 the U.S. Congress's General Accounting Office criticized the National Institutes of Health (NIH) for not following its stated policy of including women in clinical research. NIH responded by creating an Office of Research on Women's Health. In 1993, when it passed the NIH Revitalization Act, Congress mandated the inclusion of studies on women's health and of women (and minorities) as research subjects.

The following two selections take opposing views on this issue. Ruth Macklin presents an ethical analysis of women's health, placing special emphasis on the principle of distributive justice as the basis for equal treatment. Andrew G. Kadar believes, on the other hand, that the concern for women's health is misplaced and that, in fact, women have more benefits and fewer burdens than men in research and treatment.

YES   Ruth Macklin

WOMEN'S HEALTH:
AN ETHICAL PERSPECTIVE

If there is one ethical concept considered to be central to human social life it is the idea of justice. Although there are several competing principles of justice, the core concept of justice embodies the obligation to treat like cases alike, in relevant respects. Women may differ from men in some respects, but the fact that women get sick, become injured, and die from preventable causes renders them similar to men in the need to carry out biomedical research, develop therapies, and attend to health problems specific to women. An ethical perspective on women's health begins and ends with principles of justice. Although particular circumstances and conditions differ in developed and less developed countries, the ethical conclusions regarding justice are the same for women in all societies.

It is by now well known that the preponderance of biomedical research carried out in the modern era has ignored women. That fact alone signals a violation of the ethical principle of distributive justice, a principle that mandates a fair allocation of society's benefits and burdens. A singular exception to the disproportionate inclusion of men as subjects of biomedical research is the large amount of research conducted on female reproduction. The feminist philosopher Susan Sherwin explains this exception as arising out of "medicine's historical pursuit of control over women's reproductive lives."[1] Sherwin further contends that "By limiting their attention almost exclusively to means of exercising control over women's reproductive functions, medical researchers reflect a view of women as principally defined in terms of their childbearing function."[2] ...

How is ethics related to women's health? A prominent conception of ethics postulates a set of principles to guide actions and evaluate policies aimed at protecting the rights of individuals and promoting benefits to society as a whole and to its individual members. Disagreements arise in choosing which principle should take precedence when they come into conflict. Additional controversy arises over how the principles are to be interpreted and applied. However, some recent writings by philosophers and feminists have rejected the centrality of principles in favor of a casuistic approach,[3] an emphasis on

From Ruth Macklin, "Women's Health: An Ethical Perspective," *Law, Medicine, and Ethics*, vol. 21, no. 1 (Spring 1993), pp. 23–29. Copyright © 1993 by The American Society of Law, Medicine, and Ethics. Reprinted by permission.

the context of human actions,[4] or a defense of moral relativism in one form or another.[5]

For those who endorse a principled approach to ethical issues, three leading ethical principles are by now familiar for analyzing and evaluating an array of issues in biomedicine. That well-known trio comprises respect for persons, beneficence, and justice.[6] These principles state ethical ideals by articulating fundamental rights of human beings and conceptions of social justice. Some feminist writers have argued that such abstract ethical principles embody "masculinist" conceptions of ethics and fail adequately to reflect women's experiences.[7] Despite the prominence of these principles of bioethics, and perhaps because they are under attack by feminist scholars, they have only rarely been employed in the ethical analysis of women's health.[8] I contend that these principles remain sound and can be put to good use in exploring issues involving women's health.

It is not only ethical principles that create controversy. Perhaps surprisingly, disagreement also surrounds the concept of health itself. A narrow definition conceives of health as the absence of disease. A broad definition is the one adopted by the World Health Organization [WHO]: "Health is a state of complete physical, mental and social well-being and not merely the absence of disease or infirmity." While it is true that the WHO definition of health serves more as an ideal to be approached rather than an actual goal likely to be attained for most people, it serves the important function of any ideal in specifying a standard worth striving for.

... From an ethical point of view, and especially in the case of women's health, working to ensure the health of a population should be a fundamental human and social requirement in any country or region of the world. The absence of disease or infirmity is not the only goal to strive for. As a positive thesis, I argue that an ethical perspective on women's health can only be gained by construing psychological and social well-being as core ingredients in the concept of health.

Endorsing the view that health in general, and women's health in particular, should not be construed narrowly as "the absence of disease," Anne Colston Wentz and Florence Haseltine, the editors of the *Journal of Women's Health,* state that "Over and above all else, women's health is an interdisciplinary field, involving research issues certainly but also the areas of patient care, education, and health administration."[9]

HEALTH IN THE SOCIAL CONTEXT

A narrow conception of health is bound to fail to address the broad context in which numerous factors contributing to women's health are located. Furthermore, a narrow conception is unlikely to call attention to a social context that until now has largely ignored a number of salient facts: the fact that biomedical research has disproportionately involved male subjects; the fact that numerous complaints of women have been classified as psychosomatic or hysterical;[10] the fact that prevention of women's trauma and injuries from battering or rape requires sweeping social and legal changes in the attitudes and behavior of judges, lawmakers, and the police, as well as men in general.

Martha C. Romans, Director of the Jacobs Institute of Women's Health, observes that "Not too long ago, the subject of women's health was nearly synonymous with reproductive health. Now, a variety of social, scientific, and political forces have resulted in a clearer understanding of other important women's health issues."[11] In thinking about women's health, it is natural to focus on reproductive issues, on morbidity and mortality from breast cancer, on the lack of research devoted to diseases specific to women or to the fact that medical knowledge of the safety and efficacy of many drugs is largely limited to men since women have been excluded from or underrepresented in clinical trials.

But it is a mistake to focus only on these narrower issues that stem from the biomedical context. A public health perspective forces us to acknowledge a much wider set of socioeconomic and cultural determinants. As Helen Rodriguez-Trias notes: "Women live in households, communities, and cities, and in times, places, and circumstances that spell health or disease, life or death, with greater certainty than does access to health care."[12]

As a striking example, Dr. Rodriguez-Trias points to assaults by husbands, ex-husbands, and lovers, which cause more injuries to women than motor vehicle accidents, rape, and muggings combined. She cites another estimate by health officials that more than 4 million women are battered and more than 4 thousand are killed by such "intimate assaults" each year. Although medical assistance can be provided for women who survive such assaults, the issue of prevention is hardly one that the medical profession alone can address. Recently, the American Medical Association (AMA) recommended that physicians should routinely screen their female patients for domestic violence.[13] Another AMA report described domes-

tic violence as a pattern of coercion that could include repeated battering and injury, psychological abuse, sexual assault, progressive social isolation, deprivation and intimidation. Studies now indicate that at least 20 percent of adult women, 15 percent of college women, and 12 percent of adolescent girls have experienced sexual abuse and assault during their lifetimes. Studies on prevalence suggest that from one fifth to one third of all women will be physically assaulted by a partner or ex-partner during their lifetimes.[14]

These facts again make clear the importance of using a broad definition of health as not merely the absence of disease or infirmity. Psychological abuse, progressive social isolation and intimidation of women by their husbands, ex-husbands, or partners do not neatly fit a biomedical diagnosis of malady but they nonetheless represent a significant threat to women's health. It may require enhanced sensitivity and social progress to recognize that centuries-old cultural patterns of behavior of men toward their wives, sexual partners, and their daughters are ethically unacceptable. Just because these patterns have existed for centuries does not make them right. Just because they have been widespread and largely tolerated in many cultures does not make them right. The fact that a majority of people in a society accept and subscribe to certain social or cultural practices does not amount to an ethical justification of those practices. The idea that within a domestic enclave, men may do virtually whatever they want to the women under their domination violates the ethical principle of equal respect for persons. To justify domestic violence, one would have to reject the principle that women are persons, deserving of respect....

RESPECT FOR PERSONS

An ethical perspective on women's health relies on the "respect for persons" principle but starts from a broader social perspective, one that shows equal respect for women as persons. Only when women are granted a status of respect as persons equal to that traditionally given to men can the ethical problems that have plagued women's health be properly addressed.

The ethical principle of "equal respect for persons" can be understood at an individual level and as an ingredient in social justice. At the individual level, showing equal respect for women as persons means recognizing their autonomy and treating them as capable decision-makers and full participants in medical decisions. Examples include honoring women's feelings and preferences in modes of contraception and methods of abortion, even if it is more cost-effective to impose methods preferred by providers or funders; treating pregnant women with dignity and respect instead of as "fetal containers;" devoting scientific expertise and committing funds to broaden biomedical research in a wide array of areas that mainly affect women, such as breast cancer and osteoporosis; and focusing on factors that affect health at home and in the workplace as well as in the hospital and doctor's office.

The principle of "respect for persons" is violated when women who seek abortions or come for medical help after a botched abortion are treated punitively by physicians or other health-care workers. The stigma attached to sexually transmitted diseases contributes to the failure of many women to seek early treatment, leading to pelvic inflammatory disease that results in poor health status for women and often in subsequent infertility.

Coercing pregnant women by obtaining court-ordered casarean sections, intimidating them to remain in the hospital when fetal distress is suspected, and forcing pregnant Jehovah's Witnesses to accept blood transfusions, all violate the principle of respect for persons. Attempts to use the force of law to hospitalize or incarcerate drug-using women for the duration of their pregnancies represent perhaps the latest trend in lack of respect for women as persons by viewing them chiefly as an environment for optimal fetal development. Educating and seeking to persuade pregnant women to behave in ways likely to lead to the best outcome for their infants violates neither their rights nor their autonomy. But physical coercion, invoking the force of law, and psychological intimidation fail to show respect for pregnant women as persons.

JUSTICE IN WOMEN'S HEALTH

Turning now to justice in women's health, we begin with a principle of social justice maintaining that all persons within a given society deserve equal or equitable access to goods and services that fulfill basic human needs. A clear statement of equal access to the health care system is offered by the political theorist Amy Gutmann. Gutmann defines the principle as follows: "A principle of equal access to health care demands that every person who shares the same type and degree of health need must be given an equally effective chance of receiving appropriate treatment of equal quality so long as that treatment is available to anyone."[15] According to this principle, services and goods that meet health care needs should be equally available to everyone who is equally needy. An article in the journal *Women's Health Issues* notes that "Curiously ignored by providers, the public, women's health groups and women victims alike is the fact that heart disease is the leading cause of death among American women."[16]

Coronary artery disease [CAD] is the most common cause of death in women as well as in men in developed countries. In the United States, one half of all deaths from coronary artery disease occur in women. Yet that fact is not widely recognized, nor has there been as much attention paid to the risk women face from dying of this disease. One speculative explanation for this disparity is the fact that "women develop clinically apparent CAD about 10 years later than men."[17] However, we might speculate further about the speculation: If the ages were reversed, and men developed clinically apparent CAD about 10 years later than women, would that have resulted in less attention being paid to coronary artery disease in men? The undisputed focus on men and the lack of attention paid to women in both research and treatment of heart disease provide one illustration of how the equal access principle in health care has been violated.

Another example is found in the realm of reproductive health, an area that has chiefly involved women. The principle of justice mandates that all individuals who need them should have equal access to family planning and health services. From an ethical perspective, "equal access" means that use of these services should not be based on an ability to pay for them. Guaranteeing access by law has not proved sufficient for achieving social justice in societies that do not recognize a right to health care. An additional precondition for access is information about the existence and nature of the services. A moral obligation exists to ensure that women have information, as well as the means to obtain family planning services. A wide distribution of these services is also needed to ensure equitable access for everyone, in accordance with this principle of justice. These conclusions apply with even more force to women in developing countries than they do to those in developed countries. Poor women everywhere disproportionately bear the burden of restrictive abortion laws and inadequate or nonexistent family planning services....

THE PRINCIPLE OF BENEFICENCE

An ethical analysis of women's health would not be complete without discussion of the principle of beneficence. Simply stated, this principle is the obligation to strive to bring about more good consequences than harmful ones. In the medical setting, the principle is embodied in risk-benefit assessments, obligating physicians to recommend the treatment plan with the most favorable benefit-risk ratio for the patient.

An ethical perspective on women's health reveals flaws in the way risk-benefit assessments have commonly been made in the clinical setting. For many years, the standard treatment for breast cancer was radical mastectomy. That standard had not been arrived at as a result of careful assessment following clinical trials, but was instead a judgment passed on from one generation of surgeons to the next. No scientifically respectable study had been conducted comparing the outcomes of radical mastectomy with less mutilating alternatives.

And many surgeons argued against even offering women alternatives to radical mastectomy, based on their traditional belief that it was the best treatment for the condition. Not until a large-scale, randomized clinical trial was initiated by the NIH [National Institutes of Health] was there a systematic gathering of scientific data on this life-threatening condition that affects only women almost exclusively.

Making risk-benefit assessments is often not an easy task, whether they are carried out in the context of providing medical services or in research involving clinical trials. The task is made even harder by the fact that reasonable people disagree both on their evaluations of the magnitude of risks and benefits, and also on how to weigh potential risks against expected benefits. With regard to women's health, in particular, it appears that medical scientists' risk-benefit assessments are based on different criteria than those likely to be employed by women themselves who are users of a technology such as birth control.

Women's health advocates tend to define the "safety" of contraceptive methods in terms different from those typically employed by biomedical scientists. According to one report:

> Scientists' concern is to establish safety of methods according to specific measurable parameters. They assess toxicity, first in animals and then in carefully controlled studies in human volunteers. Subsequent studies address efficacy and short- to medium-term safety.... Women's health advocates... give more priority to methods that have fewer side effects and that protect against sexually transmitted diseases and their consequences such as infertility. While scientists have tended to give priority to

methods which minimize users' control, women's health advocates prefer methods controlled by the user.[18] ...

An analysis that focuses on benefits and harms has too often been ignored in contemporary ethics, despite the prominence of risk-benefit analysis in the medical context. For example, the pervasive and unending abortion debate in the United States has been carried on almost exclusively in the language of rights. Yet the long history of women's death and disease from self-induced abortions, along with data about the persistence of morbidity and mortality resulting from clandestine abortions, are well-documented harmful consequences of antiabortion policies....

Conducting an ethical analysis by balancing the good and bad consequences of actions or practices is usually connected to the principle of beneficence, but it can also be used to evaluate institutions from the standpoint of justice. Although out of favor in current philosophical thought, the conception of justice propounded by the utilitarian, John Stuart Mill, is worth recalling. Mill argued that satisfying the utilitarian principle—the greatest happiness for the greatest number of people —would succeed in fulfilling the requirements of justice. Probably the most telling criticism of that conception of justice is that it fails to account properly for the concerns of a minority. The utilitarian conception of justice could be satisfied at the expense of violating the rights of the minority or ignoring their interests.

Yet when we consider that women are not a numerical minority, but constitute half if not a slightly higher percentage of the world's population, there is no danger of ignoring the interests or violating the rights of women by using a utilitarian conception of justice. Paying attention to all aspects of women's health can only serve to increase the total amount of happiness or well-being in the world. It is true that good health alone cannot achieve the goal of making people happy. But if health is thought of as a state of complete physical, mental and social well-being, it goes at least part way toward that goal.

I began by saying that an ethical perspective on women's health begins and ends with principles of justice. I conclude by noting that refocusing efforts on women's health can begin to rectify some of the past injustices. Only by striving for the broader goals of justice that grant women status and respect equal to that enjoyed by men, and to poor women and women of color equal access to the health care system, can we hope to make overall gains in improving women's health.

REFERENCES

1. Susan Sherwin, *No Longer Patient* (Philadelphia: Temple University Press, 1992), 128.
2. Id. at 167.
3. Albert Jonsen and Stephen Toulmin, *The Abuse of Casuistry: A History of Moral Reasoning* (Berkeley: University of California Press, 1988).
4. See, for example, Ronald Christie and Barry Hoffmaster, *Ethical Issues in Family Medicine* (Oxford: Oxford University Press, 1986), and James D. Wallace, *Moral Relevance and Moral Conflict* (Ithaca: Cornell University Press, 1988).
5. See, for example, David Wong, *Ethical Relativism* (Cambridge: Cambridge University Press, 1984), and Bernard Williams, *Ethics and the Limits of Philosophy* (London: Fontanna Books, Collins, 1985).
6. See, for example, Tom L. Beauchamp and James F. Childress, *Principles of Biomedical Ethics,* Third Edition (New York: Oxford University Press, 1989).
7. See, for example, Sherwin, supra note 1.
8. For an excellent meta-analysis of bioethical principles and feminism, see Rebecca J. Cook, "Feminism and the Four Principles," in Raanan Gillon, ed., *Principles of Health Care Ethics* (Sussex, U.K.: John Wiley and Sons, Ltd., in press).
9. Anne Colston Wentz and Florence P. Haseltine, Editorial, *Journal of Women's Health,* 1 (Spring 1992), xv.
10. See, for example, Rebecca J. Cook, supra note 8; and Vicki Ratner, Debra Slade, and Kristene E. Whitmore, "Interstitial Cystitis: A Bladder Disease Finds Legitimacy," *Journal of Women's Health* 1 (1992), 63–68.
11. Martha C. Romans, Preface, *The Women's Health Data Book* (Washington, DC: The Jacobs Institute of Women's Health, 1992), vii.
12. Helen Rodriguez-Trias, "Women's Health, Women's Lives, Women's Rights," *American Journal of Public Health,* 82 (May 1992), 663.
13. Council on Ethical and Judicial Affairs, American Medical Association, "Physicians and Domestic Violence," *Journal of the American Medical Association* 267 (June 17, 1992), 3190-3193.
14. Council on Scientific Affairs, American Medical Association, "Violence Against Women," *JAMA* 267 (June 17, 1992), 3184–3189.
15. Amy Gutmann, "For and Against Equal Access to Health Care," in President's Commission for the Study of Ethical Problems in Medicine and Biomedical and Behavioral Research, *Securing Access to Health Care,* Vol. Two (U.S. Government Printing Office, 1983), 52.
16. Discussion, *Women's Health Issues* 2 (Summer 1992), 111.
17. John C. LaRosa, "Lipids and Cardiovascular Disease: Do the Findings and Therapy Apply Equally to Men and Women?" *Women's Health Issues* 2 (Summer 1992), 102.
18. Special Programme of Research, Development and Research Training in Human Reproduction and International Women's Health Coalition. *Creating Common Ground: Women's Perspectives on the Selection and Introduction of Fertility Regulation Technologies* (Geneva: World Health Organization, 1991), 11.

NO
Andrew G. Kadar

THE SEX-BIAS MYTH IN MEDICINE

"When it comes to health-care research and delivery, women can no longer be treated as second-class citizens." So said the President of the United States on October 18, 1993.

He and the First Lady had just hosted a reception for the National Breast Cancer Coalition, an advocacy group, after receiving a petition containing 2.6 million signatures which demanded increased funding for breast-cancer prevention and treatment. While the Clintons met with leaders of the group in the East Room of the White House, a thousand demonstrators rallied across the street in support. The President echoed their call, decrying the neglect of medical care for women.

Two years earlier Bernadine Healy, then the director of the National Institutes of Health [NIH], charged that "women have all too often been treated less than equally in... health care." More recently Representative Pat Schroeder, a co-chair of the Congressional Caucus for Women's Issues, sponsored legislation to "ensure that biomedical research does not once again overlook women and their health." Newspaper articles expressed similar sentiments.

The list of accusations is long and startling. Women's-health-care advocates indict "sex-biased" doctors for stereotyping women as hysterical hypochondriacs, for taking women's complaints less seriously than men's, and for giving them less thorough diagnostic workups. A study conducted at the University of California at San Diego in 1979 concluded that men's complaints of back pain, chest pain, dizziness, fatigue, and headache more often resulted in extensive workups than did similar complaints from women. Hard scientific evidence therefore seemed to confirm women's anecdotal reports.

Men more often than women undergo angiographies and coronary-artery-bypass-graft operations. Even though heart disease is the No. 1 killer of women as well as men, this sophisticated, state-of-the-art technology, critics contend, is selectively denied to women.

The problem is said to be repeated in medical research: women, critics argue, are routinely ignored in favor of men. When the NIH inventoried all the research it had funded in 1987, the money spent on studying diseases unique to women amounted to only 13.5 percent of the total research budget.

Perhaps the most emotionally charged disease for women is breast cancer. If a tumor devastated men on a similar scale, critics say, we would declare a state of national emergency and launch a no-cost-barred Apollo Project–style program to cure it. In the words of Matilda Cuomo, the wife of the governor of New York, "If we can send a woman to the moon, we can surely find a cure for breast cancer." The neglect of breast-cancer research, we have been told, is both sexist and a national disgrace.

Nearly all heart-disease research is said to be conducted on men, with the conclusions blindly generalized to women. In July of 1989 researchers from the Harvard Medical School reported the results of a five-year study on the effects of aspirin in preventing cardiovascular disease in 22,071 male physicians. Thousands of men were studied, but not one woman: women's health, critics charge, was obviously not considered important enough to explore similarly. Here, they say, we have definite, smoking-gun evidence of the neglect of women in medical research —only one example of a widespread, dangerous phenomenon....

To remedy all this neglect, we need to devote preferential attention and funds, in the words of the *Journal of the American Medical Women's Association*, to "the greatest resource this country will ever have, namely, the health of its women." Discrimination on such a large scale cries out for restitution—if the charges are true.

In fact one sex does appear to be favored in the amount of attention devoted to its medical needs. In the United States it is estimated that one sex spends twice as much money on health care as the other does. The NIH also spends twice as much money on research into the diseases specific to one sex as it does on research into those specific to the other, and only one sex has a section of the NIH devoted entirely to the study of disease afflicting it. That sex is not men, however. It is women.

*   *   *

In the United States women seek out and consequently receive more medical care than men. This is true even if pregnancy-related care is excluded. Department of Health and Human Services surveys show that women visit doctors more often than men, are hospitalized more often, and undergo more operations. Women are more likely than men to visit a doctor for a general physical exam when they are feeling well, and complain of symptoms more often. Thus two out of every three health-care dollars are spent by women.

Quantity, of course, does not guarantee quality. Do women receive second-rate diagnostic workups?

The 1979 San Diego study, which concluded that men's complaints more often led to extensive workups than did women's, used the charts of 104 men and women (fifty-two married couples) as data. This small-scale regional survey prompted a more extensive national review of 46,868 office visits. The results, reported in 1981, were quite different from those of the San Diego study.

In this larger, more representative sample, the care received by men and women was similar about two thirds of the time. When the care was different, women overall received more diagnostic tests and treatment—more lab tests, blood-pressure checks, drug prescriptions, and return appointments.

Several other, small-scale studies have weighed in on both sides of this issue. The San Diego researchers looked at another 200 men and women in 1984, and this time found "no significant differences in the extent and content" of workups. Some women's-health-care advocates have chosen to ignore data from the second San Diego study and the national survey while touting the first study as evidence that doctors, to quote once again from the *Journal of the American Medical Women's Association*, do "not take complaints as seriously" when they come from women: "an example of a double standard influencing diagnostic workups."

When prescribing care for heart disease, doctors consider such factors as age, other medical problems, and the likelihood that the patient will benefit from testing and surgery. Coronary-artery disease afflicts men at a much younger age, killing them three times as often as women until age sixty-five. Younger patients have fewer additional medical problems that preclude aggressive, high-risk procedures. And smaller patients have smaller coronary arteries, which become obstructed more often after surgery. Whereas this is true for both sexes, obviously more women fit into the smaller-patient category. When these differences are factored in, sex divergence in cardiac care begins to fade away.

To the extent that divergence remains, women may be getting better treatment. At least that was the conclusion of a University of North Carolina/Duke University study that looked at the records of 5,795 patients treated from 1969 to 1984. The most symptomatic and severely diseased men and women were equally likely to be referred for bypass surgery. Among the patients with less-severe disease—the ones to whom surgery offers little or no survival benefit over medical therapy—women were less likely to be scheduled for bypass surgery. This seems proper in light of the greater risk of surgical complications, owing to women's smaller coronary arteries. In fact, the researchers questioned the wisdom of surgery in the less symptomatic men and suggested that "the effect of gender on treatment selection may have led to more appropriate treatment of women."

As for sophisticated, pioneering technology selectively designed for the benefit of one sex, laparoscopic surgery was largely confined to gynecology for more than twenty years. Using viewing and manipulating instruments that can be inserted into the abdomen through keyhole-sized incisions, doctors are able to diagnose and repair, sparing the patient a larger incision and a longer, more painful recuperation. Laparoscopic tubal sterilization, first performed in 1936, became common practice in the late 1960s. Over time the development of more-versatile instruments and of fiber-optic video capability made possible the performance of more-complex operations. The laparoscopic removal of ectopic pregnancy was reported in 1973. Finally, in 1987, the same technology was applied in gallbladder surgery, and men began to enjoy its benefits too.

Years after ultrasound instruments were designed to look inside the uterus, the same technology was adapted to search for tumors in the prostate. Other pioneering developments conceived to improve the health care of women include mammography, bone-density testing for osteoporosis, surgery to alleviate bladder incontinence, hormone therapy to relieve the symptoms of menopause, and a host of procedures, including in vitro fertilization, developed to facilitate impregnation. Perhaps so many new developments occur in women's health care because one branch of medicine and a group of doctors, gynecologists, are explicitly concerned with the health of women. No corresponding group of doctors is dedicated to the care of men.

So women receive more care than men, sometimes receive better care than men, and benefit more than men do from some developing technologies. This hardly looks like proof that women's health is viewed as secondary in importance to men's health.

* * *

The 1987 NIH inventory did indeed find that only 13.5 percent of the NIH research budget was devoted to studying diseases unique to women. But 80 percent of the budget went into research for the benefit of both sexes, including basic research in fields such as genetics and immunology and also research into diseases such as lymphoma, arthritis, and sickle-cell anemia. Both men and women suffer from these ailments, and both sexes served as study subjects. The remaining 6.5 percent of NIH research funds were devoted to afflictions unique to men. Oddly, the women's 13.5 percent has been cited as evidence of neglect. The much smaller men's share of the budget is rarely mentioned in these references.

As for breast cancer, the second most lethal malignancy in females, investigation in that field has long received more funding from the National Cancer Institute [NCI] than any other tumor research, though lung cancer heads the list of fatal tumors for both sexes. The second most lethal malignancy in males is also a sex-specific tumor: prostate cancer. Last year approximately 46,000 women succumbed to breast cancer and 35,000 men to prostate cancer; the NCI spent $213.7 million on breast-cancer research and $51.1 million on study of the prostate. Thus although about a third more women died of breast cancer than men of prostate cancer, breast-cancer research received more than four times the funding. More than three times as much money per fatality was spent on the women's disease. Breast cancer accounted for 8.8 percent of cancer fatalities in the United States and for 13 percent of the NCI research budget; the corresponding figures for prostate cancer were 6.7 percent of fatalities and three percent of the funding. The spending for breast-cancer research is projected to increase by 23 percent this year, to $262.9 million; prostate-research spending will increase by 7.6 percent, to $55 million.

The female cancers of the cervix and the uterus accounted for 10,100 deaths and $48.5 million in research last year, and ovarian cancer accounted for 13,300 deaths and $32.5 million in research. Thus the research funding for all female-specific cancers is substantially larger per fatality than the funding for prostate cancer.

Is this level of spending on women's health just a recent development, needed to make up for years of prior neglect? The NCI is divided into sections dealing with issues such as cancer biology and diagnosis, prevention and control, etiology, and treatment. Until funding allocations for sex-specific concerns became a political issue, in the mid-1980s, the NCI did not track organ-specific spending data. The earliest information now available was reconstructed retroactively to 1981. Nevertheless, these early data provide a window on spending patterns in the era before political pressure began to intensify for more research on women. Each year from 1981 to 1985 funding for breast-cancer research exceeded funding for prostate cancer by a ratio of roughly five to one. A rational, nonpolitical explanation for this is that breast cancer attacks a larger number of patients, at a younger age. In any event, the data failed to support claims that women were neglected in that era.

Again, most medical research is conducted on diseases that afflict both sexes. Women's-health advocates charge that we collect data from studies of men and then extrapolate to women. A look at the actual data reveals a different reality.

The best-known and most ambitious study of cardiovascular health over time began in the town of Framingham, Massachusetts, in 1948. Researchers started with 2,336 men and 2,873 women aged thirty to sixty-two, and have followed the survivors of this group with biennial physical exams and lab tests for more than forty-five years. In this and many other observational studies women have been well represented.

With respect to the aspirin study, the researchers at Harvard Medical School did not focus exclusively on men. Both sexes were studied nearly concurrently. The men's study was more rigorous, because it was placebo-controlled (that is, some subjects were randomly assigned to receive placebos instead of aspirin); the women's study was based on responses to questionnaires sent to nurses and a review of medical records. The women's study, however, followed nearly four times as many subjects as the men's study (87,678 versus 22,071), and it followed its subjects for a year longer (six versus five) than the men's study did. The results of the men's study were reported in the *New England Journal of Medicine* in July of 1989 and prompted charges of sexism in medical research. The women's-study results were printed in the *Journal of the American Medical Association* in July of 1991, and were generally ignored by the nonmedical press.

Most studies on the prevention of "premature" (occurring in people under age sixty-five) coronary-artery disease have, in fact, been conducted on men. Since middle-aged women have a much lower incidence of this illness than their male counterparts (they provide less than a third as many cases), documenting the preventive effect of a given treatment in these women is much more difficult. More experiments were conducted on men not because women were considered less important but because women suffer less from this disease. Older women do develop coronary disease (albeit at a lower rate than older men), but the experiments were not performed on older men either. At most the data suggest an emphasis on the prevention of disease in younger people.

Incidentally, all clinical breast-cancer research currently funded by the NCI is being conducted on women, even though 300 men a year die of this tumor. Do studies on the prevention of breast cancer with specifically exclude males signify a neglect of men's health? Or should a disease be studied in the group most at risk? Obviously, the coronary-disease research situation and the breast-cancer research situation are not equivalent, but together they do serve to illustrate a point: diseases are most often studied in the highest-risk group, regardless of sex....

* * *

Throughout human history from antiquity until the beginning of this century men, on the average, lived slightly longer than women. By 1920 women's life expectancy in the United States was one year greater than men's (54.6 years versus 53.6). After that the gap increased steadily, to 3.5 years in 1930, 4.4 years in 1940, 5.5 in 1950, 6.5 in 1960, and 7.7 in 1970. For the past quarter of a century the gap has remained relatively steady: around seven years. In 1990 the figure was seven years (78.8 versus 71.8).

Thus in the latter part of the twentieth century women live about 10 percent longer than men. A significant part of the reason for this is medical care.

In past centuries complications during childbirth were a major cause of traumatic death in women. Medical advances have dramatically eliminated most of this risk. Infections such as smallpox, cholera, and tuberculosis killed large numbers of men and women at similar ages. The elimination of infection as the dominant cause of death has boosted the prominence of diseases that selectively afflict men earlier in life.

Age-adjusted mortality rates for men are higher for all twelve leading causes of death, including heart disease, stroke, cancer, lung disease (emphysema and pneumonia), liver disease (cirrhosis), suicide, and homicide. We have come to accept women's longer life span as natural, the consequence of their greater biological fitness. Yet this greater fitness never manifested itself in all the millennia of human history that preceded the present era and its medical-care system —the same system that women's-health advocates accuse of neglecting the female sex.

To remedy the alleged neglect, an Office of Research on Women's Health was established by the NIH in 1990. In 1991 the NIH launched its largest epidemiological project ever, the Women's Health Initiative. Costing more than $600 million, this fifteen-year program will study the effects of estrogen therapy, diet, dietary supplements, and exercise on heart disease, breast cancer, colon cancer, osteoporosis, and other diseases in 160,000 postmenopausal women. The study is ambitious in scope and may well result in many advances in the care of older women.

What it will not do is close the "medical gender gap," the difference in the quality of care given the two sexes. The reason is that the gap does not favor men. As we have seen, women receive more medical care and benefit more from medical research. The net result is the most important gap of all: seven years, 10 percent of life.

POSTSCRIPT

Is There a Gender Bias in Medicine and Research?

In July 1993 the FDA modified and revised its 1977 guidelines on the inclusion of women in early phases of clinical trials. The new guideline lifts the explicit exclusion of women from the earliest phases of drug trials, but it does not require their inclusion. Instead, the FDA will require an analysis of clinical data in drug applications to determine whether or not there is a gender difference in response to the drug and, if so, what its basis might be. Although this revision liberalized existing policy, it was criticized as inadequate by some activists.

In 1994 the Institute of Medicine, responding to a request from the NIH Office of Research on Women's Health, issued a report recommending, among other things, that investigators and Institutional Review Boards (IRBs) not exclude persons of reproductive age from participation in clinical studies. Furthermore, the institute supported the inclusion of pregnant women, declaring, "It is the responsibility of investigators and IRBs to ensure that pregnant women are provided with adequate information about the risks and benefits to themselves, their pregnancies, and their potential offspring." See *Institute of Medicine, Women and Health Research*, 2 vols., edited by Anna C. Mastroianni, Ruth Faden, and Daniel Federman (National Academy Press, 1994).

For a general review of the issues, see Judith Rodin and Jeannette R. Ickovics, "Women's Health: Review and Research Agenda as We Approach the Twenty-First Century," *American Psychologist* (September 1990), and the Council of Ethical and Judicial Affairs' "Gender Discrimination in the Medical Profession," *Women's Health Issues* (vol. 4, 1994): 1–11. In her article "The Exclusion of Pregnant, Pregnable, and Once-Pregnable People (A.K.A. Women) from Biomedical Research," *American Journal of Law and Medicine* (vol. 19, no. 4, 1993), Vanessa Merton presents legal and ethical arguments for the inclusion of pregnant women in all phases of drug trials. See also Carol Levine, "Women as Research Subjects: New Priorities, New Questions," in *Emerging Issues in Biomedical Policy: An Annual Review*, edited by Robert H. Blank and Andrea L. Bonnicksen (Columbia University Press, 1993). In "Health Law Symposium," a special issue of the *Saint Louis Law Journal* (vol. 38, no. 1, 1993), R. Alta Charo discusses the exclusion of women from research trials. For further reading on the exclusion of women from research trials on the grounds of potential fetal injury, see Hazel Sandomire's "Women in Clinical Trials: Are Sponsors Liable for Fetal Injury?" *The Journal of Law, Medicine and Ethics* (Summer 1993).

PART 5

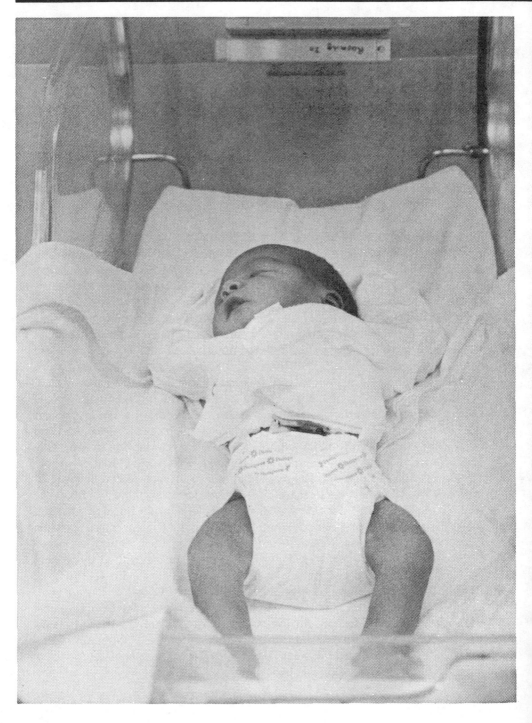

Public Policy and Bioethics

Public policy in the field of bioethics has had to struggle to respond rapidly to scientific events and technical advances. Decisions in this field can no longer be the sole province of individual doctors or patients. The availability of screening tests for disease and for genetic predisposition to disease has created many ethical puzzles. Financial and medical resources remain extremely limited, and society's demand is great. Can health care costs for all be contained without depriving some groups, such as the elderly, of some kinds of care? Will a scientific project of mapping the human genome bring back discredited eugenics policies? And perhaps most sweeping of all are considerations of reforming the U.S. health care system to provide more equitable access. This section deals with issues that have moved to the forefront of the struggle to define social values.

- Should Newborns Be Screened for HIV Infection?

- Should Newborns Without Brains Be Used as Organ Donors?

- Should There Be a Market in Body Parts?

- Should Health Care for the Elderly Be Limited?

- Is It Unfair to Tie Health Insurance to Employment?

- Should Health Insurance Companies Have Access to Information from Genetic Testing?

- Will the Human Genome Project Lead to Abuses in Genetic Engineering?

ISSUE 15

Should Newborns Be Screened for HIV Infection?

YES: Mark S. Rapoport, from "Mandatory Newborn Screening for HIV: Long Overdue, but Not Nearly Enough," *The AIDS Reader* (September/October 1994)

NO: Alan R. Fleischman, from "Mandatory Newborn Screening for HIV: The Wrong Answer to the Wrong Question," *The AIDS Reader* (September/October 1994)

ISSUE SUMMARY

YES: Pediatrician and county health commissioner Mark S. Rapoport believes that the knowledge that a baby may be HIV-infected benefits the baby's health and that parents should have this information—even if they do not want it.

NO: Pediatrician Alan R. Fleischman argues against mandatory testing, since universal counseling for women and voluntary testing will best develop the trusting relationship that is essential for providing services to both mother and child.

The first cases of what is now called AIDS (acquired immunodeficiency syndrome) were seen in 1981, and in retrospect, probably as early as the mid-1970s. The retrovirus most scientists believe causes the disease—human immunodeficiency virus, or HIV—was discovered in 1984, and a laboratory test that recognized antibodies to HIV was approved for marketing in 1985. Clinical and ethical justifications for the use of the HIV antibody test have been controversial ever since. Except for some settings (admission to the military, job corps, immigration, and some prisons), HIV testing is voluntary. There is an uneasy compromise between those who would institute compulsory, widespread testing without consent and those who would restrict the use of the test to clinical and research settings under strict consent procedures.

In 1987 the Centers for Disease Control and Prevention (CDC)—the federal agency that monitors disease—established a "family of serosurveys" in selected hospitals, drug treatment centers, and sexually transmitted disease clinics. In these settings, discarded blood was tested without any links to the patient. This method was designed to give an unbiased picture of HIV infection. Because no one in the surveys could be identified, no consent was necessary, and no one could opt out of participating.

Newborn nurseries were among the settings chosen by the CDC. Positive results on newborns give a reasonably accurate picture of the incidence of infection in women giving birth in a certain geographic area. Positive tests for the babies themselves are only suggestive of HIV infection, since at least three-quarters of the newborns who tested positive are not actually HIV-infected and lose their maternal antibodies in the first 15 months of life. A newborn's positive test result, however, almost certainly indicates HIV infection in the mother.

Pediatricians treating babies with HIV infection began to challenge this study design. As they gained more experience with HIV infection, they found that the leading cause of death in the first year of life was Pneumocystis carinii pneumonia (PCP). Prophylaxis (or preventive medicine) was proving successful in adults in forestalling PCP. Other medical benefits are also possible, although nothing so far can cure the disease or guarantee long-term survival. Pediatricians frustrated by their inability to identify potentially HIV-infected babies called for "unblinding" the serosurveys, that is, linking the positive test results to individual mothers so that they could be informed about their babies' HIV status (and by implication, their own infection).

The controversy erupted in New York State in 1993–1994 when a member of the legislature proposed that the serosurveys be unblinded and mothers be told of their infants' HIV status, even though they had not consented to the test for themselves. While the debate was raging, another study—known by its AIDS Clinical Trial Group number 076—was released. This showed that pregnant women treated with the antiviral drug zidovudine (AZT) during the last stages of pregnancy and during delivery had a much lower rate of HIV transmission to their newborns (8.3 percent compared to 25 percent in the untreated group). The newborns were also treated with AZT in the first weeks of life. This further complicated the focus and shifted the issue to screening pregnant women as well as newborns.

The following two selections summarize the debate. Mark S. Rapoport declares that the benefits of mandatory testing to the baby's health are compelling and that voluntary HIV testing programs do not achieve high enough rates of participation. Mothers, he believes, will see in retrospect (if not at the time) that testing was the right thing to do. Alan R. Fleischman argues that it is critically important that the testing of women be done with their permission and full understanding of the benefits and risks. Treatment for themselves and their babies requires trust and full cooperation, which are unlikely to be achieved with mandatory testing.

YES

Mark S. Rapoport

MANDATORY NEWBORN SCREENING FOR HIV: LONG OVERDUE, BUT NOT NEARLY ENOUGH

The very fact that New York State and New York City have been actively grappling for more than a year with the question of mandatory HIV antibody screening of all newborns tells a great deal. Multiple benefits accrue from knowing that a baby is HIV-seropositive (with actual infection easily verifiable). These include better diagnosis of febrile and pulmonary illness; antibiotic prophylaxis for pneumocystis infection and modified immunization for the baby; counseling on the risks of breast feeding and a host of other medical interventions for the mother; potential location of other cases, especially the child's father; education for prevention of additional transmission by any and all recognized routes; and a broad range of social services (especially those available via the Ryan White Care Act) for the family. None of these benefits are disputed.

For most people, in New York State and elsewhere, the case for screening is straightforward and compelling. It serves the HIV-seropositive baby's health for the data to be known, and parents should want to do well by their children. Parents should have this information, even if they do not want it. The headline on the cover of the February 21, 1994, issue of *New York* magazine may have captured that feeling. It said, "Should It Be a Crime to Treat This Baby for AIDS? The Rising Storm Over the Law That Keeps HIV-Positive Newborns from Early Treatment."

The view of the majority of people most deeply involved in AIDS policy and AIDS care, however, is very different. While they agree that real benefits accrue to both baby and mother and from knowing a baby's serostatus, other considerations take precedence. First, "coercion" is the key issue, with analogy sometimes made to testing Federal prisoners. Second, decade-old fears arise of losing insurance, spouses, and jobs (although the testing would be strictly confidential). Third, there is the unsubstantiated fear that state-mandated testing would forever estrange HIV-seropositive women from their doctors and "the system," and "drive them underground."

From Mark S. Rapoport, "Mandatory Newborn Screening for HIV: Long Overdue, but Not Nearly Enough," *The AIDS Reader* (September/October 1994). Copyright © 1994 by SCP Communications, Inc. Reprinted by permission.

I find none of these arguments convincing. The evidence for these fears being realized is very weak. Furthermore, all the perceived difficulties can be minimized by good counseling, good follow-up, and strong safeguards on confidentiality. All of these things are possible and are already being done to a substantial degree. The record of the public health enterprise in maintaining confidentiality is especially good.

A strong sense of the history of discrimination (against women, people of color, and gay men) underlies many of these fears. These sensibilities may be acknowledged, but should not be considered an eternal bar to progress in the ways we combat the plague of AIDS. AIDS is in many ways different from tuberculosis, hepatitis, and syphilis, but it is also similar in many ways. All have some stigma associated with them, nonetheless we have mounted credible efforts against them. In the course of these efforts, we often encounter suspicion, distrust, and fears, but usually we can overcome them. This has direct relevance to the arguments relating to undermining the trust of women who are indirectly tested by a newborn screening program. I think we give these women too little credit if we assume that they will be unable to see the benefits of screening (in retrospect, if not prospectively) and that this failure on their part will translate to a distrust of and unwillingness to cooperate with their doctors, nurses, and social workers. The law would emanate from the state government, not the professional at the bedside, and this distinction is not difficult to discern. Mandating testing programs for hepatitis B and syphilis has not had the feared effects and I do not believe that an HIV newborn-screening program would either. From our efforts

with these diseases, we should learn to improve our strategies and to bring AIDS care and AIDS policies closer to the norm for public health problems. Mandatory newborn screening is one such step and is long overdue.

Having said that, we must address the ACTG 076 study showing the clear benefit of giving zidovudine prenatally and intrapartum to pregnant women, and then to the newborn. The beneficial results are truly exciting. Taken together, the 3 interventions cut the rate of vertical transmission by about two-thirds, from 26% to 8%. If all HIV-infected women received the entire "package," perhaps 400 lives would be saved annually in New York State alone. There is a consensus that our emphasis now must be to identify and treat infection in pregnant women at the earliest possible time. Further, there is widespread agreement that a voluntary program would be the best first effort. I concur with this, since in the prenatal context, we confront the likelihood that substantial numbers of women (especially those with the most risk-laden medical history and social circumstances) might be deterred from seeking early prenatal care, or might be more likely to drop out of care. However, I believe that such a program would have to be well designed and continually evaluated, with a mandatory prenatal testing program as a true alternative if a voluntary program did not achieve and maintain high rates of participation.

Although a prenatal effort at testing and treatment must be the first priority, the issue of testing newborns is by no means moot. Some women will not seek prenatal care, and women at highest risk for HIV infection are likely to be over-represented in that group. Also, some women will refuse prenatal testing.

What should our response be to the needs of these women and their newborns? I believe that although the absolute number of infected babies will be lower (hopefully, a great deal lower) than under present circumstances, society's obligation to those babies remains unchanged. It is not difficult, I think, to make a case for considering the refusal to accept testing, and the attendant inability to act on the results of that testing, a form of the true "medical neglect."

As a society, we do not tolerate medical neglect of children's needs in regard to conditions other than AIDS, many of which are not nearly as lethal. We certainly need to develop a voluntary prenatal HIV program, incorporating mandatory counseling and minimizing barriers to participation; a mandatory testing program for the already-born child would not be at odds with such a program. In fact, it would reinforce it, just as it would reinforce our commitment to valuing the life of every child, and preserving and caring for those lives in the best way we know how.

NO

Alan R. Fleischman

MANDATORY NEWBORN SCREENING FOR HIV: THE WRONG ANSWER TO THE WRONG QUESTION

Pediatricians responsible for the care of children infected with the human immunodeficiency virus (HIV) increasingly voice concern that the earliest indication of HIV disease in a child is a fatal infection during the first months of life. Some of these health professionals believe that early identification of children at risk for HIV infection and the initiation of prophylactic therapies will greatly enhance the quality and quantity of children's lives. This has resulted in the recommendation that the standard newborn screening test done on all babies right after birth, which currently identifies several genetic and metabolic disorders, be utilized to find children who are infected with HIV. At first glance this recommendation seems both well-meaning and reasonable, in that the goal of protecting children from unnecessary illness is certainly laudable. However, there are many questions to be raised about the basic assumptions upon which this recommendation is made, as well as serious concerns about the consequences of universal, nonconsensual screening of newborns for HIV.

Ironically, this debate is occurring at a time when exciting new data are emerging about the prevention of transmission of HIV from pregnant women to their fetuses through the administration of zidovudine (ZDV) to the woman during pregnancy and intrapartum, and to the newborn for 6 weeks after birth. The possibility of pharmacologic primary prevention of HIV transmission during pregnancy creates a far more important question: How can we educate the entire population about the importance of knowing their HIV status in order to reduce HIV transmission from one person to another? With particular emphasis on women, how can we create a general standard of medical practice so that every woman who is of reproductive age or is at her first prenatal visit is counseled concerning the benefits of knowing her HIV status and offered appropriate comprehensive services for herself and her family?

A program of counseling and voluntary testing before or early in pregnancy can result in the identification of women who would be offered the option of antiretroviral treatment in an attempt to block HIV transmission to the fetus. Even though all of the questions concerning the use of ZDV in pregnancy have not been answered, the compelling nature of the data demands that we make this option available to women who want this intervention.

It is critically important that the testing of women be done with their permission and full understanding of the benefits and risks of the test. The health care establishment must foster an atmosphere of trust between patients and their providers that can be translated into the delivery of comprehensive services over a long period of time. The treatment of HIV disease and the potential prevention of transmission requires the full cooperation of a knowledgeable and committed patient. Mandatory programs based on coercion will only lead to greater distrust and result in patients who are appropriately reluctant to favorably consider therapeutic options presented by well-meaning health care professionals.

Knowing and accepting all of this, some legislators and health care leaders continue to press for mandatory screening of newborns for HIV. They argue that there is a need for a "safety net" to identify newborns whose mothers have not received prenatal care or who have refused to be tested. Of course, they realize that only a small proportion of the babies who test positive for antibody at birth actually will be infected (15% to 30%) while 100% of these infants' mothers will be infected. They also must be aware that the goal of a screening program is not merely the identification and labeling of a potential patient, but also the provision of needed services to that patient and family.

It is incredible to me that some physicians and politicians would consider a program that would combine voluntary testing during the prenatal period and mandatory testing after birth. Can we, as professionals, in good faith counsel women about the importance of knowing their HIV status during pregnancy and accept their voluntary decision about testing, only to test them involuntarily after birth? This seems duplicitous and inappropriate. Of course, all women who have not been tested previously should be counseled at the time of birth about the importance of testing, and we should encourage as many mothers as possible to know their and their newborns' HIV status.

We have the potential to ask the right question and create the right answer. The right question is: How can we offer appropriate counseling to all women and engage them voluntarily to learn their HIV status? If they are HIV-positive, how do we ensure that they receive needed care for themselves and potential interventions to prevent transmission to their fetus and, finally, that they provide care for their infants? This can only be accomplished through a new standard of medical practice that counsels women on the importance and appropriateness of knowing their HIV status before, during, and after pregnancy. Pregnant women should be counseled about the benefits and potential risks of HIV testing while receiving prenatal care and at the time of delivery. Testing should be linked to services and a positive test should result in referral to a program that provides comprehensive care for families.

Perhaps most critically important in the analysis of this complex problem is the issue of trust and respect among health care professionals, their patients, and the public at large. We need not create an atmosphere of fear and coercion when we have the opportunity to develop a program of screening and care that is both voluntary and comprehensive and will likely benefit the vast majority of those in need. We have available today a potential method to identify virtually all of the infants who are at risk for HIV infection through mandatory counseling and encouraged testing of women. With appropriate resources given to education and health care delivery, the desired goal of early identification and treatment of HIV-infected infants can be accomplished without mandatory newborn screening. The right question is how to develop a trusting relationship in order to provide services to those in need. The right answer is universal counseling and voluntary testing.

POSTSCRIPT

Should Newborns Be Screened for HIV Infection?

A special committee convened by the New York State AIDS Advisory Council in February 1994 rejected mandatory testing of newborns in favor of mandatory counseling of pregnant women. Several pediatricians attached a dissenting view, and the New York legislature reached a consensus that favored mandatory counseling. On the last day of the 1994 session, however, the consensus fell apart and no vote was held. Then–governor Mario Cuomo asked his Task Force on Life and the Law to look into the issue. It has not yet reported its conclusions. Other states, such as Florida, are also considering similar bills.

For legal arguments against mandatory screening of newborns see Jean R. Sternlight, "Mandatory Non-Anonymous Testing of Newborns for HIV: Should It Ever Be Allowed?" *The John Marshall Law Review* (Winter 1994), and Kevin J. Curnin, "Newborn HIV Screening and New York Assembly Bill No. 6747-B: Privacy and Equal Protection of Pregnant Women," *Fordham Urban Law Journal* (vol. 21, no. 3, 1994). An argument for mandatory screening of newborns is found in Margaret C. Heagarty and Elaine J. Abrams, "Caring for HIV-Infected Women and Children," *The New England Journal of Medicine*, (vol. 326, 1992): 887–88.

Three articles in *The New England Journal of Medicine* (November 3, 1994) discuss the impact of the results of the AIDS Clinical Trial Group number 076, which showed decreased maternal-fetal HIV transmission with AZT therapy. See "Reduction of Maternal-Infant Transmission of HIV-1 with Zidovudine Treatment," by E.M. Connor et al.; "Reducing the Risk of Maternal-Infant Transmission of HIV: A Door is Opened," by Martha F. Rogers and Harold W. Jaffe; and "Ethical Challenges Posed by Zidovudine Treatment to Reduce Vertical Transmission of HIV," by Ronald Bayer.

ISSUE 16

Should Newborns Without Brains Be Used as Organ Donors?

YES: Michael R. Harrison, from "Organ Procurement for Children: The Anencephalic Fetus as Donor," *The Lancet* (December 13, 1986)

NO: John D. Arras and Shlomo Shinnar, from "Anencephalic Newborns as Organ Donors: A Critique," *Journal of the American Medical Association* (April 15, 1988)

ISSUE SUMMARY

YES: Pediatric surgeon Michael R. Harrison asserts that if anencephalic newborns were treated as brain-dead rather than as brain-absent, their organs could be transplanted and their families could be offered the consolation that their loss provided life for another child.

NO: Philosopher John D. Arras and pediatric neurologist Shlomo Shinnar argue that the current principles of the strict definition of brain death are sound public policy and good ethics.

There are too few organs for donation for all categories of persons in need, but one of the most poignant situations occurs in newborns and infants. Only small organs are suitable for these young patients, and appropriate organs become available only when other young patients die.

Today several thousand children could benefit from transplants. Those on dialysis regimens could be given the chance to lead more normal lives with kidney transplants. Those suffering from liver failure face certain death without transplants. Others are born with heart defects so severe that only new hearts can save their lives.

The technical problems in transplanting small organs are rapidly being overcome, but the ethical problems persist. Anencephalic babies are one potential source of organs for pediatric patients. These are babies who are born without brains or with large portions missing; they may survive for a few hours or days, or even weeks, but (except in rare cases) no longer. This condition occurs about once in every 1,000 to 2,000 births and can be detected through screening of the mother's blood and confirmed through sonograms, which reveal the baby's organs in utero. About 2,000 such babies are detected each year.

The parents of these babies are faced with a difficult choice: they can choose abortion (even in the third trimester) or they can carry the pregnancy to term, knowing that their baby is doomed to die. A few parents in this situation have asked for a third option: to donate the organs of their baby so that they can feel that some good for another family has come out of their personal tragedy.

If these babies had no brain activity at all, that is, if they were brain-dead, there would be no ethical problem. Their parents could consent for the removal of their organs, just as the next of kin of a brain-dead adult can consent to organ donation. But these babies, though lacking higher brain activity, do have some rudimentary brain-stem activity. Though doomed to die, they are not yet dead. If physicians wait until the babies are brain-dead, their organs may not be suitable for transplantation.

The ethical questions thus center around the justifiability of treating anencephalic newborns as if they were brain-dead in order to achieve the goal of salvaging their organs. Is the distinction between brain-absent and brain-dead a legal technicality or does it go to the essence of human existence?

In the selections that follow, Michael R. Harrison declares that the ability to transplant fetal organs may now give us the chance to recognize the contribution of the doomed anencephalic fetus to mankind. He favors treating anencephalics as legally brain-dead. John D. Arras and Shlomo Shinnar offer a critique of this view. They argue that the attempt to reconcile the use of anencephalic newborns as organ donors with the current principles of brain death violates principles of ethics and public policy. They argue that the strict criteria for whole-brain death must be satisfied and that vital organs may not be taken from the living to benefit others.

YES

Michael R. Harrison

ORGAN PROCUREMENT FOR CHILDREN: THE ANENCEPHALIC FETUS AS DONOR

Organ transplants could give an increasing number of children with fatal childhood diseases the chance of a full life.[1, 2] However, most children die waiting for an appropriate donor organ.

THE DYING CHILD: PROMISE AT A PRICE

The need for small organs is acute and the demand is likely to grow. In the United States 300–450 children with end-stage renal disease could be taken off dialysis regimens if they received renal transplants.[3, 4] The only hope for the 400–800 children with liver failure (biliary atresia, cholestatic syndromes, and inherited metabolic defects) is liver transplantation;[5, 6] for the 400–600 children with certain forms of congenital heart disease such as hypoplastic left heart syndrome it may be cardiac transplantation;[7, 8] and for an increasing number with childhood haemopoietic and malignant diseases, it is bone-marrow transplantation.[9, 10] Finally, enzymatic, immunological, and endocrine deficiencies may be corrected by the use of cellular (rather than whole-organ) grafts.[11, 14]

For many childhood diseases, biological tissue replacement may be the only satisfactory solution because the transplant must be able to grow and adapt to increasing functional demand over the potentially long life span of the recipient. But the logistics of organ transplantation are very demanding for the young recipient, in whom rapid organ failure and lack of interim support measures make the "time window" for transplantation narrow.

The present system of obtaining vital organs from "brain-dead" accident victims cannot meet the demand for small organs. It is also logistically complex and very expensive. The cost of a new heart or liver often exceeds $100,000. Unless donor material becomes simpler and less costly to procure and transplant, these life-saving procedures will have to be rationed.

AVAILABILITY OF ANENCEPHALIC ORGANS AND TISSUES

Fetuses with defects so hopeless that they meet the requirements for pregnancy termination at any gestational age may be ideal donors. With anencephaly termination is justifiable even in the third trimester,[15] and vital organs other than the brain are usually normal. It occurs once in every 1000–2000 births,[16] is easily detected by screening for raised alphafetoprotein levels in maternal serum and amniotic fluid, and can be confirmed by sonography. When screening programmes capable of detecting 90% of all anencephalic fetuses are instituted, we can expect to detect around 2000 anencephalic fetuses in the United States each year. Even if only a small proportion proves suitable as source of donor material, it could go a long way towards satisfying estimated needs.

CAN IMMATURE ORGANS WORK?

It is unlikely that a functionally immature fetal organ can immediately replace and sustain vital organ function in a child; continued partial function of the native organ or availability of interim external support for organ function will be crucial. With support by dialysis, kidneys transplanted from newborn babies with anencephaly can show remarkable growth in size and function.[17] Technical difficulties with small-vessel anastomoses are now surmountable. Since there is no method of providing good interim support for failing liver and cardiac function, total orthotopic replacement with fetal heart or liver would be limited to neonatal recipients and near-term donors. The fetal organ would have to be large enough to fit the recipient and functionally mature enough to immediately replace life-sustaining function. But traditional whole-organ orthotopic replacement may not be necessary or even desirable. Auxiliary transplantation of immature organs that can develop until they take over the life-sustaining function of the failing native organ may prove safer, simpler, and less expensive.

Fetal liver has tremendous potential for growth and functional adaptation. We have shown experimentally that auxiliary heterotopic liver transplantation is technically feasible and physiologically sound.[18, 19] A small liver allows auxiliary placement without the elaborate manoeuvres required for enlarging a child's abdomen or reducing donor liver size.[20] And the obvious disadvantage of small vessels may be offset by circulatory peculiarities of fetal liver—eg, portal inflow can be provided via the large umbilical vein, which carries all the fetal cardiac output, rather than via the small and delicate portal vein, which carries only 20% of liver blood flow in utero.[21] Also, the ductus venosus is patent for a short time after birth and this may help to adjust the haemodynamic pressure gradient across the grafted fetal liver.[18]

Orthotopic replacement of the fetal heart, like that of the liver, is limited to late-gestation donors and neonatal recipients. But use of the small immature fetal heart as a heterotopic assist device is a promising prospect. We have developed a simple way of inserting a fetal heart in neonatal animals as a right ventricular assist (vena cava to pulmonary artery) to bypass congenital right ventricular outflow obstruction, and as a left ventricular assist (left atrium to aorta) to correct hypoplastic left heart syndrome (unpublished). Thus auxiliary heterotopic placement, which has been effective in adults,[22] may be simpler and safer than orthotopic replacement for treating both right and left hypoplastic heart syndromes in children.

FETAL TISSUES AND "SELECTIVE" TRANSPLANTATION

Perhaps the most promising use of fetal tissue is for selective cellular grafts, which do not require surgical revascularisation.[2] Suspensions of fetal thymus have been used to correct immunodeficiencies,[23] and bone-marrow grafting can restore immunocompetence and haemopoietic function.[9,10] However, the rejection and graft-versus-host disease seen with grafts from mature donors are less likely with immature haemopoietic stem cells harvested from fetal marrow or liver. Since many inherited defects (eg, thalassaemia) that may be correctable by cellular grafts can be diagnosed in the first half of gestation, it may be advantageous to reconstitute a deficient cell-line by in-utero transfusion.[11] We have shown experimentally that haemopoietic stem cells given by intraperitoneal injection in the first trimester can produce lasting haemopoietic chimerism.[24]

The difficulty of separating islets from exocrine pancreatic tissue and the rejection encountered with islet-cell transplantation, which can lead to cure of experimentally induced diabetes mellitus, may be ameliorated by the use of fetal pancreas.[13, 25] Transplantation of immature pituitary tissue[21] is also promising. Furthermore, there is the possibility that a functioning organ can be "grown" in a recipient by implanting a very primitive fetal organ as a non-vascularised free graft; fetal intestine, for example, may one day be used to treat infants with the short bowel syndrome.[26] Corneal grafts may restore sight, and fetal ventricular outflow tract has been used as a homograft valved conduit.[27]

ADVANTAGES OF USING FETAL ORGANS AND TISSUES

If fetal organs prove suitable, transplantation for children may be greatly simplified biologically, technically, and logistically. But the most important potential advantage is that use of fetal organs may need less immunosuppression than will use of mature organs. Fetal organs are not less "antigeneic" and thus less subject to rejection than mature organs because histocompatibility antigens are expressed early in fetal life. However, fetal grafts in general survive longer than do more mature grafts,[28, 29] and the use of fetal donors allows the immunological manipulations that improve graft survival. The fetus can be tissue-typed by examining amniotic fluid or fetal blood,[30] so the best possible recipient can be chosen by cross-matching. In addition, recipients can be pre-treated with donor cells (amniotic fluid or blood) by the same strategy that has led to improved graft survival in clinical renal transplantation.[31]

In the future, perhaps the unique immunological relation between mother and fetus can be exploited to facilitate graft acceptance. When the need for transplantation can be predicted before birth (eg, hypoplastic left heart, thalassaemia) it may be possible to induce specific unresponsiveness in the potential recipient antenatally, for transplantation either before or after birth. Although transplantation immunity develops early in all mammals, in early gestation the fetus is uniquely susceptible to induction of tolerance by donor cell suspensions.[32] Also, graft rejection and graft-versus-host disease may be less likely if grafting is done before the recipient becomes immunocompetent and/or the donor organ becomes populated by "passenger" leucocytes.

RISKS AND BENEFITS OF ALLOWING FETAL ORGAN DONATION

The diagnosis of fetal anencephaly is always devastating. Once the family has worked through their grief and decided how the pregnancy will be managed, the possibility of organ donation may be brought up. In my experience families are surprisingly positive about donation; they clutch at any possibility that something good might be salvaged from a seemingly wasted pregnancy. Sometimes families even bring up the subject themselves, or they become upset when organs cannot be donated because of a legal ambiguity (see below).

Would allowing organ procurement from an anencephalic fetus increase maternal risk? To be successfully transplanted, the organs must be oxygenated and perfused until harvest. If labour were induced by the usual techniques (for example, by cervical dilatation and ripening, pitocin) rather than by the more violent techniques often used in late abortions (for instance, prostaglandin injection), most anencephalic fetuses can be delivered vaginally without increased risk to mother.[33] Caesarean delivery would ordinarily not be considered except for maternal indications, even when labour is difficult to induce, or when the anencephalic fetus seems to be in distress.

ETHICAL AND LEGAL ISSUES

If further research and clinical experience shows that use of fetal organs is a biologically sound and cost-effective treatment for otherwise hopeless childhood diseases, society will have to decide what attitude to adopt towards the anencephalic fetus.

One attitude is that the anencephalic baby is a product of human conception incapable of achieving "personhood" because it lacks the physical structure (forebrain) necessary for characteristic human activity; and thus can never become a human "person". The idea that a product of human conception is biologically incapable of achieving "humanness" seems radical until we consider the many products of conception lost by early miscarriage or stillbirth because of gross abnormalities. Although this approach makes organ procurement simple by denying the anencephalic baby the legal rights of personhood, there are compelling reasons for avoiding this stance. First, it is difficult to reach a consensus about personhood and what constitutes humanness. Secondly, denying personhood denigrates the pregnancy itself and may lead to a less respectful approach to the grieving family and to medical care of the fetus and newborn. Finally, there is the possibility of abuse; other fetuses or newborn babies, possibly with less severe handicaps, might be denied personhood.

Another attitude is that the anencephalic fetus is a dying person and that death is inevitable at or shortly after birth because of brain absence. The first point in favour of this attitude is that brain absence can be clearly defined and limited only to anencephalics, so individuals with less severe anomalies or injuries cannot be classed with anencephalic babies as exceptions for brain-death guidelines. Another point in favour of this attitude is that the anencephalic fetus is considered a person, albeit one doomed to death at birth. To consider the anencephalic baby as a person who is brain absent is to recognise his devastating anatomical and functional deficiency without demeaning his existence. He has rights and deserves respect, so removal of organs must not cause suffering, detract from the dignity of dying, or abridge the right to die. This is best done in the operating theatre as is currently being done for brain-dead subjects. This approach also provides a sound ethical rationale for the present practice of allowing the family to choose termination of an anencephalic pregnancy at any gestational age, and would eliminate potential incongruities, such as insisting on care of aborted anencephalic subjects.

Current laws seem to forbid removal of organs from an anencephalic subject until vital functions cease, by which time the organs and tissues are irreparably damaged. This is because anencephalic babies are not brain dead by the widely accepted whole-brain definition of death which requires "irreversible cessation of all functions of the entire brain, including the brain stem";[34] anencephalics may have lower-brain-stem activity capable of maintaining vital functions, although precariously, for hours after birth.

The whole-brain definition of death was drafted to protect the comatose patient whose injured brain might recover function. However, failure of the brain to develop is clearly different from injury to a functioning brain, and it was simply not considered when the brain-death definition was formulated. The extreme caution and safeguards needed in pronouncing brain death after brain injury should not apply to anencephaly, in which the physical structure necessary for recovery is absent. If failure of brain development, or brain absence, is recognised as the only exception to present brain-death statutes, society and the courts can then concentrate on the legal implications of regarding the anencephalic subject as being brain absent. I believe that brain absence will come to have the same medicolegal implications as brain death, but this will have to be recognised by society and confirmed by the courts.

If the anencephalic fetus is considered to be equivalent to brain-dead subjects for legal purposes, the family should be able to allow organ donation after delivery and to arrange the timing and place of delivery to facilitate transplantation.[35] Obstetrical decisions about how and when to end the pregnancy must be independent of plans to use the organs for transplantation. Members of the transplant team should not be involved in counselling or perinatal management, and the diagnosis of anencephaly should be confirmed by a panel independent of the transplant team and include a neurologist, a bioethicist, and a neonatologist. The family should also be able to decide before delivery whether they wish to see and hold the newborn.

Because many fetal disorders can now be diagnosed and even treated antenatally, we are learning to accept the fetus as an unborn patient.[30] We are also identifying fetuses so fatally damaged that survival outside the womb is impossible. The ability to transplant fetal organs may now give us the chance to recognise the contribution of this doomed fetus to mankind. If organs from prenatally diagnosed anencephalic fetuses can be obtained with safety for mother and respect for the fetus, the family should be allowed to salvage from their tragedy the consolation that their loss can provide life to another child.

I thank Dr John C. Fletcher, Dr Albert Jonsen, Professor John A. Robertson, Dr Mitchell Golbus, and colleagues at the Fetal Treatment Program, UCSF, for suggestions and review.

REFERENCES

1. Lum CT, Wassner SJ, Martin DE. Current thinking in transplantation in infants and children. *Ped Clins North Am* 1985; **32:** 1203–32.
2. Russell PS. Selective transplantation: An emerging concept. *Ann Surg* 1985; **201:** 255–62.
3. So SKS, Nevine TE, Chang PN, et al. Preliminary results of renal transplantation. *Transpl Proc* 1985; **17:** 182–83.
4. Eggers PW, Connerton R, McMullan M. The medicare experience with end-stage renal disease: Trends in incidence, prevalence, and survival. *Hlth Care Financing Rev* 1984; **5:** 69–88.
5. Lloyd-Still JD. Mortality from liver disease in children: Implications for hepatic transplantation program. *Am J Dise Child* 1985; **139:** 381–84.
6. Gartner JC, Zatelli, BJ, Starzl TE. Orthotopic liver transplantation. Two year experience with 47 patients. *Pediatrics* 1984; **74:** 140–45.
7. Baily LL, Jang J, Johnson W, Jolley WB. Orthotopic cardiac xenografting in the newborn goat. *J Thorac Cardiovasc Surg* 1985; **89:** 242–47.
8. Penkoske PA, Freidman RM, Rowe RD, Trusler GA. The future of heart and heart-lung transplantation in children. *Heart Transplant* 1984; **3:** 233–38.
9. Thomas ED. Marrow transplantation for nonmalignant disorders. *N Engl J Med* 1985; **312:** 46–47.
10. Barranger JA. Marrow transplantation in genetic disease. *N Engl J Med* 1984; **311:** 1629–30.
11. Simpson TJ, Golbus MS. In utero fetal hematopoietic stem cell transplantation. *Sem Perinatol* 1985; **9:** 68–74.
12. Prummer O, Raghavachar A, Werner C, et al. Fetal liver transplantation in the dog. *Transplantation* 1985; **39:** 349–55.
13. Brown J, Danilovs JA, Clark WR, Mullen YS. Fetal pancreas as a donor organ. *World J Surg* 1984; **8:** 152–57.
14. Tulipan NB, Zacar HA, Allen GS. Pituitary transplantation: Part I. Successful reconstitution of pituitary dependent hormone levels. *Neurosurgery* 1985; **16:** 331–35.
15. Chervenak FA, Farley MA, Walters LR, et al. When is termination of pregnancy during the third trimester morally justifiable? *N Engl J Med* 1983; **310:** 501–04.
16. Elwood JM, Elwood JH. Epidemiology of anencephalus and spina bifida. New York: Oxford University Press, 1980: 253–99.
17. Kinnaert P, Persign G, Cohen B, et al. Transplantation of kidneys from anenephalic donors, *Transplant Proc* 1984; **16:** 71–72.
18. Flake AW, Laberge JM, Adzick NS, et al. Auxiliary transplantation of the fetal liver I. Development of a sheep model, *J Pediatr Surg* 1986; **21:** 515–20.
19. Flake AW, Harrison MA, Sauer L, et al. Auxiliary transplantation of the fetal liver II. Functional evaluation of an intra-abdominal model. *J Pediatr Surg* (in press).
20. Bismuth H, Houssin D. Reduced-sized orthotopic liver graft in hepatic transplantation in children. *Surgery* 1984; **95:** 367–70.
21. Rudolph AM. Hepatic and ductus venosus blood flow during fetal life. *Hepatology* 1983; **3:** 245–58.
22. Barnard CN, Cooper DKC. Heterotopic versus orthotopic heart transplantation. *Transplant Proc* 1984; **16:** 886–92.
23. Thong YH, Robertson EF, Rischbieth GH, et al. Successful restoration of immunity in the DiGeorge Syndrome with fetal thymic epithelial transplat. *Arch Dis Child* 1978; **53:** 580–84.
24. Flake AW, Harrison MR, Adzick NS, Zanjani ED. Transplantation of fetal lamb hematopoietic stem cells *in utero:* The creation of hematopoietic chimeras, *Science* (in press).
25. Mandel TE. Transplantation of organ-cultured fetal pancreas: Experimental studies and potential clinical application in diabetes mellitus. *World J Surg* 1984; **8:** 158–68.
26. Bass BL, Schweitzer EJ, Harmon JW, et al. Anatomic and physiologic characteristics of transplanted fetal rat intestine. *Ann Surg* 1984; **200:** 734–41.
27. Fontan F, Choussat A, Deville C, et al. Aortic valve homografts in the surgical treatment of complex cardiac malformations. *J Thorac Cardiovasc Surg* 1984; **87:** 649–57.
28. Miller I. The immunity of the human foetus and newborn infant. Boston: Martinus Nijhoff, 1983.
29. Foglia RP, LaQuaglia M, DiPreta, J, et al. Can fetal and newborn allografts survive in an immunocompetent heart? *J Pediatr Surg* 1986; **21:** 608–12.
30. Harrison MR, Golbus, MS, Filly RA. The unborn patient. New York: Grune & Stratton, 1984.
31. Monoco AP. Clinical kidney transplantation in 1984. *Transplant Proc* 1985; **17:** 5–12.
32. Billingham RE, Brent L, Medawar PB. Actively acquired tolerance of foreign cells. *Nature* 1967; **214:** 179.

33. Lawson J. Delivery of the dead or malformed fetus. Intrauterine death during pregnancy with retention of fetus. *Clins Obs Gynecol* 1982; 9: 745–56.
34. President's Commission for the Study of Ethical Problems in Medicine and Biomedical and Behavioral Research: Defining Death. US Government Printing Office, Washington DC. July 1981.
35. Harrison MR. Commentary. *Hastings Rep* 1986; 16: 21–22.

NO

John D. Arras and
Shlomo Shinnar

ANENCEPHALIC NEWBORNS AS ORGAN DONORS: A CRITIQUE

The debate over whether anencephalic newborns should be used as organ donors has entered a new phase with the recent announcements from West Germany and California (*New York Times*, Oct 19, 1987, p A1) of kidney and heart transplants from anencephalic newborns. As we move from deliberation and debate to action, there is an urgent need to reflect on the ethical implications of this controversial procedure.

THE ISSUES

The case for taking hearts, paired kidneys, and other vital organs from anencephalic newborns is based on two distinct needs. First, there are many chronically ill infants, children, and adults who may benefit from organ transplant, and there is a relative scarcity of available donors. Second, there is the need of the parents of an anencephalic infant to salvage some good from a tragic situation. Allowing the infant to be used as an organ donor may help satisfy this need.

An important feature of anencephaly is the relative certitude of diagnosis and prognosis. Ultrasonography can now detect anencephaly in utero with relative certainty. The prognosis for these infants is death within hours, days, or weeks from birth, although there is some controversy over their exact life span. In view of the need for organs and the alleged uniqueness of anencephaly, it has been proposed that society consider such infants as persons who are born "brain absent." Anencephaly would be declared the *only* legitimate exception to our current insistence that all vital organ donors meet the criteria for whole-brain death. This would be useful in procuring neonatal organs, especially since the diagnosis of whole-brain death in the neonate is extremely difficult and fraught with uncertainty. The lack of established brain death criteria in the first week of life also poses additional problems for those who would use "brain dead" neonates as organ donors (*New York Times*, Oct 19, 1987, p A1).

From John D. Arras and Shlomo Shinnar, "Anencephalic Newborns as Organ Donors: A Critique," *Journal of the American Medical Association*, vol. 259, no. 15 (April 15, 1988), pp. 2284–2285. Copyright © 1988 by The American Medical Association. Reprinted by permission. References omitted.

Advocates of the brain absent approach specifically decline to view anencephalic newborns as "nonpersons" and insist that these infants are "persons" deserving of respect. However, they state that since they are also brain absent, they should be functionally equivalent to brain dead insofar as vital organs might be harvested from them. Another approach for justifying the use of anencephalic newborns as organ donors would be to regard them as nonpersons—ie, as biologically human entities that nevertheless lack the prerequisites of "personal" life and thus lack full moral status. This perspective provides the most direct route to salvaging their organs at the expense of redefining society's views of "personhood."

Despite the manifest importance of the "gift of life" to organ recipients and the laudable desire to help parents salvage some good from a tragedy, society must consider whether allowing anencephalic infants to be used as organ donors before they meet the traditional criteria for brain death is a morally acceptable and legitimate act. We believe it is not.

BRAIN ABSENT THEORY

Let us first address the issues posed by the brain absent theory. By insisting on the personhood of these infants, proponents of this scheme commit themselves to treat the anencephalic infant as a full member of the moral community, ie, one who has rights and is worthy of respect. The question is whether prolonging the infant's life by mechanical ventilation and then abruptly terminating it by harvesting vital organs is compatible with the minimum respect due to all persons. In Kantian philosophy, which is the source of many contemporary moral theories based on the concept of personhood, using one person merely as a means to benefit another constitutes a paradigmatic violation of moral law. As "ends in themselves," persons have an intrinsic worth that cannot be reduced to their instrumental value to others. The investigators' claims notwithstanding, it is difficult to reconcile the treatment of anencephalic newborns outlined in the recent reports (*New York Times*, Oct 19, 1987, p A1) with the notion of respect for personhood.

One response to this objection is to claim that if the anencephalic infant could (miraculously) reflect on his plight, he would consent to organ donation, since losing vital organs would not deprive him of anything he would desire. Similar arguments can be made using the social contract theory of Rawls, in which the decision maker is unbiased because he does not know what role (parent, recipient, anencephalic infant, or physician) he would have in the societal drama and therefore tries to minimize the worst outcome, which may be a person in need of an organ with no available donor. However, these arguments are by no means unique to anencephalic newborns. They are equally applicable to other severely damaged infants as well as to adults in permanent vegetative states. We do not believe society is willing to harvest organs from living patients who have permanently lost the capacity for intelligent thought.

PERSONHOOD THEORY

Justifying the use of anencephalic newborns as organ donors by labeling them "nonpersons" creates the same uniqueness problem. In this philosophical theory, only beings capable of sapient life, whatever that means, have the rights and privileges of "personhood." If anencephalic newborns are nonpersons, one could perhaps justify using them as a mere means for the benefit of persons. Again, if the theory is carried out to its logical conclusion, other infants with conditions such as holoprosencephaly, hydranencephaly, and certain trisomies as well as adults in permanent vegetative states should be considered as potential organ donors.

Those who justify using anencephalic newborns as organ donors based on the fact that they will all die soon after birth must deal with two objections. First, even a dying person is still a person and is entitled to a full measure of dignity and respect as discussed above. Second, there is nothing special in this respect about anencephaly. If the crucial issue is uniform early mortality, then a number of other conditions, such as Potter's syndrome and trisomy 13, would qualify.

The availability of reliable prenatal diagnosis has led some authors to conclude that abortion of anencephalic fetuses is justified even in the third trimester. If we are willing to terminate a viable fetus just prior to term, why not terminate life just after delivery? However, the moral justification for third-trimester abortion is based on the certitude of both diagnosis and prognosis and not on any inherently unique feature of anencephaly. Many other conditions would meet the authors' criteria if reliable antenatal diagnosis were available.

BRAIN DEATH

Another fundamental objection to the proposals for amending the brain death statutes to define anencephalic infants as "dead" or "brain absent" is that this violates the spirit of our present brain death statutes regarding the definition of death. Although anencepahlic infants lack a cerebral cortex, they certainly have a brain stem that sustains and regulates a wide variety of vital bodily functions, including spontaneous respiration. Thus, it would be more accurate to describe them as "higher-brain absent" than as "brain absent." According to the present definition of brain death, ie, complete and irreversible cessation of all brain functions, including those of the brain stem, anencephalic infants are indisputably living human beings. Indeed, no one with spontaneous respirations meets the current criteria for brain death. Permitting the use of anencephalic newborns as organ donors by defining them as legally dead requires a radical reformulation of our current definition of death.

One way to accomplish this would be to reinterpret the original intent of the whole-brain definition of death. One advocate of this approach has argued that the stringent safeguards built into the current brain death statutes were put there to protect comatose patients who might eventually recover some higher cortical functions. Since anencephalic infants lack the capacity ever to achieve such a level of existence, there is no need to protect them with such rigorous definitions of brain death. Consequently, it is argued that taking organs from brain absent anencephalic newborns is ethically compatible with the spirit if not the letter of the laws governing brain death. Although the argument sounds plausible, it confuses a necessary condition for the definition of brain death with a sufficient condition. Of course, any adequate definition of brain death must preclude the possibility of meaningful recovery. However, it is one thing to note that a person is incapable of recovery of higher cortical functions and/or is imminently dying but quite another to say that he or she is dead.

Why should irreversible cessation of activity of the entire brain be necessary for a definition of death? According to the President's Commission, the brain, including the brain stem, performs an irreplaceable function in sustaining and regulating the physiological systems that keep us alive. Once it ceases to perform these vital tasks, modern technology can continue to oxygenate other organs, for a time creating a simulacrum of life, but cannot substitute for the spontaneous integrative functions that the Commission identified as the sine qua non of human life. The Commission insisted on a rigorous definition of brain death not solely to protect comatose patients, but because it believed that anything short of whole-brain death was not equivalent to the death of the human being. The Commission also specifically insisted that organ donors be *dead*, not just irrevocably brain damaged or imminently dying. This position has been cogently reiterated recently by the former executive director of the Commission. Thus, the attempt to reconcile the use of anencephalic newborns as organ donors with current principles of brain death founders on a flawed account of the rationale for accepting whole-brain death as death of the human being.

CONCLUSIONS

Current public policy and practice embody two fundamental principles: first, that vital organs may not be taken from the living for the benefit of others and, second, that for brain death to be considered the moral and legal equivalent of the death of the person, the strict criteria for whole-brain death must be satisfied. The second principle is accepted as sound public policy even by many, including one of us (J.D.A.), who do not fully agree with the President's Commission's philosophical rationale for choosing whole-brain death. The use of anencephalic newborns as organ donors is incompatible with both of these generally accepted principles. Advocates of using these infants as organ donors can invoke the more controversial "higher brain" definitions of either death or personhood to justify their proposal. However, to be consistent, infants with other severe brain malformations as well as adults in chronic vegetative states should then also be candidates for use as organ donors. We believe that the current principles of the strict definition of brain death are sound public policy and good ethics. We hope that, after careful scrutiny and debate, the use of anencephalic infants as organ donors is rejected. Admirable goals should not be advanced by improper means.

POSTSCRIPT

Should Newborns Without Brains Be Used as Organ Donors?

In the 1994 edition of its *Code of Medical Ethics*, the American Medical Association (AMA) made a limited exception to its general standard of organ transplantation because an anencephalic infant "has never experienced, and will never experience, consciousness." The AMA stated that it is ethically permissible to consider anencephalic infants as potential organ donors, "although still alive under the current definition of death," under three conditions: (1) the diagnosis of anencephaly is confirmed by two physicians who are not part of the transplant team; (2) the parents indicate in writing their desire to donate their baby's organs; and (3) there is compliance with other AMA guidelines on organ transplantation. Alternatively, the family wishing to donate may choose to support the infant with mechanical respiration until a determination of death can be made. In this case, the family must be advised that the organs might deteriorate in the process.

In March 1992 a Florida couple sought to have their newborn anencephalic daughter declared legally dead so that her organs could be transplanted to other infants. The baby was born with a partially formed brain stem but no brain cortex, the largest part of the brain. A lower court refused their request, and the Florida Supreme Court refused to hear the parents' appeal on an emergency basis. Theresa Ann Campo Pearson died ten days after birth, with only her eyes donated for research. The family continued its legal battle before the Florida Supreme Court, which denied the appeal.

"The Anencephalic Newborn as Organ Donor," a case study in *Hastings Center Report* (April 1986), offers two views of the question. Also see Larry R. Churchill and Rosa Lynn B. Pinkus, "The Use of Anencephalic Organs: Historical and Ethical Dimensions," *Milbank Quarterly* (1990). Three articles also opposing the practice are "Anencephalic Donors: Separate the Dead from the Dying," by Alexander Morgan Capron, *Hastings Center Report* (February 1987); "From Canada With Love: Anencephalic Newborns as Organ Donors?" by George J. Annas, *Hastings Center Report* (December 1987); and "The Use of Anencephalic Infants as Organ Sources: A Critique," by D. Alan Shewmon et al., *Journal of the American Medical Association* (March 24/31, 1990). Robert M. Arnold and Stuart J. Youngner consider the question of whether or not the moral framework of organ donation is outdated because it still holds to the "dead donor rule" (persons must be dead before their organs are taken) in "The Dead Donor Rule: Should We Stretch It, Bend It, Or Abandon It?" *Kennedy Institute of Ethics Journal* (vol. 3, no. 2, 1993). This issue of the journal also contains other relevant articles.

ISSUE 17

Should There Be a Market in Body Parts?

YES: Lori B. Andrews, from "My Body, My Property," *Hastings Center Report* (October 1986)

NO: Thomas H. Murray, from "Gifts of the Body and the Needs of Strangers," *Hastings Center Report* (April 1987)

ISSUE SUMMARY

YES: Attorney Lori B. Andrews believes that donors, recipients, and society will benefit from a market in body parts so long as owners—and no one else —retain control over their bodies.

NO: Ethicist Thomas H. Murray argues that the gift relationship should govern transfer of body parts because it honors important human values, which are diminished by market relationships.

In 1976 John Moore was treated for hairy-cell leukemia at the University of California at Los Angeles. His enlarged spleen was removed; Moore's condition improved. In the course of seven years of follow-up, Moore was asked by his physicians to return frequently to UCLA from his home in Seattle to have his blood tested. When he became concerned about the frequency of the visits and the amount of blood drawn, he learned that, as a by-product of his treatment, scientists had been able to use his cells to grow a potentially commercially valuable patented cell line, which they named Mo. (Cell line means cells that continuously reproduce in a culture without differentiating.) Moore sued, claiming that he had not given consent for this use of his body parts, and he asked for a share of any profits. The physicians claimed that Moore had waived his interest in his body parts when he authorized the removal of his spleen on a routine consent form.

In a similar case, Hideaki Hagiwara, a postdoctoral biology student at the University of California at San Diego, suggested to a colleague, Dr. Ivor Royston, that cancer cells from Hagiwara's mother could be used to create a human monoclonal antibody—that is, an antibody that reacts specifically with a certain kind of cancerous cell. After the new cell line was completed, Hagiwara claimed that he had an economic interest in the procedure since he had suggested the idea and the cells had come from his mother.

These cases are unusual only because they resulted in lawsuits. The practice of using patients' body parts or tissues for research with potential commercial applications is widespread. According to a survey conducted by a subcommittee of the U.S. House of Representatives, about half of 81 medical schools responding to the questionnaire use patients' fluids or tissues for research. About one-fifth of the patent applications filed by these schools in the five years previous to the survey had used materials derived from patients. Three times as many patents had originated in patients' body parts from 1980 to 1984 as had occurred between 1975 and 1979.

Should patients have the right to consent to the use of their body parts and to share in any profits that might accrue? Or does the value mainly derive from the scientists' labors? The following selections approach this problem from different viewpoints. Lori B. Andrews believes that it is time to acknowledge that body parts are personal property and that individuals must have the ability to transfer and sell them and thus to participate in any economic rewards. Thomas H. Murray, on the other hand, warns that treating body parts as property will diminish their symbolic and human value. He argues for a continuation of the gift relationship, which strengthens the bonds between strangers.

YES

Lori B. Andrews

MY BODY, MY PROPERTY

Tangible items are generally considered to be property. As new potentials for body parts unfold in research, diagnostics, and therapy, the question arises— should they be considered property as well? Current policy allows people to donate solid organs, but not to sell them. A federal law forbids sales of organs for transplant in interstate commerce[1] and certain state laws ban payment for specified organs as well.[2] This perspective—that bodily parts and products are gifts, not compensable items of property—underlies researchers' use of a patient's tissue to produce potentially marketable products.

THE PROPERTY APPROACH AND INDIVIDUAL CONTROL

Throughout the legal lore, judges have reacted with horror to the idea that body parts may be property. Nevertheless, many legal decisions treat the body as a type of property. The law allows me to make gifts of certain body parts and even to destroy my body entirely. Not only do I have a property-like interest in my own body, I may have rights that could be considered property rights in other people's bodies. Tort law allows me to recover for harm to my child, such as it allows me recovery for damage to my car. In most instances, I can collect damages if an autopsy is performed on my next of kin without my consent.

Since the legal treatment of bodies and body parts sounds suspiciously like property treatment, why is there such a reluctance to label it as such? One major fear is that bodily property could be transferred to others (the legal term is alienable) and we could become slaves, not in a market for our bodies, but in a market for body parts. However, characterizing body parts as property does not mean that they must be completely transferable. As Susan Rose-Ackerman points out, many forms of property have restrictions on alienability.[3] There may be restrictions on who holds them, what actions are required or forbidden, and what kinds of transfers are permitted. Some types of properties can be given as gifts, but not sold (items made of the fur or feathers of endangered species, for example). Other types of properties (such as the holdings of a person who is bankrupt) can be sold, but not given as gifts.

Even under current policy, the body can be considered property, the kind of property that can be transferred without payment, but not sold. However, restraints on payment need strong moral and legal justification. The Ontario Law Reform Commission recently faced the issue of paying for body parts in the context of artificial reproduction. After deciding that donating sperm, eggs, or embryos was ethically, morally, and socially acceptable, the Commission noted that any restriction on available services (for example, by prohibiting commercial banks for gametes and embryos) "must be scrutinized very carefully; it would be futile and frustrating to give with one hand, only to take with the other."[4]

The property approach recognizes people's interest in controlling what happens to their body parts. It provides a legal basis for a remedy as theories of privacy, autonomy, or assault do not when inappropriate actions are taken with respect to extracorporeal bodily materials. The presumption that the authority belongs to the individual who provided the body parts would be a starting point, which would at least assure that the regulatory and institutional policies developed be measured against some standard....

Some lawyers and researchers argue that there is no need to inform people that body parts removed in the course of treatment may be used for research or commercial purposes, so long as the patient is not exposed to any additional physical risk due to the research. Currently, under federal regulations covering federally funded research, consent is not required to do research on such pathological or diagnostic specimens, so long

as the subjects cannot be identified.[5] In such cases, consent is given under the general hospital admission form, which states that the part may be used for teaching or research before it is destroyed. But the hospital consent form does not say that the patient may refuse to allow bodily materials to be used and still retain the patient/physician relationship and be treated. Only when the human material is taken primarily for research purposes is consent required. Even then, if the research poses "no more than minimal risk" and involves only collection of some body excretions, including blood, placenta or amniotic fluid, it may be given an expedited review by an Institutional Review Board; while consent is not specifically required, presumably the IRB can seek consent if the subjects are identifiable.[6] The failure to extend consent to all categories of research on human body parts and the failure even to raise the issue of compensation puts patients at a distinct psychological and economic disadvantage....

There is support for informing patients about the potential uses of the body parts, even among groups that now gain commercially from using those parts. The Licensing Executive Society Biotechnology Committee recently surveyed its members, who generally represent organizations that use human tissues, fluids, or cells for research or development purposes. Of those responding, twenty-two believed that research or commercialization should occur *only* with the patient's prior consent; two felt consent was unnecessary. Thirteen felt that a person has a right to receive compensation for the use of his or her fluid, tissues, or cells, while eight did not.

THE MARKET'S EFFECT ON DONORS

The property approach requires the individual's consent before her body parts can be used by others. But in some instances, body parts—such as kidneys or corneas—may be in such short supply or a particular patient may have such a rare tissue or fluid type that the issue of payment to donors will arise, as it did in the Moore and Hagiwara cases....

Naturally, the need for money is not a justification for any action (we would not want the person to become a contract killer for a fee). But it is difficult to justify a prohibition on payment for what otherwise would be a legal and ethical act—giving up body parts for someone else's valid use. Similarly, the analogy to slavery is inapposite. We do not want people to sell themselves into slavery *nor* do we want them to "give" themselves into slavery without pay. In contrast, with respect to organ donation or the development of a diagnostic or therapeutic product from bodily materials, the underlying activity is one we want to encourage....

GUARDING AGAINST COERCION

Just as we would not condone a labor system that did not allow people to choose their own employers, we should insist that paid donations from living people be voluntary: that is, made by the person himself or herself. It is one thing for people to have the right to treat their own bodies as property, quite another to allow others to treat a person as property. A hospital should not be allowed to take, sell, and use blood or eggs from a comatose woman to help pay her costs of hospitalization. People should be prohibited from selling their relative's body parts when the relative dies (unless the deceased left orders to that effect). Nor should judges be allowed to sentence offenders to pay their fines in body product donations (once the property approach has established a market value for them). If this seems farfetched, consider that there already have been instances in which judges sentenced defendants to give blood transfusions. Similarly, an eighteenth-century British statute allowed judges to order anatomical dissection of hanged murderers.[7] It is possible to maintain that people are priceless by not allowing others to treat a person's body commercially either before or after death and by giving people the power to refuse to sell their body parts.

A decision to sell certain types of body parts—nonregenerative ones (such as a kidney) or parts that could give rise to offspring (sperm, eggs, and embryos)—has lifelong implications. With respect to other decisions of long-lasting consequences (such as marriage), society has sometimes adopted added protections to assure that the decision has been carefully made. A similar approach might be used with regard to body parts. In this area, only competent adults should be allowed to decide to sell. There should be a short waiting period (like the cooling-off period that protects consumers from door-to-door salesmen) between the agreement to sell an organ and its removal, and the donor should be required to observe certain formalities (such as signing a witnessed consent form).

Only the person who owns the body part should be allowed to sell it. This approach has two goals. The first is to assure that others do not treat one's body as property. For example, it will prevent the harms associated with holding the body as security until funeral costs are paid.[8] The second is to attempt to assure that the individual is adequately compensated for the body part by limiting the amount any middleman receives. If the middleman cannot "sell" the part, but can only be compensated for bringing together the donor and recipient, the donor may more likely receive adequate compensation and the transaction will less likely be viewed as excessively commercial. There might even be limitations on what the middleman (physician or entrepreneur) receives, similar to the statutory limitation in some states of "reasonableness" in the amount of money an attorney receives in connection with arranging a private adoption. . . .

Giving an individual sole rights over his or her body parts is in keeping with attitudes toward the body held in other areas of law. Attempted suicide and suicide are no longer considered crimes.[9] However, aiding and abetting a suicide is a crime. Competent individuals can refuse a readily available lifesaving treatment, but their physicians cannot withhold it. Thus, people are allowed to control what is done to their bodies (even to the point of physical damage) in ways that other individuals are not.

Ironically, our current policy is just the reverse. Other people seem to have property rights in our body parts, but we do not. In a British case, an accused man who poured his urine sample down the sink was found guilty of stealing it from the police department.[10] And although an individual has no property interest in his or her cell lines, scientists are quick to claim a property interest in those cell lines. Such a claim was the basis of a six-year conflict between microbiologist Leonard Hayflick and the National Institutes of Health. The conflict was over which side owned a cell line that Hayflick had developed with embryonic living tissue under NIH funding and then sold to scientists around the world.[11] . . .

THE MARKET'S EFFECT ON RECIPIENTS

We can protect potential donors from the market's effect by attempting to assure that donations are voluntary and by limiting donations to body parts that do not unreasonably affect the person's ability to function. But how does a market affect potential recipients? The policy of prohibiting payment for body parts and products has been justified as protecting potential recipients by raising the quality of donations and preventing a situation in which body parts are affordable only by the rich.

The work of Richard Titmuss on policies governing blood donation raised serious questions of quality control when blood is sold.[12] Among other things, he argued that paid donors have an incentive not to disclose illnesses or characteristics that might make their blood of dubious quality. Subsequent work by Harvey Sapolsky and Stan Finkelstein[13] challenged Titmuss's conclusions. They pointed to a Government Accounting Office study in which some voluntary groups in the United States reported hepatitis rates as high as the worst paid groups; and some commercially collected blood was nearly as good as the best of the volunteer blood.

Even if paid donors are more likely to misrepresent their condition than are volunteer donors, payment need not be banned on quality control grounds since tests are available to assess the fitness of the donor. In this country we allow payment for blood and sperm, although it is easy to lie about their quality; yet we do not allow payment for body organs such as kidneys, although organ transplantation offers more independent checks on quality. Nor is banning payment the only mechanism to enhance quality, since if known risks are not disclosed, liability may follow. While this may not offer sufficient protection to the recipients of blood (since donors may not be solvent), organ donors would be better paid and a portion of that money could be used to buy insurance. When a person sells organs contingent on death, payment to an estate could be withheld if it was clear that he failed to disclose a known harmful condition. Already, the Ontario Law Reform Commission has recommended enacting a criminal law prohibiting people selling their gametes from knowingly concealing infectious and genetic disorders.

A market in solid organs is also thought harmful to potential recipients because of the possibility that only the rich will be able to afford organs. On the issue of the poor selling and the rich buying body parts, Thomas Murray says, "Our consciences can tolerate considerable injustice, but such naked, undisguised profiteering in life would be too much for us."[14] Yet other equally troublesome but less visible inequities are already occurring in allocating other kinds of medical care. When a drug company prices a medication necessary for someone's life beyond a person's reach or a physician with unique skills refuses to accept patients who receive Medicare, that is also profiteering in life, but the injustice may be overlooked. Currently at least fifty different types of artificial body parts (such as artificial blood vessels and joints) have been designed to substitute for human ones.[15] It is as important ethically to address discrimination between rich and poor recipients with respect to those products as it is with respect to human body parts. A visible market in body parts may lull people out of complacency to address more general issues of allocation in health care....

THE MARKET'S EFFECT ON SOCIETY

Will a market in body parts harm society by creating an attitude that people are commodities? The body is a symbol of the whole person and degrading it can be viewed as an assault to the whole person. Our distaste with viewing the body as property is, in part, a reaction to our belief that human beings should have no price.

Certainly people are more than the sum of their parts.[16] But treating the body as property does not mean it is a person's only property. Cognitive functions can be included within the property characterization. Indeed, they already are, for example, under the legal doctrine of copyright, patent, and other so-called "intellectual property" rights. I view my uniqueness as a person as more related to my intellectual products than my bodily products. (Definitions of personhood, for example, rarely revolve around the possession of body parts, but rather focus on sentience or other cognitive traits.) Arguably it commercializes me less as a person to sell my bone marrow than to sell my intellectual products. Thus, I do not view payment of body parts as commercializing people. The danger I see in the sale of a physical (as opposed to a mental) bodily product comes from the potential for physical harm in removing the bodily material or living without it. This danger can be handled by limiting the types of body parts that can be sold and the circumstances under which they can be sold.

Selling body parts has also been criticized as harmful to society because it could diminish altruism. But in our society, the basics of life—food, shelter, health care—are already sold. Nevertheless, many people continue to act altruistically, devoting time, money, or goods to provide needy people with those basics. The possibility of selling tissue or organs seems only a modest further step toward a market, unlikely to change vastly the impulse toward altruism. Even people who take advantage of the market may engage in altruistic behavior. One patient, Ted Slavin, received up to $10.00 per milliliter from commercial enterprises for his blood, which was used in manufacturing diagnostic kits for hepatitis B virus. At the same time, he provided additional blood—at no charge—to a research project at the Fox Chase Cancer Center, which used it to develop a vaccine against hepatitis B.[17] ...

To guard against the appearance that people are commodities, we must not let other people treat one's body parts as property. Body parts will thus not be salable in the sense of cars, farm animals, or baseball cards. There will be no means for a tax man or physician to put a lien against a person's body parts. Nor can relatives choose to sell a person's parts after his or her death. However, it differs from previous notions of quasi-property by recognizing the right of an individual to compensation for certain types of body parts. Under this approach, human beings have the right to treat certain physical parts of their bodies as objects for possession, gift, and trade, but they do not become objects so long as others cannot treat them as property.

THE MARKET'S EFFECT ON THE DOCTOR/PATIENT RELATIONSHIP

The treatment of body parts as property will help curtail activities by physicians, researchers, and their attorneys that deny individuals information about or control over body parts that will be removed.

Implicit in many arguments made by physician/researchers is that the removed body part belongs to the doctor, not the patient. Why do physicians feel that way? I can only speculate that it is because society allows medical practitioners to do things to a patient's body (for example, cut it up) that no one else (other than the patient) is allowed to do. Perhaps this gives physicians the feeling that the patient's body belongs in some sense to them.

Physicians argue that getting patients' permission to use their body parts and products would change the relationship between patients and physicians or researchers. Some argue that discussing the research with the patient may imply that a patient has a right to direct the scope or direction of the study. But that is absurd. Just because IBM is required to make certain disclosures to me when I buy a share of stock does not mean that I can set policy for the operation of the company.

Related to this is an argument that paying for the patient's cells, tissue, fluids, or organs would tie up physicians in endless negotiation with their patients. But when payment for human biological material is required, it is no more disastrous to the research enterprise than payment for pipettes, microscopes, animals, or laboratory equipment. It may represent a modest increase in the cost of doing business (just as an increase in fuel prices would raise the costs of lighting the laboratory). But the money paid would go to a good cause, slightly enhancing the resources of medical patients at a time when they need money to pay for medical care. If the patient is unwilling to sell rights to the biological materials, the physician need not barter; she can simply avoid using that specimen and approach other patients. Moreover, we allow the patient to pay the physician for services without being concerned that it will lead to endless negotiations.

Just as physicians raise the price for their services to cover rising malpractice insurance rates, so they will charge slightly more for the right to use the specimens of some patients for research. If it strikes you as unfair (it does me) to force patients to pay for the research by increasing medical costs, consider that under the current system the "cost" of the human specimens is borne entirely by the patients who own them and who do not even get in return a right to refuse to participate.

Another reason has been advanced against disclosure: it would decrease patient-physician trust if the patient were aware that the physician might develop a commercial product from the patient's body parts. Yet this begs the question of whether the information is relevant. It might diminish the patient's trust to know the success rate and unnecessary surgery rates of a practitioner or health care facility; yet this information is clearly relevant to patient decision making.

There is a similar concern that disclosing the commercial potential of human body parts may tarnish the image of the researchers by making it appear that profit rather than scientific knowledge is their goal. However, the media is already informing the public about the relationship between researchers and the corporate sector. "The public cannot help but see that the goals of some scientists—clinical or basic—are different than in the past," says Leon Rosenberg, dean of the Yale University School of Medicine. "The biotechnology revolution has moved us, literally or figuratively, from the classroom to the boardroom and from the *New England Journal* to the *Wall Street Journal*."[18]

Finally people point to the difficulty of assigning values to body parts as an implicit barrier to the property approach. But the value of many items that are currently bought and sold (such as paintings or jewels) is difficult to assess. This is no reason to prohibit the market from developing a particular price....

In a variation on the value argument, physician/researchers seem to imply that the patient has already been paid for the body part by receiving the benefits of the surgery. John Moore, for example, was allegedly helped by his treatment at UCLA. (This argument is harder to make when the patient dies or otherwise does not recover.) But patients may feel they have already paid for their health benefits in the price of the surgery. The patient has a right to know about the research so that she can choose the "price" she is willing to pay for the surgery. Perhaps she would rather choose a surgeon whose price is set solely in terms of dollars and insurance coverage rather than one who commercially exploits, say, her ovaries.

THE FUTURE OF THE BODY AS PROPERTY

Some of the finest advances in society have resulted from a refusal to characterize human beings (blacks, women, children) as property. Why, then, am I arguing for a property approach here? Let me emphasize that I am advocating not that people be treated by others as property, but only that they have the autonomy to treat their own parts as property, particularly their regenerative parts. Such an approach is helpful, rather than harmful, to people's well-being. It offers potential psychological, physical, and economic benefits to individuals and provides a framework for handling evolving issues regarding the control of extracorporeal biological materials.

It is time to start acknowledging that people's body parts are their personal property. This is distinguishable from the past characterizations of people as property, which were immoral because they failed to take into account the nonbodily aspects of the individual (blacks and women were deemed incapable of rational thought) and they created the rights of ownership by others (masters, husbands, parents). Allowing people to transfer and sell their own body parts, while protecting them from coercion, does not present those dangers.

REFERENCES

1. 42 U.S.C. 274(e) (1984).
2. Cal. Penal Code § 367f (West 1986) (exception for sale by patient); D.C. Code Ann. § 6–2601 (Supp. 1985); Fla. Stat. Ann. § 873.01 (West Suppl. 1986); La. Rev. Stat. Ann. § 17.2280 (West 1982); Md. Health General Code Ann. § 5.408 (Supp. 1985); Mich. Comp. Laws Ann. § 333.10204 (West Supp. 1986); N.Y. Pub. Health Law § 4307 (McKinney 1985); Va. Code § 32.1–289.1 (1985). Additionally,

in Arkansas there is a specific prohibition on the sale of eyes after death. Ark. Stat. Ann. § 82–410.2; § 82–410.13 (1976).
3. Susan Rose-Ackerman, "Inalienability and the Theory of Property Rights," *Columbia Law Review* 931 (1985), 85.
4. Ontario Law Reform Commission, *Report on Human Artificial Reproduction and Related Matters* (Ontario: Ministry of the Attorney General, 1985).
5. 45 C.F.R. 46.101(b)(5) (1985).
6. 45 C.F.R. 46.110(b) (1985).
7. Matthews, p. 205.
8. Such practices are described in *Jefferson County Burial Soc. v. Scott,* 218 Ala. 354, 118, S. 644 (1928).
9. A 1975 law review article, "Criminal Aspects of Suicide in the United States," 7 *North Carolina Central Law Journal* 156, 158 n. 19–21 (1975) listed only three states (Oklahoma, Texas, and Washington) which still had laws against attempted suicide. Those statutes have since been repealed.
10. *R. v. Welsh,* (1974) R.T.R. 478, reported in Matthews, pp. 223–24.
11. Constance Holden, "Hayflick Case Settled," *Science* 215 (1982), 271.
12. Richard Titmuss, *The Gift Relationship: From Human Blood to Special Policy* (New York: Vintage, 1972).
13. Harvey M. Sapolsky and Stan N. Finkelstein, "Blood Policy Revisited—A New Look at 'The Gift Relationship,'" *Public Interest,* 46 (1977), 15.
14. Thomas H. Murray, "The Gift of Life Must Always Remain a Gift," *Discover* 7:3 (March 1986), 90.
15. See, e.g., L. L. Hench, "Biomaterials," *Science* 208 (1980), 826.
16. See Leon R. Kass, "Thinking About the Body," *Hastings Center Report,* 15:1 (February 1985), 20.
17. Baruch S. Blumberg, Irving Millman, W. Thomas London, et al., "Ted Slavin's Blood and the Development of HBV Vaccine," *New England Journal of Medicine* 312 (1985), 189 (letter).
18. Leon E. Rosenberg, "Using Patient Materials for Production Development: A Dean's Perspective," *Clinical Research* 33:4 (October 1985), 452–54.

NO

Thomas H. Murray

GIFTS OF THE BODY AND
THE NEEDS OF STRANGERS

Human bodies have value, and not just to the persons whose bodies they are. Organs can be transplanted; tissues used for research and product development. One way of looking at these body parts is as property, to be bought and sold.[1] Another way—the approach I want to examine—is to see them as gifts. This may seem at first a simpler concept, but it is far from that. The idea of "gift" has deep and sometimes contradictory cultural meanings, which can illuminate the appropriate stance we should take toward modern biotechnology.

There are two modern conceptions of gifts. On the one hand, William Blackstone, the great legal commentator, wrote in 1767 that "gifts are always gratuitous"—that is, requiring "no consideration or equivalent." A gift in this sense is, as the *Oxford English Dictionary* defines it, "the transference of property in a thing by one person to another, voluntarily and without any valuable consideration." Givers are free to give or not; recipients are free to accept or not, and after acceptance, free to do whatever they like with the gift.

But if gifts are so bereft of obligations of any kind, why is there a second strain of sentiment about them? Ralph Waldo Emerson, in his essay on "Gifts," illustrated the power of gifts to bind one person to another. He wrote: "It is not the office of a man to receive gifts. How dare you give them? We wish to be self-sustained. We do not quite forgive a giver."[2] In a more modern context and with a hint of irony, the historian Michael Ignatieff echoes a similar sentiment: "The bureaucratized transfer of income among strangers has freed each of us from the enslavement of gift relations."[3]

How can the notion of gifts as gratuitous and completely voluntary be reconciled with the idea that gifts are the cause of degradation, dependence, and enslavement? Neither idea captures the full significance of the gift in human relations. The first perspective sees only that gifts carry no formal *legal* obligations. This is correct, but not very important. In this sense, gifts are opposed to contracts—forms of social exchange specifying in sometimes numbing detail precisely what is being exchanged for what. Of course, the obverse is also true: anything *not* explicitly required in the contract is permitted, and no other new obligations arise outside the limited sphere of relationship created by the contract. The second perspective sees correctly that gifts may entangle people in relationships that will impose great but vague moral obligations.

The first view assumes that only legal obligations matter. The second view understands that gifts create moral obligations, but focuses only on their ugly, manipulative potential. It fails to see that relationships based on gifts can and do play positive roles in regulating family and social life, in promoting solidarity in the face of powerful forces of alienation, and in serving essential social values that are not well served by markets, commerce, and contract....

GIFTS, PRUDENCE, AND MORAL OBLIGATIONS

The notion that either donors or recipients could have obligations in gift relations seems foreign to the modern mind. The concept of "obligation," at least as it is used by moral philosophers, does not seem to fit gift relationships. Perhaps one should speak of an etiquette rather than an ethic of gifts. But such a weak term would belie the powerful ties that can be created by gifts, the strong indebtedness a recipient may feel, and the grave harm an ignorant, inconsiderate, or malicious giver may do.

There is certainly a heavy dose of prudence in many gift exchanges. Using gifts to establish personal relationships need not entail any heavy moral obligations. If you desire the relationship, then respond appropriately to the gift; if you do not, refuse the gift.

There are, however, occasions when an individual may feel obliged, morally, to make certain gifts. Suppose a member of your family was suddenly in dire need of food or shelter—or bone marrow. Perhaps not everyone will feel an obligation to give in response to this need, but many will. Some might describe it as charity or supererogation, something noble but not obligatory. But many would think they had failed more fundamentally if they did not offer some gift, however modest, that addressed the need. Another example: in a relationship of long duration characterized by great caring, one party abruptly ceases to show gratitude or to reciprocate. The harm done the other, as well as the devaluation of the relationship and of both parties, is substantial enough to count as a moral harm. Such relationships contain a set of implied promises, which were broken by the sudden, uncaring way in which they were sundered. Remember that a common way of expressing gratitude is to say "much obliged." The language of obligation may discomfit some philosophers, but it seems to reflect more accurately the importance of at least certain gift relationships.

Here are three interrelated suggestions —too informal to be called "claims" or hypotheses—that may be helpful in clarifying our thinking about gifts in general and gifts of the body in particular:

1. Significant gifts are commonly given in response to the needs of individuals and societies. I mean *need* here as opposed to mere *desire*; but human needs in a wide sense, encompassing not merely basic survival—food, clothing, and shelter—but also the requirements for flourishing in a particular society—art, beauty, preparation for participation in adult life (including, in industrialized nations, literacy and education) and, not least, peace

among groups, a measure of community, and intimate relationships.

2. The degree of *moral* (and not merely prudential) obligation one feels (and should feel) to make a gift is greatest when the recipient's need is greatest. The more universal the need (such as for adequate food) the more likely people are to feel a sense of obligation to give to those more distant.

3. Mass bureaucratic societies need to affirm what it is citizens share with their neighbors. Gifts, especially gifts to assuage needs, and most especially gifts of the body, are one of the most significant means we have to affirm that solidarity. Thomas Merton, writing of the Buddhist's begging bowl, says it "represents the ultimate theological root of the belief, not just in a right to beg, but in openness to the gifts of all beings as an expression of the interdependence of all beings...."[4] Gifts of the body, ministering to the need for health, are in this sense affirmations of interdependence....

MORAL OBLIGATIONS, GRATITUDE, AND GRACIOUSNESS

In a study of related kidney donors, Roberta Simmons and her colleagues found that when recipients did not express what the donors considered a reasonable amount of gratitude, the donor felt angry and used—a "sucker." One donor reported: "I would say for three months [the recipient] tried to avoid me. I was never so crushed. I would call him up and he would be as cold as ice. I was destroyed. To this day I don't mention the kidney in front of him. Whenever I do, it turns him off. He has never come out and said 'Thank you.'"[5]

Reciprocating the gift, in an appropriate form, at an appropriate time, is also important. Alvin Gouldner, a sociologist, argues for a "norm of reciprocity" that is "no less universal and important an element of culture than the incest taboo." He says it is "a dimension to be found in all value systems and, in particular, as one among a number of 'Principal Components' universally present in moral codes."[6] Just what constitutes appropriate reciprocation depends on particular cultural norms and the specifics of the relationship. It need not be "tit-for-tat" if, for example, the donor is a parent and the recipient a ten-year-old child, whose means are not adequate to return full economic value of the parent's gift. Similar cultural and relationship factors determine what is an appropriate time for reciprocation. Seneca's warning is correct for some situations, but not all. (Not exchanging Christmas presents simultaneously could be insulting to the person who gave the present.)

A third recipient obligation is what Camenisch calls "grateful use." He argues that "grateful acceptance of the gift indicates the concurrence of the recipient's will with the donor's and/or implies consent to comply with that will." He suggests that the moral language of "stewardship" often applies to the use of gifts. Searching for more precise criteria for grateful use, he offers two: "the nature of the gift itself and what we can discover of the donor's intention for its use." It would be wrong to treat something dear to the donor in an undignified manner, as merely a commodity; likewise it would be wrong to use it in a way the donor would disapprove of.

All three obligations—grateful use, grateful conduct, and reciprocation—stem from the purpose of gift exchange

—building moral relationships, and perhaps as well from the nature of at least certain significant gifts. Mauss says that among the Maori "to give something is to give a part of oneself.... while to receive something is to receive a part of someone's spiritual essence." It is not necessary to accept the Maori's animistic beliefs to grasp that in some gifts, the giver offers symbolically a part of himself or herself. Simply recall an occasion when someone treated with indifference a gift that you had regarded as special and important. In some way, the rejection of the gift was a personal rejection. (This is true more than metaphorically in gifts of the body.) ...

GIFTS TO STRANGERS

Perhaps Arrow's most striking criticism of Titmuss is his claim that Titmuss wishes to promote "impersonal altruism." He does not wish to encourage the "richness of family relationships or the close ties of a small community" but rather a "diffuse expression of confidence in the workings of society as a whole." But Arrow says, "Such an expression of impersonal altruism is as far removed from the feelings of personal interaction as any marketplace."

Arrow is certainly correct. It cannot be the rewards of immediate personal relationships that prompt impersonal altruism. But when he goes on to describe British blood donors as "an aristocracy of saints" and to express doubt that a voluntary system could work elsewhere, he is wrong—factually wrong—as the movement to an almost entirely voluntary system of whole blood procurement in the U.S. shows. This cannot be ascribed to the British tradition of Fabian socialism with which Arrow tries to explain the British experience.

Something more than a vague sentiment is at work in the instance of blood donation, something powerful that escapes any simple explanation in terms of pure self-interest—or pure altruism. Ignatieff grasps the problem when he notes: "We think of belonging in moral terms as direct impingement on the lives of others: fraternity implies the closeness of brothers. Yet the moral relations that exist between my income and the needs of strangers at my door pass through the arteries of the state." This would pose no problem if the needs of strangers exerted no moral pull on us; if we felt no relationship with them. But, as Ignatieff notes, "We need justice, we need liberty, and we need as much solidarity as can be reconciled with justice and liberty."

Relationships governed by markets keep moral and social dimensions to a bare minimum. Gifts, by their open-endedness, defy such minimization. Impersonal gifts such as blood or body parts or charity may not regulate relationships between specific individuals, but they serve other functions by regulating larger relationships and honoring important human values, precisely those threatened by massive and impersonal bureaucracies.

For one thing, impersonal gifts acknowledge an entire realm of moral relationships and moral obligations wider than intimate, family ones, and wider still than legal, contractual ones. Further, these obligations are often *unchosen*.

Gifts to strangers affirm the solidarity of the community over and above the depersonalizing, alienating forces of mass society and market relations. They signal that self-interest is not the only significant human motivation. And they express the moral belief that it is good to minister to fundamental human needs, needs for food, health care, and shelter, but also needs for beauty and knowledge. These universal needs irrevocably tie us together in a community of needs, with a shared desire to satisfy them, and see them satisfied in others.

Finally, these gifts remind us that wealth is merely a means to an end, and that not all valuable things can be purchased, among them love, friendship, fellow-feeling, and trust. These "moral" assets of individuals and of societies are "noneconomic" in still another way. They are not "scarce resources" that are consumed as they are offered. Arrow cautions us not "to use up recklessly the scarce resources of altruistic motivation." The truth is more likely the opposite: To a considerable extent, employing "moral assets" generously increases rather than decreases the supply.

GIFTS, SOLIDARITY, AND SOCIAL INSTITUTIONS

It may well be that the way a society structures the exchange of such "moral assets" affects their supply just as the structure of markets affects the supply of ordinary commodities. Titmuss's survey of blood donors in Great Britain revealed that the overwhelming majority, when asked why they were giving, cited non-self-interested reasons. Among them (with spelling and punctuation preserved):

Knowing I mite be saving somebody life;
    You cant get blood from supermarkets and chaine stores. People themselves must come forward;
    I thought it just a small way to help people—as a blind person other opportunities are limited.

Gratitude for good health appears in some:

Briefly because I have enjoyed good health all my life and in a small way it is a way of saying 'Thank you' and a small donation to the less fortunate.

Others write of reciprocating a gift:

To try and repay in some small way some unknown person whose blood helped me recover from two operations....;
    Some unknown person gave blood to save my wifes life.

Other reasons offered included a general sense of social duty and the perception that there was a need for blood.

A more recent study of blood procurement inspired by skepticism of Titmuss's account focused primarily on the U.S. In that work Alvin Drake, Stan N. Finkelstein, and Harvey Sapolsky found that the bleak portrait of motivation for giving and quality of blood in the U.S. painted by Titmuss was unwarranted a decade later, and may even have been an unfair picture at the time Titmuss's book was published.[7] The details of their differences are not important here. Much more significant is the authors' carefully documented research on the beliefs, values, and practices of potential blood donors in the U.S. By 1982, about 70 percent of all whole blood was being provided on a purely voluntary basis. Roughly a quarter was being given through "blood credit" or "blood insurance" programs, which could be seen as quasi-voluntary. Paid donors constituted no more than 3 to 4 percent, and that proportion was declining.

Drake, Finkelstein, and Sapolsky found that the principal impediment to fulfilling the need for whole blood was lack of coordination and competence in the regional procurement agencies. Where efforts were well organized, as they had been for years in Connecticut and in upstate New York, local needs could be met with purely voluntary programs. The researchers found a strong and consistent opposition to the use of paid donors. Americans overwhelmingly preferred to have their community's need for whole blood met with volunteer donors.

When they examined the reasons American blood donors gave for their generosity, they found it was "simply a general awareness of the continuing need for blood." "All our own experiences lead us to believe that participation in the whole-blood supply is the natural, unforced response of a great many people once they are exposed to a mild degree of personal solicitation and some convenient donation opportunities."

The saga of the transformation of the American whole-blood supply from a largely paid to a virtually all-volunteer system is not a simple one. Much of it concerns rivalries among organizations. But one important fact is clear: the voluntary agencies could not have emerged victorious unless the American people were willing to donate adequate amounts of whole blood. This willingness in turn rests, I believe, on deeply held convictions about the obligation to give to those in need, and about the ethical inappropriateness of commercializing whole blood.

It is a massive effort at giving to strangers. Roughly eight million Americans donate each year. In its scale, its lack of monetary rewards, and its distance between donor and recipient, the whole-blood procurement system in the U.S. is a remarkable example of impersonal gifts. It suggests something very important that a society would be so generous in this realm and would reject so

clearly a market approach to the supply and distribution of a good.

The gift of blood is doubly expressive. It affirms solidarity in a gift that is quintessentially human. Blood represents individual life and vitality, and at the same time it signifies the oldest, most primitive tie that affirms solidarity and binds people to one another. Perhaps one of the oldest and most persistent human problems has been to reconcile the loyalties and attachments defined by blood—the ties of family—with the need for, at a minimum, peace but, better, solidarity, with strangers—those with whom we do not share blood. From these roots comes the political importance of marriage between groups in potential conflict, and perhaps as well the symbolic value of "blood brotherhood."

Blood is life, but also kinship. Giving blood to strangers is not just any gift, but a vital one that expresses and affirms our bonds with those strangers. If, on the other hand, we would rather deny our brotherhood, then mixing blood could be a serious threat. Titmuss reports that in South Africa a set of regulations issued in 1962 required that "European" and "non-European" donors be kept separate, and that the records of their donations also be kept apart. Furthermore, "[a]ll containers of blood and blood products have to be labelled by 'racial origin.'" Although South Africa has relied primarily on voluntary donations, authorities at gold mines in the Transvaal region purchased blood from mining company employees. The rates in 1967 were four Rands per pint for whites; one Rand per pint for "Bantus, Colored and Asians."

Profiting from others' blood is sometimes seen as a particularly heinous form of exploitation. A plasmapheresis center opened in Managua, Nicaragua, in 1973 that purchased plasma and exported it. The center was owned in part by the dictator Somoza. At the funeral of a popular newspaper editor who had criticized Somoza for "inhuman trade in the blood of Nicaraguans" and who had been murdered, a large crowd burned several buildings, among them the plasmapheresis center.[8]

Blood can connect people, or it can divide them. Contemporary inhabitants in the U.S., no less than the Trobrianders or Maori or other traditional societies, seem to believe that some things are *sacra* —"sacred" in the nondenominational sense of dignified human "property" —and that it is morally preferable to procure and distribute certain kinds of property, including *sacra*, but other things as well, outside the otherwise dominant system of market and contract....

GIFTS, THE BODY, AND BIOMEDICAL RESEARCH

What has been said until now does not settle the question of what should happen to human tissues in contemporary biomedicine. It does, however, demonstrate that certain body parts are and ought to be treated as gifts and not as personal property.

Even if certain parts or products of the body are *sacra* and hence fit for gift but not commerce, it does not follow that all are equally so.[9] If I could find a buyer for my urine, it is doubtful that any great moral outcry would arise, no more than accompanies the sale of hair or fingernails. But then these products are less central to what characterizes living human persons, members of the human community, than kidneys, for example, or blood. In any case, the nature of the gift, its meaning and significance within

the community, will determine whether it belongs to the realm of commodities or the circle of gifts.

A second issue concerns the relationship between the giver—the patient or research subject in the case of biomedicine —and the recipient—the physician or researcher. The patient-physician relationship has long been described with apparently inconsistent images. On the one hand, physicians earn their money by seeing patients, and in that sense it is clearly a commercial relationship, a trade of money for service. At the same time the noncommercial aspects of the relationship are stressed. The very words used to describe what physicians do— they "take care of" patients—come from the language of personal, moral, nonmarket relationships. Physicians are expected to act in the patient's best interest, and not to try to cut the best deal for themselves; they are in a "fiduciary" relationship with their patients.

To the extent that people see their relationship with physicians as not strictly a market one, then an ethic of personal gifts may apply. (People quite commonly make gifts to their medical and nursing caretakers after an episode of illness.) With the increasing commercialization of medicine, people's expectations may be changing, and the nature of the physician-patient relationship, always an ideal only partially realized, may change accordingly. At some future time, the gift may become irrelevant to the clinic.

The emergence of the physician-researcher-entrepreneur complicates things immensely. It is one thing to have someone offer to buy something. It is quite another to give it to someone with whom we believe there is a more or less personal, noncommercial relationship, and to learn only later that what was given as a gift, especially if it was a "sacred" gift, has been diverted to commerce. The mixed roles of biomedical researchers who may also be clinicians, who may also be entrepreneurs, make it difficult to know what set of moral expectations apply. By blurring the distinctions, we jeopardize the future of physician-patient relationships. One could say cynically that such relationships always were commercial, and that it is better to be explicit about it. But if important social values were served by stressing the noncommercial dimensions of those relationships, then the threat is a serious one.

Lastly, consider the problem of how to think about impersonal gifts. Normally there is a distinction drawn between eleemosynary and civil corporations. The former are "organized for charitable purposes"; the latter, according to the Oxford English Dictionary, for "business purposes." Universities and most medical research centers, along with charities, learned societies, and the like, are eleemosynary organizations. When people are asked to make gifts of money—or of their tissues—to university-based medical research, whether or not they actually give, they see this as a reasonable request. Pleas for gifts by a profit-seeking firm, in contrast, would be perceived as ludicrous.

One of the ways to express solidarity with "strangers" is by contributing to the satisfaction of basic human needs and desires, especially those not well served by the system of trade and markets. These two systems have long existed side by side, an implicit acknowledgment that neither one alone is adequate for human flourishing and for sustaining community. In place now is an informal system of gifts of human biological materials to noncommercial organizations. Relying on this system fulfills many of the social values mentioned earlier as the justifications for gift exchanges. They include expressing solidarity in the face of illness and suffering, and declaring respect and support for biomedical research and teaching.

PURSUIT OF THE GOOD

Gifts help to create and sustain intimate personal relationships. In the face of impersonal bureaucracies, gifts to "strangers" affirm a number of vital social values including our solidarity with others in our community, and our vision of human flourishing, individual and social, that require more than the thin relationships established by markets and contracts.

Individuals in market societies, especially intellectuals, may delude themselves into believing that needs are indistinguishable from desires, that the body is merely a commodity like any other, and that we have no moral bonds with the members of our communities other than those we have freely chosen. But the evidence of charitable practices in general and gifts of the body in particular affirm the belief that there *are* human needs—biological and cultural; that the body, especially in its health-giving and life-saving manifestations, should not be treated as a mere commodity; and that we are bound together by our often needy bodies (and by our other, nonphysiological needs) into a community of needs. In this community—really multiple communities, sometimes overlapping, some like ripples extending wider and wider around a core—we can recognize the needs of others through our shared embodiment. And we can minister to those needs by sharing the fruits, the very living tissues of the body.

How we choose to handle the transfers of human biological materials from patients and research subjects to teachers and researchers will declare how we regard the human body. If certain human parts are "dignified," then our social traditions suggest they may be given, but not sold, and ownership of them is only of a special, limited kind.

Moreover, like the choice of obtaining blood for transfusions, the system chosen for obtaining human biological materials will carry whatever symbolic weight attaches to the relationship to the "strangers at our door," as Ignatieff calls our fellow inhabitants of mass society. These gifts of the body, ministering to the needs of strangers, connect us in our mutual quest to relieve suffering and to pursue our good, separately and together.

ACKNOWLEDGMENTS

I am grateful to many people whose gifts of time and thought enabled me to clarify further my own thinking on the issues discussed in this paper. Here I can mention only a few: William Winslade, Ronald Carson, and Harold Vanderpool critiqued versions of this article. I want to thank also Gladys White and the U.S. Congress Office of Technology Assessment. I did much of the research on which this paper is based for their project, "New Developments in Biotechnology: Ownership of Human Tissues and Cells."

REFERENCES

1. Lori B. Andrews, "My Body, My Property," *Hastings Center Report* 16:5 (October 1986), 28–38.

2. Ralph Waldo Emerson, "Gifts," *Essays of Ralph Waldo Emerson* (Norwalk, CT: Easton Press, 1979), pp. 212–13.

3. Michael Ignatieff, *The Needs of Strangers: An Essay on Privacy, Solidarity, and the Politics of Being Human* (New York: Viking, 1984), pp. 18–141.

4. Thomas Merton, *The Asian Journals*, eds. Naomi Burton et al. (New York: New Directions, 1973), pp. 341–42.

5. Roberta G. Simmons, Susan D. Klein, and Richard L. Simmons, *Gift of Life: The Social and Psychological Impact of Organ Transplantation* (New York: Wiley, 1977), p. 325.

6. Alvin W. Gouldner, "The Norm of Reciprocity: A Preliminary Statement," *American Sociological Review* 25:2 (1960), 171.

7. Richard M. Titmuss, *The Gift Relationship* (New York: Pantheon, 1971).

8. Piet J. Hagen, *Blood: Gift or Merchandise* (New York: Alan R. Liss, 1982), pp. 168–69.

9. Thomas H. Murray, "On the Ethics of Commercializing the Human Body." Paper prepared for U.S. Congress Office of Technology Assessment, April 1986.

POSTSCRIPT

Should There Be a Market in Body Parts?

John Moore's case was dismissed three times by state courts in California, but in August 1988 the 2d District Court of Appeals in Houston ruled that he had the right to sue UCLA. The court said, "A patient must have the ultimate power to control what becomes of his or her tissue. To hold otherwise would open the door to a massive invasion of human privacy and dignity in the name of medical progress." However, in July 1990 the California Supreme Court ruled that a patient does not have property rights over body tissue and that letting patients sue for rights in research resulting from their tissue would threaten "to destroy the economic incentive to conduct important medical research." The court also stated that the physician has a "fiduciary duty" to tell the patient if there is interest in studying his tissue. Two articles written on this subject are George J. Annas, "Whose Waste Is It Anyway? The Case of John Moore," *Hastings Center Report* (October/November 1988), and John J. Howard, "Biotechnology, Patients' Rights and the *Moore* Case," *Food Drug Cosmetic Law Journal* (July 1989).

The Hagiwara case was settled by an agreement in which the University of California was given the patent and the Hagiwara family received an exclusive license to market the cell line in Japan and Asia. For the researcher's view of this case, see Ivor Royston, "Cell Lines from Human Patients: Who Owns Them?" *Clinical Research* (vol. 33, 1985).

The Office of Technology Assessment has issued a comprehensive report called *New Developments in Biotechnology: Ownership of Human Tissue* (Government Printing Office, 1987). In an article called "Research That Could Yield Marketable Products from Human Materials: The Problem of Informed Consent," *IRB: A Review of Human Subjects Research* (January/February 1986), Robert J. Levine argues that it is unlikely that research designed to develop marketable products from human materials will present any problems to the research-subject relationship that cannot be resolved within the framework of existing informed consent regulations. See also Emanuel D. Thorne, "Tissue Transplants: The Dilemma of the Body's Growing Value," *Public Interest* (Winter 1990); Nancy E. Field, "Evolving Conceptualizations of Property: A Proposal to De-Commercialize the Value of Fetal Tissue," *Yale Law Journal* (October 1989); Margaret S. Swain and Randy W. Marusyk, "An Alternative to Property Rights in Human Tissue," *Hastings Center Report* (September/October 1990); and Courtney S. Campbell, "Body, Self, and the Property Paradigm," *Hastings Center Report* (September/October 1992).

ISSUE 18

Should Health Care for the Elderly Be Limited?

YES: Daniel Callahan, from "Limiting Health Care for the Old?" *The Nation* (August 15, 1987)

NO: Amitai Etzioni, from "Spare the Old, Save the Young," *The Nation* (June 11, 1988)

ISSUE SUMMARY

YES: Philosopher Daniel Callahan believes that since health care resources are scarce, people who have lived a full natural life span should be offered care that relieves suffering but not expensive life-prolonging technologies.

NO: Sociologist Amitai Etzioni argues that rationing health care for the elderly would encourage conflict between generations and would invite restrictions on health care for other groups.

America is aging. In 1965 the 18.5 million people over the age of 65 accounted for only 9.5 percent of the population. By 1987 the number had climbed to 29 million, or 12 percent of the population. The number of people over 85—the "old old"—is the fastest-growing age group in the United States. By the year 2040 the elderly will represent 21 percent of the population.

Older people are more likely to need health care than the young. In 1980 people over 65 accounted for 29 percent of the total American health care expenditures of $219.4 billion. By 1986 the bill had risen to $450 billion, and the share devoted to the elderly to 31 percent. The costs of Medicare —the federal program that supports the health care of people over 65—are projected to increase from $75 billion in 1986 to $114 billion in the year 2000, measured in current, not inflated, dollars.

Although Medicare coverage of nursing homes and home care remains inadequate to meet the need, organ transplants are now covered. The typical cost of such an operation is $200,000.

Many (but not all) elderly people do not want to have their lives prolonged through the use of expensive technology such as kidney dialysis, respirators, and intensive care. They fear losing control of their medical care and dying "hooked up to tubes."

There are many competing interests vying for the increasingly scarce health care dollar. Groups representing patients suffering from particular diseases —cancer, AIDS, diabetes, and heart disease, to name just a few—advocate increased spending on research and care. Those who speak for the poor, especially poor children, point out that they often do not have access to the most basic medical care, such as immunizations. The costs of treating premature, low-birth-weight infants are extremely high; yet programs that provide prenatal care and adequate nutrition to mothers at risk, which might prevent many such births, are inadequately funded.

In such a complex web of competing claims, when not all interests can be met, how should decisions to ration care be determined? Should age be one criterion? In Great Britain, which has a National Health Service and centralized planning, patients over the age of 55 have been routinely denied kidney dialysis ostensibly on "medical" grounds, even though the procedure is performed in the United States on very old patients.

Should we begin to follow this pattern in the United States? The following selections present the contrasting views. Daniel Callahan says that we must confront realities: in the interest of ensuring adequate health care for the younger generation, we must limit the kinds of care that will be available to those who have lived a full natural life span. Amitai Etzioni objects to this call to ration health care to the elderly on the grounds that it will lead to denying care to people of younger ages and other groups deemed less productive to society.

YES

Daniel Callahan

LIMITING HEALTH CARE FOR THE OLD?

Is it sensible, in the face of the rapidly increasing burden of health care costs for the elderly, to press forward with new and expensive ways of extending their lives? Is it possible even to hope to control costs while simultaneously supporting innovative research, which generates new ways to spend money? Those are now unavoidable questions....

Anyone who works closely with the elderly recognizes that the present Medicare and Medicaid programs are grossly inadequate in meeting their real and full needs. The system fails most notably in providing decent long-term care and medical care that does not constitute a heavy out-of-pocket drain. Members of minority groups and single or widowed women are particularly disadvantaged. How will it be possible, then, to provide the growing number of elderly with even present levels of care, much less to rid the system of its inadequacies and inequities, and at the same time add expensive new technologies?

The straight answer is that it will be impossible to do all those things and, worse still, it may be harmful even to try. It may be so because of the economic burdens that would impose on younger age groups, and because of the requisite skewing of national social priorities too heavily toward health care. But that suggests to both young and old that the key to a happy old age is good health care, which may not be true.

In the past few years three additional concerns about health care for the aged have surfaced. First, an increasingly large share of health care is going to the elderly rather than to youth. The Federal government, for instance, spends six times as much providing health benefits and other social services to those over 65 as it does to those under 18. And, as the demographer Samuel Preston observed in a provocative address to the Population Association of America in 1984, "Transfers from the working-age population to the elderly are also transfers away from children, since the working ages bear far more responsibility for childrearing than do the elderly."

Preston's address had an immediate impact. The mainline senior-citizen advocacy groups accused Preston of fomenting a war between the generations. But the speech also stimulated Minnesota Senator David Durenberger and others to found Americans for Generational Equity (AGE) to promote debate about the burden on future generations, particularly the Baby Boom cohort, of "our major social insurance programs." Preston's speech and the founding of AGE signaled the outbreak of a struggle over what has come to be called "intergenerational equity," which is now gaining momentum.

The second concern is that the elderly, in dying, consume a disproportionate share of health care costs. "At present," notes Stanford University economist Victor Fuchs, "the United States spends about 1 percent of the gross national product on health care for elderly persons who are in their last year of life.... One of the biggest challenges facing policy makers for the rest of this century will be how to strike an appropriate balance between care for the [elderly] dying and health services for the rest of the population."

The third issue is summed up in an observation by Dr. Jerome Avorn of the Harvard Medical School, who wrote in *Daedalus*, "With the exception of the birth-control pill, [most] of the medical-technology interventions developed since the 1950s have their most widespread impact on people who are past their fifties—the further past their fifties, the greater the impact." Many of the techniques in question were not intended for use on the elderly. Kidney dialysis, for example, was developed for those between the ages of 15 and 45. Now some 30 percent of its recipients are over 65.

The validity of those concerns has been vigorously challenged, as has the more general assertion that some form of rationing of health care for the elderly might become necessary. To the charge

that old people receive a disproportionate share of resources, the response has been that assistance to them helps every age group: It relieves the young of the burden of care they would otherwise have to bear for elderly parents and, since those young will eventually become old, promises them similar care when they need it. There is no guarantee, moreover, that any cutback in health care for the elderly would result in a transfer of the savings directly to the young. And, some ask, Why should we contemplate restricting care for the elderly when we wastefully spend hundreds of millions on an inflated defense budget?

The assertion that too large a share of funds goes to extending the lives of elderly people who are terminally ill hardly proves that it is an unjust or unreasonable amount. They are, after all, the most in need. As some important studies have shown, it is exceedingly difficult to know that someone is dying; the most expensive patients, it turns out, are those who were expected to live but died. That most new technologies benefit the old more than the young is logical; most of the killer diseases of the young have now been conquered.

There is little incentive for politicians to think about, much less talk about, limits on health care for the aged. As John Rother, director of legislation for the American Association of Retired Persons, has observed, "I think anyone who wasn't a champion of the aged is no longer in Congress." Perhaps also, as Guido Calabresi, dean of the Yale Law School, and his colleague Philip Bobbitt observed in their thoughtful 1978 book *Tragic Choices*, when we are forced to make painful allocation choices, "Evasion, disguise, temporizing ... [and]

averting our eyes enables us to save some lives even when we will not save all."

I believe that we must face this highly troubling issue. Rationing of health care under Medicare is already a fact of life, though rarely labeled as such. The requirement that Medicare recipients pay the first $520 of hospital care costs, the cutoff of reimbursement for care after 60 days and the failure to cover long-term care are nothing other than allocation and cost-saving devices. As sensitive as it is to the senior-citizen vote, the Reagan Administration agreed only grudgingly to support catastrophic health care coverage for the elderly (a benefit that will not help very many of them), and it has already expressed its opposition to the recently passed House version of the bill. It is bound to be far more resistant to long-term health care coverage, as will any administration.

But there are reasons other than the economics to think about health care for the elderly. The coming economic crisis provides a much-needed opportunity to ask some deeper questions. Just what is it that we want medicine to do for us as we age? Other cultures have believed that aging should be accepted, and that it should be in part a time of preparation for death. Our culture seems increasingly to dispute that view, preferring instead, it often seems, to think of aging as hardly more than another disease, to be fought and rejected. Which view is correct?

Let me interject my own opinion. The future goal of medical science should be to improve the quality of old people's lives, not to lengthen them. In its longstanding ambition to forestall death, medicine has reached its last frontier in the care of the aged. Of course children and young adults still die of maladies that are open to potential cure; but the highest

proportion of the dying (70 percent) are over 65. If death is ever to be humbled, that is where endless work remains to be done. But however tempting the challenge of that last frontier, medicine should restrain itself. To do otherwise would mean neglecting the needs of other age groups and of the old themselves.

Our culture has worked hard to redefine old age as a time of liberation, not decline, a time of travel, of new ventures in education and self-discovery, of the ever-accessible tennis court or golf course and of delightfully periodic but thankfully brief visits from well-behaved grandchildren. That is, to be sure, an idealized picture, but it arouses hopes that spur medicine to wage an aggressive war against the infirmities of old age. As we have seen, the costs of such a war would be prohibitive. No matter how much is spent the ultimate problem will still remain: people will grow old and die. Worse still, by pretending that old age can be turned into a kind of endless middle age, we rob it of meaning and significance for the elderly.

There is a plausible alternative: a fresh vision of what it means to live a decently long and adequate life, what might be called a "natural life span." Earlier generations accepted the idea that there was a natural life span—the biblical norm of three score and ten captures that notion (even though in fact that was a much longer life span than was typical in ancient times). It is an idea well worth reconsidering and would provide us with a meaningful and realizable goal. Modern medicine and biology have done much, however, to wean us from that kind of thinking. They have insinuated the belief that the average life span is not a natural fact at all, but instead one that is strictly dependent on the state of medical knowledge and skill. And there is much to that belief as a statistical fact: The average life expectancy continues to increase with no end in sight.

But that is not what I think we ought to mean by a natural life span. We need a notion of a full life that is based on some deeper understanding of human needs and possibilities, not on the state of medical technology or its potential. We should think of a natural life span as the achievement of a life that is sufficiently long to take advantage of those opportunities life typically offers and that we ordinarily regard as its prime benefits—loving and "living," raising a family, engaging in work that is satisfying, reading, thinking, cherishing our friends and families. People differ on what might be a full natural life span; my view is that it can be achieved by the late 70s or early 80s.

A longer life does not guarantee a better life. No matter how long medicine enables people to live, death at any time —at age 90 or 100 or 110—would frustrate some possibility, some as-yet-unrealized goal. The easily preventable death of a young child is an outrage. Death from an incurable disease of someone in the prime of young adulthood is a tragedy. But death at an old age, after a long and full life, is simply sad, a part of life itself.

As it confronts aging, medicine should have as its specific goals the averting of premature death, that is, death prior to the completion of a natural life span, and thereafter, the relief of suffering. It should pursue those goals so that the elderly can finish out their years with as little needless pain as possible—and with as much vitality as can be generated in contributing to the welfare of younger age groups and to the community of which they are a part. Above all, the elderly need to have a sense of the meaning and significance of their stage in life, one that is not dependent on economic productivity or physical vigor.

What would medicine oriented toward the relief of suffering rather than the deliberate extension of life be like? We do not have a clear answer to that question, so longstanding, central and persistent has been medicine's preoccupation with the struggle against death. But the hospice movement is providing us with much guidance. It has learned how to distinguish between the relief of suffering and the lengthening of life. Greater control by elderly persons over their own dying—and particularly an enforceable right to refuse aggressive life-extending treatment—is a minimal goal.

What does this have to do with the rising cost of health care for the elderly? Everything. The indefinite extension of life combined with an insatiable ambition to improve the health of the elderly is a recipe for monomania and bottomless spending. It fails to put health in its proper place as only one among many human goods. It fails to accept aging and death as part of the human condition. It fails to present to younger generations a model of wise stewardship.

How might we devise a plan to limit the costs of health care for the aged under public entitlement programs that is fair, humane and sensitive to their special requirements and dignity? Let me suggest three principles to undergird a quest for limits. First, government has a duty, based on our collective social obligations, to help people live out a natural life span but not to help medically extend life beyond that point. Second, government is obliged to develop under its research subsidies, and to pay for under its entitlement programs, only the kind and degree of life-extending technology necessary for medicine to achieve and serve the aim of a natural life span. Third, beyond the point of a natural life span, government should provide only the means necessary for the relief of suffering, not those for life-extending technology.

A system based on those principles would not immediately bring down the cost of care of the elderly; it would add cost. But it would set in place the beginning of a new understanding of old age, one that would admit of eventual stabilization and limits. The elderly will not be served by a belief that only a lack of resources, better financing mechanisms or political power stands between them and the limitations of their bodies. The good of younger age groups will not be served by inspiring in them a desire to live to an old age that maintains the vitality of youth indefinitely, as if old age were nothing but a sign that medicine has failed in its mission. The future of our society will not be served by allowing expenditures on health care for the elderly to escalate endlessly and uncontrollably, fueled by the false altruistic belief that anything less is to deny the elderly their dignity. Nor will it be aided by the pervasive kind of self-serving argument that urges the young to support such a crusade because they will eventually benefit from it also.

We require instead an understanding of the process of aging and death that looks to our obligation to the young and to the future, that recognizes the necessity of limits and the acceptance of decline and death, and that values the old for their age and not for their continuing youthful vitality. In the name of accepting the elderly and repudiating discrimination against them, we have succeeded mainly in pretending that, with enough will and money, the unpleasant part of old age can be abolished. In the name of medical progress we have carried out a relentless war against death and decline, failing to ask in any probing way if that will give us a better society for all.

NO

Amitai Etzioni

SPARE THE OLD, SAVE THE YOUNG

In the coming years, Daniel Callahan's call to ration health care for the elderly, put forth in his book *Setting Limits*, is likely to have a growing appeal. Practically all economic observers expect the United States to go through a difficult time as it attempts to work its way out of its domestic (budgetary) and international (trade) deficits. Practically every serious analyst realizes that such an endeavor will initially entail slower growth, if not an outright cut in our standard of living, in order to release resources to these priorities. When the national economic "pie" grows more slowly, let alone contracts, the fight over how to divide it up intensifies. The elderly make an especially inviting target because they have been taking a growing slice of the resources (at least those dedicated to health care) and are expected to take even more in the future. Old people are widely held to be "nonproductive" and to constitute a growing "burden" on an ever smaller proportion of society that is young and working. Also, the elderly are viewed as politically well-organized and powerful; hence "their" programs, especially Social Security and Medicare, have largely escaped the Reagan attempts to scale back social expenditures, while those aimed at other groups—especially the young, but even more so future generations—have been generally curtailed. There are now some signs that a backlash may be forming.

If a war between the generations, like that between the races and between the genders, does break out, historians may accord former Governor Richard Lamm of Colorado the dubious honor of having fired the opening shot in his statement that the elderly ill have "got a duty to die and get out of the way." Phillip Longman, in his book *Born to Pay*, sounded an early alarm. However, the historians may well say, it was left to Daniel Callahan, a social philosopher and ethicist, to provide a detailed rationale and blueprint for limiting the care to the elderly, explicitly in order to free resources for the young. Callahan's thesis deserves close examination because he attempts to deal with the numerous objections his approach raises. If his thesis does not hold, the champions of limiting funds available to the old may have a long wait before they will find a new set of arguments on their behalf.

In order to free up economic resources for the young, Callahan offers the older generation a deal: Trade quantity for quality; the elderly should not be given life-*extending* services but better years while alive. Instead of the relentless attempt to push death to an older age, Callahan would stop all development of life-extending technologies and prohibit the use of ones at hand for those who outlive their "natural" life span, say, the age of 75. At the same time, the old would be granted more palliative medicine (e.g., pain killers) and more nursing-home and home-health care, to make their natural years more comfortable.

Callahan's call to break an existing ethical taboo and replace it with another raises the problem known among ethicists and sociologists as the "slippery slope." Once the precept that one should do "all one can" to avert death is given up, and attempts are made to fix a specific age for a full life, why stop there? If, for instance, the American economy experiences hard times in the 1990s, should the "maximum" age be reduced to 72, 65 —or lower? And should the care for other so-called unproductive groups be cut off, even if they are even younger? Should countries that are economically worse off than the United States set their limit, say, at 55?

This is not an idle thought, because the idea of limiting the care the elderly receive in itself represents a partial slide down such a slope. Originally, Callahan, the Hastings Center (which he directs) and other think tanks played an important role in redefining the concept of death. Death used to be seen by the public at large as occurring when the lungs stopped functioning and, above all, the heart stopped beating. In numerous old movies and novels, those attending the dying would hold a mirror to their faces to see if it fogged over, or put an ear to their chests to see if the heart had stopped. However, high technology made these criteria obsolete by mechanically ventilating people and keeping their hearts pumping. Hastings et al. led the way to provide a new technological definition of death: brain death. Increasingly this has been accepted, both in the medical community and by the public at large, as the point of demise, the point at which care should stop even if it means turning off life-extending machines, because people who are brain dead do not regain consciousness. At the same time, most doctors and a majority of the public as well continue strongly to oppose terminating care to people who are conscious, even if there is little prospect for recovery, despite considerable debate about certain special cases.

Callahan now suggests turning off life-extending technology for all those above a certain age, even if they could recover their full human capacity if treated. It is instructive to look at the list of technologies he would withhold: mechanical ventilation, artificial resuscitation, antibiotics and artificial nutrition and hydration. Note that while several of these are used to maintain brain-dead bodies, they are also used for individuals who are temporarily incapacitated but able to recover fully; indeed, they are used to save young lives, say, after a car accident. But there is no way to stop the development of such new technologies and the improvement of existing ones without depriving the young of benefit as well. (Antibiotics are on the list because of an imminent "high cost" technological advance—administering them with a pump implanted in the body, which makes their introduction more reliable and better distributes dosages.)

One may say that this is Callahan's particular list; other lists may well be drawn. But any of them would start us down the slope, because the savings that are achieved by turning off the machines that keep brain-dead people alive are minimal compared with those that would result from the measures sought by the people calling for new equity between the generations. And any significant foray into deliberately withholding medical care for those who can recover does raise the question, Once society has embarked on such a slope, where will it stop?

Those opposed to Callahan, Lamm and the other advocates of limiting care to the old, but who also favor extending the frontier of life, must answer the question, Where will the resources come from? One answer is found in the realization that defining people as old at the age of 65 is obsolescent. That age limit was set generations ago, before changes in life styles and medicines much extended not only life but also the number and quality of productive years. One might recognize that many of the "elderly" can contribute to society not merely by providing love, companionship and wisdom to the young but also by continuing to work, in the traditional sense of the term. Indeed, many already work in the underground economy because of the large penalty—a cut in Social Security benefits—exacted from them if they hold a job "on the books."

Allowing elderly people to retain their Social Security benefits while working, typically part-time, would immediately raise significant tax revenues, dramatically change the much-feared dependency-to-dependent ratio, provide a much-needed source of child-care workers and increase contributions to Social Security (under the assumption that anybody who will continue to work will continue to contribute to the program). There is also evidence that people who continue to have meaningful work will live longer and healthier lives, without requiring more health care, because psychic well-being in our society is so deeply associated with meaningful work. Other policy changes, such as deferring retirement, modifying Social Security benefits by a small, gradual stretching out of the age of full-benefit entitlement, plus some other shifts under way, could be used readily to gain more resources. Such changes might be justified prima facie because as we extend life and its quality, the payouts to the old may also be stretched out.

Beyond the question of whether to cut care or stretch out Social Security payouts, policies that seek to promote intergenerational equity must be assessed as to how they deal with another matter of equity: that between the poor and the rich. A policy that would stop Federal support for certain kinds of care, as Callahan and others propose, would halt treatment for the aged, poor, the near-poor and even the less-well-off segment of the middle class (although for the latter at a later point), while the rich would continue to buy all the care they wished to. Callahan's suggestion that a consensus of doctors would stop certain kinds of care for all elderly people is quite impractical; for it to work, most if not all doctors would have to agree to participate. Even if this somehow happened, the rich would buy their services overseas either by going there or by importing the services. There is little enough we can do to significantly enhance economic equality. Do we want to exacerbate the inequalities that already exist by completely eliminating access to major categories of health care services for those who cannot afford to pay for them?

In addition to concern about slipping down the slope of less (and less) care, the *way* the limitations are to be introduced raises a serious question. The advocates of changing the intergenerational allocation of resources favor rationing health care for the elderly but nothing else. This is a major intellectual weakness of their argument. There are other major targets to consider within health care, as well as other areas, which seem, at least by some criteria, much more inviting than terminating care to those above a certain age. Within the medical sector, for example, why not stop all interventions for which there is no hard evidence that they are beneficial? Say, public financing of psychotherapy and coronary bypass operations? Why not take the $2 billion or so from plastic surgery dedicated to face lifts, reducing behinds and the like? Or require that all burials be done by low-cost cremations rather than using high-cost coffins?

Once we extend our reach beyond medical care to health care, if we cannot stop people from blowing $25 billion per year on cigarettes and convince them to use the money to serve the young, shouldn't we at least cut out public subsidies to tobacco growers before we save funds by denying antibiotics to old people? And there is the matter of profits. The high-technology medicine Callahan targets for savings is actually a minor cause of the increase in health care costs for the elderly or for anyone —about 4 percent. A major factor is the very high standard of living American doctors have, compared to those of many other nations. Indeed, many doctors tell interviewers that they love their work and would do it for half their current income as long as the incomes of their fellow practitioners were also cut. Another important area of saving is the exorbitant profits made by the nondoctor owners of dialysis units and nursing homes. If we dare ask how many years of life are enough, should we not also be able to ask how much profit is "enough"? This profit, by the way, is largely set not by the market but by public policy.

Last but not least, as the United States enters a time of economic constraints, should we draw new lines of conflict or should we focus on matters that sustain our societal fabric? During the 1960s numerous groups gained in political consciousness and actively sought to address injustices done to them. The result has been some redress and an increase in the level of societal stress (witness the deeply troubled relationships between the genders). But these conflicts occurred in an affluent society and redressed deeply felt grievances. Are the young like blacks and women, except that they have not yet discovered their oppressors—a group whose consciousness should be raised, so it will rally and gain its due share?

The answer is in the eye of the beholder. There are no objective criteria that can be used here the way they can be used between the races or between the genders. While women and minorities have the same rights to the same jobs at the same pay as white males, the needs of the young and the aged are so different that no simple criteria of equity come to mind. Thus, no one would argue that the teen-agers and those above 75 have the same need for schooling or nursing homes.

At the same time, it is easy to see that those who try to mobilize the young

—led by a new Washington research group, Americans for Generational Equity (AGE), formed to fight for the needs of the younger generation—offer many arguments that do not hold. For instance, they often argue that today's young, age 35 or less, will pay for old people's Social Security, but by the time that they come of age they will not be able to collect, because Social Security will be bankrupt. However, this argument is based on extremely farfetched assumptions about the future. In effect, Social Security is now and for the foreseeable future overprovided, and its surplus is used to reduce deficits caused by other expenditures, such as Star Wars, in what is still an integrated budget. And, if Social Security runs into the red again somewhere after the year 2020, relatively small adjustments in premiums and payouts would restore it to financial health.

Above all, it is a dubious sociological achievement to foment conflict between the generations, because, unlike the minorities and the white majority, or men and women, many millions of Americans are neither young nor old but of intermediate ages. We should not avoid issues just because we face stressing times in an already strained society; but maybe we should declare a moratorium on raising new conflicts until more compelling arguments can be found in their favor, and more evidence that this particular line of divisiveness is called for.

POSTSCRIPT

Should Health Care for the Elderly Be Limited?

Callahan's views are amplified in his book *Setting Limits: Medical Goals in an Aging Society* (Simon & Schuster, 1987). See Paul Homer and Martha Holstein, eds., *A Good Old Age: The Paradox of Setting Limits* (Touchstone, 1990) for responses to Callahan's arguments. Also see Robert L. Barry and Gerard V. Bradley, eds., *Set No Limits: A Rebuttal to Daniel Callahan's Proposal to Limit Health Care for the Elderly* (University of Illinois Press, 1991). In "Elder Choice," *American Journal of Law and Medicine* (vol. 19, no. 3, 1993), Alfred F. Conard argues that artificial prolongation of life is usually undesirable and that health care for the aged should include information about advance directives.

A study of critically ill elderly patients concluded that age alone is not an adequate predictor of long-term survival and quality of life. See L. Chelluri et al., "Long-term Outcome of Critically Ill Elderly Patients Requiring Intensive Care," *Journal of the American Medical Association* (June 23/30, 1993).

For contrasting views on age as a criterion for medical care, see David C. Thomasma, "Functional Status Care Categories and National Health Policy," *Journal of the American Geriatrics Society* (April 1993); Mark Siegler, "Should Age Be a Criterion for Health Care?" and James F. Childress, "Ensuring Care, Respect, and Fairness for the Elderly," both in the *Hastings Center Report* (October 1984); and Nancy S. Jecker and Robert A. Pearlman, "Ethical Constraints on Rationing Medical Care by Age," *Journal of the American Geriatrics Society* (November 1989). Marshall B. Kapp opposes Callahan's view in "Rationing Health Care: Will It Be Necessary? Can It Be Done Without Age or Disability Discrimination?" *Issues in Law and Medicine* (Winter 1989). Pat Milmoe McCarrick's *The Aged and the Allocation of Health Care Resources* (Scope Note No. 13, Kennedy Institute of Ethics, 1990) offers a good bibliography.

Finally, see Edward L. Schneider and Jack M. Guralnik, "The Aging of America: Impact on Health Care Costs," *Journal of the American Medical Association* (May 2, 1990) for a discussion of how the rapid increase in the elderly population will affect health care costs.

ISSUE 19

Is It Unfair to Tie Health Insurance to Employment?

YES: Nancy S. Jecker, from "Can an Employer-Based Health Insurance System Be Just?" in James A. Morone and Gary S. Belkin, eds., *The Politics of Health Care Reform: Lessons from the Past, Prospects for the Future* (Duke University Press, 1994)

NO: David A. Rochefort, from "The Pragmatic Appeal of Employment-Based Health Care Reform," in James A. Morone and Gary S. Belkin, eds., *The Politics of Health Care Reform: Lessons from the Past, Prospects for the Future* (Duke University Press, 1994)

ISSUE SUMMARY

YES: Philosopher Nancy S. Jecker asserts that the current system of employer-based health insurance arose through historical events and accidents and was not based on a morally thoughtful process. Injustice in the distribution of jobs linked to health insurance have compromised justice in health care.

NO: Political scientist David A. Rochefort believes that employment-based health insurance is America's special contribution to the international variety of approaches. Although the system is imperfect, it offers policymakers a ready-made structure for achieving their objectives of universality and cost constraint.

In 1994, for the first time in decades, the American people and Congress grappled seriously with the issue of health care reform. None of the proposed plans was adopted, however. The basic problems remained.

The American health care system is the most expensive in the world. No other country spends as much—11.5 percent of the gross national product—on health care. The American health care system is also among the most technologically advanced in the world. On the negative side, however, the American health care system is among the least equitable in the world. Approximately 37 million people have no medical insurance; some have employers who do not provide health insurance as a benefit, others are unemployed, and still others are uninsurable because of current or prior health problems such as cancer, heart disease, or AIDS. Many more millions have medical insurance that does not pay for expensive items such as prescription drugs, mental health care, or nursing home care. Publicly funded programs such as Medicare (for the elderly and those with end-stage kidney disease) and Medicaid (for the very poor) spend more and more each year to provide less and less coverage. Those who are hardest hit by the lack of financial support for health care are the poorest populations, especially children.

The United States is the only industrialized country other than South Africa that does not have some form of national health insurance. In some countries, such as the United Kingdom, health care is provided through a National Health Service, which employs physicians and other health care workers. In other countries, such as Germany, a national health insurance plan covers all citizens. In the United States the traditional form of payment for health care is "fee for service"; that is, a patient pays a doctor for an office visit, procedure, or other service, the free market sets the rates, and the costs are paid by private insurance, largely obtained as an employment benefit. There are about 1,500 private insurance companies providing health insurance, and each state regulates insurance according to its own laws. Each state also sets its own Medicaid eligibility and reimbursement standards.

Industry is trying to lower medical costs through a number of mechanisms: shifting the costs to employees; reducing hospital utilization by requiring second opinions and by limiting lengths of stay; and limiting choices of providers to those in special groups called Health Maintenance Organizations (HMOs) or Preferred Provider Organizations (PPOs). Although these cost-containment measures reduce the physician's discretion in recommending treatment, they may also reduce unnecessary surgery and other unnecessary forms of treatment. In June 1985 the U.S. Supreme Court upheld a Massachusetts statute requiring that certain health care benefits be provided to residents who are insured under employee health care plans.

No one—doctors, patients, hospital administrators, or government officials—is happy with the present system. It is generally accepted that it is too costly, inequitable, irrational, and enmeshed in red tape. However, there is no agreement as to the solution. Providing insurance through employers is a traditional American method, but in the health care reform debate many employers—especially small businesses—objected to "mandates" that they claimed would create financial hardships for them.

The following two selections look at employer-based health insurance. Nancy S. Jecker believes that employer-based health insurance cannot be fair because access to jobs is unfair. She advocates health care reform that separates health insurance from paid labor force participation. David A. Rochefort argues that the United States has extensive experience with the employer-based form of health insurance, and he maintains that policymakers understand its operational requirements, needed adaptations, and future potential better than any other model.

YES

Nancy S. Jecker

CAN AN EMPLOYER-BASED HEALTH INSURANCE SYSTEM BE JUST?

America's distinctive practice of linking private health insurance to employment is coming under increasing fire. Critics charge that the system produces inequities because it misses so many people. They also fault job-based insurance as inefficient, claiming that it feeds the problem of rising health care costs by distancing consumers from health care costs and thereby encouraging overuse; they argue that employer-based insurance restricts opportunity and lowers productivity because workers feel locked into current jobs for fear of losing benefits. Others worry that employment-sponsored insurance reduces American competitiveness in world markets by raising the cost of American products: in 1990, fully 26 percent of the average company's net earnings went for medical costs (Freudenheim 1991).

Since reform of America's health care system is very much on the political agenda today, if employment-based proposals are flawed it is important to state clearly and forcefully why they are.... Whereas many other objections to employer-sponsored health insurance can be met without abandoning an employer-based framework, the objections I raise are *endemic* to any employment-sponsored system. The objections I put forward constitute an ethical critique of any job-based insurance framework....

THE DOMINO EFFECT

To an increasing degree, doubts about the present system raise a more fundamental question: Is America's virtually unique system of linking health insurance to paid labor inherently unjust? Or is it possible to remedy justice problems within the framework of a job-based system? To address such questions, I begin by invoking the familiar idea of a domino effect. One way a domino effect can operate is when injustices in one distributive arena are compounded by linking that arena to another. For example, suppose that access to higher education was determined by invidious racial discrimination. If access to some other good, such as the right to vote, was tied to having an undergraduate degree, then injustice in education would infect the voting area as well. Assuring justice in the political sphere may then require *separating the distribution of voting rights from the awarding of undergraduate degrees....*

The relevance of the domino effect to health care is straightforward. The distribution of private health insurance is based almost entirely on participation in the paid labor force. If it can be shown that those jobs that provide health insurance are distributed in an unjust way, then tying health insurance to jobs compromises justice in health care. Since the jobs that tend to provide health insurance fall into identifiable categories, we need to examine whether the distribution of these kinds of jobs is just or whether it instead imposes disproportionate burdens on certain groups.

Clearly, there are numerous perspectives from which to evaluate justice in jobs providing health insurance. In making this evaluation, I will focus primarily on inequalities between men and women. The impact of health care financing on men compared with women is a neglected topic but an increasingly important one in light of differences in their socioeconomic status, labor force participation, and health care needs and utilization patterns. Although I use the example of sex-based discrimination, my broader aim is to show that workplace discrimination of *any* sort, whether based on race, ethnicity, religious affiliation, age, or sexual orientation, creates corresponding injustices in employment-based insurance.[1]

It should come as no surprise that the workplace insurance system, developed in the 1940s, was based on the assumption that working women are economically dependent on a wage-earning male head of household who shares his higher earnings and retirement and health insurance benefits with her. Although more women today receive health insurance directly from an employer than ever before, employed women are less likely than employed men to receive private health insurance through their job....

Working women less often receive private insurance through their employer, first, because eligibility rules continue to reflect a male model of work and male patterns of labor force participation. Full-time, full-year workers more often receive health insurance coverage through the workplace. But, partly as a result of assuming caregiving responsibilities for children and aging relatives, women are more likely to work on a part-time or part-year basis (Kasper and Soldinger 1983). Full-time, full-year employees represent two-thirds of all male workers aged fifteen and over, but only half of all female workers (Muller 1990). Whereas men average 1.3 years outside the paid labor force, women average 11.5 years (Older Women's League 1989). And, in both 1981 and 1987, nearly one in four employed women aged forty-five to sixty-four held part-time jobs (Older Women's League 1988). Women who combine child care with paid work by making themselves available as independent contractors, rather than as salaried employees, are also excluded from employer benefit plans. Although these "peripheral workers" help to meet firms' peak demands for administrative and clerical work, they make the worker the risk taker for health needs (Muller 1990).

Second, working women predominate in nonunion jobs, and this job category is less likely to provide health insurance coverage. In the twenty-five-to-thirty-four age group, 13 percent of women workers belong to unions, compared to 19 percent of men workers; at ages thirty-five to fifty-four, the gap between women and men widens, with 19.2 percent of women and 29.8 percent of men union-affiliated; by age fifty-six, union membership declines for both men and women, but more rapidly for women. Not surprisingly, unionized workers generally fare much better with respect to wages and benefits than their nonunionized counterparts, because they have an organized labor force that bargains on their behalf.

A third factor that reduces women's employment-related coverage is that the rate at which women change jobs has greatly increased over the past two decades, while the rate for men has held constant (Schorr 1991). Partly as a result of child rearing and other caregiving roles, women workers are more likely to enter and leave the work force. They are therefore increasingly vulnerable to clauses in employer insurance plans that exclude or limit coverage for preexisting conditions. A 1987 survey found that 57 percent of employers who offer health insurance have preexisting condition clauses in the policies they offer (Cotton 1991). The insurance industry uses these clauses to apply higher premiums, waiting periods, condition-specific payment denials, or complete denial of coverage to people with previously existing medical problems. In principle, these clauses are meant to control insurance industry costs by preventing adverse selection—the purchasing of insurance by people who want to pay for insurance only when they need to use it. Yet preexisting condition clauses also block access to care for women and others who participate in the paid labor force intermittently.

Fourth, low-paying jobs are less likely to offer health insurance benefits, and women predominate in such jobs. When health insurance premiums rise, many companies with a large proportion of low-wage workers find it increasingly difficult to divert money from wages to health care without reducing wages to unacceptably low levels. As a result, companies such as fast-food restaurants, gasoline stations, and other service jobs keep wages competitive by dropping benefits, including health care (Uchitelle 1991). Low pay is a marker for women's wages, partly because of the child and elder care responsibilities women assume. When women who are caregivers remain in the paid labor force, they often choose jobs with fewer demands and less pay because of caregiving duties. Thus, the average earnings of a woman who gives birth drop $3,000 the first year and stay about $5,000 below what they would otherwise be for the next two years (Muller 1990). The wage gap between women and men is greatest between the ages of forty-five and sixty-four, when full-time male workers are at the height of their earning power and women are earning basically what they did in younger years. During this period (ages forty-five to sixty-four), women working full-time earn less than two-thirds of wages of men working similar hours (Muller 1990).

In addition to gender disparities within employment-sponsored insurance, women who work at home without pay, whether because they have very young children or because they are caring for a frail elderly relative, are often denied access to private health insurance unless they are married to someone who provides it for them. The U.S. Long-Term Care Survey of 1982 found that 44 percent of daughter caregivers were not married, either because they had never married, were widowed, or were divorced or separated (Stone and Cafferata 1987). Even among married caregivers, a 50 percent divorce rate makes reliance on a spouse's health care benefits risky, and economic dependence makes women vulnerable to inequalities within the family (Weed 1980).

The significance of the sex differential in employer-based insurance lies in the fact that the *public* insurance for which working-age women are eligible is likely to be far less generous than private insurance offered through an employer. Working-age women typically are too young to qualify for Medicare, but often they are not too rich to qualify for Medicaid, the state- and federal-financed health entitlement program for the poor. For every male eighteen years of age and older covered under Medicaid, there are two females aged eighteen and over (Muller 1990). But Medicaid is a mixed blessing for women. The health benefits women receive through Medicaid are notoriously meager and inconsistent from one state to the next. Moreover, Medicaid eligibles frequently lack access to mainstream providers, because reimbursement rates are set below costs (Pare 1991). Over 25 percent of the nation's privately practicing physicians refuse to treat Medicaid patients; and participation by obstetrician-gynecologists and other key specialists is even lower (National Pharmaceutical Council 1986). Hospital admissions under the care of a personal physician, the norm for insured and self-pay patients, are precluded when Medicaid clients are not accepted by practitioners (Muller 1990). Hence, even though women are slightly more likely than men to be insured (they make up only 40.6 percent of the uninsured [Muller 1990]), the insurance benefits they receive provide only limited access to the health care system. Gender inequities will persist so long as public insurance for working-age adults remains inferior to private insurance, and the main route to private insurance continues to be through job categories in which men predominate.

The above discussion reveals quite clearly that women and men do not participate at equal levels in jobs providing health insurance benefits. Although employer-based insurance is not explicitly gender-biased, the society to which such a policy is applied is pervasively gender-structured. Women's health care access is reduced because women tend to work in lower-paying and lower-status jobs that offer fewer benefits, and they are more likely than men to work on a part-time, part-year basis. Women who stay at home to serve as caregivers for family members become dependent on a male head of household for health insurance, with women representing 70 percent of those who receive employment-based insurance through a relative (Swartz 1990). Unmarried caregivers go without health insurance or rely on inadequate public programs. To the extent that employment disparities between men and women reflect injustice, the link between employment and health insurance merely amplifies this injustice.

THE PROBLEM OF DOMINANCE

Of course, showing that men are more likely than women to fill jobs that offer health care benefits does not yet establish that such jobs are awarded *unjustly*. Some have argued, to the contrary, that gender differences in employment reflect differences in women's and men's preferences in a free market, rather than invidious discrimination. According to this line of thinking, women voluntarily forgo jobs offering higher salaries and benefits in order to pursue goals outside the paid labor force (Fuchs 1988). Yet whether or not women make such choices armed with full information and freedom is hotly debated. A growing body of feminist scholarship challenges this account, by arguing that unequal treatment begins early in life and has the effect of limiting women's aspirations to pursue careers and reducing their odds of competing successfully (Faludi 1991; Hollard and Eisenhart 1990; Gilligan 1982; Willard 1988; Abir-Am and Outram 1987). Moreover, when high-paying and prestigious occupations are heavily sex-segregated, women seeking employment in them must bear whatever stigma the society associates with being different from other, more traditional women (Goldin 1990).

To sidestep this debate, let us suppose for the purposes of argument that jobs providing health insurance coverage are justly distributed among men and women and among all groups in the society. Suppose that such jobs are allocated in conformity with ideal justice standards to which all agree. Would it then be appropriate or desirable to link the distribution of other social goods, such as health care, to the distribution of jobs?

The strongest argument against linking the distribution of one social good to another involves the problem of dominance. Michael Walzer (1983), who has written extensively in this area, describes dominance as a pattern of distributing diverse goods so that one good, or one set of goods, is determinative of value in all the different spheres of distribution. A good is dominant if the individuals who have it, because they have it, can command a wide range of other goods. For example, wealth and income are the principal dom-

inant goods in our society because they are readily convertible into power, privilege, and position in many areas....

[Walzer's] argument forbids any good from serving as the basis for access to other goods with which it has no inherent connection.

Applied to health care, this reasoning suggests that even if jobs are awarded justly, the standards for giving out jobs are not the appropriate standards for apportioning health care. Whereas criteria such as education, work experience, job skills, and freedom from caregiving responsibilities are relevant to evaluating job candidates, these factors should not determine entitlement to health care. Of course, jobs were not made convertible into health care on these grounds. But in hindsight, the de facto effect of an employer-based insurance system has been to make health care available in accordance with the standards used for distributing certain jobs.

One reply to the dominance argument might be that to reject employer-provided insurance leaves open the possibility of using a person's place of employment as a *mechanism*, rather than a *standard*, for dispensing health insurance. A mechanism for distributing goods is chosen according to standards of convenience and efficiency, rather than justice, and it can be morally neutral in a way that distributive standards cannot. For instance, provided that all people are equally able to exercise their right to vote, the difference between registering voters through driver license bureaus or through mail-in forms is morally neutral.

Yet the reply to this suggestion is that voter registration and enrollment in health insurance are different in an important sense. Whereas the right to vote is an all-or-nothing phenomenon, health insurance can be more or less generous. Even assuming that everyone has access to health insurance through workplace insurance, or through a public insurance system, *adequate* health insurance may not be universally available. So long as public insurance is inferior and adequate health benefits remain tied to jobs, labor force affiliation still functions as a standard, rather than merely a mechanism, for distributing health insurance.

A second objection to the argument based on dominance notes that we already tie many other benefits to employment, such as vacations, retirement pensions, unemployment compensation, life insurance, and child care. Are all of these ties equally unjust because they raise the problem of dominance? To answer this question, it is important to note that many of these connections are troubling for the very same reason that connecting health insurance to jobs is: such connections compound inequalities that are already endemic in American society. For instance, when a good job is readily convertible into good child care services or a generous old age pension, this spreads inequalities from jobs to other areas. Rather than establishing that the link between jobs and health insurance is benign, the presence of other job-related advantages makes the connection between health insurance and jobs more worrisome. It shows that the jobs to which health benefits are linked *already* approximate a dominant good and *already* are associated with advantages in many other areas.

Yet, notwithstanding these similarities, it is crucial to see why the coupling of jobs and superior health insurance is especially pernicious and raises unique justice concerns. Unlike the loss of other job-related perks, the loss of adequate health care coverage has potentially devastating effects in all other areas of life. For example, when persons lack access to preventive screening for various diseases, they may develop more serious forms of illness that could have been easily treated or controlled at an earlier stage. A delay in receiving treatment may result in lifelong disabilities or premature death. The loss of other job-related benefits, by contrast, does not ordinarily cause such profound losses. For example, although persons forced to go without vacations or child care benefits may find their opportunities limited, these deprivations do not have widespread effects that impinge so fundamentally upon individuals' opportunities (Daniels 1988)....

CONCLUSIONS

In conclusion, the current system of employer-based health insurance arose through historical events and accidents, rather than through a deliberate and morally thoughtful process. In its wake, patterns of injustice in the distribution of jobs linked to health insurance have compromised justice in health care. Ethical principles appropriate for distributing jobs are not the same as the ethical criteria that should govern access to health care. This more pervasive and fundamental problem provides a reason for separating the distribution of jobs and health insurance even if jobs are fairly awarded. Finally, proposals that call for mandatory employer insurance and an expanded public system for the poor and unemployed do not eliminate justice concerns. Such proposals fall short because they do not ensure that the most vulnerable members of society receive adequate protection.

Taken together, these points provide an initially compelling argument for uncoupling health insurance and jobs. If my reasoning is correct, we would be wise to explore seriously alternatives to job-based insurance. All things considered, we may then decide that future health care reforms should be fashioned without retaining a link between jobs and health care. Separating health insurance from paid labor force participation may prove a prerequisite to achieving the goal of adequate health care coverage for all.

NOTES

1. For example, critics of job-based insurance note that blacks enjoy less access than nonblacks to job-based insurance because they often live in nontraditional family structures and do not qualify for coverage as married spouses or dependent offspring (Long 1987). Other groups that fare particularly poorly include gay couples, because the uninsured partner does not qualify for family medical benefits through the employed partner, and illegal immigrants, who are not eligible for Medicaid even if they lose their jobs and become destitute.

REFERENCES

Abir-Am, P. G., and D. Outram, eds. 1987. *Uneasy Careers and Intimate Lives.* New Brunswick, NJ: Rutgers University Press.

Cotton, P. 1991. Preexisting Conditions Hold Americans Hostage to Employers and Insurance. *Journal of the American Medical Association* 265: 2451–53.

Daniels, N. 1988. *Am I My Parents' Keeper?* New York: Oxford University Press.

Faludi, S. 1991. *Backlash: The Undeclared War against American Women.* New York: Crown.

Freudenheim, M. 1991. Health Care a Growing Burden. *New York Times,* 29 January, pp. A1, C17.

Fuchs, V. 1988. *Women's Quest for Economic Equality.* Cambridge, MA: Harvard University Press.

Gilligan, C. 1982. Women's Place in Man's Life Cycle. In *In a Different Voice,* by C. Gilligan. Cambridge, MA: Harvard University Press.

Goldin, C. 1990. *Understanding the Gender Gap: An Economic History of American Women.* New York: Oxford University Press.

Hollard, D. C., and M. A. Eisenhart. 1990. *Educated in Romance: Women, Achievement and College Culture.* Chicago: University of Chicago Press.

Kasper, A. S., and E. Soldinger. 1983. Falling between the Cracks: How Health Insurance Discriminates against Women. *Women and Health* 8:77–93.

Long, S. H. 1987. Public versus Employment-related Health Insurance: Experience and Implications for Black and Nonblack Americans. *Milbank Quarterly* 65 (Suppl. 1): 200–212.

Muller, C. 1990. *Health Care and Gender.* New York: Russell Sage Foundation.

National Pharmaceutical Council. 1986. *Pharmaceutical Benefits under State Medical Assistance Programs.* Reston, VA: National Pharmaceutical Council.

Older Women's League. 1988. *The Road to Poverty: A Report on the Economic Status of Midlife and Older Women in America.* Washington, DC: Older Women's League.

———. 1989. *Failing America's Caregivers.* Washington, DC: Older Women's League.

Pare, R. 1991. Suits Force U.S. and States to Pay More for Medicaid. *New York Times,* 29 October, pp. A1, A10.

Schorr, A. L. 1991. Job Turnover—A Problem with Employer-based Health Care. *New England Journal of Medicine* 323:543–45.

Stone, R., and G. L. Cafferata. 1987. Caregivers of the Frail Elderly: A National Profile. *Gerontologist* 27:616–26.

Swartz, K. 1990. Why Requiring Employers to Provide Health Insurance Is a Bad Idea. *Journal of Health Politics, Policy and Law* 15:779–92.

Uchitelle, L. 1991. Insurance Linked to Jobs: System Showing Its Age. *New York Times,* 1 May, pp. A1, A14.

Walzer, M. 1983. *Spheres of Justice.* New York: Basic.

———. 1984. Liberalism and the Art of Separation. *Political Theory* 12:315–30.

Weed, J. A. 1980. *National Estimates of Marital Dissolution and Survivorship, Vital and Health Statistics.* Series 3, Analytic Studies, no. 19, DHHS Publ. #PHS 80-1403. Washington, DC: U.S. Department of Health and Human Services.

Willard, A. 1988. Cultural Scripts for Mothering. In *Mapping the Moral Domain,* ed. C. Gilligan, J. V. Ward, and J. M. Taylor. Cambridge, MA: Harvard University Press.

NO

David A. Rochefort

THE PRAGMATIC APPEAL OF EMPLOYMENT-BASED HEALTH CARE REFORM

That employment-related health benefits have unjustly omitted many Americans from insurance coverage is easy to see. And current state-level public health insurance programs serving welfare recipients and the poor generally do not compare favorably with private insurance plans (except in the area of long-term care). But these points, properly underscored by Nancy Jecker in her essay..., constitute more an indictment of *past* practices than a criticism of possible reforms. In fact, it is entirely feasible to design an employment-based health insurance program that would address such concerns, effectively marrying social justice with political pragmatism. To appreciate that such a program could be devised, however, it is necessary to set aside some major misconceptions about employer mandates that have entered into the national health policy debate.

A CROSSFIRE OF CRITICISM

Under a national employer mandate, the primary method for extending health insurance coverage would be to require all businesses to provide employees and their dependents with a standard basic package of benefits. Depending on the nature of this requirement, companies could do this directly or by paying a tax for employees to be covered by another source established by government Also encompassed by the government program would be the unemployed uninsured. When the latter, indirect method of coverage is given to businesses as an option, the plans are known as "play or pay."

Such employer-mandate plans represent a middle-of-the road reform strategy between providing tax subsidies to uninsured individuals, to help them purchase their own private coverage, and a total government takeover of the health care financing system—two other prominent policy positions, associated with Republicans and Democrats, respectively. As such, mandates

From David A. Rochefort, "The Pragmatic Appeal of Employment-Based Health Care Reform," in James A. Morone and Gary S. Belkin, eds., *The Politics of Health Care Reform: Lessons from the Past, Prospects for the Future* (Duke University Press, 1994). Copyright © 1994 by Duke University Press. Reprinted by permission.

have been attacked both for proposing too much public intervention and for proposing too little.

From those inclined toward a tax-based solution has come a series of ominous predictions about the economic impact of mandates (White House 1992; see also Fuchs 1992; *Businews* 1988). By increasing the cost of labor to employers, it is argued, mandates will reduce wages and jobs. Particularly hard hit will be small companies, a sector that accounts for more than half of all working uninsured. Prices of goods and services, too, are expected to rise.

On a more philosophical plane, opponents of mandates question whether guaranteeing universal health care coverage is truly a social responsibility. Or, if granting the point, they maintain that it is unfair to impose this responsibility on private employers. Not entirely consistently, others on the right, including the former Bush administration, have criticized mandates as likely to "cascade into a form of national health insurance" (White House 1992: 78)—one scenario is that more and more employers would elect to pay into the publicly operated insurance fund under the play-or-pay option. Another prediction is that a steady aggregation of older and sicker workers drawing on the public fund will lead to unacceptably rising costs for government.

Just as many complaints, albeit of a different orientation, come from those who advocate the establishment of a national public health care program in the United States (see, e.g., Russo 1991; Kerrey 1991; Glaser 1991; Swartz 1990). Some, extrapolating from defects of the current employment-based insurance system, foresee an increasing fragmentation of the insurance market, with private insurance companies calibrating products and prices according to the risk profiles of a greater number of employment groups. Also, the danger of "job lock," wherein people are hesitant to leave a position for one with less generous health benefits, would be worsened if insurers excluded the coverage of preexisting conditions for new group members. In her ethical assessment, Jecker expresses concern over the special problems this practice would create for women, who are more likely to participate intermittently in the work force. And present experience casts doubt on the ability of multiple separate employers to bargain effectively with insurance companies and health care providers to control rising costs.

In general, critics on the left characterize the employer mandate approach to health care reform as "partial" and "incremental." Their worst fear is not that the adoption of such a strategy will soon lead to national health insurance, but that it will divert needed "comprehensive" and "fundamental" policy change. At last at the point of following the road taken by other Western nations that have confronted similar health system problems, America seems ready to veer off into another historical cul-de-sac. Were a large number of employers to choose to pay into the publicly sponsored insurance plan, proponents of a single national program fear the Medicaid experience writ large—a two-class system of care, which satisfies neither recipients nor providers. Jecker, for example, describes current Medicaid benefits as "notoriously meager and inconsistent from one state to the next." Finally, the financing method of an employer mandate is judged regressive in its effects, that is, it inflicts greater burdens on lower-income workers (see, e.g., Cantor 1990).

These appraisals cast employer mandates as at best ill-considered and at worst a disastrous course of health care reform. To the extent that the brief against mandates has been constructed for political debate, however, it includes the kinds of abstractions, distortions, worst-case scenarios, and straw-man arguments typical in this context. While no analysis can dispel purely ideological preferences for more or less government, careful scrutiny of these various pitfalls can put into perspective the true potential of the mandate strategy. As Brown (1990: 794) has written, "A key policy question about mandates ... is not whether they are a good idea, or even whether they are preferable (on whatever grounds) to other approaches, but rather whether they might play a positive role in catalyzing and sustaining an effective strategic *mix*" (emphasis in original).

DISINSURANCE AND DISEMPLOYMENT DILEMMAS

Economic warnings about employer-mandated health insurance have a familiar historical ring. Conservative business elements have used a rhetoric of impending calamity whenever government has contemplated new regulation of the private sector. Had these claims been taken at face value in the past, however, the U.S. would not have child labor laws today. Nor would we ever risk increasing the minimum wage, even though experience shows that such mandated wage increases do not seem to lead to substantial job loss to the extent that this is directly measurable (Zedlewski et al. 1992: 64; Levitan 1990: 152). Recent business resistance to a family leave bill also centered

on this issue of creating unfair and burdensome new private obligations. Here again, however, the evidence from businesses already providing leaves to their employees—for example, the businesses in Dade County, Florida, the first county in the nation to pass a family leave ordinance—is that costs are lower than anticipated, while worker satisfaction and productivity have grown (Rohter 1993).

The truth is that no one can predict with precision the economic impacts on private employers of government-mandated health insurance, as numerous health care economists agree (Zedlewski et al. 1992; Kronick 1991; Swartz 1990). Without firm estimates of such components in the calculation as the "elasticity" of the demand for labor, it is possible only to delineate a likely range of outcomes based on certain assumptions....

WHO PAYS WHAT, WHEN, AND HOW?

One thing is certain. Under all proposed plans the buck stops [at] the same place. Whether it's lost wages, higher prices, higher premiums, or increased taxes, the public will have to foot the bill for expanding health insurance coverage. Within the intricacies of that money trail, however, lie varying equity issues.

Businesses that insure have to pay high premiums because hospital rates are calculated to include uncompensated care of employees of noninsuring businesses. Hence, the charge rings false that to compel noninsuring businesses to offer health benefits is unfair; in this light, it is noninsuring companies that perpetrate inequity, by "free riding" on the cross-subsidies woven into the health care financing system. More and more, business and other group health insurers attempt to resist paying these added costs for hospitals' bad debt and free care—which exceeded $300 million in Massachusetts in fiscal year 1991 (Kronick 1991)—by such means as negotiated provider discounts and self-insurance. ...

A second frequent equity criticism is that employer mandates penalize struggling small businesses, which are over-represented among the companies to be affected by new requirements. Current patterns of uninsurance make this problem a real one, although there are several mitigating factors. Any price increases and wage cuts arising from mandates should be felt by all noninsuring small businesses more or less equivalently, maintaining the competitive balance internal to that sector. Also, the leading employer mandate proposals ... contain numerous provisions specifically to soften the impact on small businesses. Included are slower phase-in schedules, small-group insurance reform, special treatment of new businesses, improved tax deductions, and new tax credits for firms with low profit margins. ...

Finally, there is the question of "regressivity" under employer mandates. The problem is straightforward: assuming some trade-off between new health benefits, payroll taxes, and wages, low-wage earners will be losing a greater proportion of their income. To be sure, a wholly publicly funded program supported by outlays from a progressive income tax would be more egalitarian. However, several points complicate the choice of most suitable funding for health reform.

First, there is the force of tradition to reckon with. The major social insurance entitlements of the American welfare state for unemployment, disability, Medicare, and old-age pensions are all financed primarily by payroll taxes, not general revenues. With government using a sliding-scale fee for enrollees in the publicly sponsored plan and for the premiums of low-income workers in employer plans, ... an employer mandate would be that much more progressive than these established programs. The opportunity to reduce tax liability by making pretax health plan contributions would be another monetary bonus that mandates would give to those presently working without insurance. Second, although it may be regressive at "take-in," universal health insurance would be progressive at payout to the extent that lower socioeconomic and minority groups have greater need for health services. Third, this awkward combination of regressive and progressive principles, with the regressive dimension outermost, could be critical to avoiding the public perception of universal health care as "welfare." This, in turn, would enhance the initiative's long-term political viability.

A TROJAN HORSE

The idea that job lock, more extensive "redlining" of groups and individuals, and other private insurance abuses would worsen under an employer mandate system assumes a half-measure type of reform that is not under serious consideration. Current leading mandate proposals do much more than merely require universal workplace coverage, leaving present market dynamics to shape the outcome. They also embody an array of interventions to remedy the inefficiencies and ineffectiveness of that health care market. Such changes include requirements for communitywide insurance rating and no coverage exclusions on the basis of health status or preexisting conditions. Other pieces of this omnibus overhaul strategy are malpractice reform and administrative and billing simplification. Whether all of these actions will be pursued far enough and buttressed with adequate monitoring is a fair concern. Much of the legislative and administrative process will consist of bargaining with powerful interests over just these issues. Admittedly, this is not a struggle to be taken lightly. But it is simply incorrect at this stage of the national debate to portray mandate reformers as unmindful of such problems.

Another fundamental component of leading mandate plans is payment reform. Many include rate setting to establish standard reimbursements for providers from all third-party payers and an independent Federal Reserve type of health expenditure board to specify national and state spending ceilings. These cost-containment measures draw simultaneously on the lessons of national health care programs in other countries like Canada and Germany, as well as innovative state programs inside the U.S., whose impressive successes are discussed elsewhere in this issue.

The specter of a monster Medicaid program likewise misconstrues the nature of the employer-mandate strategy. If the public plan under play or pay, as is generally proposed, featured a standard package of benefits across states equivalent to basic private coverage, higher provider reimbursement levels, and substantial working- and middle-class enrollments,... would the resulting program still equal Medicaid?

Alternatively, instead of playing the role of direct insurer, public authorities could function like "the health benefits manager of a large employer ... contract[ing] for health benefits with a se-lection of high-quality health plans," and giving a choice of these plans to those not insured by their employer (Kronick 1991: 28). Hawaii's state health insurance plan supplies a working example, albeit with limited benefits (Dukakis 1992). This approach is also consistent with current "managed competition" reforms. In short, there is no reason why a mixed private-public system of universal health insurance must perpetuate the current problem of two standards of care reflecting different sources of coverage.

Morone and Dunham (1986) have suggested that fundamental policy shifts in the American political system sometimes assume the guise of incremental changes. Reviewing the development, refinement, and spread of diagnosis-related group reimbursement from the state to national levels in the 1980s, they mused whether the country might not be "slouching toward national health insurance." Heavily regulated employer mandate plans exhibit something of this same deceptive innocuousness, appearing merely to extend current private insurance arrangements, while introducing sweeping new public controls over the health care system. They are also, in this sense, a kind of Trojan horse of reform. Terminology aside, the similarities with both the aims and means of national health insurance outweigh the differences.

POLITICAL CALCULUS

... A predominantly employment-based system is America's indigenous contribution to the international panoply of health insurance approaches. Moreover, of the roughly 35 million Americans who now lack health insurance, 85 percent are workers and their dependents (Fuchs 1992), making the workplace a logical and effective vehicle for addressing the problem of no insurance for the bulk of the population affected. Labor market analysts report a rising trend in businesses' use of part-time and temporary help, "disposable workers," who can be paid lower wages with few fringe benefits (Kilborn 1993). This development makes more comprehensive regulation of privately provided benefit packages not just desirable but an absolute necessity, in order to stem rampant shifting of costs onto private households and government.

Although it is now imperfect, employment-based health insurance nonetheless offers to policymakers a ready-made structure for achieving their objectives of universality and cost constraint. We understand its operational requirements, needed adaptations, and future potential far better than any other model.

REFERENCES

Brown, L. D. 1990. The Merits of Mandates. *Journal of Health Politics, Policy and Law* 15 (4): 793–96.

Businews. 1988. Government Mandates: Will Small Business Survive? September/October, p. 1.

Cantor, J. C. 1990. Expanding Health Insurance Coverage: Who Will Pay? *Journal of Health Politics, Policy and Law* 15 (4): 755–78.

Dukakis, M. S. 1992. Hawaii and Massachusetts: Lessons from the States. *Yale Law and Policy Review* 10 (2): 397–408.

Fuchs, B. C. 1992. *Mandated Employer-provided Health Insurance.* Washington, DC: Congressional Research Service, 24 February update.

Glaser, W. A. 1991. *Health Insurance in Practice.* San Francisco, CA: Jossey-Bass.

Kerrey, R. 1991. Why America Will Adopt Comprehensive Health Care Reform. *American Prospect* 2 (Summer): 81–91.

Kilborn, P. T. 1993. New Jobs Lack the Old Security in a Time of "Disposable Workers." *New York Times,* 15 March, p. A1.

Kronick, R. 1991. Can Massachusetts Pay for Health Care for All? *Health Affairs* 10 (1): 26–44.

Levitan, S. A. 1990. *Programs in Aid of the Poor,* 6th ed. Baltimore: Johns Hopkins University Press.

Morone, J. A., and A. B. Dunham. 1986. Slouching toward National Health Insurance. *Bulletin of the New York Academy of Medicine* 62 (6): 646–62.

Rohter, L. 1993. In Florida, Family Bill Wins Converts. *New York Times,* 5 February, p. A14.

Russo, M. 1991. Single-Payer System Guarantees Health Care for Less. *Christian Science Monitor,* 10 September, p. 18.

Swartz, K. 1990. Why Requiring Employers to Provide Health Insurance Is a Bad Idea. *Journal of Health Politics, Policy and Law* 15 (4): 779–92.

White House. 1992. *The President's Comprehensive Health Reform Program.* Washington, DC: White House.

Zedlewski, S. R., G. P. Acs, and C. W. Winterbottom. 1992. Play-or-Pay Employer Mandates: Potential Effects. *Health Affairs* 11 (1): 62–83.

POSTSCRIPT

Is It Unfair to Tie Health Insurance to Employment?

Tired of waiting for a federal solution, several states have attacked the problem of attaching health insurance to employment on their own. Hawaii has a long-standing plan to provide universal access to health care. Massachusetts tried but has failed: its 1988 Health Security Act, which enjoyed broad support at the outset, has run into severe economic and political difficulties. Especially damaging has been the burden on employers in a recession. In January 1991, New York began covering primary and preventive care for children under 13 whose families have incomes below a certain level. The plan does not cover costs of hospitalization or specialized dental, vision, or speech treatment. In addition, the New York State Department of Health has developed a proposal for universal health insurance.

Another approach has been taken by Oregon, which developed a list of priorities for health care financing under Medicaid (which covers health care for some categories of very poor people). Under the Oregon plan, access to health care would be expanded by 50 percent but Medicaid would no longer pay for procedures that fell near the bottom of the list of 709 procedures, no matter how compelling the individual case.

Minnesota has enacted a plan called "HealthRight." Its name to the contrary, the plan does not entitle any state resident to health care but seeks to expand access by making health insurance more affordable. The state's 370,000 uninsured residents (about 8.6 percent of the population) will be able to buy insurance at subsidized rates. Many other states are at various stages of considering or implementing partial reform proposals. For a review of health care reform in the states, see Emily Friedman, "Getting a Head Start: The States and Health Care Reform," *Journal of the American Medical Association* (March 16, 1994).

The 1994 health care reform debate produced a vast amount of literature. See, for example, Dan W. Brock and Norman Daniels, "Ethical Foundations of the Clinton Administration's Proposed Health Care System," *Journal of the American Medical Association* (April 20, 1994). A special 1993 supplement to *Health Affairs* presents a variety of articles on health care reform, and Susan M. Wolf looks at "Health Care Reform and the Future of Physician Ethics," in the *Hastings Center Report* (March–April 1994).

For further reading see articles by Uwe E. Reinhardt, Ruth B. Putilo, and Sidney Dean Watson in the Summer 1994 issue of *The Journal of Law, Medicine and Ethics*, and Lawrence O. Gostin, "Health Care Reform in the United States," *The Journal of Law, Medicine and Ethics* (Spring 1993).

ISSUE 20

Should Health Insurance Companies Have Access to Information from Genetic Testing?

YES: American Council of Life Insurance and Health Insurance Association of America, from *Report of the ACLI-HIAA Task Force on Genetic Testing* (ACLI-HIAA, 1991)

NO: Thomas H. Murray, from "Genetics and the Moral Mission of Health Insurance," *Hastings Center Report* (November/December 1992)

ISSUE SUMMARY

YES: The American Council of Life Insurance and the Health Insurance Association of America assert that while insurers do not currently plan to use genetic information, if they are denied access to genetic test results, the amount paid out in insurance claims could increase, resulting in higher premiums for most policyholders.

NO: Thomas H. Murray, a professor of biomedical ethics, believes that actuarial fairness—the insurance industry's standard—fails to accomplish the social goals of health insurance and that genetic tests should not be used to deny people access to health insurance.

Genetic diseases and predisposition to disease are not uncommon. An estimated 4,000 to 5,000 genetic diseases have already been identified. Some of these diseases are detectable prenatally, such as Down's syndrome, a form of mental retardation, and sickle-cell anemia, a blood disorder. Others are detected at birth, such as PKU, a metabolic disorder. Still others become manifest only in adults, such as Huntington's disease, a lethal neurological disorder.

Approximately 1,100 genes that cause disease have been identified, many of them because of the work of the Human Genome Project and the existence of newer DNA-based technologies. (A gene for a relatively rare type of breast and ovarian cancer was identified only in 1990.) Genetic disorders come in several varieties. Inherited disorders are passed on from parent to child. Acquired disorders appear later in life as a result of genetic alteration, perhaps due to chemical or environmental toxicities. In addition to diseases directly related to a single gene or a pair of genes, a number of common illnesses—such as most breast cancers, Alzheimer's disease, which causes mental and physical deterioration, and coronary artery disease—are most likely caused by a combination of genetics and environment.

Once a disease-causing gene is identified, a test to determine whether a particular individual carries that gene is often developed. The ability to test for such genes has benefits and burdens. The most common use is in prenatal screening, in which a fetus can be tested for a number of chromosomal abnormalities. Premarital screening is also used—particularly among ethnic groups predisposed to certain diseases—so that couples can make informed reproductive choices. The knowledge that one is prone to develop a certain disease can lead to preventive measures such as changes in diet, exercise, and early treatment. The knowledge that these tests provide can be reassuring, or it can force difficult choices—such as whether to marry, conceive a child, or abort a pregnancy.

Choices become more problematic in diseases where children may be affected later in life. For example, should a child be tested for Huntington's disease? If the child is tested and found to be carrying the gene, should he or she be told? How would a young person weigh the concern of becoming demented in adult life against the importance of having that information for his or her future mate and potential children?

Whatever the personal decisions made in these cases, nearly everyone concerned about genetic testing worries about its impact on insurance. As the number of genetic tests increases, and as they become routine in medical practice, more and more diseases and predispositions will be identified and entered into a person's medical record. Who will have access to that information? For what purposes? Medical information of all kinds is now transmitted routinely to insurance companies who use it to validate claims, accept or deny applications for insurance, and to set actuarial standards (making estimates of future claims).

The following two selections present different points of view about the use of genetic tests for insurance. The American Council of Life Insurance and the Health Insurance Association of America, both large trade associations, assert that while they do not currently use or plan to use genetic test results in their evaluation of individuals, they must remain free to use whatever information is relevant to maintaining fair rates for all their policy holders. Thomas H. Murray sees this use of "fairness" as flawed, particularly because health insurance is a system with social and moral responsibilities to maintain access to medical care for those in need.

YES

American Council of
Life Insurance and
Health Insurance
Association of America

REPORT OF THE ACLI-HIAA TASK FORCE ON GENETIC TESTING

THE ADVENT OF GENETIC TESTING

Genetic science has advanced dramatically in recent years. From gene splicing to gene mapping to gene therapy, astounding scientific breakthroughs have occurred frequently with each discovery being more impressive than the last. The federal government's creation in 1988 of the Human Genome Initiative has further accelerated the pace of discovery and captured the public's attention.

Hope abounds that the Human Genome Initiative will find new ways to prevent and cure disease. But there is also real fear that genetic science may unleash undesirable social problems. Some of the deepest concerns that have been raised relate to how insurance companies and employers might someday use genetic test results to infringe on the right to privacy and improperly deny people access to jobs or insurance coverage.

The American Council of life Insurance (ACLI) and the Health Insurance Association of America (HIAA) recognize the public's hopes and fears about genetic testing. The ACLI and the HIAA are acutely aware that the advent of genetic testing will bring with it many questions about the insurance industry's practices in the areas of risk selection, medical expense reimbursement and protection of medical information. Inevitably, insurance issues occupy a central place in the discussions of the legal, ethical and social dimensions of this new-found technology....

PUBLIC CONCERNS ABOUT INSURANCE

The public policy debate already under way in academic circles is raising significant policy issues for the insurance business. At numerous conferences held across the country during the past year, speakers routinely expressed concern for how insurers might use genetic test information. They expressed fears that insurers would begin using genetic information to deny coverage for large segments of the population. And they questioned whether insurers can be trusted to keep sensitive genetic testing records confidential.

The Task Force believes that for insurers, the two most controversial issues to emerge from the debate will be how genetic information might be used in risk classification to determine insurability and how the confidentiality of such information will be protected. Risk classification, at its center, is the ability of the insurer to appraise an applicant's insurability so that coverage may be offered at an appropriate and fair premium. Confidentiality is the protection of personal information obtained in the course of underwriting an application or administering a claim. Genetic testing promises to draw keen public attention to these two aspects of the insurance business.

Public Concerns: Risk Classification and Insurability

The cornerstone of a private voluntary insurance system is risk classification. Insurers must be able to appraise risks in order to group similar risks together, to forecast costs, and to establish fair and adequate premium rates. As fundamental as this may seem to the insurance industry, however, it is a concept seldom comprehended and oftentimes found objectionable by the public at large.

What the public does understand is insurance availability. This is especially true in the area of health insurance, where in recent years accessibility and affordability have been seriously jeopardized by soaring health care costs. Given this orientation towards insurance, the pub-lic tends to view genetic testing as yet another threat to insurance accessibility. A concern widely expressed is that genetic testing will create a "genetic underclass" and swell the ranks of uninsured individuals.

At various forums where knowledgeable people have gathered together to discuss genetic testing, some of the strongest concerns have focused on whether genetic testing will foreclose large numbers of people from the health insurance market. Life insurance availability seems not to arouse the same fervent sentiments, presumably because life insurance is not perceived as an entitlement to the same extent as health insurance.

Those who have reflected on genetic testing and insurance have raised a myriad of questions. Would insurers deny coverage to healthy individuals with a genetic predisposition for a particular disease? Will insurers refrain from using genetic tests until they are proven reliable? Would insurers cancel existing coverages based on genetic test results? Would insurers refuse coverage for new-borns if insured parents are asymptomatic carriers of a disease or disorder?

To some extent, it seems that those who ask the questions already have preconceived notions that insurers will use genetic testing to unfairly discriminate against genetically "inferior" individuals. Such questions are often asked in rhetorical fashion as though it were a foregone conclusion that the insurance industry stands ready to fully embrace genetic testing as a means to achieve perfect risk selection.

The truth is that the insurance industry is approaching genetic testing with great caution and a certain degree of trepidation. No one—either inside or outside the insurance industry—knows for sure how genetic testing will affect existing insurance practices. At this point, what is known is that genetic testing has had little or no impact on insurance. And as for the future, there is ample reason to doubt whether genetic testing will ever significantly alter insurance as we know it today.

The Task Force believes that it is important, amidst the rhetoric and anecdotal stories about genetic discrimination, not to lose sight of the important facts we do know about genetic testing and insurance. Those should serve to allay much of the public's uneasiness about genetic testing and ought to serve as a starting point for establishing any public policy with regard to genetic testing and insurance. Here are some of the points which the Task Force finds noteworthy:

• Life insurance is widely available today and likely to stay that way. Statistics show that an overwhelming 97 percent of applications for ordinary life insurance are accepted—92 percent at standard rates and 5 percent substandard. Only 3 percent of those who apply for coverage are declined. The fact is that insurance underwriting is not a barrier to the vast majority of Americans seeking life insurance. It has yet to be shown whether introducing genetic testing into the underwriting process would substantially change the industry's broad acceptance of applicants.

• Most health insurance is not individually underwritten and so genetic testing would have no effect on the vast majority of health insurance consumers. About 85–90 percent of health insurance is currently purchased through group plans which accept all full-time employees and dependents without evidence of insurability. For those individuals who are not members of an employer group and cannot get health insurance today, the issue is more often cost than insurability. Admittedly, there are gaps in our health insurance system for which workable solutions are needed —such as high-risk insurance pools, small-employer market reforms, and increased Medicaid coverage of the poor. However, the fact remains that genetic testing is unlikely to affect the typical American health insurance consumer who gets coverage through an existing employer-based group health plan.

• The difficulty that small employers face in securing health insurance coverage for their employees when one or more of them is high risk has been of tremendous concern to the industry. In response, the HIAA has developed a comprehensive set of legislative reforms aimed at assuring that private insurance coverage is always available to small employers regardless of the health of their employees. Most important for the concerns posed by genetic testing is that these market reforms will assure that high-risk employees are not denied coverage. Furthermore, people with existing health conditions would be required to satisfy pre-existing condition exclusions for a single, specified time only. If the employer were to change insurers or the employee to change jobs, new pre-existing exclusion time periods would not be imposed. Under these reforms, if enacted, genetic conditions would not affect the ability of employees to obtain and maintain affordable health insurance coverage.

- No insurer—life or health—currently requires genetic tests. One simple and practical reason is cost. Most available tests are far too expensive to be routinely used in the underwriting process. The test for Huntington's disease, for example, costs thousands of dollars. Though costs may come down over time (a cystic fibrosis test now exists for about $200) it will be years and perhaps decades before insurers could realistically afford genetic testing on any wide-scale basis.
- Although an estimated 4,000 genetic disorders and diseases have been identified, predispositions to many of these illnesses are already detectable, to some extent. For example, predisposition to heart disease is already detected through high cholesterol and high blood pressure levels. Family history already gives insurers information about an individual's possible predisposition to diseases like Alzheimer's and some cancers.
- Sickle cell anemia can be detected at a very young age without a genetic test. Thus, many of the illnesses potentially predictable through genetic testing are already known and factored into insurers' underwriting decisions.
- Genetic testing is no crystal ball. Genetic tests will not tell when an illness will strike nor will most of them tell for sure whether an illness will strike. Experts agree that environmental and lifestyle factors can have a large influence on inherited diseases. Such factors include diet, smoking, drinking, exercise, stress and occupation. Also, early detection will enable individuals to take precautions or possibly seek treatment to control or eliminate increased risk. Because there are so many variables that influence the onset of a genetic disease, it cannot be assumed insurers would deny coverage based merely on a genetic test result.
- It is estimated that the average person carries six to eight genes that could lead to diseases. Obviously, insurers would soon go out of business if they denied coverage to everyone with a genetically-diagnosed predisposition.

Above all, it cannot be emphasized enough that insurers are not using genetic tests in risk assessment, nor are there any plans to do so. Genetic tests are not of immediate concern for the life and health insurance industry, because health care providers are using them infrequently.

The Task Force believes that genetic research should be allowed to run its course independent of insurance considerations. Premature legal constraints on the use of such technology at this point in time would only serve to preclude the development of balanced guidelines for the responsible use of genetic testing information. In the meantime, however, the insurance industry should be monitoring the progress of genetic testing, periodically re-assessing the potential ramifications of genetic testing on insurance availability, and developing lines of communication with public policymakers on how to harness the positive aspects of genetic testing while mitigating potentially adverse consequences....

INSURERS' CONCERNS ABOUT ADVERSE SELECTION

It is interesting to note that insurers may be more fearful of genetic testing than are consumers. While customers fear how insurers may use genetic testing to deny coverage or invade privacy, insurers fear how consumers could use genetic testing to foresee coverage needs and exploit the insurance system. Insurers are concerned about a phenomenon known as "adverse selection" which ultimately drives up the cost of insurance for most people. Adverse selection (also called, "anti-selection") is the disproportionately heavy purchase of insurance by persons who are higher risks than their insurers are aware.[1] It is notable that a recent survey conducted by the Task Force into the attitudes of insurance underwriting officials reveals that few, if any, insurers see genetic testing as a means to improve risk selection. But those same officials expressed grave concerns about the potential for adverse selection if insurers were ever denied access to the results of genetic tests already known to the applicant.

Based on preliminary actuarial analyses and fundamental principles of anti-selection, these concerns of insurance underwriters are well-founded. Actuarial experts, who took a closer look at the potential for adverse selection in the event insurers were ever denied access to genetic testing information, concluded that the costs of adverse selection would vary widely depending on the particular disease, but that the cumulative cost of adverse selection for the total spectrum of genetic diseases could be quite significant. Simply put, if insurers are denied access to genetic test results, the amount paid out in insurance claims could increase substantially and the result would be higher premiums for most policyholders.

Though it should be self-evident why insurers need all relevant medical information to perform accurate risk assessment and avoid anti-selection, the unfortunate reality is that many policymakers give short shrift to such concerns. Too often there is a failure to appreciate how adverse selection harms the average, well-meaning policyholder. As a result, simplistic proposals to prohibit insurers from obtaining genetic testing information are introduced and advanced in the name of consumer protection.

The Task Force believes legislative initiatives to limit insurer access to genetic test results are forthcoming and will garner considerable political support. Given the ground swell of public awareness and apprehension towards genetic testing, defeating such proposals will be no small task. The challenge facing the insurance industry, as is so often the case with issues involving risk classification, will be to educate lawmakers on the ramifications of adverse selection and to prove the need for full disclosure by the insurance applicants, including the disclosure of genetic test results.

NOTES

1. It is important to distinguish clearly between insurers requiring genetic tests and insurers having access to genetic test information. As discussed above, the prospect of insurers ordering genetic tests in the course of reviewing an insurance application seems highly remote at this time. But genetic testing is slowly seeping into clinical medicine. There will likely be an increasing amount of genetic testing performed by medical specialists. It is the results of those tests—ordered not by the insurers but by the patients and doctors themselves —which may give rise to the problem of adverse selection.

NO

Thomas H. Murray

GENETICS AND THE MORAL MISSION OF HEALTH INSURANCE

All men are created equal. So reads one of the United States of America's founding political documents. This stirring affirmation of equality was not meant as a claim that all people are equivalent in all respects. Surely the drafters of the Declaration of Independence and the Constitution were as aware then as we are now of the wondrous variety of humankind. People differ in their appearance, their talents, and their character, among other things, and those differences matter enormously.

The commitment to equality embodied in our political tradition is not a claim that people, in fact, are indistinguishable from one another. Rather it is an assertion that before this government, this system of laws and courts, all persons are to be given equal standing, and all persons must be treated with equal regard.

Human genetics, in contrast, is a *science of inequality*—a study of human particularity and difference. One of the most difficult challenges facing us in the coming flood tide of genetic information is how to assimilate these evidences of human differences without undermining our commitment to political, legal, and moral equality.

The information about human differences pouring forth from the science of human genetics provides us with a multitude of opportunities to treat people differently according to some aspect of their genetic makeup. Deciding which uses of this information are just and which are unjust will require us to reexamine the ethical significance of a wide variety of human differences and the larger social purposes of a variety of institutions, among them health, life, and other forms of insurance.

Health insurance in the United States has moved from a system based mostly on community rating where, in a given community, all people pay comparable rates, to a system where the cost to the purchasers of insurance is based on the expected claims—a risk- or experienced-based system. This movement has significant ethical as well as economic overtones. Community rating was a system that reflected a notion of community responsibility for providing health care for its members, where the qualifying principle was

From Thomas H. Murray, "Genetics and the Moral Mission of Health Insurance," *Hastings Center Report*, vol. 22, no. 6 (November/December 1992). Copyright © 1992 by The Hastings Center. Reprinted by permission.

community membership. Other differences, such as preexisting risks, did not count as morally relevant distinctions. Risk-and experience-based systems presume that it is fair to charge different prices, or to refuse to insure people entirely, if they will need expensive health care. Such systems treat predicted need for care as a morally relevant difference among persons that justifies differential access to health insurance, and through it, to health care. But this presumes precisely what is in question: what are good moral reasons for treating people differently with respect to access to health insurance and health care? ...

GENETICS AND DISTRIBUTIVE JUSTICE

Distributive justice, as the term implies, concerns the distribution of social goods or ills: in its simplest formulation it holds that like cases are to be treated alike and unlike cases are to be treated differently. All depends, obviously, on how we fill in the material conditions of this purely formal statement of comparative justice. When we are asking about a particular occasion of just or unjust treatment, the question commonly takes the form, What makes these cases like or unlike in a morally relevant way? Failure to state a morally relevant reason for treating people differently opens one to the charge that one's action was arbitrary, capricious, and unjust.

Human genetics provides a large and rapidly growing set of differences among persons that may be used to try to justify unequal treatment. For many genetic differences and many distributions of social goods, the moral relevance of the difference seems transparently obvious. Height, for example, is largely determined by genetics. Does it make any sense to say that it was unfair to allow Kareem Abdul Jabaar to play center in the National Basketball Association for many years, but not me, just because he is taller than I am, and our differences in height are genetic, rather than anything we can claim credit for accomplishing? Most people would judge that to be absurd. In this instance a genetic difference —height—constitutes a morally relevant difference that justifies treating people differently. That same difference, however, would not justify treating us differently if, for example, we were accused of a crime, or being judged on our literary accomplishments, or in need of health care....

Having health insurance is a way to pay for ... treatment—the cost of treating a serious illness can easily exceed an average family's ability to pay for it. Health insurance is, for most people, the means to the end of health care. It is not the good of health care itself. But to the extent that it determines who does and who does not have access to care, and who has the peace of mind that comes with knowing that if care is needed it will be available, access to health insurance is a matter of justice.

GENETIC TESTING: THE CHALLENGE FOR HEALTH INSURANCE

Research in human genetics, such as the Genome Project, is likely to increase dramatically our ability to predict whether individuals are at risk for particular diseases. There are tests currently offered for diseases such as Huntington's, where the presence of the gene assures that the individual will develop the disease if he or she lives long enough. There are tests for carrier status such as cystic fibrosis where two copies of the defective gene —one from each parent—must be inherited in order for symptomatic disease to occur. And there will be tests for diseases of complex etiology such as heart disease, cancer, stroke, lung disease, and the like. For certain relatively rare genes there will be a strong connection between having the gene and having the disease. Yet most of the common killing and disabling diseases are more likely to have a complex variety of causes, including perhaps several genes each of which has some predictive relationship with the disease. These risk-oriented genetic predictors potentially are very interesting to employers and insurers.

Genetic information, in fact, is used now by insurers. There may be considerable genetic information in one's medical record. If your policy is being individually underwritten, that entire record can be copied and shipped to the prospective insurer and that information used to justify increasing the price or denying health insurance altogether. But this begs a prior question: should information about genetic differences be used at all in health insurance?

One argument against paying any special attention to genetic predictors of risk is that insurers already use risk predictors that have genetic components. Coronary artery disease is an example. It is well known that people with higher levels of cholesterol, especially the low-density-lipoprotein component, are at higher risk of coronary artery disease and subsequent heart attacks. It also seems clear that an individual's cholesterol level is at least in part determined by genetics. Variations in individual metabolism can have a substantial impact on a person's cholesterol level, such that two people can be equally virtuous (or careless) in diet and exercise and yet have very different cholesterol levels, and, presumably, very different risks for coronary artery disease and heart attack.

In time it is likely that researchers will discover a number of genes that affect cholesterol metabolism and, presumably, cholesterol level, arterial disease, and the risk of a heart attack. We may be able to construct a genetic profile of an individual's risk of heart disease. Does such a predictive index differ in any ethically significant way from today's cholesterol test, which has not evoked similar objections?

Genetic tests differ from a cholesterol test in that the latter, even if significantly influenced by genetics, is still in some measure under the individual's control. The risk of heart attack is affected by a variety of health-related behaviors including diet, exercise, stress, and smoking. To the extent that people can be held responsible for their behavior, their cholesterol level is something for which they have some responsibility. On the other hand, people cannot be said to be responsible for their genes. An old maxim in ethics is "Ought implies can." You should not be held morally accountable for that which you were powerless to influence.

Genetic tests may also have more direct distributional consequences. Alleles occur in different frequencies in different ethnic groups; it would not be surprising to find that an allele associated with an epidemiologically significant disease such as coronary artery disease was more prevalent in some ethnic groups than in others. Alpha-1 antitrypsin deficiency, associated with lung disease, appears to be more common among people of Scandinavian ancestry. If the group in which the allele occurs more often was not historically a target of discrimination, we might not be particularly concerned. If, however, the allele was more common in a group that continues to suffer discrimination, such as sickle-cell trait in people of African descent, we would have good reason for concern. The mere fact that genetic predictors have the potential to affect differentially ethnic groups that experience discrimination does not uniquely distinguish them from other risk predictors. Hypertension, for example, is more prevalent among Americans of African heritage. But the immediate and direct tie between genetcs and ethnicity may make genetic testing a more blatant use of a potentially explosive and discriminatory social classification scheme.

A third response to the claim that we need not worry about genetic risk testing because it is essentially similar to things like cholesterol testing is to question the premise that people know about the genetic component of cholesterol. Discussions of cholesterol in the media emphasize the things people can do to lower it. Reminders that cholesterol level is also significantly affected by genetics appear less frequently, and it may well be that most people are unaware that cholesterol level has a substantial genetic component. If people did understand that, perhaps they would be less tolerant of the widespread use of cholesterol testing to determine insurance eligibility, precisely because it was to that extent outside of individuals' control.

There is yet another possibility: that the central notion underlying commercial health insurance underwriting—the greater the likelihood of illness, the more one should pay for coverage—is morally unsound.

ACTUARIAL FAIRNESS

Insurers take a particular view of fairness: actuarial fairness. Actuarial fairness claims that "policyholders with the same expected risk of loss should be treated equally.... An insurance company has the responsibility to treat all its policyholders fairly by establishing premiums at a level consistent with the risk represented by each individual policyholder."[1] This definition of fairness begs the question: Why should we count differences in risk of disease as an ethically relevant justification for treating people differently in their access to health insurance and health care?

Actuarial fairness does have a realm of application in which it seems reasonable. Call it the Lloyds of London model: if two oil tanker companies ask to have their cargoes and vessels insured, one for a trip up the Atlantic to a U.S. port, the other for a voyage through the Arabian Gulf during the height of the war in Kuwait and Iraq, the owner of the first ship would cry foul if she were charged the same extraordinarily high rate as the owner of the second. Most of us, I suspect, would agree that charging the two owners the same rate would be unfair. What makes it so?

For one thing, the two ships are exposed to vastly different risks, and it seems only fair to charge them accordingly. (The process of assessing risks is called underwriting.) Furthermore, the risks were assumed voluntarily. Third, the goal of both owners is profit, and it seems reasonable to ask them to bear the expense of voluntarily assumed risks. We could also ask how commercial insurance divides up the world. In this hypothetical [situation] it divides it into those who prefer prudent business ventures and those willing to take great risks. That does not seem to be an objectionable way to parse the world for the purpose of insuring oil tankers.

In practice, insurers do not behave as if actuarial fairness were an ironclad moral rule. Valid predictors may not be used for a variety of reasons, typically having to do with other notions of fairness —for example, not discriminating on the basis of race, sex, class, or locale, even though these characteristics are related to the likelihood of insurance claims. Deborah Stone, who has studied insurance practices for HIV infection, dismisses the idea of actuarial fairness and argues instead that:

> insurability is the set of policy decisions by insurers about whom to accept. It is not a trait, but a concept of *membership*.... Treated as a scientific fact about individuals, the notion of insurability disguises fundamentally political decisions about membership in a community of mutual responsibility.[2] ...

UNDERWRITING AND THE SOCIAL PURPOSES OF INSURANCE

The threat genetic testing poses to the future of insurance for health-related risks —including health, life, and disability insurance—compels us to reexamine the social purposes served by insurance. Two points are obvious: first, that different types of insurance can have different purposes; and second, that the purpose of a particular form of insurance must be understood within its social context.

Life insurance, for example, is meant to provide financial security for one's dependents in the event that one dies. In the contemporary United States we must evaluate the role of such insurance in the context of a not particularly generous social welfare system that would otherwise leave the surviving dependents of a deceased breadwinner in very poor financial condition. The typical purchaser is an individual with one or more dependents who are unlikely to become financially independent in the immediate future. The benefits from life insurance are intended to tide survivors over until they can become financially self-sufficient, or live out their lives decently; they are not meant to provide windfalls to friends of the deceased. To the extent that life insurance is perceived as serving a need rather than being merely a commodity, we are likely to regard it as something that ought to be available to all. Our public policies toward life insurance suggest we view it otherwise, however. We prohibit certain actuarially valid distinctions such as ethnicity in setting life insurance rates. But we do not require that all persons, whatever their age, employment, or health, be permitted to buy life insurance at identical prices or at all. In consequence, the financial dependents of a person unable to obtain life insurance may suffer devastating changes in their life prospects if the principal earner dies.

Does the Lloyds of London model fit health care? Despite the current enthusiasm for tying voluntary behavior to health, most illness and disability is neither chosen nor in any sense "deserved," distinguishing it from the risks of shipping oil in a war zone. Neither is the goal of health care for those who seek it profit. Daniels argues that "justice requires that we protect *fair equality of opportunity* for individuals in a society." Reasonable access to health care in the contemporary United States is a necessary condition for fair equality of opportunity to pursue other goods that life affords. The social purpose of health insurance, understood in this way, is to provide access to the health care that people need to have a fair opportunity in life.

Lastly, how does underwriting in health insurance divide the world? It sets off the well from the ill and those likely to become ill. For insurers, the concept of actuarial fairness provides a rationale for charging much higher rates or declining to insure persons with a substantial possibility of illness or disability, reasoning that such persons should bear the costs associated with their particular risks. Persons at risk could find it difficult to obtain insurance at affordable rates, or at all....

IMPLICATIONS FOR POLICY

The era of predictive genetic testing coincides with a period of grave public concern about health care....

There is little doubt that the current ragged system of private and public programs, with its many holes and frayed edges, must be changed. The conviction that health care ought to be available to those who need it seems to be widely shared. That conviction, together with a growing sense that the current patchwork is failing, may be strong enough to overcome the citizenry's hesitations about government inefficiency. Indeed, it seems likely that private health insurance would not have survived this long if not for government intervention. Tax subsidies for employer-sponsored health insurance programs amounted to $39.5 billion in 1991.[3] In addition, we provide direct government coverage for the health needs of people that commercial insurers want to avoid: Medicare, for those much more likely to need health care; and Medicaid, for some of those unable to pay for their own insurance.

Public programs such as Medicare and Medicaid tell us something important about our moral convictions on health care. They suggest that we are not content to allow the old and the poor simply to languish without access to care. Had we not passed such legislation, we well might have overturned or radically restructured the existing system of commercial health insurance decades ago.

There are good reasons to doubt that actuarial fairness is an adequate description of genuine fairness in health insurance. It may be a sufficient principle for commercial insurance against losses of ships at sea, but even a brief inquiry into the social purpose of health insurance suggests that apportioning by risks, as actuarial fairness dictates, fails to accomplish the primary social goals of health insurance. Genetic tests, like other predictors of the need for health care, are not good reasons for treating people differently with respect to access to health insurance.

REFERENCES

Karen A. Clifford and R. P. Iuculano, "AIDS and Insurance: The Rationale for AIDS-Related Testing," *Harvard Law Review* 100 (1987): 1806–24.

Deborah A. Stone, "AIDS and the Moral Economy of Insurance," *American Prospect* 1 (1990): 62–73.

John K. Iglehart, "The American Health Care System: Private Insurance," *NEJM* 326 (1992): 1715–20.

POSTSCRIPT

Should Health Insurance Companies Have Access to Information from Genetic Testing?

The failure of health care reform in 1994 meant that the question of genetic testing for health insurance went unanswered. Most of the proposals would have banned insurance companies from denying insurance to anyone with pre-existing conditions, a category that would include genetic diseases. The Human Genome Project's Task Force on Genetic Information and Insurance recommended in 1993 that, in the case of health insurance, "information about past, present or future health status, including genetic information, should not be used to deny health care coverage or services to anyone."

Further readings on the topic address some of the major concerns about genetic testing. In "Genetic Testing and the Social Responsibility of Private Health Insurance Companies," *The Journal of Law, Medicine and Ethics* (Spring 1993), for example, Nancy S. Jecker argues that "socially responsible insurance companies will avoid genetic discrimination." The existence of discrimination as a consequence of genetic testing is documented in an article by Paul R. Billings et al. in the *American Journal of Human Genetics* (vol. 50, 1992). The American Medical Association's position on the use of genetic testing by employers, outlined in the *Journal of the American Medical Association* (October 2, 1991), is that it generally opposes genetic testing by employers, while recognizing a limited exception in excluding workers who have a genetic susceptibility to occupational illness. See also Barbara B. Biesecker et al., "Genetic Counseling for Families with Inherited Susceptibility to Breast and Ovarian Cancer," *Journal of the American Medical Association* (April 21, 1993).

For more general readings on genetic screening, social policy, and the history of modern genetics, see Lori B. Andrews et al., *Assessing Genetic Risks: Implication for Health and Social Policy* (National Academy Press, 1994); Robert F. Weir, Susan C. Lawrence, and Evan Fales, eds., *Genes and Human Self-Knowledge: Historical and Philosophical Reflections on Modern Genetics* (University of Iowa Press, 1994); and Pat Milmoe McCarrick, *Genetic Testing and Genetic Screening* (Scope Note No. 22, Kennedy Institute of Ethics, 1993).

In September 1994 the American Council of Life Insurance submitted a statement to the National Association of Insurance Commissioners that opposed limiting or prohibiting underwriting on the basis of genetic information. It reiterated its view that "the continued existence of the current insurance market is dependent on insurers' ability to fully and appropriately select and classify risks."

ISSUE 21

Will the Human Genome Project Lead to Abuses in Genetic Engineering?

YES: Evelyn Fox Keller, from "Nature, Nurture, and the Human Genome Project," in Daniel J. Kevles and Leroy Hood, eds., *The Code of Codes: Scientific and Social Issues in the Human Genome Project* (Harvard University Press, 1992)

NO: Daniel J. Kevles and Leroy Hood, from "Preface" and "Reflections," in Daniel J. Kevles and Leroy Hood, eds., *The Code of Codes: Scientific and Social Issues in the Human Genome Project* (Harvard University Press, 1992)

ISSUE SUMMARY

YES: Professor of history and philosophy of science Evelyn Fox Keller warns that the Human Genome Project's beneficent focus on "disease-causing genes" may lead to a "eugenics of normality," in which inherently ambiguous standards of normality and individual responsibility may be abused.

NO: Professor of humanities Daniel J. Kevles and professor of biology Leroy Hood discount fears of a resurgence of negative eugenics because enlightened public opinion and contemporary political democracies, as well as technological difficulties, would make it unlikely.

The Human Genome Project is big science, the first venture in biology that compares to huge projects in space exploration or astrophysics. This international project began in 1988, will take 15 years, and will cost somewhere between $300 million and $3 billion. A genome refers to all the genetic material contained within the chromosomes of a particular organism.

The origins of such a vast undertaking spans the century. In 1900 the earlier work of Gregor Mendel in explaining the scientific laws of heredity was resurrected by botanists and biologists. In 1953 James Watson (now director of the Human Genome Project) and Francis Crick discovered the double-helix structure of deoxyribonucleic acid (DNA), the long molecule that is the building block of human life. In 1973 the technology of recombinant DNA made it possible to take a fragment of DNA from one genome and splice it (recombine it) with another. Using recombinant DNA, scientists began to isolate single human genes and discover their function. Proposals to characterize the entire human genome began in the 1980s.

To comprehend the scale of the human genome project, consider these numbers: Each human cell is made up of 23 chromosome pairs (rod-like structures composed of proteins and cellular DNA). The chromosomes are believed to contain 100,000 or more genes (the fundamental unit of heredity). Each gene is an ordered sequence of nucleotides (subunits of DNA or RNA, which are designated by the four letters of the DNA alphabet A [adenine], T [thymine], G [guanine], and C [cytosine]). These subunits are paired as A and T or G and C, and it is the bonds between these base pairs that hold together the double strands of DNA. The size of a genome is generally given as the number of its base pairs, in the human about 3 billion. According to Walter Gilbert, a molecular biologist, the amount of information contained in these base pairs is equal to a thousand thousand-page telephone books.

The Human Genome Project has been enthusiastically hailed and vigorously criticized. Professor Gilbert calls the project "a vision of the Grail," a reference to the plate from which Jesus ate at the Last Supper and a central object of medieval Christian pursuits and legends. Some geneticists and physicians look to the project as an unprecedented resource that will aid in understanding the genes involved in human biology and eventually in diagnosing and treating some of the approximately 4,000 known human genetic diseases as well as some diseases that may have genetic factors.

Some critics, on the other hand, have pointed out that only a minor percentage of DNA, perhaps less than 10 percent, represents genes and their regulatory sequences. The rest are repetitive or have an unknown function. In this view, the map of the human genome would be incredibly detailed but not much of a guide to major landmarks. Another view is that the millions that will be spent on the Human Genome Project might be more fruitfully allocated to other areas of basic or clinical research.

The most serious criticisms, however, concern not the possibility of failure but the probability of success. What will happen to individual rights and freedoms if genetic information is readily available to employers, insurers, schools, courts, and others who might make decisions based on prejudice, risk-avoidance, or misunderstanding of the limits of genetic data? At its best genetic information is usually only one factor in determining a particular individual's development of disease, intelligence, skills, or behavior.

Another, even more far-reaching concern, is discussed in the following selections. That is the possibility that the Human Genome Project might bring back eugenics. Eugenics (literally "good in birth"), involving efforts to alter human heredity by selective breeding, was popular earlier in this century. It reached its most repressive form in the Nazi attempts to establish their superiority in their campaign of "racial hygiene," which involved mass murders of so-called inferior people. Evelyn Fox Keller warns that today's version of eugenics is more sophisticated but still dangerous. In her view the Human Genome Project fails to appreciate the complexity of human development and promotes an ambiguous definition of "normality." Daniel J. Kevles and Leroy Hood, on the other hand, look to today's political democracies and informed public opinion as protection against the authoritarian abuses of eugenics that characterized earlier decades.

YES   Evelyn Fox Keller

NATURE, NURTURE, AND THE HUMAN GENOME PROJECT

Genes became big business in the 1980s, and they are likely to become even bigger business in the decades to come. Plant genes, mouse genes, bacterial genes, and human genes are all in the news, but over the last couple of years it is human genes that have become the focus of particular interest. Daily, we are told—by Barbara Walters, by newspaper journalists, and above all, by proponents of the human genome project—that it is our genes that make us "what we are," that make some of us musical geniuses, Olympic athletes, or theoretical physicists and others alcoholics, manic-depressives, schizophrenics—even homeless. The Office of Technology Assessment concludes that "one of the strongest arguments for supporting human genome projects is that they will provide knowledge about the determinants of the human condition"; that, especially, the human genome project promises to illuminate the determinants of human disease, even of those diseases "that are at the root of many current societal problems."[1]

Some may worry about the "desirability of using genetic information to control and shape the future of human society," but others worry, perhaps equally, about a possible failure of courage.[2] To withhold support for this ambitious and expensive undertaking, writes Daniel Koshland, the editor of *Science* magazine, is to incur "the immorality of omission—the failure to apply a great new technology to aid the poor, the infirm, and the underprivileged."[3]

Thanks largely to the remarkable progress of molecular biology, it is claimed that the controversy between nature and nurture that has plagued us for so long has finally been resolved. To quote Koshland again, we now know what "may seem obvious to a scientist, but our judges, journalists, legislators, and philosophers have been slow to learn"—namely, that if we want to induce children to behave, to rehabilitate prisoners, to prevent suicides, we must recognize that

> we are dealing with a very complex problem in which the structure of society and chemical therapy will [both] play roles. Better schools, a better environment, better counseling, and better rehabilitation will help some individuals, but not all.

From Evelyn Fox Keller, "Nature, Nurture, and the Human Genome Project," in Daniel J. Kevles and Leroy Hood, eds., *The Code of Codes: Scientific and Social Issues in the Human Genome Project* (Harvard University Press, 1992). Copyright © 1992 by Daniel J. Kevles and Leroy Hood. Reprinted by permission of Harvard University Press. Some notes omitted.

Better drugs and genetic engineering will help others, but not all. It is not going to be easy for those without scientific training to cope with these complicated relationships even when all the factors are well understood.[4] ...

Most responsible advocates are of course careful to acknowledge the role of *both* nature and nurture, but rhetorically, as well as in scientific practice, it is "nature" that emerges as the decisive victor. ...

The shifts that Plomin, Koshland, and others note are real, and the usual assumption is that they are a direct consequence of developments in our scientific understanding of genetics. It is important to note, however, that our beliefs in nature and nurture have a cultural as well as a scientific history. There is indeed something new in the current configuration of our beliefs, and if we are to understand that novelty properly we must examine both histories, their mutual entwinement and their interdependence. ...

* * *

Of signal importance in the transfiguration of genetic determinism is the fact that, in the late 1960s, molecular biologists began to develop techniques by which they themselves could manipulate the "Master Molecule." They learned how to sequence it, how to synthesize it, and how to alter it. Out of molecular biology emerged a technological know-how that decisively altered our historical sense of the immutability of "nature." Where the traditional view had been that "nature" spelled destiny and "nurture" freedom, now the roles appeared to be reversed. The technological innovations of molecular biology invited

a vastly extended discursive prowess, encouraging the notion that we could more readily control the former than the latter—not simply as a long-term goal but as an immediate prospect. This notion, though far in excess of the actual capabilities of molecular biology of that time, transformed the very terms of the nature-nurture debate; eventually, it would transform the terms of molecular biology as well.

For the first twenty years of molecular biology, research focused on organisms at the opposite end of the phylogenetic scale from humans, and to most people the implications for human beings seemed remote. For some, however, the distance from *Escherichia coli* to *Homo sapiens* had never seemed very large, and certainly by the late 1960s, with the development of new techniques for working with eukaryotic genes and mammalian viruses, that gap began to close. It was perhaps inevitable that the prospects of control invited by the new research would soon extend into the reaches of human nature. The first explicit formulations of such ambitions by molecular biologists began to appear around 1969. Even then, however, when molecular biology was just beginning to move into the domain of higher organisms, the kinds of control envisioned were already presented as crucially distinct from those of the older eugenics.

Whereas the eugenics programs of the earlier part of the century had had to rely on massive social programs, and hence were subject to social control, molecular genetics seemed to enable what Robert Sinsheimer called "a new eugenics"—a eugenics that "could, at least in principle, be implemented on a quite individual basis."[5] Sinsheimer added,

> The old eugenics was limited to a numerical enhancement of the best of our existing gene pool. The new eugenics would permit in principle the conversion of all the unfit to the highest genetic level.[6]

In short, in the vision inspired by the successes of molecular biology, "nature" became newly malleable, perhaps infinitely so; certainly it was vastly more malleable than anyone had ever imagined "nurture" to be....

The themes in these scientific/utopian scenarios that had particular influence on popular belief are (1) the newly acclaimed malleability of "nature"; (2) the reach across the divide between biology and culture that had been at least tacitly in place since World War II; and (3) the emphasis on the role of individual choice in the kinds of interventions the new genetics would make possible. In turn, of course, the influence of such arguments on popular belief would prove critical for making available the resources and support required for these aspirations to exert a practical influence over the future course of research in molecular biology....

Without doubt, the 1970s was a decade of extraordinary expansion for molecular biology: technically, institutionally, culturally, and economically. My aim is not to question that expansion per se, but rather to question the conventional understanding that the institutional, cultural, and economic expansion of molecular biology proceeded directly, and as a matter of course, from its technical successes. In particular, I want to focus on the ideological expansion of molecular biology into both popular culture and

medicine, and at least to raise a question about the effect of this ideological expansion on subsequent technical developments. To this end, the historian Edward Yoxen's exploration of the construction of the idea of "genetic disease" provides an absolutely essential starting point, for it is this concept which both has provided the ground for the cultural and medical expansion of molecular genetics and, at the same time, distinguishes current formulations of genetic determinism from those of the earlier part of the century.[7]

As Yoxen points out, one need not dispute the fact that "many of the phenomena of genetic disease are grounded in material reality" in order to ask "why we isolate or delineate certain phenomena for analysis, why we say that they constitute diseases, and why we seek to explain their nature and cause in genetical terms."[8] Although an earlier generation of geneticists may not have doubted the power of genes to determine (and thus ultimately to transform) human well-being, they did not (except in isolated instances) link their claims to a concept of genetic disease, and their medical colleagues, failing to see any direct relation between genes and treatment even for those diseases that were understood to be genetic, regarded genetics as being of little relevance to medical practice. Today, however, the relation between genetics and the medical sciences has dramatically changed. Even though, in actuality, genetics remains of quite limited practical relevance to the healing arts, the concept of disease—now extended throughout the domain of human behavior—has increasingly come to be understood by health scientists in terms of genetics. Indeed, the volume of medical literature on genetic disease has increased exponentially over the past decade,* and much of this literature suggests a conceptual shift that one commentator describes as follows:

> [In the past,] most physicians and investigators have perceived that deleterious influences on human health are of two kinds: either a deficiency of a basic resource such as food or vitamins, or exposure to hazards that may be either natural... or man-made... Genetics is now showing that this view of the determinants of health as being external is too simplistic. It neglects a major determinant of disease—an internal one. Far from being a rare cause of disease, genetic factors are a very important determinant of health or illness in developed countries.[9]

But as Yoxen points out, in the course of this conceptual shift "genetic disease" has become an extremely large category, encompassing not only genetic disorders that are thought of as diseases but also genetic abnormalities associated with no known disorder as well as disorders that may be neither genetic nor diseases.[10]

Many factors (both technical and cultural) have contributed to the expansion of the concept of genetic disease and, with it, the domain of clinical genetics. Among these one might note: increasingly general acceptance of the explanatory framework of molecular biology; the postwar diminution of the burden of acute disease; intensification of scientific training for medical practice; changing expectations for health in the general public; and patterns of resource distribution for scientific research. For example, Yoxen notes

*A count of review articles on genetic disease listed in Medline reveals a more than sevenfold increase over the years 1986 to 1989 alone. Fifty-one articles are listed for 1986, 152 for 1987, 288 for 1988, and 366 in 1989.

that, in the early 1970s, the National Institute of General Medical Sciences (a subdivision of the NIH) sought

> to mobilize support for its programs by representing genetic disorders as a significant cause of ill health. Here, genetics offers a strategy of territorial expansion through the redefinition of the causes of disease to a relatively low status institution.[11]

Yoxen's main point, however, is to indicate the many social, economic, political, and technical issues that must be taken into account if we are to understand how the "basic explanatory form of a 'genetic disease' has been constructed to fit the contemporary context."[12]

My point is an even more general one. It is to note that the concept of genetic disease, enthusiastically appropriated by the medical sciences for complex institutional and economic reasons, represents an ideological expansion of molecular biology far beyond its technical successes. I also want to argue that the general acceptance of this concept has, in turn, proved critical for the direction that subsequent technical developments in molecular biology have now begun to take. Without question, it was the technical prowess that molecular biology had achieved by the early 1980s that made it possible even to imagine a task as formidable as that of sequencing what has come to be called "the human genome." But it was the concept of genetic disease that created the climate in which such a project could appear both reasonable and desirable.

* * *

I want to focus on two arguments that surfaced early in the advocacy of the human genome project. First is the startling promise that the full sequence of the human genome will teach us, finally, "what it means to be human"; it will enable us to "decipher the mysteries" of our own existence. In spite of the fact that the actual genomes of any two individuals will differ by as much as three million bases, from a molecular biological point of view, the "essential underlying definition" of the human being is a single entity.[13] Advocates for the human genome project continue by arguing that the characterization of this entity (namely, its genetic sequence) therefore constitutes a critical question for medicine. But what is sometimes presented as a sequitur is more commonly presented as an independent appeal to the "major [or 'revolutionary'] impact" such a data base will have "on health care and disease prevention." In the official report issued in 1988 by the National Research Council Committee on Mapping and Sequencing the Human Genome, the value of this information for the "diagnosis, treatment, and prevention" of human disease is repeatedly emphasized. It is argued:

Encoded in the DNA sequence are fundamental determinants of those mental capacities—learning, language, memory —essential to human culture. Encoded there as well are the mutations and variations that cause or increase susceptibility to many diseases responsible for much human suffering.[14]

The committee concludes "that a project to map and sequence the human genome should be undertaken" in order to "allow rapid progress to occur in the diagnosis and ultimate control of many human diseases."[15] James Watson makes the point even more strongly. For him, the human genome project is "our best go at diseases." Indeed, he goes further.

Referring to manic depression as an instance of the kind of disease we seek to control, he argues that we must find the gene because without it "we are lost."[16]

The two central images of the rhetoric employed here—on the one hand the idea of a base-line norm, indicated by "the human genome," and on the other the specter of a panoply of genetic diseases (currently estimated at well over 3,000) —definitively distinguish this discourse from its precursors. The emphasis now is not so much on the "cultural perfection of man" or on the "conscious" and "direct" employment of genetic technology to engineer our "transition to a whole new pitch of evolution,"[17] or even on improving the quality of our genetic pool, but rather on the use of genetics—through diagnosis, treatment, and prevention—to guarantee to all human beings an individual and natural right, the right to health. In its 1988 report on the human genome project, the Office of Technology Assessment concluded that "new technologies for identifying traits and altering genes make it possible for eugenic goals to be achieved through technological as opposed to social control."[18] But even more important, the report sets the project's eugenic implications apart from earlier precedents by distinguishing a "eugenics of normalcy": that is, "the use of genetic information . . . to ensure that . . . each individual has at least a modicum of normal genes." The report cites an argument that "individuals have a paramount right to be born with a normal, adequate hereditary endowment."[19]

Just as Sinsheimer predicted twenty years ago, the nineties version of the "new eugenics" (though the word *eugenics* is not now used) is no longer construed as a matter of social policy, the good of the species, or the quality of our collective gene pool; the current concern is the problem (as Watson puts it) of the "disease-causing genes" that "some of us as individuals have inherited [my italics]." Accordingly, it is presented in terms of the choices that "they as individuals" will have to make.[20] Genetics merely provides the information enabling the individual to realize an inalienable right to health, where "health" is defined in reference to a tacit norm, signified by "the human genome," and in contradistinction to a state of unhealth (or abnormality), indicated by an ever growing list of conditions characterized as "genetic disease."

A number of fairly obvious questions come to mind at this point about the concepts of both "individual" and "choice" that are invoked in this discourse, but first, some basic points stand in need of clarification. The first is that, despite the repeated emphasis on health care, on the diagnosis, treatment, and prevention of genetic disease, it is in fact primarily the possibility of diagnosis that is considered of practical relevance for the near future by even the most enthusiastic proponents of the human genome project; estimates of arrival times for therapeutic benefits run, optimistically, as long as fifty years hence. Thus, "treatment" is at best a long-term goal, and "prevention" means preventing the births of individuals diagnosed as genetically aberrant—in a word, it means abortion. The choices "individuals" are asked to make are therefore choices not on behalf of their own health but on behalf of the health of their offspring and, implicitly, on behalf of the nation's health costs. Pointing to schizophrenia, which he claimed currently accounts for one-half of all hospital beds, Charles Cantor, the former head of the Human Genome Center at the Lawrence Berkeley Laboratory, recently argued in a lecture that the project would more than pay for itself by preventing the occurrence of just this one disease. When asked how such a saving could be effected he could only say: "by preventing the birth" of schizophrenics.[21]

Which brings us to the second point requiring clarification: namely, that these newly available choices, though ostensibly made by individuals, are in fairly obvious ways preconstructed by the categories of disease already presented to the decisionmaker, often on the basis of rather dubious evidence. Psychiatric disorders are a good case in point. In 1987, reports of a genetic locus for manic depression received extensive publicity, as did a similar report for a genetic locus for schizophrenia published in 1988. Less well publicized was the retraction of both these claims in 1989. Three months before Cantor's lecture, Nature had reported that the retraction "leaves us with no persuasive evidence linking any psychiatric disease to a single locus." As David Baltimore, then Director of the Whitehead Institute at MIT, said, "Setting myself up as an average reader of Nature, what am I to believe?"[22] Even more pressing for my point is the question of what the average reader of Time and Newsweek is to believe. If the scientific community were in closer agreement on genetic definitions of disease, an individual's choices might be clearer, but they would not be any more "autonomous."

The current disarray surrounding attempts to define "genetic disease" bears in part on a third point that I briefly indicated earlier—namely, the elusiveness of a norm against which the concept of abnormality is implicitly defined. Molecular analysis of human DNA indicates that the genomes of any two individuals will, on average, differ in approximately three million bases. In an attempt to bypass the enormous diversity among even "normal" human beings, a composite genome, with different chromosomes obtained from different individuals, has been adopted as the standard for genomic analysis. This "solution" does nothing, however, to address either the de facto variability in nucleotide sequence within individual chromosomes or the consequent difficulty in deciding what a "normal" sequence would be.

A fourth and final point that needs at least to be mentioned is that many of the categories of genetic disease —especially those referring to mental competence—put into question the very capacity of those individuals who carry the purported "disease-causing genes" to make choices. Such individuals might well be expected, in Watson's own words, to be "genetically incapable of being responsible."[23]

* * *

Forty years ago, when the specter of eugenics aroused such intense anxiety, the aims of genetics were made safe by a clear demarcation between biology and culture. The province of genetics, particularly of molecular genetics, was biology—primarily, the biology of lower organisms. To most people in or out of genetics, molecular biology seemed to have little if any bearing on human behavior. At that time, it was culture, not biology, that "made us human"; culture was simultaneously the source and the object of our special, human, freedom to make choices. Today we are being told— and judging from media accounts, we are apparently coming to believe—that what makes us human is our genes. Indeed, the very notion of "culture" as distinct from "biology" seems to have vanished;

in the terms that increasingly dominate contemporary discourse, "culture" has become subsumed under biology.

But if culture is to be subsumed under biology, and if it is our biological or genetic future that we now seek to shape, where are we to locate the domain of freedom by which this future can be charted? The disarming suggestion that is put forth is that this domain of freedom is to be found in the elusive realm of "individual choice"—a suggestion that invokes a democratic and egalitarian ideal somewhere beyond biology. But since there is in this discourse no domain "beyond biology," since it is our genes that "make us what we are," and since they do so with a definitive inequality that compromises even those choices some of us can make, we are obliged to look elsewhere for the implied realm of freedom. I suggest that the locus of freedom on which this discourse tacitly depends is to be found not in the domain of "individual choice," comforting as such a notion might be, but rather in a domain protected by the ambiguous designation of "normality." More generally, I suggest that the distinction that had earlier been made by the demarcation between culture and biology (or between nurture and nature) is now made by a demarcation between the normal and the abnormal; the force of destiny is no longer attached to culture, or even to biology in general, but rather more specifically to the biology (or genetics) of disease. Far from teaching us "what it means to be human," in actual practice, the burden of the new human genetics turns on the elucidation not of human order but of human disorder. Our genes may make us "what we are," but, it would appear, they do so more forcefully for some of us than for others. By general consensus, molecular geneticists do not seek genetic loci for traits that they—and we—accept as normal. Indeed, they, like us, do not even seek to define the meaning of "normal."

It is perhaps inevitable that the appeal to the desire for health translates into a search for the genetic basis of unhealth, but the net effect of this translation is that the nature of normality is allowed silently to elude the gaze of genetic scrutiny—and thereby tacitly to evade its determinist grip. The freedom molecular biology promises to bring is the freedom to rout the domain of destiny inhering in "disease-causing genes" in the name of an unspecified standard of normality—a standard that remains unexamined not simply by oversight but by the internal logic of the endeavor. The "normal" state can be specified in this endeavor only by negation—by the absence of those alleles said to cause disease.

More problematic still is the insistent ambiguity inhering in the very term *normal*, an ambiguity that the philosopher and historian of science Ian Hacking traces to Auguste Comte:

> Comte... expressed and to some extent invented a fundamental tension in the idea of the normal—the normal as existing average, and the normal as figure of perfection to which we may progress. This is an even richer source of hidden power than the fact/value ambiguity that had always been present in the idea of the normal... On the one hand there is the thought that the normal is what is right, so that talk of the normal is a splendid way of preserving or returning to the status quo... On the other hand is the idea that the normal is only average, and so is something to be improved upon.[24]

This ambiguity permits all of us a certain latitude in our hopes and expectations for a "eugenics of normalcy." It also clears a large field for the operation of distinctly nongenetic, ideological forces.

Both the definition and the routing of genetic disease express human choices, and even if "individual choice" is an inadequate model for describing the process by which choices actually get made, the very possibility of choice depends on a residual domain of agency that can remain free only to the extent that it remains unexamined. The question, of course, is where, and how, this residual domain of agency gets constructed and articulated, how the authority for prescribing the meaning of "normal" is distributed. The notion of culture (like that of nurture) may have vanished from contemporary biological discourse, but it is here, hidden from view, that the facts of culture continue to exert their undeniable force.

There is no question that eugenics has become a vastly more realizable prospect than it was in the earlier part of the century, and it must be granted that, in many ways, the very notion remains as disturbing as it was in 1945. As Watson has written,

> We have only to look at how the Nazis used leading members of the German human genetics and psychiatry communities to justify their genocide programs, first against the mentally ill and then the Jews and the Gypsies. We need no more vivid reminders that science in the wrong hands can do incalculable harm.[25]

It is of course true that, in 1990, we have no Nazi conspiracy to fear. All we have to fear today is our own complacency that there are some "right hands" in which to invest this responsibility—above all, the responsibility for arbitrating normality.

NOTES

1. U.S. Congress, Office of Technology Assessment, *Mapping Our Genes* (Washington, D.C.: Government Printing Office, 1988), p. 85; Daniel Koshland, "Sequences and Consequences of the Human Genome," *Science*, 146 (1989), 189.

2. Office of Technology Assessment, *Mapping Our Genes*, p. 79.

3. Koshland, "Sequences and Consequences," p. 189. In the address on which this editorial was based, delivered at the First Human Genome Conference in October 1989, Koshland was even more explicit. In response to the oft-raised question, "Why not give this money to the homeless?" he said, "What these people don't realize is that the homeless are impaired... Indeed, no group will benefit more from the application of human genetics." Just how the human genome project will aid "the poor, the infirm, and the underprivileged," Koshland did not say.

4. Daniel Koshland, "Nature, Nurture, and Behavior," *Science*, 235 (1987), 1445.

5. Robert Sinsheimer, "The Prospect of Designed Genetic Change," *Engineering and Science*, 32 (1969), 8–13; reprinted in Ruth Chadwick, ed., *Ethics, Reproduction, and Genetic Control* (London: Croom Helm, 1987), p. 145.

6. Ibid.

7. Edward J. Yoxen, "Constructing Genetic Diseases," in Troy Duster and Karen Garett, eds., *Cultural Perspectives on Biological Knowledge* (Norwood, N.J.: Ablex, 1984).

8. Yoxen, "Constructing Genetic Diseases," p. 41.

9. P. A. Baird, "Genetics and Health Care," *Perspectives in Biology and Medicine*, 33 (1990), 203–213.

10. Yoxen, "Constructing Genetic Diseases," p. 49.

11. Ibid., p. 50.

12. Ibid., p. 48.

13. See the chapter by Walter Gilbert in *The Code of Codes: Scientific and Social Issues in the Human Genome Project* (1992), "A Vision of the Grail," pp. 83–97.

14. National Research Council, *Mapping and Sequencing the Human Genome* (Washington, D.C.: National Academy Press, 1988), pp. 1, 12–13, 45.

15. Ibid., p. 11.

16. The quotations are taken from a lecture that Watson gave at the California Institute of Technology, May 9, 1990.

17. Sinsheimer, "Prospect of Designed Genetic Change," p. 146.

18. Office of Technology Assessment, *Mapping Our Genes*, p. 84.

19. Ibid., p. 86.

20. James D. Watson, "The Human Genome Project—Past, Present, and Future," *Science* 248 (April 6, 1990), 44–49.

21. Charles Cantor, informal lecture at the University of California, Berkeley, 1990.

22. Miranda Robertson, "False Start on Manic Depression," *Nature*, 342 (November 18, 1989), 222.

23. Watson lecture, May 9, 1990.

24. Ian Hacking, *The Taming of Chance* (Cambridge: Cambridge University Press, 1990), p. 168.

25. Watson, "The Human Genome Project," p. 46.

NO

Daniel J. Kevles
and Leroy Hood

THE CODE OF CODES

The human genome comprises, in its totality, all the different genes found in the cells of human beings. The Nobel laureate Walter Gilbert has called it the "grail of human genetics," the key to what makes us human, what defines our possibilities and limits as members of the species *Homo sapiens*. What makes us human beings instead of chimpanzees, for example, is a mere 1 percent difference between the ape genome and our own. That distinction amounts to no more than a gross reckoning, however. The substance and versatility of the human genome lie in its details, in specific information about all the genes we possess—the number has been variously estimated at between 50,000 and 100,000—about how they contribute to the vast array of human characteristics, about the role they play (or do not play) in disease, development, and behavior.

The search for the biological grail has been going on since the turn of the century, but it has now entered its culminating phase with the recent creation of the human genome project, the ultimate goal of which is the acquisition of all the details of our genome. That knowledge will undoubtedly revolutionize understanding of human development, including the development of both normal characteristics, such as organ function, and abnormal ones, such as disease. It will transform our capacities to predict what we may become and, ultimately, it may enable us to enhance or prevent our genetic fates, medically or otherwise.

Unquestionably, the connotations of power and fear associated with the holy grail accompany the genome project, its biological counterpart. The project itself has raised professional apprehensions as well as high intellectual expectations. Undoubtedly, it will affect the way that much of biology is pursued in the twenty-first century. Whatever the shape of that effect, the quest for the biological grail will, sooner or later, achieve its end, and we believe that it is not too early to begin thinking about how to control the power so as to diminish—better yet, abolish—the legitimate social and scientific fears....

It is our conviction that the social and ethical issues of human genetics —which the project is not so much raising as intensifying—are analyzed most usefully when they are tied to the present and prospective realities of the science and its technological capacities. Science-fiction fantasies about the genetic future distract attention from the genuine problems posed by advances in the study of heredity....

* * *

In April 1991, an exposition opened in the hall atop the great arch of La Defense, in Paris, under the title *La Vie en Kit: Éthique et Biologie*. This exhibit concerning "life in a test tube" included displays about molecular genetics and the human genome project. The ethical worries were manifest in a statement by the writer Monette Vaquin that was printed in the catalogue and was also prominently placarded at the genome display:

> Today, astounding paradox, the gener-ation following Nazism is giving the world the tools of eugenics beyond the wildest Hitlerian dreams. It is as if the preposterous ideas of the fathers' gen-eration haunted the discoveries of the sons. scientists of tomorrow will have a power that exceeds all the powers known to mankind: that of manipulating the genome. Who can say for sure that it will be used only to avoid hereditary illnesses?[1]

Vaquin's apprehensions, echoed fre-quently by scientists and social analysts alike, indicate that the shadow of eugen-ics continues to hang over the genome project. Commentators have suggested that the project may stimulate state at-tempts at positive eugenics, the use of genetic engineering to foster or enhance characteristics such as scholastic, scien-tific, and mathematical intelligence, mu-sical ability, or athletic prowess. The ul-timate goal will be the creation of new Einsteins, Mozarts, or Kareem Abdul-Jabbars (curiously, brilliantly talented women—such as Marie Curie or Nadia Boulanger or Martina Navratilova—are rarely if ever mentioned in the pan-theon of superpeople). Other commen-tators have warned that the project will more likely spark a revival of negative eugenics—state programs of intervention in reproductive behavior so as to discour-age the transmission of "bad" genes in the population.

Negative-eugenic programs could well be prompted by economic incentives. Concern for financial costs played a role in the eugenics movement of the early twentieth century, when social patholo-gies were said to be increasing at a terrible rate. At the Sesquicentennial Exposition in Philadelphia, in 1926, the American Eugenics Society exhibit included a board that, in the manner of the population counters of a later day, revealed with flashing lights that every fifteen seconds a hundred dollars of the observer's money went for the care of persons with "bad heredity" and that every forty-eight sec-onds a mentally deficient person was born in the United States. The display implied that restricting the reproduction of people with deleterious genes would not only benefit the gene pool but reduce state and local expenditures for "feeble-mindedness" in public institutional set-tings—that is, state institutions and state hospitals for the mentally deficient and physically disabled or diseased. Perhaps indicative of this reasoning is that, in California and several other states, eu-genic sterilization rates increased signifi-cantly during the 1930s, when state bud-gets for the mentally handicapped were squeezed.[2]

In our own day, the more that health care becomes a public responsibility, payable through the tax system, and the more expensive this care becomes, the greater the possibility that taxpayers will rebel against paying for the care of those whom genetics dooms to severe disease or disability. Public policy might feel pressure to encourage, or even to compel, people not to bring genetically disadvantaged children into the world— not for the sake of the gene pool but in the interest of keeping public health costs down.

Eugenic promptings might also come from scientists, who, having been lured by ideas of biological imperatives in the past, could find them equally seductive in the future. It is worth bearing in mind that eugenics was not an aberration, the commitment merely of a few oddball scientists and mean-spirited social theorists. It was embraced by leading biologists—not only of the political right but of the progressive left—and it was integral to the research programs of prominent, powerful institutions devoted to the study of human heredity. Indeed, eugenics remained a powerfully attractive idea even after the social prejudice of its early form was recognized and exposed. Objective, socially unprejudiced knowledge is not ipso facto inconsistent with eugenic goals of some type. Indeed, such knowledge may assist in seeking them. The enrichment of human genetics by molecular biology moved Robert Sinsheimer, in 1969, to raise with enthusiasm the possibility of a "new eugenics"—a eugenics that could be free of social bias and, as a result of DNA engineering, scientifically achievable. The more that is learned in the future about human genetics, the more might some biologists be tempted to reunite it with eugenic goals.

In recent years, crude eugenic policies have been promulgated by several governments. In Singapore in 1984, Prime Minister Lee Kwan Yew deplored the relatively low birth rate among educated women, resorting to the fallacy that their intelligence was higher than average and that they were thus allowing the quality of the country's gene pool to diminish. Since then, the government has adopted a variety of incentives—for example, preferential school enrollment for offspring —to increase the fecundity of educated women, and it has offered a similar incentive to their less-educated sisters who would have themselves sterilized after the birth of a first or second child. In 1988, China's Gansu Province adopted a eugenic law that would—so the authorities said—improve "population quality" by banning the marriages of mentally retarded people unless they first submit to sterilization. Since then, similar laws have been adopted in other provinces and have been endorsed by Prime Minister Li Peng. The official newspaper *Peasants Daily* explained, "Idiots give birth to idiots."[3]

Geneticists know that idiots do not necessarily give birth to idiots and that mental retardation may arise from many nongenetic causes. Analysts of civil liberty also know that reproductive freedom is much more easily curtailed in dictatorial governments than in democratic ones. Eugenics profits from authoritarianism—indeed, almost requires it. The institutions of political democracy may not have been robust enough to resist altogether the violations of civil liberties characteristic of the early eugenics movement, but they did contest them effectively in many places. The British government refused to pass eugenic sterilization laws. So did many American states, and where eugenic laws were enacted, they were often unenforced. It is far-fetched to expect a Nazi-like eugenic program to develop in the contemporary United States so long as political democracy and the Bill of Rights continue in force. If a Nazi-like eugenic program becomes a threatening reality, the country will have a good deal more to be worried about politically than just eugenics.

What makes contemporary political democracies unlikely to embrace eugenics is that they contain powerful anti-eugenic constituencies. Awareness of the barbarities and cruelties of state-sponsored eugenics in the past has tended to set most geneticists and the public at large against such programs. Geneticists today know better than their early-twentieth-century predecessors that ideas concerning what is "good for the gene pool" are highly problematic. (We might add, however, that even though they know better, they may not know enough and that, given the human genome project, education in the social and ethical implications of genetic research and genetic claims should probably become a required part of every biologist's professional training.) Then, too, although prejudice continues against persons living with a variety of disabilities and diseases, today such people are politically empowered, as are minority groups, to a degree that they were not in the early twentieth century. For example, in 1990 they obtained passage of the Americans with Disabilities Act, which, among other things, prohibits discrimination against disabled people in employment, public services, and public accommodations. They may not be sufficiently empowered to counter all quasi-eugenic threats to themselves, but they are politically positioned, with allies in the media, the medical profession, and elsewhere, to block or at least to hinder eugenic proposals that might affect them.

The advance of human genetics and biotechnology has created the capacity for a kind of "homemade eugenics," to use the insightful term of the analyst Robert Wright—"individual families deciding what kinds of kids they want to have." At the moment, the kinds they can choose are those without certain disabilities or diseases, such as Down's syndrome or Tay-Sachs. Most parents would probably prefer a healthy baby. In the future, they might have the opportunity —for example, via genetic analysis of embryos—to have improved babies, children who are likely to be more intelligent or more athletic or better looking (whatever that might mean).[4]

Will people exploit such possibilities? Quite possibly, given the interest that some parents have shown in choosing the sex of their child or that others have pursued in the administration of growth hormone to offspring who they think will grow up too short. Benedikt Härlin's report to the European Parliament on the human genome project noted that the increasing availability of genetic tests was generating increasingly widespread pressure from families for "individual eugenic choice in order to give one's own child the best possible start in a society in which hereditary traits become a criterion of social hierarchy." A 1989 editorial in Trends in Biotechnology recognized a major source of the pressure: " 'Human improvement' is a fact of life, not because of the state eugenics committee, but because of consumer demand. How can we expect to deal responsibly with human genetic information in such a culture?"[5]

However, genetic enhancement would inevitably involve the manipulation of human embryos, and, for better or for worse, human-embryo research faces governmental prohibitions in the United States and powerful opposition in virtually all the major western democracies, especially from Roman Catholics. The European Parliament did resolve in 1989 to allow for research on human embryos, but only under very restricted circumstances—for example, only if it would be "of direct and otherwise unattainable benefit in terms of the welfare of the child concerned and its mother." The Parliament's action was based on a report from its Committee on Legal Affairs and Citizens' Rights entitled *Ethical and Legal Problems of Genetic Engineering and Human Artificial Insemination.* The rapporteur for the section of the report concerned with genetic engineering was Willi Rothley, who is not only a Green but a Catholic, and the report itself argued against genetic manipulation of the embryo on several philosophical grounds, including the claim that "each generation must be allowed to wrestle with human nature as it is given to them, and not with the irreversible biological results of their forebears' actions."[6]

The idea of human genetic engineering as such offends many non-Catholics, too. A broad spectrum of lay and religious opinion on both sides of the Atlantic agrees with the European Parliament's 1989 declaration that genetic analysis "must on no account be used for the scientifically dubious and politically unacceptable purpose of 'positively improving' the population's gene pool" and its call for "an absolute ban on all experiments designed to reorganize on an arbitrary basis the genetic make-up of humans."[7] In any event, human genetic improvement is not likely to yield to human effort for some time to come. While the human genome project will undoubtedly accelerate the identification of genes

for physical and medically related traits, it is unlikely to reveal with any speed how genes contribute to the formation of those qualities—particularly talent, creativity, behavior, appearance—that the world so much wants and admires. The idea that genetic knowledge will soon permit the engineering of Einsteins or even the enhancement of general intelligence is simply preposterous.[8] Equally important, the engineering of designer human genomes is not possible under current reproductive technologies and is not likely in the near future to become much easier technically.

NOTES

1. *La Vie en Kit: Éthique et Biologie* (Paris: L'Arche de la Defense, 1991), p. 25.

2. Philip R. Reilly, *The Surgical Solution: A History of Involuntary Sterilization in the United States* (Baltimore: The Johns Hopkins University Press, 1991), pp. 91–93. The last state eugenic sterilization law was passed in 1937, in Georgia, partly in response to conditions of overcrowding in the state's institutions for the mentally handicapped. Edward J. Larson, "Breeding Better Georgians," *Georgia Journal of Southern Legal History*, 1 (Spring/Summer 1991), 53–79.

3. Steven Jay Gould, *The Flamingo's Smile: Reflections in Natural History* (New York: W. W. Norton, 1985), pp. 292–295, 301–303; *The New York Times*, August 15, 1991, p. 1.

4. Robert Wright, "Achilles' Helix," p. 27; Joseph Bishop and Michael Waldholz, *Genome: The Story of the Most Astonishing Scientific Adventure of Our Time—The Attempt to Map All the Genes in the Human Body* (New York: Simon and Schuster, 1990), pp. 310–322.

5. Jane E. Brody, "Personal Health," *The New York Times*, November 8, 1990, p. B7; Barry Werth, "How Short Is Too Short?" *The New York Times Magazine*, June 16, 1991, pp. 15, 17, 28–29; European Parliament, Committee on Energy, Research, and Technology, *Report Drawn up on Behalf of the Committee on Energy, Research and Technology on the Proposal from the Commission to the Council (COM/88/424-C2-119/88) for a Decision Adopting a Specific Research Programme in the Field of Health: Predictive Medicine: Human Genome Analysis (1989–1991)*, Rapporteur Benedikt Härlin, European Parliament Session Documents, 1988–89, 30.01.1989, Series A, Doc A2–0370/88 SYN 146,

pp. 25–26; John Hodgson, "Editorial: Geneticism and Freedom of Choice," *Trends in Biotechnology,* September 1989, p. 221.

6. "Resolutions Adopted by the European Parliament on 16 March 1989," in European Parliament, Committee on Legal Affairs and Citizens' Rights, Rapporteurs: Mr. Willi Rothley and Mr. Carlo Casini, *Ethical and Legal Problems of Genetic Engineering and Human Artificial Insemination* (Luxembourg: Office for Publications of the European Communities, 1990), pp. 15, 38–39. Carlo Casini, from Italy, the rapporteur for the section of the report concerned with human artificial insemination, is known in the circles of the Parliament as virtually a papal representative to the legislative body. Embryo research and germ-line engineering are also opposed by many adherents of Islamic religion and by many Protestants, most recently in a 1989 report by the World Council of Churches. Lectures by Azeddine Guessos and Jack Stotts, "II Workshop on International Cooperation for the Human Genome Project: Ethics," Valencia, Spain, November 12, 1990.

7. "Resolutions Adopted by the European Parliament on 16 March 1989," in European Parliament, Committee on Legal Affairs and Citizens' Rights, *Ethical and Legal Problems of Genetic Engineering and Human Artificial Insemination,* p. 12; Daniel J. Kevles, "Unholy Alliance," *The Sciences,* September/October 1986, pp. 25–30.

8. Bishop and Waldholz, *Genome,* pp. 314–316; Sharon Kingman, "Buried Treasure in Human Genes," *New Scientist,* July 8, 1989, p. 37.

POSTSCRIPT

Will the Human Genome Project Lead to Abuses in Genetic Engineering?

The Human Genome Project is currently ahead of schedule and under budget. A significant interim goal—the construction of a genetic linkage map showing the relative positions of genes and DNA sequences on the chromosomes— was not expected until the end of 1995 but was achieved in 1994. For a review of this progress, see the special issue of *Science* (September 30, 1994) devoted to the genome initiative. Although the discovery of "disease genes" is progressing rapidly, new treatments will take much more time.

In September 1992 the National Institutes of Health was forced to cancel a conference at the University of Maryland on genetic factors in crime that was part of the Human Genome Project's ethics program. Critics led by psychiatrist Peter Breggin claimed that the conference would foster racist attempts to identify individuals as prone to criminal behavior. University officials asserted that the aim of the conference was to examine the evidence and not to endorse ideas of a genetic predisposition to crime.

In "The Human Genome Project and Eugenic Concerns," *American Journal of Human Genetics* (vol. 54, no. 1, 1994), Kenneth L. Garver and Bettylee Garver analyze German and American eugenics programs in the early twentieth century and conclude that, given present-day social problems and the growing demand for cost-effective genetic services, a resurgence of eugenics is possible. From a different viewpoint, W. French Anderson argues that genetic engineering should not be considered a threat to our humanness, because it can alter only quantitative human characteristics and not our unique, qualitative abilities. See "Genetic Engineering and Our Humanness," *Human Gene Therapy* (vol. 5, 1994).

For other supportive accounts of the Human Genome Project, see Joel Davis, *Mapping the Code: The Human Genome Project and the Choices of Modern Science* (John Wiley, 1990), and Lois Wingerson, *Mapping Our Genes: The Genome Project and the Future of Medicine* (E. P. Dutton, 1990). Also see Tom Wilkie, *Perilous Knowledge: The Human Genome Project and Its Implications* (Faber & Faber, 1993), and George J. Annas and Sherman Elias, *Gene Mapping: Using Law and Ethics as Guides.* (Oxford University Press, 1992). Sharon J. Durfy and Amy E. Grotevant have compiled a bibliography, *The Human Genome Project* (Scope Note No. 17, Kennedy Institute of Ethics, 1992), and the U.S. Department of Energy's Office of Energy Research has published *ELSI Bibliography: Ethical, Legal, and Social Implications of the Human Genome Project* edited by Michael S. Yelsey (1993).

CONTRIBUTORS
TO THIS VOLUME

EDITOR

CAROL LEVINE is the executive director of the Orphan Project: The HIV Epidemic and New York City's Children, and she is the recipient of a 1993 fellowship from the MacArthur Foundation. She is a former executive director of the Citizens Commission on AIDS for New York City and Northern New Jersey. She is an associate editor of *IRB: A Review of Human Subjects Research* and a former editor of the *Hastings Center Report*, both of which are published by the Hastings Center in Briarcliff Manor, New York. Ms. Levine received a B.A. in history from Cornell University and an M.A. in public law and government from Columbia University. She writes and lectures widely on AIDS and other issues in bioethics.

STAFF

Mimi Egan   Publisher
Brenda S. Filley   Production Manager
Libra Ann Cusack   Typesetting Supervisor
Juliana Arbo   Typesetter
Lara Johnson   Graphics
Diane Barker   Proofreader
David Brackley   Copy Editor
David Dean   Administrative Editor
Richard Tietjen   Systems Manager

AUTHORS

FELICIA ACKERMAN is a professor of philosophy at Brown University in Providence, Rhode Island. Her articles have appeared in various philosophy journals and anthologies, including *Philosophical Perspectives* and the *Midwest Studies in Philosophy* book series.

DAVID B. ALLEN is an associate professor of pediatrics and the director of pediatric endocrinology at the University of Wisconsin Children's Hospital.

AMERICAN COUNCIL OF LIFE INSURANCE in Washington, D.C., an association of legal reserve life insurance companies authorized to do business in the United States, was founded in 1976 to advance the interests of the life insurance industry and to provide effective government relations.

AMERICAN MEDICAL ASSOCIATION is a society of physicians that was organized in 1847 to promote the science and art of medicine and the betterment of public health. Its main activities include evaluating drugs, foods, and medical equipment; coordinating research; and improving medical education standards.

LORI B. ANDREWS is a research fellow with the American Bar Foundation and a senior scholar at the University of Chicago's Center for Clinical Medical Ethics in Chicago, Illinois. She is the author of *Between Strangers: Surrogate Mothers, Expectant Fathers, and Brave New Babies* (Harper & Row, 1989).

JOHN D. ARRAS is an associate professor of bioethics at Montefiore Medical Center/Albert Einstein College of Medicine and an adjunct associate professor of philosophy at Barnard College in New York City. He is also a fellow of the Hastings Center and a member of the New York State Task Force on Life and Law. His research interests include the forgoing of life-sustaining treatments and clinical issues in AIDS treatment and research.

SISSELA BOK is a faculty member of the Center for Advanced Study in the Behavioral Sciences in Stanford, California, and a former associate professor of philosophy at Brandeis University in Waltham, Massachusetts. Her publications include *Secrets: On the Ethics of Concealment and Revelation* (Vintage Books, 1983) and *A Strategy for Peace: Human Values and the Threat of War* (Pantheon Books, 1989).

DANIEL CALLAHAN, a philosopher, is the cofounder and director of the Hastings Center's Institute of Society, Ethics, and the Life Sciences. He received a Ph.D. in philosophy from Harvard University, and he is the author or editor of over 31 publications, including *Ethics in Hard Times* (Plenum Press, 1981), coauthored with Arthur L. Caplan; *Setting Limits: Medical Goals in an Aging Society* (Simon & Schuster, 1987); and *The Troubled Dream of Life: Living With Mortality* (1993).

SIDNEY CALLAHAN is a professor in the Department of Psychology at Mercy College in Dobbs Ferry, New York. She is the author of many articles and books, including *Abortion: Understanding Differences* (Plenum Press, 1984); *With All Our Heart and Mind: The Spiritual Works of Mercy in a Psychological Age* (Crossroad, 1987); and *In Good Conscience: Reason and Emotion in Moral Decision Making* (HarperCollins, 1991).

JAMES F. CHILDRESS is the Edwin B. Kyle Professor of Religious Studies and a professor of medical education at the University of Virginia in Charlottesville, Virginia, where he also chairs the Department of Religious Studies and codirects the Virginia Health Policy Research Center. He is the author of *Who Should Decide: Paternalism in Health Care* (Oxford University Press, 1982) and the coauthor, with Tom L. Beauchamp, of *Principles of Biomedical Ethics*, 4th ed. (Oxford University Press, 1993).

INGE B. CORLESS is an associate professor in the Graduate Program in Nursing at the Massachusetts General Hospital Institute of Health Professions in Boston, Massachusetts. She is a co-editor of *Dying, Death, and Bereavement: Theoretical Perspectives and Other Ways of Knowing* (Jones & Bartlett, 1994).

AMITAI ETZIONI, a senior adviser to the White House from 1979 to 1980, is a professor in the Department of Sociology at George Washington University in Washington, D.C., where he has been teaching since 1968. He is also the founder of the Society for the Advancement of Socio-Economics and the founder and director of the Center for Policy Research, a nonprofit organization dedicated to public policy. His publications include *A Responsive Society: Collected Essays on Guiding Deliberate Social Change* (Jossey-Bass, 1991).

ALAN R. FLEISCHMAN is a physician with the Albert Einstein College of Medicine in New York City.

KAREN G. GERVAIS is an associate for the Center for Biomedical Ethics at the University of Minnesota in Minneapolis, Minnesota, a coordinator for the Minnesota Network for Institutional Ethics Committees, and an associate professor of philosophy at St. Olaf College in Northfield, Minnesota.

MICHAEL R. HARRISON, an attending surgeon in the San Francisco area, is a professor in and the chief of the division of pediatric surgery in the Department of Surgery at the University of California, San Francisco. His research interests focus on the clinical application of fetal therapy, including fetal stem cell transplantation, fetal wound healing, and Wilms' tumor research.

HEALTH INSURANCE ASSOCIATION OF AMERICA in Washington, D.C., an association of accident and health insurance firms, was founded in 1956 to promote the development of voluntary insurance against loss of income and financial burdens resulting from accident and sickness.

LEROY HOOD is the William Gates III Professor of Molecular Biology at the University of Washington in Seattle, Washington. He is the former Bowles Professor of Biology at the California Institute of Technology.

NANCY S. JECKER is an associate professor in the School of Medicine at the University of Washington in Seattle, Washington.

ANDREW G. KADAR is an attending physician at Cedars-Sinai Medical Center in Los Angeles, California, and a clinical instructor in the School of Medicine at the University of California, Los Angeles.

EVELYN FOX KELLER is a professor of history and philosophy of science in the Program in Science, Technology, and Society at the Massachusetts Institute of Technology in Cambridge, Massachusetts. She received her Ph.D. in theoretical physics at Harvard University, and her research interests focus on the history of developmental biology. Her publications include *Secrets of Life/Secrets of Death* (Routledge, 1991) and *Keywords in Evolutionary Biology* (Harvard University Press, 1992)

DANIEL J. KEVLES is the Koepfli Professor of the Humanities at the California Institute of Technology in Pasedena, California. He is the author of *The Physicists: The History of a Scientific Community in Modern America* (Harvard University Press, 1987).

MICHAEL H. KOTTOW is a physician at Olga Children's Hospital in Stuttgart, Germany. He is the author of *Anterior Segment Fluorescein Anpiography* (Kreiger, 1978).

JOHN D. LANTOS is an assistant professor of pediatrics at the University of Chicago in Chicago, Illinois, and an associate director of clinical medical ethics at La Rabida Children's Hospital and Research Center.

JEROD M. LOEB is the assistant vice president for science and technology at the American Medical Association in Chicago, Illinois, and an adjunct professor of physiology at Northwestern University Medical School in Evanston, Illinois. He is also a cardiovascular physiologist, and he has published widely in areas related to the heart, the use of animals in biomedical research, science education, and science policy.

JOANNE LYNN is a professor of medicine and of community and family medicine and a senior associate in the Center for the Evaluative Clinical Sciences at the Dartmouth-Hitchcock Medical Center in Hanover, New Hampshire.

She is a member of the board of directors of the American Geriatrics Society, and in April 1992, she received the National Board's Outstanding Woman Physician or Biomedical Scientist Award.

RUTH MACKLIN, a philosopher and medical ethicist, is an ethicist in residence at the Albert Einstein College of Medicine and its affiliate hospitals in New York City. Her published works on medical ethics, behavior control, and informed consent include *Mortal Choices: Bioethics in Today's World* (Pantheon Books, 1987).

DOUGLAS K. MARTIN is a Ph.D. candidate at the University of Toronto Centre for Bioethics in Toronto, Ontario, Canada. He is also a secretary and research assistant to the group assigned to revise the Canadian Ethics Guidelines for Research Involving Humans. He has applied his expertise in qualitative research methods to complex bioethical issues, including euthanasia, advance directives, end-of-life care, and fetal tissue transplantation.

RICHARD A. McCORMICK is the John A. O'Brian Professor of Christian Ethics at the University of Notre Dame in Notre Dame, Indiana. He has also held an academic appointment as the Rose F. Kennedy Professor of Christian Ethics at Georgetown University, and he is the author of *The Critical Calling: Reflections on Moral Dilemmas Since Vatican II* (Georgetown University Press, 1989).

GILBERT MEILAENDER is a professor of religion in the Department of Religion at Oberlin College in Oberlin, Ohio. He is the author of *Friendship: A Study in Theological Ethics* (University of North Dakota Press, 1981); *The Theory and Practice of Virtue* (University of North Dakota Press, 1984); and *The Limits of Love:*

Some Theological Explorations (Pennsylvania State University Press, 1987).

BERNARD C. MEYER is a psychiatrist in New York City.

STEVEN H. MILES is an associate professor of medicine in the division of geriatric medicine at the Hennepin County Medical Center and in the Center for Biomedical Ethics at the University of Minnesota in Minneapolis, Minnesota.

FRANKLIN G. MILLER is a professor in the School of Medicine at the University of Virginia in Charlottesville, Virginia.

THOMAS H. MURRAY is a professor of biomedical ethics and the director of the Center for Biomedical Ethics in the School of Medicine at Case Western Reserve University in Cleveland, Ohio. His research interests cover a wide range of ethical issues in medicine and science, including genetics, aging, children, and health policy. He is a founding editor of the journal *Medical Humanities Review* and the author or editor of over 100 publications, including *Feeling Good, Doing Better* (Humana Press, 1984) and *Which Babies Shall Live?* (Humana Press, 1985), coauthored with Arthur L. Caplan.

DAVID ORENTLICHER is the ethics and health policy counsel for the American Medical Association in Chicago, Illinois. He is also a lecturer in law at the University of Chicago Law School and an adjunct assistant professor of medicine at Northwestern University Medical School. He recieved an M.D. and a J.D. from Harvard University.

JIM PERSELS is the editor in chief of the *Southern Illinois University Law Journal.* He has taught organizational behavior and health systems management, and he has contributed numerous articles on health management and bioethical issues to professional journals and anthologies.

MARK S. RAPOPORT is a physician and the commissioner of public health for Westchester County, New York.

TOM REGAN is a professor of philosophy at North Carolina State University in Raleigh, North Carolina, where he has been teaching since 1967. He has published many books and articles on animal rights and environmental ethics, including *All That Dwell Therein: Animal Rights and Environmental Ethics* (University of California Press, 1982) and *The Struggle for Animal Rights* (ISAR, Inc., 1987).

JOHN A. ROBERTSON is the Thomas Watt Gregory Professor of Law at the University of Texas School of Law in Austin, Texas. He is also a fellow of the Hastings Center, and he has served on a federal task force on organ transplantation, on the National Institutes of Health Panel on Fetal Tissue Transplantation Research, and on the Ethics Committee of the American Fertility Society. He has written widely on law and bioethics issues, reproductive rights, organ transplantation, and human experimentation.

DAVID A. ROCHEFORT is an associate professor of political science and public policy at Northeastern University in Boston, Massachusetts.

CARMEL SHALEV is a legislation officer with the Israel Ministry of Justice who also teaches feminist jurisprudence as an adjunct professor at the Tel Aviv University Faculty of Law. She studied law at Hebrew University in Jerusalem and at the Yale University School of Law.

THOMAS A. SHANNON is the Paris Fletcher Distinguished Professor of the Humanities in the Department of the Humanities at Worcester Polytechnic Institute in Worcester, Massachusetts. He is the author or editor of several publications in bioethics, including *Bioethics*, 3rd ed. (Paulist Press, 1987) and, coedited with James J. Walter, *Quality of Life: The New Ethical Dilemma* (Paulist Press, 1991).

SHLOMO SHINNAR is an associate professor of neurology and pediatrics and the director of the Montefiore/Einstein Epilepsy Management Center at Montefiore Medical Center/Albert Einstein College of Medicine in New York City. He is a member of the professional advisory board, the children's subcommittee, and the research grants subcommittee of the Epilepsy Foundation of America.

MARK SIEGLER, recognized as one of the leaders in the field of medical ethics, is the director of the Center for Clinical Medical Ethics at the University of Chicago in Chicago, Illinois. In the 1970s he did pioneering work in developing the field of clinical medical ethics, which integrated the theoretical observations of philosophers and legal scholars with the practical experiences of clinicians from a wide range of clinical disciplines.

BONNIE STEINBOCK is a professor of philosophy at the State University of New York at Albany, where she holds joint appointments in the Department of Public Policy in Rockefeller College and the Department of Health Policy in the School of Public Health. She is also a fellow and former vice president of the Hastings Center, and her research interests focus on the intersection of law, medicine, and ethics.

CARSON STRONG is a professor in the Department of Human Values and Ethics in the College of Medicine at the University of Tennessee in Memphis, Tennessee.

DOROTHY E. VAWTER is an associate director of the Minnesota Center for Health Care Ethics and an adjunct associate professor in the Department of Philosophy at the College of St. Catherine in St. Paul, Minnesota. She has also held academic appointments in bioethics at Michigan State University and at the University of Arkansas, and she has written extensively on the use of human fetal tissue. Her other research interests include ethical and policy issues in reproductive health, organ donation and transplantation, research with human subjects, and individual responsibility for health.

INDEX